Hobbes on Politics and Religion

Hobbes on Politics and Religion

EDITED BY
Laurens van Apeldoorn
and Robin Douglass

OXFORD
UNIVERSITY PRESS

OXFORD
UNIVERSITY PRESS

Great Clarendon Street, Oxford, OX2 6DP,
United Kingdom

Oxford University Press is a department of the University of Oxford.
It furthers the University's objective of excellence in research, scholarship,
and education by publishing worldwide. Oxford is a registered trade mark of
Oxford University Press in the UK and in certain other countries

First Edition published in 2018
Impression: 1

Published in the United States of America by Oxford University Press
198 Madison Avenue, New York, NY 10016, United States of America

British Library Cataloguing in Publication Data
Data available

Library of Congress Control Number: 2018932424

ISBN 978–0–19–880340–9

Printed and bound by
CPI Group (UK) Ltd, Croydon, CR0 4YY

Contents

Acknowledgements   vii
Contributors   ix
Abbreviations   xiii

Introduction   1 √
Laurens van Apeldoorn and Robin Douglass

1. The Theocratic *Leviathan*: Hobbes's Arguments for the Identity of
    Church and State   10
    Johan Olsthoorn

2. Natural Sovereignty and Omnipotence in Hobbes's *Leviathan*   29
    A. P. Martinich

3. First Impressions: Hobbes on Religion, Education, and the
    Metaphor of Imprinting   45
    Teresa M. Bejan

4. Tolerance as a Dimension of Hobbes's Absolutism   63
    Franck Lessay

5. Hobbes on the Motives of Martyrs   79
    Alexandra Chadwick

6. Hobbes, Calvinism, and Determinism   95
    Alan Cromartie

7. Mosaic Leviathan: Religion and Rhetoric in Hobbes's Political Thought   116
    Alison McQueen

8. Devil in the Details: Hobbes's Use and Abuse of Scripture   135
    Paul B. Davis

9. The Politics of Hobbes's *Historia Ecclesiastica*   150
    Patricia Springborg

10. A Profile in Cowardice? Hobbes, Personation, and the Trinity   167
    Glen Newey

11. Hobbes and the Future of Religion   184
    Jon Parkin

12. Hobbes and Early English Deism   202
    Elad Carmel

13. All the Wars of Christendom: Hobbes's Theory of Religious Conflict   219
    Jeffrey Collins

14. Religious Conflict and Moral Consensus: Hobbes, Rawls, and
    Two Types of Moral Justification   239
    Daniel Eggers

15. Hobbes on the Duty Not to Act on Conscience   256
    S. A. Lloyd

Bibliography   273
Index   295

Acknowledgements

This volume marks the culmination of the inaugural research project of the European Hobbes Society. The Society originated as an informal network of European-based Hobbes scholars in 2011, which was later formalized—that is, we launched a website—in 2015. We would like to take this opportunity to thank everyone who helped to get the Society off the ground in its early days, without whom we would not be where we are now: Adrian Blau, Dirk Brantl, Alexandra Chadwick, Daniel Eggers, Signy Gutnick Allen, Johan Olsthoorn, Dietrich Schotte, Gabriella Slomp, and Luciano Venezia. Thanks are also due to all those who have more recently joined the Society and are helping to take it forward as we write.

The majority of chapters in this volume were presented at two workshops in 2015, the first at King's College London and the second at Leiden University. We are very grateful for the financial support of both institutions, and, most of all, to everyone who attended and helped to make this volume possible. We would especially like to thank Adrian Blau, who was closely involved in the early stages of organizing the project. We are also very grateful to the two referees for Oxford University Press, who offered invaluable feedback on a full draft of the volume.

One of the aims of the European Hobbes Society is to bring together the most promising young Hobbes scholars with established experts in the field. We hope this volume does justice to that aspiration and sets the mark for more to come.

* * *

While this volume was in press, we were saddened to learn of the untimely death of Glen Newey. Glen was a fine scholar and a good friend of the European Hobbes Society. His chapter in this volume showcases the philosophical and historical nuance—along with just the right measure of dry wit—that characterized all his research and made it so enjoyable to read. We would like to take this opportunity to acknowledge Glen's considerable contribution to Hobbes scholarship and all his support for the Society.

Contributors

LAURENS VAN APELDOORN is Assistant Professor of Philosophy and a member of the Centre for Political Philosophy at Leiden University, the Netherlands. His research has appeared in journals including *Archiv für Geschichte der Philosophie*, *History of European Ideas*, and *Hobbes Studies*.

TERESA M. BEJAN is Associate Professor of Political Theory at the University of Oxford. She is the author of *Mere Civility: Disagreement and the Limits of Toleration* (2017) and her research on early modern political thought and contemporary theory has appeared in journals including the *Journal of Politics*, *History of Political Thought*, *Review of Politics*, and *History of European Ideas*.

ELAD CARMEL is a Postdoctoral Fellow at the Hebrew University of Jerusalem. His DPhil thesis, completed at the University of Oxford, is entitled ' "When Reason Is Against a Man, a Man Will Be Against Reason": Hobbes, Deism, and Politics' (2016).

ALEXANDRA CHADWICK is a Postdoctoral Researcher in the Department of the History of Philosophy at the University of Groningen. She completed her PhD in 2016, and from 2016–17 was a Max Weber Fellow in the Department for History and Civilization at the European University Institute.

JEFFREY COLLINS is an Associate Professor of History at Queen's University in Kingston, Ontario. He is the author of *The Allegiance of Thomas Hobbes* (2005) and of many journal articles and chapters on both Hobbes and the religious and political history of seventeenth-century Britain.

ALAN CROMARTIE is Professor of the History of Political Thought at the University of Reading. He is the author of *The Constitutionalist Revolution* (2006) and the editor of Thomas Hobbes, *A Dialogue between a Philosopher and a Student, of the Common Laws of England* (2005).

PAUL B. DAVIS studied history as an undergraduate at Harvard University and a graduate student at Princeton University. From 2014 to 2016, he worked at the New York Public Library. Since 2016 he has worked in the biopharmaceutical industry, managing corporate communications for Roivant Sciences.

ROBIN DOUGLASS is Senior Lecturer of Political Theory at King's College London. He is the author of *Rousseau and Hobbes: Nature, Free Will, and the Passions* (2015) and his research on Hobbes has appeared in journals including the *European Journal of Political Theory*, *History of European Ideas*, and *History of Political Thought*.

DANIEL EGGERS is Assistant Professor in Moral and Political Philosophy at the University of Cologne. He is the author of *Die Naturzustandstheorie des Thomas*

Hobbes: Eine vergleichende Analyse von 'The Elements of Law', 'De Cive' und den eng-lischen und lateinischen Fassungen des 'Leviathan' (2008). His works on the history of political philosophy have appeared in *Archiv für Geschichte der Philosophie, The Southern Journal of Philosophy, Intellectual History Review*, and *Hobbes Studies*.

FRANCK LESSAY is Emeritus Professor at the Sorbonne Nouvelle-Paris 3 University. He has published *Souveraineté et légitimité chez Hobbes* (1988), *Le débat Locke-Filmer* (1998), *Les fondements philosophiques de la tolérance* (2002, as co-editor), and about a hundred articles on various subjects of political theory in French, English, and Italian journals. He has translated several short treatises of Hobbes into French.

S. A. LLOYD is Professor of Philosophy and Law at the University of Southern California. She is author of *Ideals as Interests in Hobbes's Leviathan* (1992) and *Morality in the Philosophy of Thomas Hobbes: Cases in the Law of Nature* (2009), and editor of *Hobbes Today* (2012), *The Bloomsbury Companion to Hobbes* (2012), and *Interpreting Hobbes's Political Thought* (forthcoming).

A. P. MARTINICH is Vaughan Centennial Professor in Philosophy and Professor of History and Government at the University of Texas at Austin. He is the author of *The Two Gods of Leviathan* (1992), *A Hobbes Dictionary* (1995), *Hobbes: A Biography* (1999), *Hobbes* (2005), and co-editor (with Kinch Hoekstra) of *The Oxford Handbook of Hobbes* (2016).

ALISON MCQUEEN is an Assistant Professor in the Department of Political Science at Stanford University. Her work focuses on religion in early modern political thought, political realism, and the ethics and politics of catastrophe. She is the author of *Political Realism in Apocalyptic Times* (2018). Her work has appeared in *The Journal of Politics, Perspectives on Politics, European Journal of Political Theory*, and *American Political Thought*.

GLEN NEWEY was, until his death in 2017, Professor of Practical Philosophy at Leiden University in the Netherlands. He was the author of *Hobbes and Leviathan* (London: Routledge; revised and expanded edition 2014), and several other books on political philosophy, as well as numerous articles.

JOHAN OLSTHOORN is Assistant Professor in Political Theory at the University of Amsterdam and Postdoctoral Fellow of the Research Foundation—Flanders (FWO) (2015–21) at KU Leuven. He has published widely on Hobbes and early modern moral and political philosophy.

JON PARKIN is Fellow and Tutor in History at St Hugh's College Oxford. He has held posts at Cambridge, London, and York and is the author of *Science, Religion, and Politics in Restoration England* (1999), *Taming the Leviathan* (2007) and co-editor (with Timothy Stanton) of *Natural Law and Toleration in the Early Enlightenment* (2013).

PATRICIA SPRINGBORG is Guest Professor and Fellow at the Centre for British Studies of the Humboldt University, Berlin. She edited *Mary Astell: Political Writings* (1996) and *The Cambridge Companion to Hobbes's Leviathan* (2007), and co-authored the first English translation and critical edition of Hobbes's *Historia Ecclesiastica* (2008). Her research in political theory has been published in the *American Political Science Review*, *Political Theory*, *Political Studies*, *History of Political Thought*, *Journal of the History of Ideas*, and the *British Journal for the History of Philosophy*.

Abbreviations

The following abbreviations are used for frequently cited works of Hobbes:

AW   *Thomas White's De Mundo Examined*, trans. Harold Whitmore Jones (London: Bradford University Press, 1976).

B   *Behemoth or The Long Parliament*, ed. Paul Seaward (Oxford: Clarendon Press, 2010).

C   *The Correspondence*, ed. Noel Malcolm, 2 vols (Oxford: Clarendon Press, 1994).

DCo   *De Corpore*, trans. as *Elements of Philosophy. The First Section, Concerning Body*, in *The English Works of Thomas Hobbes of Malmesbury*, i, ed. William Molesworth (London: John Bohn, 1839), 388–90.

DCv   *De Cive*, trans. as *On the Citizen*, ed. Richard Tuck and Michael Silverthorne (Cambridge: Cambridge University Press, 1998).

DH   *De Homine*, trans. in *Man and Citizen*, ed. Bernard Gert (Indianapolis, IN: Hackett, 1991).

DPS   *A Dialogue between a Philosopher and a Student, of the Common Laws of England*, in *Writings on Common Law and Hereditary Right*, ed. Alan Cromartie and Quentin Skinner (Oxford: Clarendon Press, 2005), 1–152.

EL   *The Elements of Law, Natural and Politic: Part I, Human Nature, Part II, De Corpore Politico*, ed. J. C. A. Gaskin (Oxford: Oxford University Press, 1994).

EW   *The English Works of Thomas Hobbes of Malmesbury*, ed. William Molesworth, 10 vols (London: John Bohn, 1839–45).

HE   *Historia Ecclesiastica*, ed. and trans. Patricia Springborg, Patricia Stablein, and Paul Wilson (Paris: Champion, 2008).

L   *Leviathan: The English and Latin Texts*, ed. Noel Malcolm (Oxford: Clarendon Press, 2012).

LL   Latin *Leviathan*, in *Leviathan: The English and Latin Texts*, ed. Noel Malcolm (Oxford: Clarendon Press, 2012).

LLA   'Appendix to *Leviathan*', in *Leviathan: The English and Latin Texts*, ed. Noel Malcolm (Oxford: Clarendon Press, 2012).

OL   *Thomae Hobbes malmesburiensis opera philosophica quae latine scripsit omnia*, ed. William Molesworth, 5 vols (London: John Bohn, 1839–45).

QLNC *Questions Concerning Liberty, Necessity, and Chance* (London, 1656).

References to AW, DCo, DCv, DH, and EL are given by chapter and section numbers. References to EW and OL are given by volume and page numbers. References to L and

LL are given by chapter and page numbers in the Clarendon edition. For other works, references are given by page number to the edition cited. For full details of works of Hobbes cited see the Bibliography.

Spelling, capitalization, and punctuation generally follow the conventions in the editions cited, although rounded and pointed forms of 'u' and 'v' have been modernized appropriately. When not quoting directly from Hobbes, chapter contributors have been given the freedom to decide whether to follow seventeenth-century conventions of referring to 'man' and use of the male pronoun, or to update such language into gender-neutral terms.

Introduction

Laurens van Apeldoorn and Robin Douglass

This volume investigates the complex and rich intersections between Thomas Hobbes's political and religious thought. Hobbes is often credited with being one of the first great theorists of the modern state,[1] but the state he theorized, as the title of his most famous work announces, was a commonwealth ecclesiastical and civil. One of the main goals of *Leviathan* (1651) was to unite 'the two heads of the eagle', to use Jean-Jacques Rousseau's memorable phrase,[2] for '*Temporall and Spirituall* Government, are but two words brought into the world, to make men see double, and mistake their *Lawfull Soveraign*'.[3]

Religion is central to an understanding of seventeenth-century politics, and so too Hobbes's politics. Politics is, amongst other things, a response to problems of human conflict and disagreement, and the greatest conflicts and disagreements of Hobbes's day were of religious inspiration. As early as 1641 he wrote to William Cavendish, third Earl of Devonshire, that 'the dispute for precedence betwene the *spirituall* and *civill power*, has of late more than any other thing in the world, bene the cause of *civill warres*, in all *places of Christendome*'.[4] The English Civil War soon served to confirm this, which Hobbes later diagnosed as arising from the conflicts between Catholicism and Anglicanism, and within Anglicanism between Episcopalians and Presbyterians.[5] The kingdom of darkness, propagated chiefly by the Roman clergy and Presbyterian ministers, looms whenever people believe that the church has greater authority than the sovereign. Long-lasting peace could only ever be attained by overcoming the disputes between spiritual and civil powers, for which people would need to understand that the authority of any church derives from that of the sovereign.

---

[1] E.g. Quentin Skinner, 'A Genealogy of the Modern State', *Proceedings of the British Academy* 162 (2009), 325–70.

[2] Jean-Jacques Rousseau, *Du contrat social; ou principes du droit politique* (Amsterdam, 1762), book 4, chapter 8.

[3] L, 39, pp. 732–4.

[4] C, p. 120. Cf. DCv, 6.11. Referring to religious views supporting the belief that citizens 'have the right and the duty to refuse obedience to the commonwealth', Hobbes wrote: 'What war ever broke out in the Christian world that did not spring from this root or was fed by it?'

[5] LLA, p. 1226; B, pp. 181, 232.

In *The Elements of Law* (1640), the first instalment of his political philosophy, Hobbes had argued for the authority of the supreme magistrate over all doctrinal matters largely on the basis of secular premises. After the Civil War he became increasingly aware of the need to show that his position would also be acceptable from a theological point of view, giving rise to the two-pronged approach so characteristic of *Leviathan*: while the first two books develop a defence of absolutism on the basis of a naturalistic human psychology, the second two books do so on the basis of a study of Scripture and church history. This strategy does much to explain the complex relationship between his political and religious views.

In considering the appropriate place of religious institutions in society, Hobbes approached religion primarily as a political phenomenon of natural origins. Religious institutions, he recognized, serve to exercise power over others. This led him, on the one hand, to engage in notorious invectives against deceiving theologians who deny the supremacy of civil over religious authorities. He exposed them as envious and ambitious men who abuse Scripture and the 'Vain philosophy' of Aristotle for their own 'worldly Benefits'—sovereign power first among them, but also the right to determine successions in hereditary kingdoms, and exemptions from taxation.[6] He explained their motives from his conception of human nature, which reserved a prominent role for the pursuit of glory and power, while simultaneously drawing on his epistemology, most fully developed in *De Corpore* (1655), to denounce their teachings as meaningless canting.

On the other hand, Hobbes also recognized that religious institutions could be enlisted in support of social tranquillity. The seeds of religion are natural to humans and are cultivated in society 'with a purpose to make those men that relyed on them, the more apt to Obedience, Lawes, Peace, Charity, and civill Society'.[7] While it is tempting to focus solely on Hobbes's biting criticisms of certain religious doctrines and sects, it is also worth keeping in mind, as Sarah Mortimer has recently reminded us, that he appreciated the power of Christianity 'not only to destroy commonwealths but to support them'.[8] To this end, for instance, he proposed ambitious reforms of the universities, which he condemned as a hotbed of seditious teaching, and in *Behemoth* (1681) expressed his hope that 'the Polyticks there taught be made to be (as true Polyticks should be) such as are fit to make men know that it is their duty to obey all Laws whatsoever shall by the Authority of the King be enacted'.[9] Hobbes was a theorist of civil religion and many of his criticisms of specific religious ideas and practices are based on their failing to serve the ends of the state.[10]

---

[6] L, 47, pp. 1104–10.   [7] L, 12, p. 170.

[8] Sarah Mortimer, 'Christianity and Civil Religion in Hobbes's *Leviathan*', in *The Oxford Handbook of Hobbes*, ed. A. P. Martinich and Kinch Hoekstra (Oxford: Oxford University Press, 2016), 517.

[9] B, p. 182.

[10] L, 29, p. 517. On Hobbes's civil religion see e.g. Richard Tuck, 'The "Christian Atheism" of Thomas Hobbes', in *Atheism from Reformation to the Enlightenment*, ed. M. Hunter and D. Wootton (Oxford: Oxford University Press, 1992), 111–30; Tuck, 'The Civil Religion of Thomas Hobbes', in *Political Discourse in Early Modern Britain,* ed. Nicholas Phillipson and Quentin Skinner (Cambridge: Cambridge University

To make his political doctrines acceptable to a religious audience Hobbes pursued an elaborate rereading of Scripture. He understood all too well that if one were to be required to obey a command 'as cannot be obeyed, without being damned to Eternall Death, then it were madnesse to obey it'.[11] That is why he sought to show the consistency of the near unlimited obedience he demanded from citizens of a well-ordered commonwealth with the requirements for their salvation. His engagement with Scripture, moreover, aimed to square the teachings of the Bible with the ontological and epistemological commitments that informed his conception of human nature and ultimately underpinned his politics. This led him, for example, to find scriptural evidence for the corporality of God and the soul, and for the temporary nature of the torments of Hell.[12] After writing *Leviathan* he increasingly turned to ecclesiastical history. In works such as *Behemoth* (his history of the Civil War), the *Historia Ecclesiastica* (1688), and *A Historical Narration Concerning Heresy* (1668), he further defended— and, as in the case of his highly inflammatory reading of the Trinity, revised—his theological positions. One of the persistent themes in these writings remained his critique of the clergy, 'for whom war was useful',[13] and who attempted to undermine the authority of civil authorities with potentially grave consequences.

Hobbes's project, then, committed him to dangerously heterodox theological positions and it is unsurprising that, in his own day, his religious views courted at least as much controversy as his civil ones. Commentators expressed outrage over his materialistic metaphysics, which they regarded as coming dangerously close to denying the existence of God and rendering the grounds of religion and morality uncertain.[14] Henry More, in *The Immortality of the Soul* (1659), worried that Hobbes held that 'there is no Religion, no Piety nor Impiety, no Vertue nor Vice, Justice nor Injustice, but what it pleases him that has the longest Sword to call so'.[15] Hobbes's critics were equally concerned by his scriptural interpretations. Upon reading *Leviathan*'s deflationary account of Hell and eternal suffering, Bishop John Bramhall remarked, quite accurately, that Hobbes 'hath killed the great infernal Devil, and all his black angels, and left no devils to be feared, but devils incarnate, that is, wicked men'.[16] Hobbes's Erastianism

Press, 2010), 120–38; Patricia Springborg, 'Hobbes's Theory of Civil Religion', in *Pluralismo e religione civile*, ed. Gianni Paganini and Edoardo Tortarolo (Milan: Bruno Mondatori, 2003), 61–98; Ronald Beiner, *Civil Religion: A Dialogue in the History of Political Philosophy* (Cambridge: Cambridge University Press, 2010), especially chapters 5–6; Mortimer, 'Christianity and Civil Religion'.

[11] L, 43, pp. 928–30.
[12] EW 4, p. 313; L, 38, pp. 716–18; LLA, pp. 1128–30.   [13] HE, line 29, p. 307.
[14] Responding to Hobbes's materialism, John Wallis in *Elenchus Geometriae Hobbianae* wrote: 'Who does not see that thereby you not only deny . . . angels and immortal souls, but the great and good God himself', quoted in Jon Parkin, *Taming the Leviathan: The Reception of the Political and Religious Ideas of Thomas Hobbes in England, 1640–1700* (Cambridge: Cambridge University Press, 2007), 152.
[15] Henry More, *The Immortality of the Soul, So farre forth as it is Demonstrable from the Knowledge of Nature and the Light of Reason* (London, 1659), 56.
[16] John Bramhall, quoted in EW 4, p. 356. For evidence that these fears were better grounded than is often suspected, see Jon Parkin, 'Baiting the Bear: The Anglican Attack on Hobbes in the Later 1660s', *History of Political Thought* 34.3 (2013), 421–58.

was also attacked, with George Lawson maintaining that it is 'as great an offence for the State to encroach upon the Church, as for the Church to encroach upon the State'.[17] By the late 1660s, as John Aubrey famously reported, the opposition Hobbes's views had generated apparently left him fearful of a motion proposed to Parliament by some of the bishops 'to have the good old gentleman burn't for a heretique'.[18]

If Hobbes's seventeenth-century readers appreciated that questions of religion and politics are inextricably bound, this did not last. By the middle of the twentieth century Hobbes had been recast as a secular forefather of modernity. His lengthy discussions of religion and the Bible could thus be abridged with no great loss.[19] Even John Rawls, who praised *Leviathan* as 'the greatest single work of political thought in the English language', taught his students that Hobbes's 'secular political and moral system is fully intelligible as regards its structure of ideas and the content of its principles when [its] theological assumptions are left aside'.[20] One of the most important developments of late twentieth-century Hobbes scholarship was the rediscovery of the importance of religion, but even in 1992, in what remains one of the most comprehensive studies of the relationship between Hobbes's political and religious thought, A. P. Martinich could write that: 'Most Hobbes scholars are secularists. One consequence is that they present a bowdlerized version of his philosophy from which all the religious elements have been expurgated.'[21] Happily, things have continued to improve over the last twenty-five years and increased scholarly attention has been devoted to the religious dimensions of Hobbes's thought. Yet it arguably remains the case, as Jeffrey Collins remarked in his landmark study of 2005, that 'there has been a pronounced tendency to treat Hobbes's religion and his political views as discrete subjects', such that conventional scholarship 'has failed to grasp the fundamentally religious nature of the Hobbesian project'.[22]

This volume seeks to bring these two subjects together, exploring the relationship between Hobbes's political and religious thought from various perspectives. The focus is principally on Hobbes's religious politics, rather than his own religious beliefs, or lack thereof.[23] All chapters in this volume engage, in one way or another, with his treatment of religion as a political phenomenon or with the political dimensions of his

[17] George Lawson, *An Examination of the Political Part of Mr. Hobbs his Leviathan* (London, 1657), 138.

[18] John Aubrey, *Brief Lives, Chiefly of Contemporaries*, ed. A. Clark (Oxford: Clarendon Press, 1898), i, 339.

[19] See Sterling P. Lamprecht's edition of *De Cive* (New York: Appleton-Century-Crofts, 1949), and Herbert W. Schneider's edition of *Leviathan: Parts One and Two* (New York: Liberal Arts Press, 1958). Thanks to Paul Davis for these references.

[20] John Rawls, *Lectures on the History of Political Philosophy*, ed. Samuel Freeman (Cambridge, MA: Belknap Press of Harvard University Press, 2007), 23, 26. Even if this view is less widely endorsed by Hobbes scholars today, it remains the impression that many undergraduate students encountering Hobbes for the first time, especially those studying philosophy or politics, will be left with.

[21] A. P. Martinich, *Two Gods of Leviathan: Thomas Hobbes on Religion and Politics* (Cambridge: Cambridge University Press, 1992), 14.

[22] Jeffrey Collins, *The Allegiance of Thomas Hobbes* (Oxford: Oxford University Press, 2005), 4.

[23] A contrast adopted from Glen Newey, *Routledge Philosophy Guidebook to Hobbes' Leviathan*, 2nd edition (New York: Routledge, 2014), 232.

engagement with Christian doctrines and their history. In particular, the volume seeks to move beyond questions that have attracted much scholarly attention in the past—most notably, 'was Hobbes an atheist?',[24] or 'should the laws of nature be understood as divine commands?'[25]—to open up new directions for thinking about the relationship between politics and religion in Hobbes. Our aim is not to provide exhaustive coverage of this relationship, but rather to ask new questions and illuminate perspectives that have not previously received the attention they deserve.

In order to open up new directions of research it helps to take a pluralistic approach, which is reflected in the methodological diversity of the chapters in this volume. Some authors pursue mainly historical inquiries about the motives and circumstances of Hobbes's political and religious writings. These contributions seek to unearth the pressures that led him to pursue certain lines of argument over others, allowing us to better understand the meaning of his ideas. Others test their philosophical coherence and examine their relevance for contemporary concerns. We, too, live in an age of religious diversity, which often manifests itself in disagreement and conflict. While Hobbes's world was no doubt very different from ours, these authors show that we may profit from looking closely at his strategies to overcome religious disagreement in the pursuit of peace.

In Chapter 1, Johan Olsthoorn traces the development of Hobbes's views on the relationship between civil and religious authority from *De Cive* (1642, 2nd edition 1647) to *Leviathan*. He shows that Hobbes defended a view that went beyond Erastianism—requiring that the church is subordinate to the state—arguing for the much stronger thesis that the church is identical with the state. Olsthoorn reveals that Hobbes's arguments for this identity change in *Leviathan*, based on his new authorization and representation doctrine, and highlights that the work introduces a number of 'theocratic' elements, so substituting 'a Priesthood of Kings' for 'a Kingdome of Priests'. Where Olsthoorn examines how Hobbes's theory of civil sovereignty comes to encompass the church, in Chapter 2, A. P. Martinich focuses on Hobbes's account of God's

---

[24] E.g. J. G. A. Pocock, 'Time, History and Eschatology in the Thought of Thomas Hobbes', in his *Politics, Language, and Time: Essays on Political Thought and History* (New York: Athenaeum, 1971), 148–201; Willis B. Glover, 'God and Thomas Hobbes', in *Hobbes Studies*, ed. K. C. Brown (Oxford: Blackwell, 1965), 141–68; Arrigo Pacchi, 'Hobbes and the Problem of God', in *Perspective on Thomas Hobbes*, ed. G. A. J. Rogers and Alan Ryan (Oxford: Oxford University Press, 1988), 171–88; Martinich, *Two Gods*, especially chapter 1; Edwin Curley, ' "I durst not write so boldly" or, How to Read Hobbes' Theological-Political Treatise', in *Hobbes and Spinoza: Science and Politics*, ed. D. Bostrenghi (Napoli: Bibliopolis, 1992), 497–593; Curley, 'Calvin and Hobbes, or Hobbes as an Orthodox Christian', *Journal of the History of Philosophy*, 34.2 (1996), 257–71; Douglas M. Jesseph, 'Hobbes's Atheism', *Midwest Studies in Philosophy* 26 (2002), 140–66; Alan Cromartie, 'The God of Thomas Hobbes', *The Historical Journal* 51.4 (2008), 857–79.

[25] E.g. A. E. Taylor, 'The Ethical Doctrine of Hobbes', *Philosophy* 13.52 (1938), 406–24; Howard Warrender, *The Political Philosophy of Hobbes: His Theory of Obligation* (Oxford: Clarendon Press, 1957); John Plamenatz, 'Mr. Warrender's Hobbes', *Political Studies* 5.3 (1957), 295–308; F. C. Hood, *The Divine Politics of Thomas Hobbes: An Interpretation of Leviathan* (Oxford: Clarendon Press, 1964); Brian Barry, 'Warrender and His Critics', *Philosophy* 43.64 (1968), 117–37; Martinich, *Two Gods*, especially chapter 4; David Gauthier, 'Hobbes: The Laws of Nature', *Pacific Philosophy Quarterly* 82.3–4 (2001), 258–84; Perez Zagorin, *Hobbes and the Law of Nature* (Princeton, NJ: Princeton University Press, 2009).

natural sovereignty and explores its implications for understanding civil sovereignty. Taking as his starting point the position that the rights of sovereignty derive directly from omnipotence, Martinich analyses the nature of divine sovereignty and argues that Hobbes may have been led to argue for this thesis in order to facilitate the comparison of the powers of earthly sovereigns—Hobbes called them 'mortal Gods'—with those of the deity. He also shows that the comparison runs both ways and that Hobbes may have had in mind specific psalms and other biblical texts when he attributed properties to the earthly sovereign that were traditionally attributed to God.

The chapters by Teresa M. Bejan and Franck Lessay address the contentious problem of the place of private religious belief in a Hobbesian commonwealth and thereby offer original—and contrasting—perspectives on the 'tolerant Hobbes?' debate.[26] In Chapter 3, Bejan challenges the widely held assumption that Hobbesian sovereigns are unable to affect inward belief and instead reveals how, through education, they could shape the religious convictions of their subjects. She pursues this argument through an examination of Hobbes's rich metaphor of imprinting and, in doing so, brings to light an aspect of his thought neglected by those who read him as an advocate of toleration or proponent of popular enlightenment. That position is evaluated further in Chapter 4, in which Franck Lessay argues that the secular justification Hobbes offers for the sovereign's absolute power supports a tolerant approach towards religion, such that tolerance should be viewed as a dimension of Hobbesian absolutism. On Lessay's reading, Hobbes's doctrinal minimalism and focus on civil peace as the relevant criterion for assessing questions of tolerance led him to demarcate a private sphere for religious judgements, beyond the reach of the sovereign.

In Chapter 5, Alexandra Chadwick addresses Hobbes's project of reconciling salvation and obedience from a very different angle, by assessing the apparent tension between his deterministic-materialist psychology and his explanation of the motives of martyrs who prioritize eternal salvation over bodily preservation. Chadwick shows not only that Hobbes's materialist psychology is compatible with his discussion of martyrdom, but also that those who choose martyrdom are mistaken about the powers and purposes of human beings. Where Hobbes's theology reveals that martyrs misunderstand what is required for salvation, Chadwick argues, his psychology reveals that they more fundamentally misunderstand their own nature as humans.

Chapter 6 plunges deeper into the historical context in which Hobbes developed the philosophical arguments for his deterministic-materialist psychology, by addressing his relation to Calvinism. Alan Cromartie charts the collapse of Calvinist doctrine in early seventeenth-century England and relates this to developments in Hobbes's philosophical career up until his debates with Bishop John Bramhall on free will and determinism. Cromartie shows that Hobbes's determinism was not an eccentric

---

[26] For an overview of the main contours of the debate, see Teresa M. Bejan, 'Difference without Disagreement: Rethinking Hobbes on "Independency" and Toleration', *The Review of Politics* 78.1 (2016), 1–6.

variant on well-established views, but very much at odds with standard Protestant assumptions. By setting Hobbes's determinism against this background, Cromartie helps us to appreciate its sheer novelty and, more speculatively, raises further questions about the place of religion in motivating Hobbes's philosophy—questions that are problematic for both those who read him as a loyal Calvinist and those who see his determinism as wholly secular.

Alison McQueen and Paul B. Davis both focus, in different respects, on the biblical context of Hobbes's political thought. In Chapter 7, McQueen discusses the place that biblical Israel occupied in seventeenth-century political and religious debates and, against this background, identifies a 'Mosaic turn' in *Leviathan*, where Moses is presented as the scriptural exemplar of a civil sovereign. McQueen shows how the Mosaic turn intervened in debates between defenders of monarchical rule and parliamentarians, who drew respectively on the period of Davidic kings and the polity of the Israelites under Moses in support of their political positions. She argues that this should be understood as a polemical move whereby Hobbes sought to appropriate and thereby subvert the parliamentarian appeal to the Mosaic polity. In Chapter 8, Davis advances our understanding of Hobbes's use of Scripture by documenting where and how his scriptural quotations diverged from contemporary translations of the Bible. While Hobbes usually relied on these translations, Davis reveals that on some points—especially regarding supernatural phenomena—he took considerable liberties to reconcile the Bible with the key tenets of his own political philosophy. Davis also shows that attending to Hobbes's translations both helps to locate some of the key sources for his biblical exegesis, such as work by the biblical scholar Joseph Mede, and provides further evidence confirming that a Latin text of *Leviathan* did not predate the English version.

The chapters by Patricia Springborg and Glen Newey turn to the explosive political environment facing Hobbes after the Restoration, when he became increasingly engrossed in questions of theology and church history. In Chapter 9, Springborg considers the dating and context of the *Historia Ecclesiastica*, which further develops material that Hobbes had added to the Latin *Leviathan* (1668), and argues that the poem aimed to appeal to humanist Christian historiographers, perhaps with the aim of responding to the accusations of heresy and atheism he was facing. In Chapter 10, Newey challenges the widespread view that the changes Hobbes made in the Latin *Leviathan* and its Appendix—in particular with regard to his radically deflationary conception of the Trinity—were occasioned by these accusations of heresy. If Hobbes was really set on avoiding prosecution for heretical views, then adducing further scriptural support for eccentric theological views unpersuasive to his Anglican audience was a needlessly risky strategy. It seems more likely, Newey argues, that he published these views in those later works simply because he thought they were correct.

In Chapter 11, Jon Parkin addresses the question of Hobbes's audience from a different perspective, by showing how Hobbes hoped to ensure that the legacy of his religious ideas would be amenable to different readers who might take them forward. While Hobbes never articulated a clear vision of the future of religion, Parkin argues that he aimed to produce a deliberately ambiguous religious identity, precisely so that he could engage with the diversity of religious audiences of his day. This is not just reflected in his doctrinal minimalism, but also in the distinctive writing strategies he deployed to convey his religious ideas. Many of those ideas, Parkin argues, could be accommodated by multiple possible religious futures and, in each case, a Hobbesian version of that future would provide more stable foundations for a Christian commonwealth.

One such possible future is teased out in Chapter 12, in which Elad Carmel charts Hobbes's considerable influence on the development of early English deism. Hobbes's anticlericalism and criticisms of revelation proved especially attractive to the deists and Carmel argues that their and Hobbes's political projects, while different in crucial respects, were animated by similar concerns, which are obscured when Hobbes is straightforwardly read as an authoritarian and the deists as proponents of toleration. Foregrounding their anticlericalism, however, brings their common goal into view and, Carmel suggests, reveals deism to be one possible highway to Hobbesian enlightenment.

In Chapter 13, Jeffrey Collins addresses Hobbes's more long-lasting contribution to enlightenment, liberal, or secular narratives of modernity, by focusing on the problem of religious warfare. On the one hand, Collins argues that recruiting Hobbes as a secular theorist of sovereignty who helped to resolve this problem presupposes a generic account of religious violence in tension with Hobbes's own analysis of the English Civil War, which emphasized its historical specificity. On the other hand, Collins suggests that Hobbes actually contributed to this confusion by at times having offered psychological and proto-sociological accounts of religion that anticipated later enlightened or liberal narratives. Collins is thus able to explain why Hobbes has come to occupy such an important place in such narratives, while at the same time revealing their partiality.

In the final two chapters of the volume, Daniel Eggers and S. A. Lloyd each seek to evaluate whether Hobbes's political philosophy remains instructive for thinking about how to overcome problems of religious disagreement. In Chapter 14, Eggers pits Hobbes (and modern-day Hobbesians) against John Rawls by evaluating two different approaches for forming moral consensus in the face of religious diversity. Eggers argues that the Hobbesian approach should be understood as a form of extra-moral justification, derived from non-moral premises, whereas the Rawlsian approach is a form of intra-moral justification that takes certain moral principles for granted. Eggers assesses the merits of each approach and maintains that, on balance, the Rawlsian approach is better equipped to address religious disagreement. In Chapter 15, Lloyd focuses on Hobbes's controversial principle that we have a duty not to act on our conscience in cases where the demands of conscience conflict with the sovereign's commands. Lloyd argues that while this principle is widely considered suspect—having been repudiated at Nuremberg—there is nonetheless something defensible about it, which any plausible theory of political obligation will have to accommodate. Lloyd also considers the extent to which Hobbes's reasoning relies on indispensable theological premises, and thus takes a stance on the vexed question of whether a purely secular interpretation of his political philosophy can adequately explain his central commitments.

As this brief overview indicates, the chapters in this volume provide wide-ranging and sometimes conflicting assessments of Hobbes's political and religious thought. As such, the volume does not advance any single overarching interpretative claim about precisely how the relationship between Hobbes's political and religious ideas should be understood, beyond showing how closely intertwined they are. In their different ways, however, the chapters all showcase how this perspective can help us to better understand his thought, lest we see double when we read Hobbes.

1

The Theocratic *Leviathan*

Hobbes's Arguments for the Identity of Church and State

Johan Olsthoorn

a Church, such a one as is capable to Command, to Judge, Absolve, Condemn, or do any other act, is the same thing with a Civil Common-wealth, consisting of Christian men; and is called a *Civill State*, for that the subjects of it are *Men*; and a *Church*, for that the subjects thereof are *Christians*[1]

Hobbes is commonly read as expounding an Erastian theory of church–state relations.[2] Taking its name from the Swiss Protestant theologian Thomas Erastus (1524–83), Erastianism is the view that the state holds supreme authority over religious and ecclesiastical as well as civil affairs.[3] Hobbes certainly endorses lay control over the clergy. But as the introductory quotation attests, he also defends a stronger claim: a church, properly understood, is *identical with* a state headed by a Christian ruler. '[A] *commonwealth* [*civitas*] and a *church* [*ecclesia*] of the same *Christian* men are exactly the same thing under two names'.[4] There are hence as many churches as there are commonwealths governed by a Christian sovereign, and none of these

For helpful comments on earlier drafts of this chapter, I would like to thank Robin Douglass, Franck Lessay, Jan Machielsen, A. P. Martinich, Lodi Nauta, Laurens van Apeldoorn, George Wright, and audiences at KU Leuven, UC Berkeley, and the Renaissance Society of America Conference 2016.

[1] L, 39, p. 732.

[2] E.g. J. P. Sommerville, 'Hobbes, Selden, Erastianism, and the History of the Jews', in *Hobbes and History*, ed. G. A. J. Rogers and Tom Sorell (London: Routledge, 2000), 160–88; Jeffrey Collins, *The Allegiance of Thomas Hobbes* (Oxford: Oxford University Press, 2005); Eric Brandon, *The Coherence of Hobbes's 'Leviathan': Civil and Religious Authority Combined* (London: Bloomsbury, 2007), 75–94; A. P. Martinich, 'Hobbes's Erastianism and Interpretation', *Journal of the History of Ideas* 70.1 (2009), 143–63. Cf. J. P. Sommerville, *Thomas Hobbes: Political Ideas in Historical Context* (Basingstoke: Macmillan Press, 1992), 127–34.

[3] J. Neville Figgis, 'Erastus and Erastianism', *Journal of Theological Studies* 2.5 (1900), 66–101.

[4] DCv, 17.21. Also DCv, 17.26–8, 18.1, 18.13; L, 33, p. 606; L, 39, p. 732; L, 42, pp. 864–6; L, 42, p. 916; L, 47, p. 1104; LLA, p. 1196; EW 4, pp. 337–8; EW 7, p. 345.

commonwealths has an institutional structure distinct from its national church (the reverse also holds).[5]

How are we to understand the church–state identity thesis? And what is Hobbes's argument for it? Erastianism does not by itself entail or require the identification of church and state. The doctrine is compatible with the more moderate contention that the church is a separate body subordinate to the state, as well as with Erastus's own identification of 'church' in its sword-wielding sense with the civil magistracy.[6] Hobbes's well-known arguments for the sovereign's absolute authority over civil as well as religious affairs—as being required for peace and political stability and as vouch-safed by Scripture—do not therefore suffice to establish that 'a Christian Church and a Christian commonwealth are the same thing'.[7] An additional argument is needed. What is it?

This chapter argues that Hobbes advanced two distinct arguments for the church–state identity thesis. Both understand 'church' as a congregation of Christians. And both are premised on the idea of personation: a church, properly understood, consists of a multitude of Christians united into one person (section 1.1). The two arguments differ, however, with respect to how this personation is achieved.

On *De Cive*'s Summon & Bind model of personation, analysed in section 1.2, personating a disparate mob of Christians into a church requires some authority 'by which individuals are obliged to attend the meeting either in person or through others'.[8] Absent this obligation, no words and actions can be attributed to the assembled individuals *qua* crowd; the multitude would consist of many persons rather than of one. Only the sovereign, Hobbes argues, has the authority requisite for uniting a multitude of Christians into a personified church. Since states lack jurisdiction across borders, it follows that 'a Christian commonwealth is a Christian Church...and is co-extensive with it'.[9] On Summon & Bind, the sovereign is head of the church. But she does not necessarily *represent* the church (an idea Hobbes had not yet fully developed at the time). All the sovereign does is provide the conditions for church personation to be possible. Summon & Bind does not therefore imply or require that the sovereign speaks on behalf of the church. The model is compatible with mere state control

---

[5] According to Sommerville, *Thomas Hobbes*, 117, Hobbes's identity thesis was unoriginal: 'Anglicans commonly held that in any Christian country, church and commonwealth are simply terms describing two different aspects of a single community'. See also J. P. Sommerville, '*Leviathan* and its Anglican Context', in *The Cambridge Companion to Hobbes's Leviathan*, ed. Patricia Springborg (Cambridge: Cambridge University Press, 2007), 363; Martinich, 'Hobbes's Erastianism', 157. The Anglican Bishop Bramhall was not of this opinion: 'All other men distinguish between the church and the commonwealth; only *T. H.* maketh them to be one and the same thing' (quoted in EW 4, p. 336). On shifts in Anglican views on this issue during the 1640–50s, see Sarah Mortimer, 'Christianity and Civil Religion in Hobbes's *Leviathan*', in *The Oxford Handbook of Hobbes*, ed. A. P. Martinich and Kinch Hoekstra (Oxford: Oxford University Press, 2016), 501–19.

[6] Thomas Erastus, *The Nullity of Church-Censures* (London, 1659), 49: 'But there are solid Arguments to prove that Christ in this place [Matt. 18.17] by the word Church will not have us understand the multitude, and common meetings of the *Jews*, but the *Jewish* Magistracy or Senate' (also pp. 51, 59). For Hobbes, both 'church' and 'commonwealth' denote the entire unified body of citizens living within a territory.

[7] DCv, 18.13.   [8] DCv, 17.20.   [9] DCv, 17.26.

over the ecclesiastical councils and synods whose words and actions are attributed to the church.

On *Leviathan*'s Representation model of personation, by contrast, the church is a civil person created through representation by the sovereign (section 1.3). The sovereign bears the person of the church just as she bears that of the commonwealth. More precisely, since the church *is* the commonwealth, the sovereign actually bears only one person: that of the people. While theoretically parsimonious, we cannot straightforwardly apply representation to church personation. Unlike the commonwealth, the church is not formed through an original covenant in which individuals mutually agree to authorize and henceforth obey a common representative. This raises the question why the civil sovereign, and not someone else, represents the church? Section 1.4 argues that actors other than the sovereign can represent the church without contravening either political absolutism or Erastianism. *Leviathan* has the conceptual and theoretical resources to portray churches as regular subordinate systems: associations of citizens united into one civil person by an internal representative, subject to the higher authority of the state.

But that is a road not taken. In *Leviathan*, Christian sovereigns represent the church. This is somewhat surprising. Hobbes's masterpiece is often read as outlining a modern, secular theory of the state.[10] But as section 1.5 reveals, the account of church–state relations developed in the second half of the book is anything but secular. *Leviathan*'s Christian commonwealth incorporates several strikingly theocratic features not present in the earlier works. The sovereign is the 'Supreme Pastor', an office she ostensibly holds by divine right. Moreover, *Leviathan* endows Christian sovereigns with full spiritual and sacerdotal powers *ex officio*, including powers of consecration and baptism. As Ronald Beiner aptly observes: 'Hobbes's object is not to divorce theology and politics, but rather, as he puts it, to substitute "a Priesthood of Kings" for "a Kingdom of Priests".'[11] This chapter contends that *Leviathan*'s Representation model of church personation explains this shift: the sovereign representative of the church must have full sacerdotal powers since subordinate priests act in her name and by her right.

1.1   Of the Signification of the Word 'Church'

Hobbes's discussions of the scriptural meanings of 'church' in *De Cive* and *Leviathan* proceed along similar lines.[12] *Leviathan* mentions five distinct scriptural senses of the

---

[10] Indeed, Hobbes has been called 'the master theorist of the modern state'. See Christopher W. Morris, *An Essay on the Modern State* (Cambridge: Cambridge University Press, 1998), 40, and his 'The State', in *The Oxford Handbook of the History of Political Philosophy*, ed. George Klosko (Oxford: Oxford University Press, 2011), 549.

[11] Ronald Beiner, *Civil Religion: A Dialogue in the History of Political Philosophy* (Cambridge: Cambridge University Press, 2010), 59; and his 'Machiavelli, Hobbes, and Rousseau on Civil Religion', *The Review of Politics* 55.4 (1993), 630. Citing L, 35, p. 642.

[12] *The Elements of Law*, chapter 26, contains a prolonged discussion of church government without, however, discussing what a church is.

term 'church'. Only the first of these, [A] as a religious building (temple), is not found in *De Cive*. This sense of 'church' is metaphorical, Hobbes claims, 'for the Congregation there assembled'.[13] As Greek etymology attests, in its proper signification 'church' means [B] 'a Congregation, or an Assembly of Citizens, called forth, to hear the Magistrate speak unto them'. Assemblies summoned by a proper authority are called 'lawful churches', all other assemblies are 'confused' or 'disordered'.[14] Underlying Hobbes's biblical exegesis of the meanings of 'church' is a nominalist ontology of collective bodies (including the commonwealth). Collective bodies are ontologically differentiated not in terms of any institutional or legal features, but primarily by the individuals composing the body.

So much is clear. Hobbes proceeds to distinguish four subcategories of 'church' in its non-figurative sense, differentiated by the kind of congregation referred to. 'Church' sometimes signifies [B1] all individuals who 'have right to be of the Congregation, though not actually assembled', i.e. 'the whole multitude of Christian men, how far soever they be dispersed'.[15] The church, in this sense, presumably consists of all baptized individuals worldwide—the entire Christian *ummah*, of which Christ is the head.[16] What Hobbes calls the 'universal' or 'general' church is probably [B1]. Sometimes 'church' refers to some but not all Christians: [B2] a spatially restricted subset ('the Church that is in his house'), or [B3] the elect alone. The latter is not really a church yet; rather, it is a 'Church to come'.[17] Finally, 'church' could mean [B4] an actually assembled number of individuals professing Christianity, sincerely or not. 'And in this last sense only it is that the *Church* can be taken for one Person; that is to say, that it can be said to have power to will, to pronounce, to command, to be obeyed, to make laws, or to doe any other action whatsoever'.[18]

Whether having personality is essential for church-hood, as it is for commonwealths, is not entirely clear. In reply to Bramhall, Hobbes claims that what is 'properly called' a church is 'a company of Christian men on earth incorporated into one person that can speak, command, or do any act of a person'.[19] Another passage states that 'a dissolute number of individuall persons' 'is no more a Church'.[20] Yet the non-personified 'universal' church [B1] is elsewhere criticized, not for failing to be a church, but for lacking personality.[21] Regardless of what view we take on this issue, church and state are identical only insofar as the church is personified—i.e. insofar as a multitude of Christians is united into one person. '[T]he Church, if it be one person, is the same thing with a Common-wealth of Christians'.[22] How is this personation achieved? And what is the role of the sovereign in the process of unification?

[13] L, 39, p. 730.   [14] L, 39, p. 730; DCv, 17.19.
[15] L, 39, p. 730.   [16] DCv, 17.19; L, 39, p. 730; LLA, p. 1196; cf. DCv, 17.22.
[17] L, 39, p. 730; also DCv, 17.19, 22. Cf. John Calvin, *Institutes of the Christian Religion*, trans. Henry Beveridge (Peabody, MA: Hendrickson Publishers, 2008), 4.1.7: 'Holy Scripture speaks of the church in two ways'. It either signifies 'the whole multitude of men spread over the earth who profess to worship one God and Christ' or only the elect.
[18] L, 39, p. 732.   [19] EW 4, p. 337.   [20] L, 42, p. 804.
[21] E.g. DCv, 17.22, 26; L, 33, p. 606; L, 42, p. 916; EW 4, p. 337.
[22] L, 33, p. 606; also L, 39, p. 732.

1.2 The Summon & Bind Model of Personation

On *De Cive*'s model of personation, uniting a multitude into one person presupposes some legal authority capable of summoning and binding that multitude. A church is personified only insofar as it can 'assemble as a group when necessary'. 'For a Church cannot speak or decide or give audience except as a group'. Legal authority is required for two reasons. First, members of the multitude must be individually bound to accept the majority decision: 'for a crowd is said to decide something when each one is obligated by the decision of the majority'.[23] Otherwise the words uttered by congregated Christians are merely private opinions. Second, legal authority is required to coercively summon together church members. Individuals gathering on their private initiative cannot be said to speak in the name of those absent, over whom they have no right.[24] The church has unity, Hobbes concludes, 'not because it has uniformity of doctrine, but because it has unity of authority to summon Synods and assemblies of Christians; otherwise it is merely a crowd, and several distinct *persons*'.[25] 'Hence a *church* only exists where there is a definite and recognized, i.e. legitimate, authority by which individuals are obliged to attend the meeting either in person or through others'. *De Cive* defines a church accordingly as:

a crowd [multitudo] of men who have entered into a new agreement with God through Christ (i.e. a crowd of people who have undergone the Sacrament of Baptism), and a crowd which may be rightly summoned into one place by someone, at whose summons all are obliged to attend either in person or through others[26]

Lawful assemblies of Christians and personified churches are not coextensive on Summon & Bind. A sovereign may *permit* a crowd of Christians to assemble, e.g. for church services or in ecclesiastical synods, without turning its judgements into binding law for all others. Such lawful assemblies do not count as personified churches since their words and actions neither bind dissenters nor those absent. *Leviathan* reiterates the idea that legal authority is required for church personation.

For without authority from a lawfull Congregation, whatsoever act be done in a concourse of people, it is the particular act of every one of those that were present, and gave their aid to the performance of it; and not the act of them all in grosse, as of one body; much lesse the act of them that were absent, or that being present, were not willing it should be done[27]

Hobbes's political absolutism implies that the authority to summon and bind Christians within a commonwealth must ultimately belong to the civil sovereign.

---

[23] DCv, 17.20.   [24] DCv, 17.20; EW 4, p. 337.
[25] DCv, 17.20. Cf. Erastus, *The Nullity of Church-Censures*, 2–3: 'But we are made Consorts of the externall and visible Church, by the profession of the same Faith, by the content we give to the same Doctrine, and by the using of the same Sacraments'.
[26] DCv, 17.20.   [27] L, 39, p. 732; cf. DCv, 6.1n., 12.8.

'If the secular sovereign is not identical with the head of the church, then there will be two sovereigns (one for religious matters and one for nonreligious matters); but that is absurd'.[28] Sovereignty, understood as the highest legal authority within a territory, is indivisible. Divided sovereignty is incompatible with the concept of a commonwealth, the nature of which consists in '*union or subjection*'.[29] Consequently, 'citizens who believe themselves obliged to comply with an external Authority for doctrines necessary for salvation, do not constitute a commonwealth in themselves but are subjects of that foreigner'.[30]

Hobbes rejects papal and clerical claims to independent ecclesiastical authority by arguing on scriptural grounds that bishops lack the authority requisite for summoning and binding Christians into a personified church.[31] Even if the entire clergy of a Christian state would gather, without the sovereign's authority none of their words and actions can be properly attributed to the church.[32] The apostolic mission was one of teaching, not governing. Christ ordered his disciples 'out as Sheep unto Wolves, not as Kings to their Subjects . . . consequently they could not make their Writings obligatory Canons, without the help of the Soveraign Civill Power'.[33] All legislative power derives from human consent and belongs exclusively to the civil sovereign. An anti-papalist conclusion follows: 'there is on Earth, no such universall Church, as all Christians are bound to obey; because there is no power on Earth, to which all other Commonwealths are subject'.[34]

The claim that the sovereign is the only authority capable of incorporating Christians into a church informs the first premise of Hobbes's Summon & Bind argument for the church–state identity thesis. It establishes their 'formal' identity.

For the *material* of the *commonwealth* and of the *church* are the same, namely the same Christian men. And the *form* which consists in the legal authority to summon them is also the same; for it is common ground that individual citizens are obliged to come to the spot to which they are summoned by the commonwealth[35]

The argument for material identity may seem questionable to the modern reader. Are we really to assume that all citizens in a commonwealth ruled by a Christian sovereign are, or are to count as, Christians? Hobbes provides no further support for this claim, perhaps because it was uncontroversial at the time. Richard Hooker's defence of church–state identity, for instance, rested on the very same premise, and exclusively

---

[28] A. P. Martinich, *The Two Gods of Leviathan: Thomas Hobbes on Religion and Politics* (Cambridge: Cambridge University Press, 1992), 280.

[29] DCv, 6.3; cf. DCv, 6.13.   [30] DCv, 17.27; cf. DCv, 12.5.

[31] On the intellectual background for episcopal claims to independent authority, see J. P. Sommerville, 'The Royal Supremacy and Episcopacy "Jure Divino", 1603–1640', *The Journal of Ecclesiastical History* 34.4 (1983), 548–58.

[32] EW 4, p. 337.   [33] L, 42, p. 824.

[34] L, 39, p. 732; also DCv, 17.26; EW 4, p. 337.   [35] DCv, 17.21.

so.[36] In a book that 'may be taken as a representative statement of Anglican doctrine on the subject of the relations of church and state',[37] Hooker writes:

For if all that believe be contained in the name of the Church, how should the Church remain by personal subsistence divided from the commonwealth, when the whole commonwealth doth believe? The Church and the commonwealth therefore are in this case personally one society, which society being termed a commonwealth as it liveth under whatsoever form of secular law and regiment, a church as it hath the spiritual law of Jesus Christ.[38]

Like Hobbes, Hooker conceives of both church and state as 'politic societies of men'. The two are identical since the 'selfsame multitude' constitutes the substance of both.[39] This substance is called 'church' with respect to some of its properties and 'commonwealth' in light of others.[40] Hobbes adds a second token of identity: the same agent (the sovereign) gives form to the same matter (Christian individuals), thus shaping the multitude into a church/commonwealth.

Interpretive accuracy demands that we refrain from reading into *De Cive*'s remarks about church personation *Leviathan*'s later and better-known theory of representation. It has hitherto gone unnoticed that *De Cive* presents an interesting theory of *personation without representation*. In *Leviathan*, personation is brought about by representation. The agent unifying a disparate crowd is thus the same one bearing their person (the people's representative). In *De Cive*, by contrast, personation is achieved not by representation, but rather by summoning together an assembly and binding its members by authoritative decree. Summon & Bind is by and large compatible with *Leviathan*'s theory of representation. But unlike the latter model, it permits the intriguing possibility that spokesperson and unifier are not the same agent. This possibility exists *ex silentio*. *Leviathan*'s doctrine of representation serves to demonstrate theoretically whose words and actions count as those of a corporate body. The spokesperson of the church is its representative: the sovereign. All Hobbes establishes in *De Cive* is that the sovereign alone can have the right to determine who shall speak in the name of the church. Hobbes does not argue, nor does his argument imply, that the sovereign herself must speak in the name of the church.

Hence *De Cive*'s emphasis on the sovereign's exclusive right to summon and disassemble ecclesiastical synods and assemblies as she sees fit and to determine who shall partake in them.[41] While decisions of the assembled Christians can be attributed to the

---

[36]   David Eppley, 'Royal Supremacy', in *A Companion to Richard Hooker*, ed. Torrance Kirby (Leiden and Boston, MA: Brill, 2008), 504–7.

[37]   Weldon S. Crowley, 'Erastianism in England to 1640', *Journal of Church and State* 32.3 (1990), 559.

[38]   Richard Hooker, *Of the Laws of Ecclesiastical Polity*, ed. A. S. McGrade, 3 vols (Oxford: Oxford University Press, 2013), 8.1.4; also 8.1.1–6; 8.3.6. On Hooker's influence on views on church–state identity in seventeenth-century England, see Sarah Mortimer, 'Kingship and the "Apostolic Church", 1620–1650', *Reformation & Renaissance Review* 13.2 (2011), 225–46.

[39]   Hooker, *Ecclesiastical Polity*, 8.1.2.

[40]   Jacqueline Rose, *Godly Kingship in Restoration England: The Politics of the Royal Supremacy, 1660–1688* (Cambridge: Cambridge University Press, 2011), 208.

[41]   DCv, 17.24, 17.27.

church and become law only by the sovereign's authority, it can—but need not—be the sovereign who speaks on behalf of the church. State-sanctioned clerical assemblies and synods can do so as well. Lacking independent authority, these synods need (but obviously cannot compel) the sovereign to make their decisions law. Summon & Bind thus presupposes Erastianism: the sovereign has the right to issue religious legislation, turning clerical judgements into binding law for all church members. Hobbes's ecclesiastical histories chime well with Summon & Bind. As the posthumously published *Historia Ecclesiastica* stresses, early Christian councils like that of Nicaea and Chalcedon were called together by the emperor and their decrees made 'law' by his command.[42]

Richard Tuck has argued at length that *De Cive* and *Leviathan* set forth contrasting ecclesiological views.[43] Both texts grant the sovereign supreme authority over religious and ecclesiastical affairs. But in *De Cive* Hobbes 'allowed (albeit in a kind of advisory position) a crucial role to the Church in the formation of public doctrine'.[44] In his earlier works Hobbes favoured 'an autonomous national church headed by the civil sovereign, but with the sovereign under a duty to use apostolically ordained clergymen in deciding doctrine'.[45] While 'in his works of 1640 to 1643, Hobbes denied that the sovereign should use his own natural reason to interpret [theological] doctrine', *Leviathan*, we shall see, endows the sovereign with full spiritual and doctrinal powers in virtue of her office.[46] Tuck calls Hobbes's turn away from doctrinal hegemony of the clergy 'a dramatic difference in his religious theory'.[47] The direct textual evidence in favour of Tuck's claim is slim. It rests primarily on *De Cive*'s claim that the sovereign is 'obliged to interpret holy scripture...by means of duly ordained *Ecclesiastics*'.[48] I shall argue that Hobbes's shift from Summon & Bind to the Representation model of church personation provides additional philosophical evidence for Tuck's discontinuity thesis.

Nauta has pressed an objection against Tuck. The sovereign's duty to interpret Scripture by means of duly ordained ecclesiastics must be 'a self-imposed obligation to listen to people to whom he had delegated some power', Nauta contends, since the

[42] HE, pp. 367, 403–5; LLA, p. 1238.

[43] Richard Tuck, 'Warrender's *De Cive*', *Political Studies* 33.2 (1985), 313–15; also Tuck's *Hobbes* (Oxford: Oxford University Press, 1989), 85–6; and his 'Hobbes and Locke on Toleration', in *Thomas Hobbes and Political Theory*, ed. Mary G. Dietz (Lawrence, KS: University of Kansas Press, 1990), 161–6. See also by Richard Tuck: 'The "Christian Atheism" of Thomas Hobbes', in *Atheism from the Reformation to the Enlightenment*, ed. Michael Hunter and David Wootton (Oxford: Oxford University Press, 1992), 122–8; 'The Civil Religion of Thomas Hobbes', in *Political Discourse in Early Modern Britain*, ed. Nicholas Phillipson and Quentin Skinner (Cambridge: Cambridge University Press, 1993), 120–38; 'Introduction', in *Thomas Hobbes: Leviathan* (Cambridge: Cambridge University Press, 1996), pp. xxxviii–xliv; and 'Hobbes, Conscience, and Christianity', in *Oxford Handbook of Hobbes*, 495–8.

[44] Tuck, *Hobbes*, 85.   [45] Tuck, 'Civil Religion', 124.

[46] Ibid.   [47] Tuck, *Hobbes*, 86.

[48] DCv, 17.28; also DCv, 18.13. Cf. also EL, 11.9–10. The passage Tuck ('Civil Religion', 127) quotes from the 1643 *Anti-White*—'the leaders of the Church, whose task it is to regulate all dogmas' (AW, 39.8)—is indecisive since Hobbes insists that the sovereign is head of the church.

clergy holds no authority over the sovereign.[49] This objection contradicts a key premise of Hobbes's political absolutism. The sovereign cannot have obligations owed to herself alone. Anyone 'bound to himself only is not bound' since he can release himself at will.[50] The duty to consult duly ordained clergy is rather a positional one, owed to God and incurred through baptism: 'As a Christian therefore, the holder of sovereign power is obliged to interpret holy scripture, when it is a question about the *mysteries of faith*, by means of duly ordained *Ecclesiastics*'.[51] That Christian sovereigns have special duties owed to God alone is compatible with political absolutism and repeated in *Leviathan*. 'Soveraigns are supreme Teachers (in generall) by their Office; and therefore oblige themselves (by their Baptisme) to teach the Doctrine of Christ: And when they suffer others to teach their people, they doe it at the perill of their own souls'.[52] In neither text has the sovereign any duties owed *to* the clergy. But in *De Cive* she does have a duty to consult the clergy, owed to God.

Tuck occasionally overstates his position, for instance when maintaining that in *De Cive* 'the church could have a *right* of interpretation independent of the civil sovereign'.[53] In fact, *De Cive* grants the sovereign the exclusive right to authoritatively interpret Scripture and divine law, primarily on the grounds that social peace requires this. '[I]n every *Christian Church*, i.e. in every *Christian commonwealth*, the *interpretation* of holy scripture, i.e. the *right to settle* all *disputes*, should depend on and be derived from' the sovereign.[54] Interpretive questions depending on natural reason and the meaning of words the sovereign may settle herself. However, questions about faith, which 'cannot be examined by natural reason',[55] require clerical support. '[T]o decide questions of faith, i.e. questions *about God*, which are beyond human understanding, one needs God's blessing... and this comes from CHRIST himself by *laying on hands*'.[56] Not having been ordained herself, the sovereign is obliged, as a Christian, to consult the clergy. In *De Cive* bishops thus hold certain spiritual powers exclusively and independently of the sovereign—though none that generates political authority. In *Leviathan*, we shall see, *every* clerical power derives from the sovereign, a veritable priest herself.[57]

---

[49] Lodi Nauta, 'Hobbes on Religion and the Church between *The Elements of Law* and *Leviathan*: A Dramatic Change of Direction?', *Journal of the History of Ideas* 63.4 (2002), 592. Also Sommerville, '*Leviathan* and its Anglican Context', 369–70.

[50] L, 26, p. 416. Also e.g. EL, 15.12; DCv, 6.14; DCv, 7.7; DCv, 12.4; EW 5, p. 144.

[51] DCv, 17.28. Cf. Erastus, *The Nullity of Church-Censures*, 89: 'For that Ecclesiastick judgment-Seat of manners, (for Doctrine the Magistrates ought ever to consult them that are most acquainted therewith) it is not to be found commanded in any place of the holy Scriptures'.

[52] L, 42, p. 882.   [53] Tuck, 'Hobbes and Locke', 166 (emphasis added).

[54] DCv, 17.27; also DCv, 6.11n.

[55] This idea underlies Hobbes's claim that theology is not a science. E.g. EW 1, p. 10.

[56] DCv, 17.28; also DCv, 17.13–14. The role and significance of the imposition of hands for clerical ordination became a highly contested issue after the Reformation. See Paul F. Bradshaw, *Rites of Ordination: Their History and Theology* (Collegeville, MN: Liturgical Press, 2013), especially 11–14, 150–76.

[57] Nauta, 'Hobbes on Religion', 588–9, argues that Hobbes endorses priestly kingship already in *Elements*. Kings may take upon them 'ministerial priesthood' 'if it pleased them' (EL, 26.11). Yet as Sommerville, '*Leviathan* and its Anglican Context', 373–4n. notes, it is unclear whether this means that sovereigns can exercise priestly functions in virtue of their office, i.e. without ordination.

Denying the sovereign the requisite spiritual powers to explicate theological doctrine does not contravene Hobbes's Erastian commitments. The sovereign alone can give ecclesiastical pronouncements about theology's legal force. *De Cive* thus advances the complex but coherent view that the sovereign alone has the authority to issue binding religious decrees, despite being obliged, as a Christian, to rely on the clergy to interpret theological doctrine.[58] This 'division of spiritual labour' model chimes well with Summon & Bind. In matters of doctrine, the ecclesiastical councils consulted by the sovereign speak on behalf of the church, even though these councils lack the authority to unify the multitude of Christians into a church. Moreover, a synod's permission to settle theological doctrine derives from and remains dependent on the sovereign, as she alone can make such doctrine legally binding.[59]

1.3 The Representation Model

Leviathan introduces a highly innovative theory of representation and authorization to explain personation. 'A Multitude of men, are made *One* Person, when they are by one man, or one Person, Represented'.[60] In the original covenant, a crowd authorizes 'one Man, or Assembly of men, to beare their Person', thus allowing that other party to speak and act in their name.[61] As Hobbes explains, 'to *Personate*, is to *Act*, or *Represent* himselfe, or an other; and he that acteth another, is said to beare his Person, or act in his name'.[62] The set of individuals thus united into one person is called a commonwealth. Sovereign is now defined as she who bears the person of the commonwealth/the people.[63]

It is tempting to think of church personation along the lines of commonwealth for-mation. A personified church would then consist of Christians united into one person through representation by the head of church (the sovereign). Ample textual evidence attests that Hobbes indeed tried to apply *Leviathan*'s new theory of representation to church personation. Neither the English nor the Latin *Leviathan* mentions 'represen-tative' or its cognates in chapter 39 (on the nature of the church). But that chapter's definition of church does indicate that the sovereign herself personates the church:

I define a CHURCH to be, *A company of men professing Christian Religion, united in the person of one Sovereign; at whose command they ought to assemble, and without whose authority they ought not to assemble*[64]

Elsewhere representation is explicitly invoked to describe church personation: 'they that are the Representants of a Christian People, are Representants of the Church: for a

---

[58] DCv, 17.27–8. *Pace* Collins, *Allegiance*, 67–9, 122.   [59] DCv, 18.13.

[60] L, 16, p. 248.   [61] L, 17, p. 260.

[62] L, 16, p. 244.   [63] L, 17, p. 262.

[64] L, 39, p. 732. Also LLA, p. 1238; L, 33, p. 606: 'the Church, if it be one person, is the same thing with a Common-wealth of Christians; called a *Common-wealth*, because it consisteth of men united in one per-son, their Sovereign; and a *Church*, because it consisteth in Christian men, united in one Christian sover-eign'. Cf. LL, 39, p. 731.

Church, and a commonwealth of Christian people are the same thing';[65] 'by the Authority of the King, or other true Representant of the Church';[66] and:

> severall Bodies of Christians; that is to say, severall Churches: And their severall Soveraigns Represent them, whereby they are capable of commanding and obeying, of doing and suffering, as a naturall man; which no Generall or Universall Church is, till it have a Representant[67]

Such clear textual evidence for Representation notwithstanding, upon second thoughts it may seem that the model cannot be straightforwardly applied to church personation. For the covenants individuals enter to become citizens (the social contract) and to become Christians (baptism) differ in nature. Individuals become citizens by mutually agreeing to lay down the natural right to everything and by authorizing a common representative to speak in their names; in other words, by pledging allegiance to the sovereign. By contrast, baptism involves neither authorization nor alienation of right: 'we do not in Baptisme constitute over us another authority, by which our externall actions are to bee governed in this life'.[68] Citizens cannot bind themselves to obey any religious leader in baptism as that would be a violation of the original covenant's promise of simple obedience and hence unjust. Baptism is a 'Pact with God', not a covenant with men.[69] Since bishops have been authorized neither by citizens in the covenant of baptism nor by Christ himself (who made them teachers, not leaders), they do not have independent religious authority.

Since it does not include authorization, baptism cannot make you a member of a personified church; it only makes you a member of the non-personified 'universal church'. This raises the question of why and when individuals have consented to be subject to a head of church. Summon & Bind provides a top-down model of church personation: membership in a personified church is imposed on Christians from above by a pre-existing legal authority. Top-down personation is incompatible with Representation insofar as the relevant representation is *authorized*. Personation by authorized representation is of necessity a bottom-up affair.[70] Only *your* authorization can make my words and actions bindingly count as your own. The sovereign cannot unilaterally make herself the church's representative, obliging Christians to accept her

---

[65] L, 42, p. 866.   [66] L, 45, p. 1034.

[67] L, 42, p. 916. Compare the parallel passage in LL, 42, p. 917: 'several churches: and their sovereigns are different persons, *by means of whom* they can speak, act, consult, etc., in the way that individual men do; which no universal church can do, since it has no representative person on Earth' (emphasis added). The third appendix to the Latin *Leviathan* defines 'church' as a lawful synod: 'by Church [Hobbes] understands a synod with the authority to make decrees, and whose decrees it was unjust to disobey. Now, such synods cannot exist without sovereign power' (LLA, p. 1238; also EW 4, p. 363). The textual context—a discussion of the history of the church—may explain this definition.

[68] L, 42, p. 792.

[69] L, 41, p. 762. Hobbes calls baptism a 'covenant' in L, 35, p. 636. On the nature of baptism, see DCv, 17.25; EW 4, p. 363; L, 42, p. 792.

[70] Not every artificial person (representative) has his words and actions authorized and hence owned by those whom he claims to represent, thus rendering it possible for him to wrong the represented (L, 16, p. 244). The Neapolitan mafia did not authorize Roberto Saviano to personify them in his 2008 movie *Gomorrah*. Representation is thus not a sufficient condition for attaining authority over a crowd.

words and actions as their own. These contrary directions of fit render the Summon & Bind and Representation models of personation ultimately incompatible.

This complicates extending *Leviathan*'s theory of representation to church personation. I can think of only one way to resolve the resulting complication. Citizens should be understood as having authorized the sovereign in the original covenant to represent them *qua Christians* as well as *qua citizens*. This may seem problematic. Not so much because it presupposes that individuals, threatened by temporal death in the state of nature, have authorized the sovereign to take care of their otherworldly welfare as well—after all, sovereigns are morally obliged to do what is necessary for citizens' salvation.[71] But because of what may be called the Conversion Objection. Suppose citizens have promised obedience in the original covenant to a pagan ruler who subsequently converts to Christianity. Church and commonwealth thereupon become identical. Should we understand the citizens, perhaps pagans themselves, as having conditionally authorized the sovereign to represent the church as well in case she happens to convert to Christianity? That seems a stretch. The Conversion Objection should be rejected, however. It relies on the false premise that the church and the commonwealth are distinct civil persons. They are not. The sovereign represents the *people*. And the selfsame people can be seen either as a collection of citizens (the commonwealth) or as a congregation of Christians (the church). I conclude that Hobbes is best read as holding that in the original covenant individuals have authorized the civil sovereign to be (or, upon conversion, to become) the representative of the church, i.e. of a Christian people.

1.4 Subordinate Systems

Hobbes's political absolutism ensures that the legal authority unifying the multitude of Christians into a church is the civil sovereign (section 1.2). Sovereignty is by definition absolute, rendering the existence of two highest authorities (one civil, one religious) within the same body politic logically impossible. This section argues that the existence of two *representatives* within the same commonwealth is not similarly oxymoronic. *Leviathan* contains the conceptual and theoretical resources to envision churches as internally coercive civil bodies subordinate to the sovereign, akin to universities, guilds, and colonies. Christians can be incorporated into a church by an internal representative subordinate to the sovereign, without violating either political absolutism or Erastianism.[72] The Representation model of personation does not, therefore, entail the church–state identity thesis.

---

[71] EL, 28.2; DCv, 13.5; L, 42, p. 916.

[72] Confusion abounds around Hobbes's distinction between natural and artificial persons. Here is my currently preferred reading. A natural person is he whose words and actions are considered his own, an artificial person he whose words and actions represent another (L, 16, p. 244). Civil persons such as corporations, guilds, and universities need human spokespersons to have voice and agency. Civil persons thus

Hobbes's theory of subordinate systems has received only cursory treatment in the existing literature.[73] Subordinate systems are not discussed at great length prior to *Leviathan*.[74] It was the latter's theory of representation that first allowed Hobbes to explain what makes 'subordinate corporations...to be one person in law'.[75] Subordinate systems belong to the same genus as commonwealths ('systems of citizens' in the Latin *Leviathan*'s terminology). Unlike commonwealths, subordinate systems are not absolute: they are 'Subordinate to some Soveraign Power, to which every one, as also their Representative is *Subject*'.[76] Subordinate systems can either be political or private. Political subordinate systems (like towns, colonies, and certain universities) are 'made by authority from the Soveraign Power'. Private subordinate systems (like families, businesses, and football clubs) are set up either by citizens themselves or by foreign agents. Many private systems are permitted by the state and thus lawful. Both political and private subordinate systems are 'regular': 'One Man, or Assembly of men, is constituted Representative of the whole number'.[77] 'Irregular' systems are 'those which having no Representative [Personam], consist only in concourse of People'.[78] Examples are markets, theatre shows, and other popular gatherings. This subcategory confirms that Hobbes regards systems primarily as *congregations* of citizens.

All subordinate systems are subject to the sovereign—the 'absolute' and 'unlimited' representative of the people.[79] Crucially, subjection to state authority does not make the sovereign the representative of subordinate systems. State control over a university does not imply or require that the sovereign *represents* the university—that task is the rector's. Each regular subordinate system has its own internal representative, whose power is necessarily limited by that of the sovereign.[80] Hobbes is quite clear that the representative of a subordinate system holds authority over the individuals composing the system. A subordinate system, he writes, requires a 'Common Representative to oblige them to any other Law, than that which is common to all other subjects'.[81] Likewise, families are 'united in one Person Representative', usually the father, who 'obligeth his Children, and Servants, as farre as the Law permitteth, though not further, because none of them are bound to obedience in those actions, which the Law hath forbidden to be done'.[82] Hobbes's discussion of the family reveals that it is possible for

---

form a third category, not to be confused with the artificial person that personates these collectives. The commonwealth is thus a civil person represented by an artificial person (the sovereign).

[73] The most elaborate discussions are found in Otto von Gierke, *Natural Law and the Theory of Society, 1500–1800*, trans. Ernest Barker (Cambridge: Cambridge University Press, 1934), i, 79–84; Deborah Baumgold, *Hobbes's Political Thought* (Cambridge: Cambridge University Press, 1988), 84–5; Franck Lessay, 'La vocabulaire de la personne', in *Hobbes et son vocabulaire: Études de lexicographie philosophique*, ed. Yves Charles Zarka (Paris: Vrin, 1992), 167–79; Norberto Bobbio, *Thomas Hobbes and the Natural Law Tradition*, trans. Daniela Gobetti (Chicago, IL: University of Chicago Press, 1993), 172–96; Mónica Brito Vieira, *The Elements of Representation in Hobbes: Aesthetics, Theatre, Law, and Theology in the Construction of Hobbes's Theory of the State* (Leiden and Boston, MA: Brill, 2009), 193–8.

[74] Corporations are briefly discussed in EL, 19.9; DCv, 5.10.

[75] EL, 27.7.   [76] L, 22, p. 348.   [77] L, 22, p. 348.

[78] L, 22, p. 348; also L, 22, p. 370.   [79] L, 22, p. 350; L, 22, p. 352.

[80] L, 22, p. 350.   [81] L, 22, p. 362.   [82] L, 22, p. 368.

representatives of subordinate systems to get their authority directly from their subjects, rather than from the state. Parental authority is pre-political and diminished by civil law, rather than constituted by it.[83] Much of chapter 22 deals with the extent of the authority of representatives of subordinate systems, its relation to civil authority, and with corporate liability.

I see no reason why a church cannot be seen as a regular subordinate system, internally governed by its representative while remaining subject to the higher authority of the state. Hobbes explicitly mentions churches as examples of regular subordinate systems.[84] The parallel passage in the Latin *Leviathan* has 'Ecclesiae' rather than 'templum', attesting that Hobbes had a congregation of Christians in mind rather than a building.[85] The English *Leviathan* further mentions 'church' in the context of irregular popular gatherings.[86] Interestingly, the Latin *Leviathan* changes this to 'theatre', perhaps because Hobbes preferred to portray 'churches' as personified systems.[87] Churches can either be private (set up by Christians themselves) or political (set up by the state); the former are lawful only insofar as the government tolerates their existence. While no church is directly created through the covenant of baptism, I see no reason why, the sovereign permitting it, citizens cannot institute private churches in a separate act, just as they can create private businesses and football clubs. Depicting churches as regular subordinate systems neither contradicts Hobbes's political absolutism nor his Erastianism. Like any subordinate system, churches would remain subject to the authority of the sovereign, who can assemble and disassemble such congregations as she sees fit. Moreover, the sovereign would retain ultimate authority over religious and ecclesiastical affairs (just as she can issue legislation concerning corporations like businesses and families). On *De Cive*'s Summon & Bind, sovereign authority is a necessary condition for church personation. On *Leviathan*'s Representation model, by contrast, sovereignty is merely a sufficient condition: the church can in theory be represented by other actors as well.

I conclude that Hobbes could have coherently presented churches as regular subordinate systems. Doing so would have been incompatible with the church–state identity thesis, however. Recall that 'in Christian commonwealths, the kingdom and the Church are the same people'.[88] It is not logically possible for a subordinate system to be coextensive with the state. What makes an assembly of citizens a regular subordinate system is their personation by an internal representative, subordinate to the sovereign. Were any subordinate system to be coextensive with the state, then the sovereign would be a member of it. Were someone other than the sovereign to be the representative, then that person would both be and not be subject to the sovereign. And that is contradictory. Political absolutism requires that the sovereign be the representative of

[83] Here I disagree with Von Gierke, *Natural Law and the Theory of Society*, 81. While the authority of every subordinate body is indeed *limited by* civil law, the authority of private subordinate systems is not *derived from* the sovereign.

[84] L, 22, p. 360; also L, 16, p. 246.   [85] LL, 22, p. 361.   [86] L, 22, p. 374.

[87] LL, 22, p. 375.   [88] LLA, p. 1196. Also DCv, 17.21; L, 42, p. 864; L, 47, p. 1104.

that subordinate system—which, in turn, is incompatible with the latter's status as a subordinate system. The church–state identity thesis, in conjunction with political absolutism, thus rules out that anyone other than the sovereign can be the church's representative.

I have argued that the Representation model does not necessitate the church–state identity thesis. It permits the existence of a number of churches within a territory, each only internally binding. Only if we assume that church and state are materially coextensive, i.e. that every citizen is a member of the same church, does the Representation model entail that the sovereign must be the church's representative. *Leviathan* contains the theoretical resources to develop a more liberal theory of church–state relations. This would have brought him closer to the Independents, with whom Hobbes is sometimes allied.[89] But instead of discarding the church–state identity thesis and sanctioning the existence of several, perhaps denominationally distinct churches subordinate to the state, *Leviathan* takes a decidedly theocratic turn.

1.5 Hobbes's Theocratic Turn

Tuck has argued that in *Leviathan* Hobbes pushes his position on religion 'in a remarkably utopian direction'.[90] This section argues that the shift is better labelled 'Hobbes's theocratic turn'. *Leviathan* defends the startling thesis that the sovereign is by divine right the supreme pastor, responsible for the spiritual well-being of her citizens and in possession of full spiritual powers.[91] My contention is that *Leviathan*'s claim that the sovereign represents the church herself mandated introduction of these theocratic features. It should be noted, however, that Hobbes reinterprets the meaning of each of these features, thus 'civilizing' theocracy considerably.

From *Leviathan* onwards, Hobbes insists that the sovereign is the 'chief Pastor'.[92] 'And therefore Christian Kings are still the Supreme Pastors of their people, and have power to ordain what Pastors they please, to teach the Church, that is, to teach the People committed to their charge'.[93] The force of this highly provocative claim is

---

[89] According to Collins, *Allegiance*, 129, Hobbes considered 'Independency...the church model most likely to secure religious peace and protect the ecclesiastical supremacy of the state' (also pp. 123–30). Observe that the passage usually cited in support, 'reduced to the Independency of the Primitive Christians to follow Paul, or Cephas, or Apollos, every man as he liketh best' (L, 47, p. 1116), does not refer to a personified church; Martinich, 'Hobbes's Erastianism', 153. Arash Abizadeh, 'Publicity, Privacy, and Religious Toleration in Hobbes's *Leviathan*', *Modern Intellectual History* 10.2 (2013), 261–91, highlights Hobbes's surprising degree of toleration for private worship: worship not performed in the name of the people. His argument is compatible with mine if we accept that sub-state religious congregations engaging in private worship are not personified churches, capable of obligating their members.

[90] Tuck, 'Introduction', p. xxxix. Cf. Richard Tuck, 'The Utopianism of *Leviathan*', in *Leviathan After 350 Years*, ed. Tom Sorell and Luc Foisneau (Oxford: Oxford University Press, 2004), 137.

[91] For an insightful analysis of Hobbes's views on biblical theocracy, here left undiscussed, see Beiner, 'Machiavelli, Hobbes, and Rousseau', 625–30; and his *Civil Religion*, 49–58.

[92] L, 39, p. 734.

[93] L, 42, p. 852. Also L, 42, pp. 852–4; L, 42, p. 872; L, 42, p. 882; L, 42, p. 894; EW 4, p. 345; EW 4, p. 374.

diminished by Hobbes's deflationary understanding of pastor (and its namesake 'bishop') as anyone ruling either by law or by doctrine. 'Bishop' originally merely meant 'an Overseer, or Superintendent of any businesse, and particularly a Pastor, or Shepherd'. The term later became metaphorically applied to the office of king as well.[94] So in calling the sovereign 'the supreme shepherd of his people',[95] Hobbes is not per se attributing any spiritual powers to her. Still, Hobbes never calls kings 'pastors' prior to *Leviathan*; moreover, we shall see that the sovereign is in fact given full sacerdotal authority.

Furthermore, Hobbes claims, remarkably, that the sovereign exercises her 'Office of Supreme Pastor, by immediate Authority from God, that is to say, *in Gods Right*, or *Iure Divino*'.[96] Hobbes is widely read as rejecting a divine right theory of political authority in favour of a social contract one. Is he here endorsing a divine right theory of *spiritual* authority, thus smuggling in supernatural justification by the backdoor? Well, no. Recall that 'right' for Hobbes simply means 'liberty' or 'permission'.[97] When saying that the sovereign rules *jure divino*, Hobbes is claiming that she is accountable to God alone. By contrast, all ecclesiastics, including bishops and the pope, rule *jure civili*— that is, by permission of the sovereign.[98] This is how we should understand the claim that '[a]ll lawfull Power is of God, immediately in the Supreme Governour, and mediately in those that have Authority under him'.[99] Hobbes is emphatic that Christ did not endow the apostles with any right of government; all political authority derives from the consent of the governed.

Leviathan's most salient theocratic departure from *De Cive* concerns its rejection of the spiritual importance of the imposition of hands. Ecclesiastical infallibility underwrote both clerical doctrinal supremacy and the Summon & Bind model of church personation in *De Cive*. 'Our Saviour promised this Infallibility (in matters essential to salvation) to the *Apostles* until the day of judgement, i.e. to the *Apostles* and to the *Pastors* who were to be consecrated by the *Apostles* in succession by the *laying on of hands*'.[100] The imposition of hands no longer has any spiritual importance in *Leviathan*. The ceremony, we read, was simply used as a sign to direct attention towards the object of prayer or consecration.[101] Since sovereigns already have the power to teach in virtue of their office, if baptized, 'they needed no Imposition of Hands . . . to authorize them to exercise any part of the Pastorall Function, as namely, to Baptize, and Consecrate'.[102] The upshot is that:

every Christian King is not only a Bishop, but an Arch-Bishop, and his whole Dominion his Diocesse. And though it were granted that Imposition of hands is necessary from a Priest, yet seeing Kings have the Government of the Clergy that are his subjects, even before Baptisme, the Baptisme it selfe wherein he is received as a Christian is a sufficient Imposition of hands; so that whereas before he was a Bishop, now he is a Christian Bishop[103]

---

[94] L, 42, p. 834; also B, p. 125; cf. DCv, 17.23.   [95] HE, p. 529.
[96] L, 42, p. 854.   [97] E.g. DCv, 14.3; L, 14, p. 198; L, 26, p. 450.
[98] L, 42, p. 866; L, 42, p. 906; EW 4, pp. 345–6.
[99] L, 42, p. 900.   [100] DCv, 17.28.   [101] L, 42, pp. 858–62.
[102] L, 42, p. 862; also L, 42, p. 882; EW 7, pp. 397–8.   [103] B, p. 125.

From *Leviathan* onwards, Hobbes attributes full spiritual powers to Christian kings, including 'the Authority, not only to Preach … but also to Baptize, and to Administer the Sacrament of the Lords Supper; and to Consecrate both Temples, and Pastors to Gods service'.[104] In a striking departure from *De Cive*, Christian rulers have become both priests and kings.[105]

These observations amply demonstrate *Leviathan*'s theocratic turn. Throughout his works, Hobbes insists that 'church' and 'commonwealth' are different labels for the same thing. But only from *Leviathan* onwards does he say the same about 'pastors' and 'kings'. This dramatic change has not gone entirely unnoticed. Existing explanations of this shift appeal to the changing historical context, however, rather than to an underlying philosophical rationale.[106]

My contention is that *Leviathan*'s theory of representation and authorization *requires* sacerdotal sovereignty. In *De Cive*, Hobbes denied emphatically that the clergy held any independent powers of government. But he was happy to grant them independent doctrinal and spiritual powers. *Leviathan*, by contrast, maintains that the sovereign *represents* the church. That means that subordinate priests, like any civil servant, act in name and by right of the sovereign. 'All Pastors, except the Supreme, execute their charges in the Right, that is by the Authority of the Civill Soveraign, that is, *Iure Civili*'.[107] Agents cannot act by authority of another party if that other party lacks the right to perform the action herself. 'So that by Authority, is always understood a Right of doing any act: and *done by Authority*, done by Commission, or Licence from him whose right it is'.[108] Had the sovereign lacked the right to consecrate, then priests could not have consecrated in the sovereign's name (by her right). Sovereigns who are not priests themselves can at most permit priests to consecrate, not authorize them. Attributing full sacerdotal powers to the sovereign allows Hobbes to claim that *every* power bishops have, including non-binding spiritual ones like the powers to consecrate and baptize, derives from the sovereign.

the Civill Soveraign is the Supreme Pastor [and…] it is by his authority, that all other Pastors are made, and have power to teach, and perform all other Pastorall offices; it followeth also,

---

[104] L, 42, p. 856.

[105] The idea of sacerdotal kingship was widely discussed in Reformation England. Some of its protagonists drew inspiration from the Protestant doctrine of the priesthood and kingship of *all* true Christians. Malcolm B. Yarnell III, *Royal Priesthood in the English Reformation* (Oxford: Oxford University Press, 2013).

[106] In her recent study of early modern views on royal supremacy, Jacqueline Rose highlights Hobbes's endorsement of sacerdotal kingship. Rose, *Godly Kingship*, 204–5, 214–21. Rose sees no substantial changes between *De Cive* and *Leviathan* in Hobbes's account of church personation (pp. 210–11) and thus does not connect *Leviathan*'s sacerdotal sovereign to church personation. In *Civil Religion*, Ronald Beiner highlights Hobbes's attempt to 'retheocratize politics' (p. 57) and stresses that *Leviathan* advances a more ambitious project of civil religion than *De Cive* (p. 53). Beiner's analysis focuses on Hobbes's 'bizarre interpretation' of scriptural history (p. 55). He neither discusses *Leviathan*'s attribution of spiritual powers to the sovereign, nor church personation.

[107] L, 42, p. 854.

[108] L, 16, p. 244; also DH 15.2. Cf. Michael J. Green, 'Authorization and Political Authority in Hobbes', *Journal of the History of Philosophy* 53.1 (2015), 29–32.

that it is from the Civill Sovereign, that all other Pastors derive their right of Teaching, Preaching, and other functions pertaining to that Office; and that they are but his Ministers; in the same manner as the Magistrates of Towns; Judges in Courts of Justice, and Commanders of Armies, are all but Ministers of him that is the Magistrate of the whole Common-wealth, Judge of all Causes, and Commander of the whole Militia[109]

Before the conversion of Constantine, bishops obtained these spiritual powers through the imposition of hands; afterwards, they derived them from the sovereign.

On *Leviathan*'s Representation model, the church has personality because the sovereign's words and actions can be attributed to it. For practical reasons, the sovereign will delegate ecclesiastical responsibilities to subordinate pastors, letting them speak in her name while retaining final authority. Likewise, 'by the same Right of his Office' whereby the sovereign institutes university lecturers, he may 'read Lectures [in the Sciences] himself'. But 'because the care of the summe of the businesse of the Common-wealth taketh up his whole time, it were not convenient for him to apply himself in Person to that particular'.[110] The sovereign cannot authorize priests to baptize and consecrate in her name unless she has full sacerdotal powers herself. The Representation Model thus *requires* that the sovereign is a veritable priest in virtue of her office. Church personation and sacerdotal kingship are thus logically linked in *Leviathan*. Indeed, Hobbes concludes his discussion of the sovereign's sacerdotal powers by pointing out that the sovereign

hath the Supreme Power in all causes, as well Ecclesiastical, as Civill . . . And these Rights are incident to all Soveraigns, whether Monarchs, or Assemblies: for they that are the Representants of a Christian People, are Representants of the Church: for a Church, and a Common-wealth of Christian people, are the same thing[111]

1.6 Conclusion

This chapter aimed to further our understanding not only of Hobbes's views on church–state relations, but also of his theories of personation, representation, and subordinate systems. Much has been written on Hobbes's application of representation and personation to the commonwealth and the Trinity.[112] Church personation, by contrast, has received very little scholarly attention.[113] This is the more lamentable if my contention is right that *De Cive* develops a theory of church personation without representation. On its hitherto overlooked Summon & Bind model, the sovereign unifies a congregation of Christians into a personified church by summoning and binding them.

---

[109] L, 42, p. 852.   [110] L, 42, p. 856.   [111] L, 42, p. 866.

[112] The supreme governor of the church bears the person of God (e.g. L, 45, p. 1044; LLA, p. 1232; DH, 15.3). It does not follow that the supreme governor therefore also bears the person of the *church*. The two types of personation are logically independent. On Hobbes's peculiar interpretation of the Trinity, see George Wright, *Religion, Politics and Thomas Hobbes* (Dordrecht: Springer, 2006), 175–210.

[113] Brito Vieira, for example, mentions church personation only in passing in *Elements of Representation*, 153.

On *Leviathan*'s Representation model, by contrast, church personation is brought about by representation by the sovereign. By altering the way churches are personated, *Leviathan* significantly revises Hobbes's account of church–state relations. Summon & Bind permits government-mandated synods and assemblies to speak on behalf of the church; Representation explicitly rules this out. I have argued that *Leviathan*'s new ideas on authorization and representation explain Hobbes's theocratic turn: for subordinate priests to act in the name of the sovereign, the sovereign must have full sacerdotal powers. This chapter thus provides new ammunition to the debate about whether Hobbes's views on church–state relations changed between *De Cive* and *Leviathan*. The proffered analysis of church personation supports the discontinuity view of Tuck. Indeed, the change is in one respect considerably larger than previously thought: *Leviathan* departs from earlier works by advancing a theocratic theory of government, a change mandated by its Representation model of church personation.

2

Natural Sovereignty and Omnipotence in Hobbes's *Leviathan*

A. P. Martinich

The relationship between omnipotence and natural sovereignty is discussed in chapter 31 of *Leviathan*, 'Of God's Natural Kingdom', the last chapter of Part Two in 'Of the Commonwealth'. That is an appropriate place for it because the natural kingdom of God belongs in the philosophical part of *Leviathan* precisely because it is natural. Also, God's natural sovereignty is relevant to the matter of the laws of nature being his commands, known by reason, as he sometimes says they are.[1] In addition to these timeless reasons, there was at least one time-bound reason for discussing the issue. A standard understanding of the authority of kings or of any absolute human monarch was modelled on divine sovereignty. The sovereign's properties represented or resembled God's properties. While it was possible to question whether any monarch was an absolute sovereign or ought to be one, it was not practically possible to question that God was an absolute sovereign. God's absolute sovereignty is asserted as a matter of course in books of the 1630s and 1640s.[2] The properties of the sovereign God could be used to figure out the properties of an absolute human sovereign, or those of the

I want to thank Laurens van Apeldoorn, Robin Douglass, Jake Galgon, Leslie Martinich, Johan Olsthoorn, two anonymous readers for Oxford University Press, and the participants at the European Hobbes Society Meeting, 8 April 2015, King's College London, for their comments on earlier versions of this chapter.

[1] L, 15, p. 242. On the issue of the laws of nature being commands, see A. P. Martinich, 'The Laws of Nature are the Laws of God in *Leviathan*', European Hobbes Society, <http://www.europeanhobbessociety. org/newpublications/debate-martinich-deigh-on-law-1-martinich/> and John Deigh, 'Reply to Martinich', European Hobbes Society, <http://www.europeanhobbessociety.org/newpublications/debate-martinich-deigh-on-law-2-deigh/>, both accessed 16 June 2017.

[2] Another reason to discuss God's natural sovereignty would be to fill out Hobbes's position that subjects have no right to rebel. In a sovereign-making covenant, subjects transfer their right of governing themselves to the civil sovereign. They might have an excuse to disobey if they could argue that God desires disobedience. But they cannot argue that way if God is a natural sovereign and if a law of nature, in particular, the law that enjoins keeping one's covenants, is a genuine law. See L, 31, p. 570; see also L, 43, pp. 928–9 and 950–4.

human sovereign to get a better idea of the sovereignty of God. Sometimes it is hard to know which direction the comparison is going. Thomas Adams seems to reason from God's sovereign properties to those of human sovereigns although he indicates that he will proceed by 'comparing earthly things with heavenly' ones. Notice in the following passage how the properties of God are passed down to human sovereigns:

the king eternall, immortall, invisible...All inferiour kingdomes are derived from him...he doth not take away temporall kingdomes, that gives an eternall kingdome. He who is the blessed and only Potentate, the king of kings, and Lord of Lords; is content to distribute some honour among certaine men. Of [human kings it is]...presumptuous to say, *Divisum imperium cum Iove Caesar habet*: but *Imperium summum sub Iove Caesar habet*.[3]

Caesar has the highest authority under God. Shortly later, Adams continued in the same vein:

There is *Deus naturaliter*, a God by nature, the one only God himselfe....*Deus est immortalis Rex, Rex est mortalis deus*: God is an immortal king, the king is a mortall god....We distinguish betweene the eternal GOD, and the temporal LORD: but we obey the temporall LORD, for his [God's] sake that is the eternall God. And certainely he that refuseth obedience to the temporall King, hath yet made no gracious entrance into the everlasting kingdome of Iesus Christ.[4]

For Adams too, there can be no conflict between the commands of God and the commands of a Christian king.

Hobbes and Adams are also alike in calling the human sovereign 'a mortal god' in a favourable sense.[5] The concept of a human sovereign as a 'mortal god' is suggested by the famous line, 'I [God] said, "you are gods"'. Adams mentions this text and refers the reader to the Gospel according to John, chapter 10, verse 34, rather than the original source, Psalm 82:6. Adams had used the phrase 'mortal gods' twenty years before the publication of *Leviathan*.[6] He and Hobbes wrote in the same spirit because both were non-Puritan, episcopal, Calvinist, anti-Catholic supporters of King James I.[7]

---

[3] Thomas Adams, *Commentary or, Exposition upon the Divine Second Latin Epistle General, Written by the Blessed Apostle St. Peter* (London, 1633), 239. The first Latin sentence at the end of the quotation above was attributed to Virgil and appears in his biography by Aelius Donatus. See Virgilius Maro, *Opera P. Virgilii Maronis* (Cambridge, 1632). Adams corrects the thought of that sentence in the next clause.
[4] Adams, *Commentary*, 239–40.   [5] L, 17, p. 260.
[6] To my knowledge, the only favourable use of 'mortal God' earlier than Adams's is that of John Bill, printer to the king, in his preface to William Camden in *The Abridgment of Camden's Britania* (London, 1626), [1]. Earlier uses of the phrase, 'mortal god' are unfavourable.
[7] I have argued for this understanding of Hobbes in various places, first in *The Two Gods of Leviathan: Thomas Hobbes on Religion and Politics* (Cambridge: Cambridge University Press, 1992), and later several times, for example in 'On the Proper Interpretation of Hobbes's Philosophy', *Journal of the History of Philosophy* 34.2 (1996), 272–83. On Adams's beliefs, see J. Sears McGee, 'On Misidentifying Puritans: The Case of Thomas Adams', *Albion* 30.3 (1998), 401–18, and J. Sears McGee, 'Thomas Adams', in *The Dictionary of National Biography* (online), <http://www.oxforddnb.com.ezproxy.lib.utexas.edu/view/article/131?docPos=3>, accessed 16 June 2017.

The properties of the human sovereign mirror God's because he was God's representative or vicegerent.[8] In short, an investigation of God as the natural, absolute sovereign is instructive with respect to the properties of the human, absolute sovereign. Near the end of this chapter, I will describe how the properties that Hobbes attributes to human sovereigns were properties traditionally attributed to God.

Since the Christian conception of God as an absolute sovereign was rooted in favoured texts from the Bible, it is important to study these texts. Such a study complements what Hobbes says as a philosopher.[9] The similarity between the properties of a civil sovereign and the Lord God psychologically reinforces belief in the authority of the sovereign. To paraphrase the adage, 'like father, like son', like sovereign, like God.

In the first paragraph of chapter 31, Hobbes wrote:

Subjects owe to Soveraigns, simple Obedience, in all things, wherein their obedience is not repugnant to the Lawes of God...There wants onely, for the entire knowledge of Civill duty, to know what are those Lawes of God. For without that, a man knows not...whether it be contrary to the Law of God, or not: and so, either by too much civill obedience, offends the Divine Majesty, or through feare of offending God, transgresses the commandements of the Common-wealth. To avoyd both these Rocks, it is necessary to know what are the Laws Divine.[10]

A century earlier, John Calvin had raised the same issue of whether people should obey God or their human sovereign in case their commands conflicted. His view is unsurprising, 'Obedience to man must not become disobedience to God.' He went on: 'How absurd it would be that in satisfying men you should incur the displeasure of him for whose sake you obey men themselves!'[11] If we momentarily think about the human predicament from a Christian perspective, Hobbes's answer is better than Calvin's because his forestalls the difficulty of figuring out exactly when God's commands might conflict with those of the secular sovereign. That is, subjects are never faced with the hard choice of choosing between God and their sovereign because God commands people to obey their earthly sovereigns.[12]

Hobbes's use of 'the Divine Majesty' suggests what his audience presupposed: God is a natural sovereign and had a law from the beginning. Seventeenth-century texts are replete with the phrase 'Lord God' and variations on it, such as 'Lord Almighty' and

---

[8] This idea can be found in other thinkers of the time, for example, Edmund Hall, *Lazarus's Sores Licked* (London, 1650), 17, and [Anon.], *Discourse presented to those Who Seek Reformation of the Church of England* (London, 1642), 116. See also Camden, *Abridgment*, [1].

[9] For the purposes of this discussion, we can put aside the issue of whether Hobbes genuinely believed what he wrote. I want to explain how he represented his position and suggest that it is inspired by the Bible. Also, I am not precluding other influences on Hobbes's views.

[10] L, 31, p. 554.

[11] John Calvin, *Institutes of the Christian Religion*, ed. John T. McNeill, trans. Ford Lewis Battles (Philadelphia, PA: The Westminster Press, 1960), 1520.

[12] If one doubts that choosing between God and one's sovereign can ever be a hard choice, consider that that situation involves a judgement about what God commands, what the sovereign commands, and whether there is a genuine conflict. Also, for Hobbesian humans, there is the conflict between the desire to avoid death or pain relatively soon versus the desire to avoid long-term pain in the relatively distant future.

'Almighty God'. Early English Books Online cites almost two thousand works that use 'Lord God' in the thirty years between 1620 and 1650. The other two phrases are also used regularly. As the context of the use of these phrases by English divines shows, they are closely connected with biblical texts, especially some of the psalms, as we shall see. These phrases are never or virtually never used to explain the relation between God's almightiness or omnipotence and his sovereignty, probably because the connection is too close to require explanation. Also, many divines, especially Laudian ones, preferred to relate God's sovereignty to his justice and goodness.

Hobbes asserted the connection between sovereignty and omnipotence in a marginal note in chapter 31: 'The right of God's sovereignty is derived from his omnipotence'. The paragraph adjacent to the note says, "The Right of Nature, whereby God reigneth over men, and punisheth those that break his Lawes, is to be derived... from his *Irresistible Power*'.[13] According to Hobbes, the criterion for irresistible power is power that can 'never [be] taken away'.[14] Because we know that the power of human beings is finite, we know that human sovereigns do not have irresistible power.[15]

Although people in the state of nature have unlimited rights, no one is sovereign because the right to rule 'could not be obtained by force'. No one has omnipotent power. If anyone had 'Power Irresistible; there had been no reason, why he should not by that Power have ruled, and defended both himselfe' and others. And 'consequently it is from that Power, that the Kingdome over men, and the Right of Afflicting men at his pleasure, belongeth Naturally to God Almighty... as Omnipotent'.[16] In *De Cive*, Hobbes momentarily gives the impression that a human being could theoretically be a natural sovereign because he discusses natural sovereignty as it might occur in the state of nature: 'in the natural state of men, *sure and irresistible power gives the right of ruling and commanding those who cannot resist*'.[17] However, the next clause cancels the suggestion: 'so that the right to do anything whatsoever is an essential and direct attribute of omnipotence'.[18] But why should 'sure and irresistible power [*potentiam certam et irresistibilem*]' be equated with omnipotence? I believe that Hobbes intuited that anyone who had such power would be the sovereign only as long as that irresistible power lasted, since no one had authorized the sovereign to represent them or transferred their power to him. Since the strength of every human being begins to fail, a group with a natural sovereign would be inherently unstable. But God's strength and hence his authority never fails because he is omnipotent.

---

[13] L, 31, p. 558; see also QLNC, p. 111. Most likely, Hobbes did not believe that 'God is omnipotent' is literally true. But he writes as if it is in chapter 31. See Thomas Holden, 'Hobbes's First Cause', *Journal of the History of Philosophy* 53.4 (2015), 647–67.

[14] L, 31, p. 558.

[15] Hobbes considers the sense in which human beings have dominion over lions and bears and lions have dominion over individual people. It concerns which thing has more physical power. But whichever has dominion in this sense, 'it may be called dominion... [but] properly it cannot', QLNC, pp. 141–2. In DCv, 8.10, Hobbes says that people have right and dominion over beasts.

[16] L, 31, p. 558; also EL, 14.13–14.   [17] DCv, 1.14.   [18] DCv, 1.14.

It is easy to interpret the opening verse of the Bible as evidence for and an expression of God's omnipotence: 'In the beginning, God created the heavens and the earth.'[19] To create is to make something from nothing. To bring something from being nothing to being something is, metaphorically, to traverse an infinite metaphysical distance, which can be accomplished only by an infinite, that is, an omnipotent power. Scholastic and scholastically trained philosophers often explained God's omnipotence in connection with his creating: 'From him, through him, and in him are all things.'[20] His creating 'pertains to God's essence ... [as] his omnipotence'.[21] Almost all early modern theists thought that the opening chapter of Genesis would confirm their view that the efficient cause of everything is a creative cause. Omnipotence is tied to God's sovereignty when, near the end of the first creation story, God gives human beings dominion over the other animals.[22] An axiom of Western medieval and early modern philosophy was that a thing cannot give what it does not have.

Hobbes's view contrasts with three of the standard accounts of God's sovereignty, each of which he rejects. One is that God is sovereign because he is good.[23] Evidence of God's goodness is reported in the first creation story. At the end of several of the days of creating, God sees that what he has made is good; and at the end of the sixth day, the end of his creating, he says that what he had made was 'very good'.[24] Hobbes could have explained the goodness of creation in two ways. One is that the things of creation are desired by human beings, namely, light, air with birds, water with fish, and land with plants and beasts. The other is that creation was good because God desired it, as evidenced by his creating.[25] The second way is not literally true because God does not literally have desires according to Hobbes. In any case, neither explanation of the source of goodness is relevant to God's sovereignty. There is also no logical connection between making good things and obligation. And there is no connection between creation, gratitude, and obligation: 'The right of nature whereby God reigneth over men ... [comes] not from his creating them, as if he required obedience as of gratitude for benefits.'[26] Owing a debt of gratitude to someone does not make

---

[19] Genesis 1:1. God's sovereignty, based upon his creating the world, is described as 'the intuitive logic of monotheism'. See Roy Rosenberg, 'Yahweh Becomes King', *Journal of Biblical Literature* 85.3 (1966), 297; see also p. 302.

[20] William Ames, quoting Romans 11:36, in *The Marrow of All Theology* (Durham, NC: Labyrinth Press, 1968), 91; see also pp. 90, 94, 100. On the general issue of the relevance of the Bible to political theory in the seventeenth century, see Eric Nelson, *The Hebrew Republic* (Cambridge, MA: Harvard University Press, 2010).

[21] Ames, *Marrow*, 92. Ames supports his view with various quotations from such diverse texts of the Bible as Isaiah 9:6, Jeremiah 32:18, 2 Chronicles 20:6, Luke 1:37, Philippians 3:21, 1 Timothy 6:15.

[22] See also Robert Filmer, *Patriarcha and Other Writings*, ed. J. P. Sommerville (Cambridge: Cambridge University Press, 1991), 7.

[23] See, for example, Gottfried Leibniz, 'The Common Concept of Justice', in *Political Writings*, ed. Patrick Riley (Cambridge: Cambridge University Press, 1988), 45–7, 57–9.

[24] Genesis 1:31.   [25] L, 6, p. 80.

[26] Hobbes may have conflated the arguments from ownership and gratitude because at the end of the discussion he says that God's sovereignty does not depend on his being 'Creator, and Gracious', as if these amounted to the same thing, L, 31, p. 558. Other philosophers and divines distinguished between the creator and ownership arguments and the gracious and goodness arguments, as we shall see.

that person a sovereign. Few saints were sovereigns; and no one became sovereign by doing good works.

A second explanation for the natural sovereignty of God comes from considering only God's making of the world. The opening chapter of Genesis can be interpreted as indicating that God was sovereign of the world because he made it.[27] A third explanation is that God was sovereign because he owned the world. If God owns the world, then there is no mystery about how he can give Adam dominion over the animals. The second and third explanations sometimes go together: God owns the world because he made it. Psalm 24 begins: 'The earth is the Lord's, and the fullness thereof; | the world, and they that dwell therein. | For he hath founded it upon the seas, and established it upon the floods.'[28] Hobbes did not deny Yahweh's ownership; he simply thought that ownership was not the foundation of sovereignty.[29] George Lawson, one of Hobbes's earliest critics, combines the two explanations:

Dominion in general is twofold:...of possession or government. That of possession we call propriety: in which respect God is absolute Lord of all his creatures, because he createth and preserveth them, so that their very being is more his then theirs.[30]

Neither the making nor the owning explanations are cogent according to Hobbes. It is evident that making something does not confer ownership of it. Parents make children and have authority over them, but they do not own them. Hobbes's explanation for parental authority is complicated and possibly inconsistent. In any case, he does not connect parental authority with either making or owning.[31] Unless a person has sold or contracted out their labour, it is plausible that a person owns what he makes. God was

---

[27]   The biblical author may well have thought that God's sovereignty was based in his making; see e.g. John Gibson, *Genesis* (Edinburgh: The St. Andrew Press, 1981), i, 5.

[28]   Psalms 24:1–2, *The Bible, King James Version, with the Apocrypha* (London: Penguin Classics, 2006), 695. The New Revised Version translates these verses as: 'The earth is the Lord's and all that is in it, | the world, and those who live in it; for he has founded it on the seas, | and established it on the rivers'. *The New Oxford Annotated Bible*, College Edition, 3rd edition (New York: Oxford University Press, 2001), 794. Cf. Luc Foisneau, *Hobbes et la Toute-Puissance de Dieu* (Paris: Presses Universitaires de France, 2000), 29.

[29]   Because the biblical authors conceived of God in various ways, the texts are not always consistent. Some passages suggest that God does not bestow dominion but only something more like stewardship. Even if that is true, God's sovereignty is implied by passages such as 'all the earth is mine' (Ex. 19:5; see also Ps. 89:11). Although human ownership of property depends on the existence of sovereigns who protect the property of their subjects, if the entire earth is said to belong to one person and that person has the power to control it, the fair inference is that the 'owner' of the earth is its sovereign. The fact that Yahweh's ownership seems to be even more restricted in other passages—He owns Canaan or Israel and not necessarily other places (Gen. 14:19, 22 and L, 35, p. 634)—is also not a viable objection to God's sovereignty. God's special kingship is compatible with his universal kingship. See A. P. Martinich, 'The Interpretation of Covenants in *Leviathan*', in *Leviathan After 350 Years*, ed. Tom Sorell and Luc Foisneau (Oxford: Clarendon Press, 2004), 217–40.

[30]   George Lawson, *Examination of the Political Part of Mr. Hobbs his Leviathan* (London, 1657), 150.

[31]   The ability of a parent to kill an infant or young child is tantamount to omnipotence. But Hobbes cannot make this explicit without giving the impression that human sovereignty does not depend on a covenant. In fact, he is often interpreted as holding that sovereignty by acquisition does not depend on a covenant. Cf. A. P. Martinich, *Hobbes* (London: Routledge, 2005), 125–8.

in that position at creation. Hobbes does not give any reasons for holding that making is logically independent of owning. Nor does he explain why owning does not confer sovereignty. However, it is not hard to think of a Hobbesian explanation. Ownership is correlative with property; and property presupposes sovereignty. It is the sovereign's commands about what people may do or not do with respect to things that constitutes property. Property owners as such do not have any authority to command others. Hobbes's attribution of omnipotence to God may seem somewhat odd, for he sometimes says that the only thing that human beings can know of him is that he exists.[32]

Arash Abizadeh has argued that God is an artificial person by fiction for Hobbes. In brief, his argument is this. When Hobbes discusses representation 'by fiction', he discusses five groups, in five successive paragraphs, (1) inanimate things, (2) children and madmen, (3) idols, (4) God, and (5) a sovereign. Concerning the first three types, Hobbes says that the things represented are not authors. But Hobbes does not say this about God (4).[33] Abizadeh claims that Hobbes implies that the reader should add 'and God can be no author'. While space does not allow me to explain the problems with Abizadeh's position in detail, some of them can be stated briefly. One concerns his claim that because Hobbes says of the examples in the first three groups, that they cannot be authors, and because he does not say that God can be an author, he expects the reader to supply the proposition that God cannot be an author. Abizadeh thinks that Hobbes can expect his reader to provide the extra proposition because it is required by 'the rhythm already set in motion by Hobbes's prose'.[34] But there is no such rhythm. Each paragraph contains a slightly different structure, as demanded by the group of examples being discussed. Also, there was no need to say that God was an author since that was the presupposition of his readers. My guess is that if Hobbes had written, 'Of course, God is an author', a just-so story would be told to explain why Hobbes meant it as sarcasm. Another problem is that as the fifth group of examples shows, a person by fiction can have authors. So it is not necessary to think that Hobbes is implying that God cannot be an author. Yet another problem is that Abizadeh's position does not fit with the Latin version of *Leviathan*. The relevant passage is, 'Etiam Dei veri Persona geritur, & gesta est. Mundum enim in propria Persona creavit. In redimendo genere Humano Personam Dei gessit Iesus Christus' ['Also, the Person of the true God is borne and has been borne. For in his own person, he created the world. In redeeming human kind, Jesus Christ bore the Person of God'].[35] God the Father acts 'in propria Persona', and 'Persona *Propria*' is Hobbes's term for a natural person.[36] Finally, a general

---

[32] AW, 36.16.

[33] Arash Abizadeh, 'The Representation of Hobbesian Sovereignty', in *Hobbes Today*, ed. S. A. Lloyd (Cambridge: Cambridge University Press, 2013), 137–9.

[34] Ibid., p. 139. Cf. L, 22, pp. 386–7.   [35] LL, 16, p. 249, my translation.

[36] LL, 16, p. 245. In a later formidable article, Abizadeh claims that Hobbes changed the wording in the Latin translation in order 'to avoid the charge of heresy'; see Arash Abizadeh, 'Hobbes's Conventionalist Theology, The Trinity, and God as an Artificial Person by Fiction', *The Historical Journal* 60.4 (2017), 915–41. This assertion seems to be made only to neutralize contrary evidence. Abizadeh's main position in the later

problem is that Abizadeh does not consider all the relevant evidence. His interpretation cannot accommodate straightforward statements by Hobbes such as that Leviathan is the '*Mortall God,* to which wee owe under the *Immortall God*, our peace and defence',[37] although Abizadeh quotes it.

In one place, Hobbes implies that his proof for the existence of God is a proof that something that is 'Eternall, Infinite, and Omnipotent' exists.[38] About eternity, he may think that he has to assert it of God because if God began to exist at some particular time, there would have to be some moving body that caused God to come to exist; and so God would not be the first cause. About infinity, Hobbes may have thought that he could assert it because he was not committing himself to very much. God is infinite because everything that human beings sense is finite. God, who cannot be sensed, is not finite, and so, infinite. It was easier for a seventeenth-century geometer like Hobbes to have a deflationary idea of infinity than an arithmetician.

Because God's natural sovereignty is grounded in his omnipotence, he enjoys carte blanche in his treatment of human beings:

To those therefore whose Power is irresistible [omnipotent], the dominion of all men adhereth naturally by their excellence of Power; and consequently it is from that Power, that the Kingdome over men, and the Right of afflicting men at his pleasure, belongeth Naturally to God Almighty...as Omnipotent. And though Punishment be due for Sinne onely, because by that word is understood Affliction for Sinne; yet the Right of Afflicting, is not always from mens Sinne, but from Gods Power.[39]

One benefit of Hobbes's position is that it provides a straightforward solution to the problem of evil:[40]

This question, *Why Evill men often Prosper; and Good men suffer Adversity*, has been much disputed by the Antient, and is the same with this of ours, *by what Right God dispenseth the Prosperities and Adversities of this life*; and is of that difficulty, as it hath shaken the faith, not onely of the Vulgar, but of Philosophers, and which is more, of the Saints, concerning the Divine Providence. *How Good* (saith *David*), *is the God of Israel to those that are Upright in Heart; and yet my feet were almost gone, my treadings had well-nigh slipt; for I was grieved at the Wicked, when I saw the Ungodly in such Prosperity.* [Ps. 72:1–3] And *Job*, how earnestly does he expostulate

article is that Hobbes is a theist, whose God of course acted in history, as narrated in the Bible, and is 'constructed artificially by human convention'. His thesis is paradoxical according to Hobbes's standards. In non-technical language, this makes Hobbes's God both fictive and a fictional character. Cf. Roy Sorenson, 'Fictional Theism', *Analysis* 75.4 (2015), 539–50. Limitations of space preclude the full answer that Abizadeh's article deserves.

[37] L, 17, p. 260.   [38] L, 12, p. 166. But cf. Holden, 'Hobbes's First Cause'.

[39] L, 31, p. 558. Hobbes's view that nothing that God can do to creatures can be an injury was a mainstream view. See for example Arthur Hildersham, *CLII Lectures upon Psalme LI preached at Ashby-Delazouch in Leicester-shire* (London, 1635), 520.

[40] The book of Job proposes many solutions to the problem of evil. Hobbes's preferred solution might be called the 'God-Above-Justice Solution'. As almighty, God has a natural authority over humans, that is, is sovereign over them and hence cannot be unjust to them.

with God, for the many Afflictions he suffered, notwithstanding his Righteousnesse? This question in the case of *Job*, is decided by God himselfe, not by arguments derived from *Job's* Sinne, but his own Power. For whereas the friends of *Job* drew their arguments from his Affliction to his Sinne, and he defended himselfe by the conscience of his Innocence, God himselfe taketh up the matter, and having justified the Affliction by arguments drawn from his Power, such as this, *Where wast thou when I layd the foundations of the earth*,[41] [Job 38:4] and the like, both approved *Job's* Innocence, and reproved the Erroneous doctrine of his friends. Conformable to this doctrine is the sentence of our Saviour, concerning the man that was born Blind, in these words, *Neither hath this man sinned, nor his fathers; but that the works of God might be made manifest in him*.[42] And though it be said, *That Death entered into the world by sinne*, (by which is meant that if *Adam* had never sinned, he had never dyed, that is, never suffered any separation of his soule from his body,) it follows not thence, that God could not justly have Afflicted him, though he had not Sinned, as well as he afflicteth other living creatures, that cannot sinne.[43]

Hobbes's solution is true to part of the book of Job.[44] In reply to one of his friends' speeches, Job says:

> He is not a man as I am, that I can answer him
> Or that we can confront one another in court.
> If only there were one to arbitrate between us
> And impose his authority on both.[45]

Job is oblivious to the irony of his comments. Indeed, no one can arbitrate between him and God because God is not on the same legal or moral level as human beings. God is not subject to any laws, and hence cannot be just by following them or unjust by breaking them.[46] Hobbes could have quoted another part of Job in support of his view. The passage 'And God appeared to Job out of the whirlwind' may be interpreted as referring to God's power. Similarly, human sovereigns cannot be just or unjust with respect to the laws of their commonwealth. It was part of the common law that the king could do no wrong. Human sovereigns approach omnipotence as much as a non-divine person can insofar as they have all the political power in a civil state. However, I think that Hobbes's considered view is that absolute sovereigns are above justice and injustice because they make laws, not because they approximate to omnipotence.

---

[41] This verse contains a solution to the problem of evil that may be called the 'Unanswerable-Question Solution'. Humans do not have enough information to be able to answer the question. This solution is different from the God-Above-Justice Solution.

[42] This verse from the Gospel of John 9:3 expresses yet another solution, different from those mentioned above. It does not occur in Job.

[43] L, 31, pp. 558–60; see also QLNC, pp. 102, 104–5.

[44] There are at least seven solutions proposed in the book of Job. Most of them are obviously unacceptable such as that Job is not good and that he is rewarded in the end.

[45] Job 9:32–3; see also 9:2–4, 9:15–19, 13:3, 13:15, 16:21, 23:3–5, 31:35–7.

[46] Thomas Aquinas wrestles with the issue of God's justice at *Summa theologiae* I, Q. 21, art. 1.

Hobbes's view that God is a natural sovereign in virtue of his extraordinary power was not peculiar in the mid-seventeenth century. People as distant from Hobbes politically as the Leveller John Lilburne conjoined power and kingship:

God, the absolute sovereign Lord and King of all things in heaven and earth, the original fountain and cause of all causes, who is circumscribed, governed, and limited by no rules, but doth all things merely and only by his sovereign will and unlimited good pleasure.[47]

The connection between omnipotence and obedience is implicit in some of the work of William Ames. His answer to the question 'by what motives a man may be stird up to embrace the call of God' is that he is called by 'an omnipotent God, to whom we ought to hearken and give eare'.[48] The idea goes back to the Fathers of the Church. Saint Ambrose wrote: 'you Princes, and Potentates of the earth, yee ought your selves...live under the command, and obedience of the omnipotent God'.[49] God's absolute sovereignty immunizes him against criticism about predestination. Arthur Hildersham wrote: 'God had done no wrong, if in his eternall decree he had chosen no man unto life but reprobated all men unto destruction. For he is our absolute soveraigne Lord as we have heard; and it was lawfull for him, to doe with his owne what himselfe pleased.'[50] The reasons that God cannot injure any creature are divided into two by Hildersham:

1. In regard of his Soveraignty, and Supreame, and undependent power he hath over all things that he hath made, even as the potter hath over his clay.... In respect of this Soveraignty, and Supreame power of God, *Elihu* saith, *Iob* 33.13. that *God giveth no account of any of his matters*....2. In regard of his will, it is not possible he should wrong any of his creatures, for his will is the rule of all righteousnesse, and every thing is therefore just &, because his will is so.[51]

To say that God may treat people in whatever way he sees fit, as Hobbes and others say or imply, is not to deny that he treats most good people well.[52] In fact, an important part

---

[47] John Lilburne, *The Free-man's Freedom Vindicated* (London, 1646). Lilburne does not use the word 'omnipotence'. But omnipotence is suggested by the phrase 'fountain and cause of all causes' and more particularly, 'cause of all causes', which imitates other biblical phrases applied to God such as 'lord of lords' and 'king of kings'. Only God is lord and only God is king; and only God is cause of causes. The connection between unlimited power and kingship seems to supervene on the clustered ideas of absolute sovereignty, lordship, universal kingship, being cause of causes, being absolutely unlimited, and legitimately arbitrary. The glue holding them together is psychological association. Neither Lilburne nor the other seventeenth-century intellectuals who string together some or all of these ideas analyses their logical relationships. More important than the fact that they were not philosophers is the fact that these ideas occur together in the Bible without analysis. Concerning Lilburne's statement that God's 'will is the rule of all righteousness', see also Hildersham, *CLII Psalms*, 520: 'the only thing' that justifies God is his 'will and good pleasure'.

[48] William Ames, *Conscience with the Power and Cases thereof Devided into V. books* ([Leyden and London], 1639), 11–12.

[49] Ambrose, *Christian Offices Crystal Glass* (London, 1637), 1.

[50] Hildersham, *CLII Lectures*, 249.

[51] Ibid., 248. See also John Arrowsmith, *Armilla Catechetica. A Chain of Principles* (London, 1659), 345; Christopher Cartwright, *A Practical and Polemical Commentary or Exposition on the Whole Fifteenth Psalm* (London, 1658), 50; and Henry Church, *Miscellanea Philo-theologica. Or, God, & Man* (London, 1637), 107.

[52] Hildersham, *CLII Lectures*, 249.

of the biblical conception of the divine king is that he uses his strength to protect his people. The moral of the Deuteronomistic history, which covers the history of the Israelites in the desert after the Exodus up to the Babylonian Captivity, is that Yahweh protects the Israelites and they prosper when Yahweh is obeyed; and they suffer when they disobey.[53] This reciprocal relationship between protection and obedience is similar to Hobbes's 'protection and obedience' formula, in the 'Review and Conclusion' of *Leviathan*.

Returning to the separation of power from goodness, we should consider the biblical passages in which Yahweh behaves abominably, as when he orders the slaughter of the inhabitants of Jericho, Ai, Hazor, and other cities:

Joshua said, 'The city and all that is in it shall be devoted to the Lord [Yahweh] for destruction. Only Rahab the prostitute and all who are with her in her house shall live'...

Then the Lord [Yahweh] said to Joshua, 'do not fear or be dismayed...You shall do to Ai and its king as you did to Jericho and its king'...

When Israel had finished slaughtering all the inhabitants of Ai...and when all of them to the very last had fallen by the edge of the sword, all Israel returned to Ai, and attacked it with the edge of the sword. The total of those who fell that day, both men and women, was twelve thousand—all the people of Ai. For Joshua did not draw back his hand, with which he stretched out the sword, until he had utterly destroyed all the inhabitants of Ai...according to the word of the Lord [Yahweh].[54]

Joshua might have said about Yahweh what several American politicians have reportedly said about one or another dictator, 'He's a son of a bitch, but he is our son of a bitch'.[55] If we think that these tales of slaughter in the name of God must have been so abhorrent to Hobbes that he could not have accepted them, recall that both sides in the English Civil War justified or excused their barbarities because they were fighting on the side of God. General histories typically mention that 'God's Englishman', Oliver Cromwell, killed the inhabitants of Drogheda and Wexford after those cities surrendered; but the killing of non-combatants including women and children occurred on a smaller scale during most of the war. The 'godly' soldiers on the parliamentary side believed that they were slaughtering Catholics, who corrupted Christianity, and atheists.[56] Christians accepted that some horrific behaviour was approved of or performed by God (see e.g. Genesis 22). While we may not like Hobbes's view about God's sovereignty and his solution to the problem of evil, the discrepancy in attitude is due in large part to the deep differences between his moral world and our own.

Hobbes does not have to show that God's apparently bad behaviour is incompatible with his goodness because he, like other negative theologians, does not think that

---

[53] Although early modern intellectuals did not use the term 'Deuteronomistic history', they believed that the Bible taught that good behaviour was rewarded and that bad behaviour was punished.

[54] Joshua 6:17; Joshua 8:1–2; Joshua 8:24–7, in *The Bible*, 217, 279, 280, respectively.

[55] For other stories about Yahweh's horrific commands, see Joshua 10:16–11:23.

[56] Diane Purkiss, *The English Civil War* (New York: Basic Books, 2006), 288–99.

God is literally good.[57] In saying this, Hobbes is not contradicting anything in the three most important creeds of the Christian Church. The Apostles' Creed begins, 'I believe in God the Father Almighty, Creator of heaven and earth.' It says nothing about his supposed goodness. The Nicene Creed begins, 'I believe in one God, the Father Almighty, Maker of heaven and earth, and of all things visible and invisible.' Again, nothing about goodness. While it takes some time for the Athanasian Creed to get to the properties of God, when it does, the first property attributed to him is being almighty, and it never adds that God is good. Rather, since human beings consider calling someone good to be a way of honouring a person, they ought to call God 'good'. Hobbes's position does seem to be incompatible with the Thirty-Nine Articles, but they, undergoing various revisions, have an unusual status in English history; and have much less weight than the early creeds. Bishop John Bramhall wrote of them:

Some of them are the very same that are contained in the Creed; some others of them are practical truths, which come not within the proper list of points or articles to be believed; lastly, some of them are pious opinions or inferior truths, which are proposed by the Church of England to all her sons, as not to be opposed; not as essentials of Faith necessary to be believed by all Christians *necessitate medii*, under pain of damnation.[58]

One apparent problem with Hobbes's treatment of God's being a natural sovereign is that it does not fit the definition of a sovereign that he gave in *Leviathan*. A sovereign is:

One Person, of whose Acts a great Multitude, by mutuall Covenants one with another, have made themselves every one the Author, to the end he may use the strength and means of them all, as he shall think expedient, for their Peace and Common Defence.[59]

In *Leviathan*, Hobbes never said that God was a party to a sovereign-making covenant involving Adam and Eve.[60] The text of Genesis 3 and 4 presupposes that God's authority was independent of any covenant. It would have been absurd to interpret 'Do not eat of the tree…' as counsel. As shown by their behaviour after disobeying God and the punishment they receive from him, they were commanded—given a law—not to eat of the tree of the knowledge of good and evil. The easiest way to explain the discrepancy between Hobbes's definition and what he said about God's sovereignty is that Hobbes intended his definition to define only human sovereignty. This interpretation is made plausible by two things. One is the context in which it appears. Hobbes is beginning to explain how human sovereigns are created by a covenant. The other is that it is plausible that a sovereign is a person who has the right to command, that is, the right to have people obey simply because the person desires it.[61] Also, whoever has a right to the end

---

[57] L, 31, p. 566. That is Hobbes's official position. In other places, he explains God's goodness as if it were literally applied to him. In his debate with John Bramhall, he holds that God's goodness is a consequence of his irresistible power, QLNC, p. 159.

[58] John Bramhall, *Schism Guarded and Beaten Back upon the Right Owners* (London, 1658), 200.

[59] L, 17, pp. 260–2.   [60] Cf. Martinich, *Two Gods*, 147–9, 277–8, 286–7, 291–2, 383–4.

[61] See L, 25, p. 398. For almost all seventeenth-century thinkers, to have sovereignty over a person would mean that the person has an obligation to obey the sovereign's commands. Hobbes's comment that God is a natural sovereign in virtue of his omnipotence, but that human beings have an obligation to obey

has a right to the means. And both a human sovereign in virtue of a covenant, and the natural, divine sovereign in virtue of his power have that right.

About the fact that God does not have to act for the safety and defence of his subjects, as a sovereign does, one might begin by saying that it is 'God's prerogative',[62] as a natural sovereign, and then go on to say that as a matter of fact God typically saves those who obey him.

Hobbes's discussion of the nature of God's sovereignty prepares the reader for the main point he wanted to make in chapter 31:

It remaineth therefore that we consider, what Praecepts are dictated to men, by their Naturall Reason onely, without other word of God, touching the Honour and Worship of the Divine Majesty.

Honour consisteth in the inward thought, and opinion of the Power, and Goodnesse of another: and therefore to Honour God, is to think as Highly of his Power and Goodnesse, as is possible. And of that opinion, the externall signes appearing in the Words, and Actions of men, are called Worship.[63]

Although goodness does not literally apply to God, power irresistible does. Hobbes likely first learned about the unique power of God by hearing and having explained to him the opening chapter of the Bible, as suggested above. In any case, for more than a millennium before, philosophers had thought that creation required omnipotence. So the commitment to God's omnipotence comes from (representing oneself as) accepting the Bible.[64]

The Old Testament expresses some ambivalence towards monarchy. However, the history of Israel from the latter part of II Samuel to the end of II Kings and in the two books of Chronicles is a history of government by kings. Both King David and King Solomon are among the most admired figures in the Old Testament. It is much easier to see one's god reflected in a 'unitary executive' than it is to see it reflected in a council: 'The kingship of YHWH has its earthly counterpart in the rule of the Davidic dynasty...'.[65] Hobbes's practical commitment to monarchy is strong enough that he interprets the key anti-monarchical passage in the Old Testament as endorsing absolute sovereignty:

This shall be the Right of the King you will have to reigne over you. He shall take your sons, and set them to drive his Chariots and to be his horsemen, and to run before his chariots; and gather in his harvest; and to make his engines of War, and Instruments of his chariots; and shall take your daughters to make perfumes, to be his Cookes, and Bakers. He shall take your fields, your vineyards, and your olive-yards, and give them to his servants. He shall take the tyth of your corn and

---

him in virtue of their weakness may be odd. However, he gives an argument for his view. Suppose two beings were omnipotent. Then neither would have sovereignty over the other because neither could compel the other. Also, neither would have an obligation towards the other. So obligation has to arise from strength that is less than omnipotent, DCv 15.7.

[62] Decades ago, a philosopher and theist told me this.   [63] L, 31, p. 560. See also AW, 35.16.

[64] Biblical scholars recognize that God does not actually create the world from nothing since primeval water and a formless earth are present before creation begins.

[65] John Collins, *Introduction to the Hebrew Bible* (Minneapolis: Fortress Press, 2004), 477.

wine, and give it to the men of his chamber, and to his other servants. He shall take your man-servants, and your maid-servants, and the choice of your youth, and employ them in his businesse. He shall take the tyth of your flocks; and you shall be his servants.[66]

Hobbes's interpretation of this passage has at least this much sense. Both he and its author thought of God as a king.

God as king is the dominant representation of him in the Psalms and other books. The second paragraph of Hobbes's discussion of omnipotence and natural sovereignty begins with two quotations from Psalms: 'God is King, let the earth rejoyce, saith the Psalmist. And again, God is King though the Nations be angry; and he that sitteth on the Cherubims, though the earth be moved.'[67] Hobbes is translating from the Vulgate. And his translation is a bit free. Twice, he puts 'God is King' for 'Dominus regnavit'.[68] Hobbes's use of these passages is appropriate because the theme of God's kingship and his power are closely associated: 'The central image used to portray God is that of kingship, and the emphasis is on ... power.'[69] More of Psalm 97 supports Hobbes's view:

> Clouds and darkness are round about him;
> righteousness and judgement are the habitation of his throne.
> A fire goeth before him,
> and burneth up his enemies round about.
> His lightnings enlightened the world:
> the earth saw, and trembled.
> The hills melt like wax at the presence of the Lord [Yahweh],
> at the presence of the Lord of the whole earth.[70]

The same is true for Psalm 99. After saying that Yahweh has been enthroned, the psalmist says, 'The Lord [Yahweh] is great in Zion: | and he is high above all people. | Let them praise thy great and terrible name.'[71] Divinity, power, and kingship are inseparable for the psalmist:

> The Lord [Yahweh] reigneth, he is clothed with majesty;
> the Lord is clothed with strength, wherewith he hath girded himself:
> the world also is established, that it cannot be moved.
> Thy throne is established of old:
> thou art from everlasting.[72]

The psalmist often expressed power figuratively, especially in terms of storms and water. And so Psalm 93 continues:

> The floods have lifted up, O Lord, the floods have lifted up their voice;
> the floods have lifted up their waves.

---

[66] 1 Samuel 8:11–17; quoted in L, 20, p. 316.

[67] L, 31, p. 554. Because natural sovereignty depends on omnipotence and only God is omnipotent, sovereignty by acquisition cannot depend on power alone.

[68] See L, 31, p. 555.   [69] Collins, *Hebrew Bible*, 475.   [70] Psalm 97:1–5, in *The Bible*, 767.

[71] Psalm 99:2–3, in *The Bible*, 768.   [72] Psalm 93:1–2, in *The Bible*, 764.

> The Lord on high is mightier than the noise of many waters,
> yea, than the mighty waves of the seas.[73]

Another powerful natural phenomenon associated with God was thunder and lightning on mountain tops. Certain mountains were associated with the Israelite God. Just as Zeus lived atop Mt Olympus and Baal on Zaphon, Yahweh too lived on a mountain.[74] One of the earliest epithets of Yahweh, 'El Shaddai', is usually translated as 'God Almighty' and is understood as referring to a mountain god.[75] Because the concept of omnipotence is more sophisticated than great power, older parts of the Bible associated kingship with a power less than omnipotence. The paradigm of a powerful leader was the warrior king, for example, the first two kings of Israel. Since a nation's God was supposed to protect the people from its enemies, God was portrayed as a warrior.[76] One of the oldest passages in the Bible is a song to Yahweh as a warrior:

> I will sing unto the Lord [Yahweh], for he has triumphed gloriously:
> The horse and his rider hath he thrown into the sea.
> … The Lord is a man of war:
> The Lord [Yahweh] is his name.[77]

Divinity, kingship, and the power of a warrior occur together in this passage:

> Who is this King of glory?
> The Lord, strong and mighty,
> the Lord, mighty in battle.…
> Who is this King of glory?
> The Lord of hosts, he is the King of glory.[78]

And Hobbes could have referred to passages in other books of the Bible, for example, Isaiah 3:1 and 42:13.

The concept of a warrior God and the fact that the king was preceded by tribal chiefs who established their authority through military prowess may raise the question of which came first: warrior chief or warrior god? My guess is that the one concept reinforced the other. Kings liked to represent themselves as having divine qualities. In defence of his claim to absolute sovereignty in a speech to Parliament (1610), King James said, 'even by God himself they [kings] are called gods'.

---

[73] Psalm 93:3–4, in *The Bible*, 764. Also: 'The voice of the Lord [Yahweh] is upon the waters: | the God of glory thundereth… | The voice of the Lord [Yahweh] is powerful; | the voice of the Lord [Yahweh] is full of majesty' (Psalm 29:32, in *The Bible*, 699). And: 'Thou rulest the raging of the sea' (Psalm 89:9, in *The Bible*, 759).

[74] Cf. Harold Attridge (ed.), *HarperCollins Study Bible* (New York: Harper One, 2000), 804, n. 89.12.

[75] Although the literal meaning is conjectural, most scholars believe that El Shaddai means *God of the Mountain*.

[76] The idea of a warrior king in the ancient Near East goes back to the third millennium BCE. See Steven Garfinkle, 'Ancient Near Eastern City-States', in *The Oxford Handbook of the State in the Ancient Near East and Mediterranean*, ed. P. Fibiger Bang and W. Scheidel (New York: Oxford University Press, 2013), 94–120.

[77] Ex. 15:1, 3, in *The Bible*, 85.   [78] Psalm 24:8, 10, in *The Bible*, 695.

I began this chapter by discussing Hobbes's belief that omnipotence is sufficient for sovereignty; I then discussed how having great power, more precisely, more power than one's enemies, is sufficient for being a sovereign, divine or non-divine. I now want to point out how Hobbes may predicate the properties standardly attributed to God to sovereigns in an attenuated sense.

The sovereign approaches omnipotence with respect to its subjects,[79] as alluded to above, in that they have transferred their rights of government to the sovereign, and by the principle that whoever has a right to an end has a right to the means, they have potentially transferred all their power to him.[80] The sovereign approaches omniscience in that whenever a dispute arises about a matter of fact or science, he has the right to decide what the truth shall be taken to be.[81] The sovereign approaches omnibenevolence in that he can do no wrong and what he desires is good; and the sovereign is just in the sense that he is the judge of all disputes and above justice and injustice in that he cannot break any law since he makes the law.[82] Finally, the sovereign is the redeemer because he saves his subjects from the impending death of the state of nature.

Hobbes's view can be considered an answer to those enemies of Charles I, who would have denied that kings are like gods, for example, Henry Parker who wrote that those who look upon the king 'the efficient…cause, and the Subject of all power' and 'maintain, That all Kings are in all things and commands…to be obeyed, as being like Gods, unlimitable, and as well in evil, as in good unquestionable' are 'sordid flatterers'.[83]

Because of his historical situation, Hobbes thought that the proper understanding of Christianity should be biblical.[84] The biblical conception of God that prevailed from at least the fourth century on was the conception of an omnipotent and sovereign God; and that conception was salient because it appears at the beginning of the Bible. Another part of that conception, or another conception that was not distinguished from the first, was that God, as king, was a great warrior because he had great power. This God punished the Israelites and human beings generally when they disobeyed him; and he protected people when they obeyed him. This reciprocal relationship between protection by and obedience to God was understood as being essential. Goodness had little to do with it.

---

[79] I will not repeat the phrase 'with respect to his subjects' for the other properties.

[80] See A. P. Martinich, 'Authorization and Representation in Hobbes's *Leviathan*', in *The Oxford Handbook of Hobbes*, ed. A. P. Martinich and K. Hoekstra (Oxford: Oxford University Press, 2016), 315–38.

[81] L, 18, pp. 268–74.   [82] L, 18, pp. 270, 272–4.

[83] Henry Parker, *Observations upon Some of his Majesties Late Answers and Expresses* (London, 1642), 44, spelling modernized.

[84] Hobbes may have thought biblical religion was important because Christianity does not challenge the established government and that in Israelite religion, the king was the head of the religion, as much as anything else.

3

First Impressions

Hobbes on Religion, Education, and the Metaphor of Imprinting

Teresa M. Bejan

Ever since Alan Ryan's recovery of a 'more tolerant' Hobbes three decades ago, scholarly support for a kinder, gentler Monster of Malmesbury has only grown.[1] While few commentators go as far as Richard Tuck in characterizing *Leviathan* as a 'passionate defense of toleration',[2] many have likewise sought to correct the dominant picture of an *intolerant* Hobbes by highlighting the passages in his works that seem to call for a significant degree of freedom of thought in and about religion.[3] Above all, they point to *Leviathan*'s apparent endorsement of the 'Independency of the Primitive Christians' as proof that Hobbes's project was one of popular enlightenment intended to liberate individuals from the clerical yoke and so to secure their spiritual and intellectual independence thereafter.[4]

For proponents of a tolerant Hobbes *qua* defender of popular enlightenment, the first reason offered in favour of religious 'Independency' is particularly significant: 'Because there ought to be no Power over the Consciences of men but the Word it selfe, working Faith in every one, not always according to the purpose of them that Plant

The author is grateful to Zak Black for research assistance.

[1] Alan Ryan, 'Hobbes, Toleration and the Inner Life', in *The Nature of Political Theory*, ed. David Miller and Larry Siedentop (Oxford: Oxford University Press, 1983), 197–218; and his 'A More Tolerant Hobbes?', in *Justifying Toleration: Conceptual and Historical Perspectives*, ed. Susan Mendus (Cambridge: Cambridge University Press, 1988), 37–59.

[2] Richard Tuck, 'Hobbes and Locke on Toleration', in *Thomas Hobbes and Political Theory*, ed. Mary G. Dietz (Lawrence, KS: University of Kansas Press, 1990), 163.

[3] See Richard E. Flathman, *Thomas Hobbes: Skepticism, Individuality, and Chastened Politics* (Lanham, MD: Rowman & Littlefield, 2002); J. Judd Owen, 'The Tolerant Leviathan: Hobbes and the Paradox of Liberalism', *Polity* 37.1 (2005), 130–48; Edwin Curley, 'Hobbes and the Cause of Religious Toleration', in *The Cambridge Companion to Leviathan*, ed. Patricia Springborg (Cambridge: Cambridge University Press, 2007), 309–36; Arash Abizadeh, 'Publicity, Privacy, and Religious Toleration in Hobbes's *Leviathan*', *Modern Intellectual History* 10.2 (2013), 261–91.

[4] L, 47, p. 1116. See also Teresa M. Bejan, 'Difference without Disagreement: Rethinking Hobbes on "Independency" and Toleration', *The Review of Politics* 78.1 (2016), 1–25.

and Water, but of God himself, that giveth the Increase'.[5] Many commentators recognize in this and other passages a claim central to the arguments of later tolerationists: that force cannot compel belief, hence the state should not seek to 'impose' on its citizens in matters of religious doctrine or worship.[6] While the soundness of this normative conclusion, drawn most famously by Locke in *A Letter Concerning Toleration* (1689), was and is a matter of dispute—the Anglican clergyman Jonas Proast's rejoinder that force very well could influence belief, if 'indirectly and at a distance', goaded Locke into writing three additional *Letters on Toleration* of several hundred pages each—Hobbes explicitly denied it. 'A private man has always the liberty, (because thought is free,) to beleeve, or not beleeve in his heart... but when it comes to confession of that faith, the Private Reason must submit to the Publique'.[7]

But what of the empirical claim, about the inefficacy of sovereign power *in foro interno*? The idea that Hobbes was committed to this, and so drew an insuperable boundary between the inward and the outward realm, is a staple of many 'tolerant Hobbes' arguments. Yet this would seem to be, at the very least, in tension with his materialist metaphysics, which understood human cognition as a product of matter in motion, rendering 'thinking-bodies' subject to the physical forces of action and reaction like any other.[8] More importantly, Hobbes's enthusiasm for educational reform as a key right and duty of sovereignty raises important questions about how or to what extent he believed it possible for sovereigns to shape subjects' 'internal' religious beliefs—both directly and 'at a distance'.[9]

Hobbes was certainly not unique in foregrounding the political, as well as the religious, significance of education. Several prominent contemporaries, including Samuel Hartlib and John Milton, also advocated for universal provision and public oversight,[10] and even Locke would insist that 'of all the men we meet with, nine parts of ten are what they are, good or evil, useful or not, by their education'.[11] This chapter will argue, however, that Hobbes was unique, not simply in the scope and grandeur of his proposed reforms, which included replacing all of Aristotle with *Leviathan* in the university curriculum, but in the distinctive image he used to illustrate his educational project as well. While Locke described 'a Gentleman's son... as white Paper, or wax, to be moulded

---

[5] L, 47, p. 1116.

[6] See Franck Lessay's chapter, 'Tolerance as a Dimension of Hobbes's Absolutism', in this volume; J. Judd Owen, *Making Religion Safe for Democracy* (Cambridge: Cambridge University Press, 2014), 51–4; Steven B. Smith, *Modernity and its Discontents* (New Haven, CT: Yale University Press, 2016), 83, 86–7.

[7] L, 37, p. 696.

[8] For a powerful critique of the persistent dualism attributed to Hobbes, see Samantha Frost, 'Faking It: Hobbes's Thinking-Bodies and the Ethics of Dissimulation', *Political Theory* 29.1 (2001), 30–57.

[9] See Teresa M. Bejan, 'Teaching the *Leviathan*', *Oxford Review of Education* 36 (2010), 607–26 and Douglas Jesseph, *Squaring the Circle: The War Between Hobbes and Wallis* (Chicago, IL: University of Chicago Press, 1999), chapter 2.

[10] Bejan, 'Teaching the *Leviathan*', 610–11.

[11] John Locke, *Some Thoughts Concerning Education*, ed. Jean S. Yolton and John W. Yolton (Oxford: Clarendon Press, 1989), §1. See Nathan Tarcov, *Locke's Education for Liberty* (Lanham, MD: Lexington Books, 1999), and Mark E. Button, *Contract, Culture, and Citizenship: Transformative Liberalism from Hobbes to Rawls* (University Park, PA: Pennsylvania State University Press, 2010).

or fashioned as one pleases',[12] Hobbes turned his attention beyond elites and insisted that 'the Common-peoples minds, unlesse they be tainted with dependance on the Potent, or scribbled over with the opinions of their Doctors, are like clean paper, fit to receive whatsoever by Publique Authority shall be imprinted in them'.[13]

While this metaphor of educational 'imprinting' has long captured the imagination of commentators inclined to view Hobbes as a harbinger of totalitarian modernity,[14] no one has tackled Hobbes's metaphor and its obvious significance for the (in)tolerant Hobbes debate directly.[15] This chapter will thus examine the metaphor of imprinting in the broader context of Hobbes's life and works in order to understand its implications for the sovereign's role in regulating religion in the *inward*, as well as the outward, forum. Doing so reveals 'imprinting', like all of Hobbes's metaphors, to have been well and carefully chosen.[16] As a self-conscious play on both an ancient pedagogical analogy developed by Plato and a biblical maxim, 'Faith cometh by hearing', put forward by St Paul, it reflected Hobbes's sensitivity to the curious moment in which he wrote—a moment in which the rise of a new culture of mass media and older traditions of philosophical and religious reflection on education would collide.

3.1 Imagining Education

Although imprinting may be the most memorable, it was certainly not the only metaphor Hobbes used to describe the process of education, and unlike the others—for instance, animal 'training' or agriculture—which recur across his writings, 'imprinting' on the 'clean paper' of the common people's minds appears only in *Leviathan*. Indeed, the Oxford English Dictionary cites Hobbes's 1651 usage as exemplary of a key transition in the meaning of the verb 'to imprint' in early modern English inaugurated by William Caxton in the 1470s: that is, from the general sense of applying pressure to some medium in order to 'stamp' or 'impress' a mark upon it, to the process of *printing* by fixing letters or characters on paper through the combined technologies of the printing press and movable type.[17]

---

[12] Locke, *Thoughts*, §216.   [13] L, 30, p. 524.

[14] See Eric Voegelin, 'The Political Religions', in *Modernity Without Restraint*, ed. Manfred Henningsen (Columbia, MO: University of Missouri Press, 2000), 19–73; and Hannah Arendt, 'Truth and Politics', in her *Between Past and Future* (New York: Penguin, 2006), 223–59. Today, the alternative picture of Hobbesian education as enlightened liberation has gained a surprising amount of traction. S. A. Lloyd, 'Coercion, Ideology, and Education in Hobbes's *Leviathan*', in *Reclaiming the History of Ethics*, ed. A. Reath, B. Herman, and C. Korsgaard (Cambridge: Cambridge University Press, 1997), 32–65; Jeremy Waldron, 'Hobbes: Truth, Publicity, and Civil Doctrine', and Richard Tuck, 'Hobbes on Education', both in *Philosophers on Education*, ed. Amelie Oksenberg Rorty (London and New York: Routledge, 1998), 139–46, 147–56, respectively.

[15] The tolerant Hobbists have largely ignored it, with the exception of Noel Malcolm, *Aspects of Hobbes* (Oxford: Clarendon Press, 2002), 544.

[16] The view of Hobbes as an enemy of metaphor has rightly been criticized by Noel Malcolm and Quentin Skinner, among others. See Malcolm, *Aspects of Hobbes*; Quentin Skinner, *Reason and Rhetoric in the Philosophy of Hobbes* (Cambridge: Cambridge University Press, 1996), 363–72.

[17] 'Imprint, v. : Oxford English Dictionary', <www.oed.com>, accessed 28 July 2016.

On the surface, then, *Leviathan*'s appeal to imprinting appears to represent Hobbes at his most self-consciously modern, popular, and perhaps even democratic. Not only does it occur in the context of a discussion of the comprehensive instruction of the Commonwealth, beyond the rarefied circles of university-educated elites; the metaphor also appealed to a technology that, while not exactly new, was rapidly transforming the political world in which he lived and wrote.[18] *Leviathan* appeared at a time when rates of early education and literacy in England—particularly in the commercial centre of London—were at an all-time high.[19] In his own history of the civil wars, *Behemoth*, Hobbes would highlight explicitly the role played by the nascent mass medium of pamphleteering, which allowed preachers and politicians to popularize their 'paper war' by appealing to 'the Judgement of the people ... by printing'.[20]

Despite the growing scholarly literature on Hobbes and language, little has been said about the importance of these two so-called 'revolutions'—in education and in printing—in early modern England for his works.[21] Yet he enjoyed a front-row seat to both. As a bright young man of little means (the son of a disgraced country curate) in Elizabethan England, Hobbes owed everything to his education. Robert Latimer, an Oxford graduate who ran a small school in Westport, was the first to recognize his talents. After graduating Oxford himself, Hobbes would become a teacher to multiple generations of Cavendishes, in addition to serving as a tutor, if only in Geometry, to the future Charles II.[22] According to Aubrey, he even attempted to endow a 'free-schoole' of his own at Malmesbury in 1665, a plan foiled by the machinations of the 'queen's priests'.[23] As for printing, Noel Malcolm has detailed how, after circulating *The Elements of Law* in manuscript, Hobbes adopted a hands-on

---

[18] For a good overview of this process, see Elizabeth L. Eisenstein, *The Printing Revolution in Early Modern Europe* (Cambridge: Cambridge University Press, 2012). See also Peter Lake and Steve Pincus, 'Rethinking the Public Sphere in Early Modern England', *Journal of British Studies* 45.2 (2006), 270–92.

[19] Lawrence Stone, 'The Educational Revolution in England, 1560–1640', *Past & Present* 28.1 (1964), 41–80. Stone estimates that over half the adult male population was literate. See also Eisenstein, *Printing Revolution*.

[20] B, p. 217.

[21] See Philip Pettit, *Made with Words: Hobbes on Language, Mind, and Politics* (Princeton, NJ: Princeton University Press, 2008), 25. The rare book-length treatment of Hobbes's views on education comes in Geoffrey Vaughan, *Behemoth Teaches Leviathan: Thomas Hobbes on Political Education* (Lanham, MD: Lexington Books, 2002). Of course, the seminal treatment of Hobbes's own education remains Quentin Skinner's *Reason and Rhetoric*. Many scholars focus on Hobbes's involvement in the printing of his works in the context of explicating *Leviathan*'s frontispiece. See, in particular, Malcolm, *Aspects of Hobbes*, 336–82, and his 'Textual Introduction' to volume 1 of his edition of *Leviathan* (Oxford: Clarendon Press, 2012); Justin Champion, 'Decoding the *Leviathan*: Doing the History of Ideas through Images, 1651–1714', in *Printed Images in Early Modern Britain: Essays in Interpretation*, ed. Michael Cyril William Hunter (Farnham: Ashgate, 2010), 255–76; Magnus Kristiansson and Johan Tralau, 'Hobbes's Hidden Monster: A New Interpretation of the Frontispiece of *Leviathan*', *European Journal of Political Theory* 13.3 (2014), 299–320.

[22] For Hobbes's experience as 'princely tutor' as a possible inspiration for *Leviathan*, see Noel Malcolm's 'General Introduction' to *Leviathan*, i, 11, 53–60.

[23] John Aubrey, *Brief Lives, Chiefly of Contemporaries*, ed. Andrew Clark (Oxford: Clarendon Press, 1898), i, 342–3. I am grateful to Jon Parkin for bringing this design to my attention.

approach to the publication of his later works, corresponding frequently with his publishers in Amsterdam and London.[24]

Hobbes's own views on educational reform received their fullest exposition in *Leviathan*, culminating in the much-maligned suggestion that his book become the basis of the university curriculum.[25] Yet *The Elements of Law* had also argued that 'if the true [civil] doctrine…were perspicuously set down, and taught in the Universities', young men might 'easily receive the same, and afterward teach it to the people',[26] and *De Cive* affirmed that 'it is a duty of sovereigns to have…the true Elements of civil doctrine written and to order that it be taught in all the Universities in the commonwealth'.[27] Hobbes's appeal to 'imprinting' in *Leviathan* was thus not simply a reflection of the educational and technological revolutions of the age, but the culmination of a discussion begun in his earlier political works, albeit with the aid of different images. 'If the minds of men were all of white paper', Hobbes had argued in *The Elements*, they could as easily be taught true doctrine as false, 'but when men have once acquiesced in untrue opinions, and registered them as authentical records in their minds; it is no less impossible to speak intelligibly to [them], than to *write* legibly upon a paper already scribbled over'.[28] *De Cive* likewise traced the seditious doctrines that 'crept into the minds of uneducated people' to the universities, hence 'anyone who wants to introduce a sound doctrine has to begin [there]': 'after the young men are *steeped* in [it], they can instruct the common people in private and in public'.[29]

While there is no mention of men's minds as paper in *De Cive*, as in the *Elements*, the Latin *imbuti* (from *imbuere*), which Michael Silverthorne translates as 'steeped', conveys a sense of being stained by dye or ink. The shift between these precursor passages and *Leviathan* thus marks an increase in technological sophistication, from writing or dying to printing, as well as a shift in the locus of educational concern, from the minds of the elite future teachers of the people, educated at Oxford and Cambridge, to the 'common people' themselves. On this view, Hobbes's turn to imprinting would seem to reflect precisely the sort of secular modernity and democratization of learning to which proponents of the popular enlightenment thesis appeal. But before one gets swept away by the democratic promise of his chosen metaphor, one must recognize that in adopting such an apparently forward-looking image, Hobbes was also playing on other, much older educational traditions and themes. Indeed, *Leviathan* deliberately downplayed the significance of 'the Invention of *Printing*' which 'though ingenious…is no great matter' when compared with the earlier invention of letters, 'a profitable

---

[24] See, for example, Malcolm's biographical sketches of Samuel Sorbière (who worked for Hobbes's publishers, the Blaeus, in Amsterdam as a young man) and Andrew and William Crooke in C, pp. 893–8. For more on William Crooke's role in the formation and dissemination of 'Hobbism', see William Bulman, 'Hobbes's Publisher and the Political Business of Enlightenment', *The Historical Journal* 59.2 (2016), 339–64.

[25] For the critical reaction from Hobbes's contemporaries, see Bejan, 'Teaching the *Leviathan*', 608.

[26] EL, 28.8.   [27] DCv, 13.9.   [28] EL, 10.8 (my emphasis).

[29] DCv, 13.9 (my emphasis).

Invention for continuing the memory of time past, and the conjunction of mankind'
introduced long ago in ancient Greece.[30]

To tease out the origins of Hobbesian imprinting, then, and to understand why
Hobbes chose to highlight this educational metaphor above all others in *Leviathan*, it
is fruitful to compare his account of sovereign imprinting with the exemplary ancient
pedagogue to whom he compares himself explicitly in that work: Plato.

3.2 *Plattein* with Plato

Book Two of *Leviathan* ends with the following memorable declaration: 'I am at the
point of believing this my labour, as useless, as the Common-Wealth of *Plato*; For
he also is of opinion that it is impossible for the disorders of State…ever to be taken
away, till Soveraigns be Philosophers.' However, Hobbes concludes on a cautiously
optimistic note:

But when I consider again, that the Science of Naturall Justice, is the onely Science necessary
for Soveraigns…and that they need not be charged with the Sciences Mathematicall, (as by
Plato they are,)…and that neither *Plato*, nor any other Philosopher hitherto, hath put into
order, and sufficiently…I recover some hope, that one time or other, this writing of mine, may
fall into the hands of a Soveraign, who will consider it himselfe, (for it is short, and I think
clear,)…and by the exercise of entire Soveraignty, in protecting the Publique teaching of it,
convert this Truth of Speculation, into the Utility of Practice.[31]

The suggestion that knowledge of mathematics was not necessary for would-be sovereigns strikes a nicely ironic note, given Hobbes's employment as the crown-prince's
geometry tutor at the time! Still, contemporary critics within the universities read this
passage as clear evidence of Hobbes's megalomaniacal educational pretensions.[32]
Modern commentators, by contrast, have generally overlooked the significance of
this comparison, coming (as it does) as the culmination of the turn to educational
reform in the previous chapter.[33]

However, this placement is, to say the least, suggestive. In presenting education as
the key to translating political theory into practice, Hobbes was on firm, Platonic
ground.[34] Moreover, Plato also employed a host of metaphors, organic and inorganic,
to describe the process of education, with each figuring the nature of the student, the
activity of the teacher, and the interrelationship between the medium, method,
and message of instruction in different ways. To the first group belong the frequent
comparisons of students to young animals (puppies or colts) that must be trained, or to

---

[30] L, 4, p. 48.   [31] L, 31, p. 574.

[32] Seth Ward and John Wallis, *Vindiciae academiarum* (Oxford, 1654), 51–2.

[33] While Vaughan mentions it in passing (*Behemoth Teaches Leviathan*, 7, 93), Leon Craig depicts
Hobbes as a covert 'Platonist' without mentioning education at all, *The Platonian Leviathan* (Toronto:
University of Toronto Press, 2013).

[34] Of course, Aristotle also had a lot to say about the importance of the laws and early education to
character formation. Hobbes's antipathy to the malign effects of Aristotelian philosophy on the educational
system of his day perhaps explains why he focused exclusively on Plato as a pedagogical exemplar.

'sprouting' plants, the seeds of which must be 'implanted' and carefully cultivated.[35] Hobbes employed a similar image of education as 'training' [*disciplina*] in *De Cive* in describing how the antisocial animal, man, might be 'made fit for Society',[36] but the agricultural metaphor occurs more often in his works, especially in discussions of religion. As in the endorsement of Independency, Hobbes presented the clergy, those who 'plant and water' the 'naturall seeds' of religion, as teachers *qua* cultivators, and he noted that the English 'worship' derived from the Latin *cultus*, 'which signifieth properly... the labour which a man bestowes on any thing, with a purpose to make a benefit by it', just as 'the labour bestowed on the Earth, is called *Culture*; and the education of Children a *Culture* of their mindes'. [37]

These organic metaphors presented the nature of the pupil as paramount in determining the appropriate form and content of instruction. Plato's favourite inorganic metaphor, however, reduced the student to the formless, plastic medium of wax, while the teacher and his teaching took centre stage. This manipulation of the wax pupil took two chief forms. The first is the familiar idea of 'moulding' or 'shaping' the student invoked by Locke and captured in the Greek word *plattein*. This metaphor, particularly prominent in the *Republic*, derived from the ancient technique of lost-wax casting used to create bronze statues—'lost' because the heat of the metal melted the wax, destroying the model each time.[38] The second is that of *graphein* or 'writing'—in this case, by pressing down on a wax tablet with a stylus.[39] While the technology of writing on papyrus with ink was available in classical Greece, wax tablets were much cheaper, with the added advantage of being erasable. By heating the wax, one could wipe or scrape away yesterday's impressions and start afresh.

In contrast with animal training or agriculture, Plato's inorganic metaphors focused firmly on the virtuoso teacher, who must not only possess wisdom, but also know how to manipulate his medium by softening his students' souls—specifically, by making them *impressionable* through heat. In *The Elements*, Hobbes linked this Platonic ideal of passionate pedagogy with the agricultural metaphor of 'implanting' in a characteristically deflationary way:

The opinion of Plato concerning honourable love... is this: that a man full and pregnant with wisdom... naturally seeketh out some beautiful person, of age and capacity to conceive... and this is the idea of the then noted love of Socrates wise and continent, to Alcibiades young and beautiful... which maketh me suspect this platonic love for merely sensual; but with an honourable pretence for the old to haunt the company of the young and beautiful.[40]

---

[35] E.g. *Theages* 121b–d; *Republic* 375a–376b; *The Laws* 788d. *Symposium* gives the agricultural metaphor a memorably sexual spin.

[36] DCv, 1.2.   [37] L, 31, pp. 560–2.

[38] While today Greek sculpture is primarily associated with marble, bronze was likely a much more common, if more recycled, medium.

[39] Cf. *Republic*, 488a. Danielle Allen, *Why Plato Wrote* (Chichester: John Wiley & Sons, 2010), 30.

[40] EL, 9.17. As Richard A. Talaska notes, it is difficult to determine precisely which edition of Plato's *Opera* Hobbes would have had to hand, *The Hardwick Library and Hobbes's Early Intellectual Development* (Charlottesville, VA: Philosophy Documentation Center, 2013), 101.

Still, the Hobbesian education described in *Leviathan* bears the unmistakable imprint of a different Platonic metaphor. In the *Theaetetus*, Socrates proposes yet another method for manipulating wax to illustrate the creation of memories in the mind. 'Suppose, for the sake of argument,' he bids his young interlocutor, 'that our souls contain a waxen block...and that we imprint [*apotypousthai*] on it whatever we wish to remember...as if we were making impressions [marks/*semeia*] from signet rings [*daktylios*]; whatever is imprinted on the block, we remember and know for as long as its image is in the wax, while whatever is wiped off or proves incapable of being imprinted we have forgotten.'[41]

Of course, Plato was not the only ancient author to adopt this image.[42] Still, it has left its deepest impression on the history of philosophy thanks to the epistemological debates about empiricism inspired by Locke's *Essay Concerning Human Understanding* (1689), which gave this metaphor of the mind as *tabula rasa*—not the 'blank slate' of popular imagination, but rather a scraped wax tablet—a new lease of life.[43] Plato's emphasis, however (like Hobbes's in *Leviathan*), was not on the receiving medium (the wax), but the method. The technology of authenticating documents through the stamping or sealing of wax (in Greek, *apotypoo*; in Latin, *impremere*) with a ring was prevalent throughout the ancient world. It is in this sense that the 'light of God's countenance' is said to be '*signed* upon us' in the Psalms,[44] an image that Christian theologians later associated with man's creation *imago Dei*. Augustine would compare this to 'a coin stamped with the king's picture',[45] and centuries later, Thomas Aquinas would deploy the image to describe '[God's] truth' as 'a likeness of his own eternal light, that shines within one's soul, as a light that is impressed within us...it impresses a definite sign, or seal', by which 'one [who] is signed, or sealed with the Sacred Spirit' can 'know goodness'.[46]

We shall see Bramhall take up these Christian arguments about divine imprinting in his debates with Hobbes about free will in the 1640s and 1650s. But first, we must note that as a metaphor for education, both Platonic and Augustinian imprinting had two key features: reproducibility and fixity. Unlike writing or moulding by hand, imprinting with a ring afforded the possibility of a highly individual and

---

[41] Plato, 'Theaetetus', in *Plato: Theaetetus and Sophist*, ed. Christopher Rowe (Cambridge: Cambridge University Press, 2015), 191d–e.

[42] See also *Republic*, 377a–b and Aristotle's *De Memoria*: 'Memory...marks in a sort of imprint, as it were, of the sense-image, as people do who seal things with signet rings' (450a25). Richard Sorabji, *Aristotle on Memory* (Providence, RI: Brown University Press, 1972), 50.

[43] Of course, Locke himself never used either phrase—*tabula rasa* or 'blank slate'—in the *Essay*, helping himself instead to Hobbes's image of 'white paper, void of all characters'. John Locke, *An Essay Concerning Human Understanding*, ed. Peter Nidditch (Oxford: Clarendon Press, 1975), 104.

[44] See Psalm 4:6–7. Here, the KJV ('Lord, lift up the light of thy countenance upon us') loses the sense of the Vulgate ('signatum est super nos lumen vultus tui Domine').

[45] Augustine, 'Expositions of the Psalms 4.8', in *Psalms 1–50*, ed. Craig A. Blaising and Carmen S. Hardin (Downers Grove, IL: InterVarsity Press, 2008), 34.

[46] 'Aquinas: Psalm 4', trans. F. F. Reilly, <http://dhspriory.org/thomas/PsalmsAquinas/ThoPs4.htm>, accessed 19 June 2017.

individuated mark that was nevertheless *reproducible* in the form of nearly identical impressions—unlike handwriting or lost-wax casting, the latter of which, quite literally, broke the mould every time. Secondly, like the metaphors of *graphein* and *plattein*, imprinting foregrounded the teacher above the student by conveying an idea of education as the impressions made by an authoritative mind on a passive, plastic medium that hardens over time.

'Don't you know', says Socrates to Adeimantus in *The Republic*, 'that the beginning is the most important part of every work, and that it is especially so with anything young and tender? For at that stage it's most plastic, and each thing assimilates itself to the model whose stamp anyone wishes to give it'.[47] This idea of human nature as moving from plasticity to fixity is essential for understanding the central place of education [*paideia*] in political theory not only for Plato, but for Aristotle, as well. While wax was more malleable than metal, Plato's emphasis on the significance of early education reflected a shared faith in the power of first impressions, especially through music and poetry, to 'shape' the soul and 'imprint' the fundamental beliefs that establish the unreflective preconditions of action thereafter.

3.3 'Faith Cometh by Hearing'

In introducing 'imprinting' as a metaphor for education in *Leviathan*, Hobbes seems to have had Plato's indelible impressions in mind. His translation of the relevant passage in the *Opera Latina* described the same process as making an 'impression' (*impressio*) on *chartae purae*.[48] Years later in the *Historia Ecclesiastica*, he would liken the papal invention of the scholastic university to the moulding or *plattein* of wax directly: 'Perhaps you think that folly can't be taught: it's difficult to teach a hard old man (in my opinion). | But in his tender years, like soft wax, a man will take any form you please'.[49]

Thus, Hobbes's thoroughly modern metaphor of imprinting evidently had ancient roots, and its appearance elsewhere in *Leviathan* and in other works composed around the same time confirms this impression. The first comes in chapter 8, in which Hobbes adapts an anecdote from Lucian in which the inhabitants of the Greek city of Abdera went mad after watching Euripides's tragedy, *Andromeda*, 'upon an extream hot day', and from 'the heat, and the Tragedy together... did nothing but pronounce Iambiques... And this madness was thought to proceed from the Passion imprinted by the Tragedy'.[50] The capacity of poetry to leave so deep an impression on an audience as to fundamentally transform their behaviour and apprehension of reality is described again by Hobbes, albeit in a more laudatory and less humorous fashion (and without the assistance of accidental overheating), in his *Answer* to William Davenant's epic poem *Gondibert*: 'The virtues you distribute there amongst so many noble persons... [are] so

---

[47] *Republic*, 377a–b.   [48] LL, 30, p. 525.
[49] HE, p. 531. Compare this with Locke's comments at the end of *Some Thoughts* and Plato's *Laws*, 789e.
[50] L, 8, p. 116.

deeply imprinted, as to stay for ever [in my fancy], and govern all the rest of thoughts and affections.'[51]

Although Aubrey reports that he enjoyed music, Hobbes evidently did not share Plato's emphasis on its power, in particular, to 'penetrate' and mould the souls of men.[52] Still, the practical and moral significance of the arts in general to make deep impressions upon the mind is picked up again in chapter 12 of *Leviathan*, 'Of Religion'. There, Hobbes describes how their sensitivity to human credulity led 'the first Founders, and Legislators of Common-wealths amongst the Gentiles'—above all Numa Pompilius—'in all places [to take] care...to imprint in [the people's] minds a beliefe, that those precepts which they gave concerning Religion, might not be thought to proceed from their own device, but from the dictates of some God, or other Spirit'.[53] Here, Hobbes describes as 'imprinting' the process whereby one's basic orientation towards epistemic authority becomes fixed, which establishes the implicit metaphysical preconditions governing one's actions, in turn. As in the *Republic*, poetry fills the epistemic breach when it comes to religious beliefs—about the gods, the soul, and the afterlife—in particular, and so undergirds all of our implicit claims to knowledge about these things thereafter.[54]

The power of imprinting to determine not simply what and how one believes, but *whom*—and the special place of religion in the unreflective, cultural context in which this process takes place—is made explicit in Hobbes's discussion of education as a duty of sovereignty. As evidence that the people's minds are, indeed, 'fit to receive whatsoever by public authority shall be imprinted in them', he cites the example of Christianity: If 'whole Nations be brought to *acquiesce* in the great Mysteries of Christian Religion, which are above Reason...shall not men be able, by their teaching, and preaching, protected by the Law, to make that received, which is so consonant to Reason, that any unprejudicated man, needs no more to learn, than to hear it?'[55] The true mysteries of Christianity, unlike the Catholic belief in the miracle of transubstantiation, may be 'above' not 'against' reason; nevertheless, Hobbes implies that they, too, are believed only because they have been 'imprinted' in the public mind through preaching and teaching.

Here, in characteristic fashion, Hobbes adduces a Pauline maxim—in this case, the injunction towards evangelism, 'Faith cometh by hearing' (KJV Romans 10:17)—only to turn it on its ear. 'The most ordinary immediate cause of our beleef, concerning any point of Christian Faith, is that wee beleeve the Bible to be the word of God.' But, 'the means of *making them beleeve*, which God is pleased to afford men ordinarily, is according to the way of Nature, that is to say, from their Teachers'.[56] Hobbes then draws the sceptical conclusion that Christians believe Christianity to be true because they have been taught to believe it from an early age: '[I]t is evident, that the ordinary cause

---

[51] EW 4, pp. 457–8.   [52] Plato, *Republic*, 401d–402c.

[53] L, 12, p. 176. Hobbes's other examples include the King of Peru and Muhammad. Cf. Niccolò Machiavelli, *Discourses on Livy*, ed. and trans. Harvey C. Mansfield and Nathan Tarcov (Chicago, IL: University of Chicago Press, 1996), i, 11.

[54] Allen, *Why Plato Wrote*, 32.   [55] L, 30, p. 524.   [56] L, 43, pp. 934–6 (my emphasis).

of beleeving that the Scriptures are the Word of God, is the same with the cause of the beleeving of all other Articles of our Faith, namely, the Hearing of those that are by the Law allowed and appointed to Teach us, as our Parents in their Houses, and our Pastors in the Churches.' It does not follow that Christianity is false; but it *does* follow that most Christians have no better reason for believing the Gospel to be the revealed word of God than do Muslims the Quran. 'For what other cause can there bee assigned, why in Christian Common-wealths all men either beleeve, or at least professe the Scripture to bee the Word of God, and in other Common-wealths scarce any; but that in Christian Common-wealths they are taught it from their infancy; and in other places they are taught otherwise?'[57]

Hobbes would go on to deploy these sceptical arguments about the role of religious imprinting against Bramhall in their public debates.[58] In *Catching of Leviathan* (1658), Bramhall insisted that 'religion towards God' and 'justice towards man' were laws of nature, 'those rays of heavenly light, those natural seeds of religion, which God himself hath imprinted in the heart of man'.[59] In his *Answer*, Hobbes was incredulous: 'did [Bramhall] hope to make any wise man believe, that when this nation very lately was an anarchy [with] dissolute multitude of men, doing every one what his own reason or *imprinted light* suggested, they did out of the same light call in the king, and peace again...rather than out of fear of perpetual danger and hope for preservation?'[60]

This description of the self-styled prophet's claim to divine inspiration as 'imprinted light' was a succinct encapsulation of the 'accidental' nature of enthusiasm illustrated years earlier in *Leviathan* by the Abderites, who had the misfortune to attend the theatre in extreme heat. Yet crucially for Hobbes, enthusiasts were not alone in mistaking the effects of education for privileged access to religious truth. No matter how elaborate the theological edifice, the foundations of everyone's religious beliefs were equally accidental, based on the first culture the 'seeds of religion' received from our parents and teachers. Thus in religion, we all navigate by imprinted light.

3.4 Making an Impression

Hobbes was not the only seventeenth-century author to emphasize the religious importance of our first impressions. In his *Philosophical Commentary* (1686–8), Pierre Bayle argued that religious beliefs were the result of 'the almost invincible Impressions [of] Education' and drew the tolerationist conclusion: 'It is not always for want of

---

[57] L, 43, p. 936. Compare: 'But if Teaching be the cause of Faith, why doe not all believe?...Faith is the gift of God, and hee giveth it to whom he will. Neverthelesse, because to them to whom he giveth it, he giveth it by the means of Teachers, the immediate cause of Faith is Hearing. In a School, where many are taught, and some profit, others profit not, the cause of learning in them that profit, is the Master; yet it cannot be thence inferred that learning is not the gift of God'.

[58] Thomas Hobbes and John Bramhall, *Hobbes and Bramhall on Liberty and Necessity*, ed. Vere Chappell (Cambridge: Cambridge University Press, 1999), 45, 77.

[59] Quoted in EW 4, p. 286.   [60] EW 4, p. 287 (my emphasis).

Application, of Zeal, of Sincerity, of Good-Will, that Men continue in Errors, but from [the] too strong Impressions made on us by Custom.'[61] Compulsion in religion was therefore unjust as well as ineffective. Men cannot be held responsible for their beliefs; moreover, the 'wonderful impressions' made by the spectacular punishment of heretics on 'the Machine of the Body' are insufficient to counteract all of the educational 'Impressions' since youth that produced the error.[62] Despite any intervening lessons of reason or experience, 'the greatest part of [men] remain persuaded of what they had bin taught to believe from their Childhood: [neither] a plain argument…nor the Advantages of this World, are able to efface the Impressions of Religion.'[63]

While Hobbes's apparent influence on Bayle once lent succour to those intent on proving his atheism,[64] today it is cited more often as evidence of his tolerationism.[65] Yet Hobbes clearly did not share Bayle's doubts about the state's power to shape the 'first impressions' received by the 'machine of the body'. We may have less control over the mental transformations of education than the Platonic metaphor of *plattein* would suggest, but for 'thinking-bodies' imprinting is a physical process like any other.[66] The force of sovereign laws and punishments cannot compel belief; nevertheless, they can and do make an impact.

To get a sense of that impact, it helps to consider the complementary account of imprinting in Hobbes's physics as described in *De Corpore* (1655). The English translation, which appeared in print one year after the Latin original, appeals to the metaphor of 'imprinting' repeatedly to describe the physical effects of one moving body on another, from the 'motion imprinted [*impressus*] by any movent' on a 'fluid medium',[67] to the 'shining of glow-worms' caused by the 'simple motion imprinted [*impressum*] in them by the sun',[68] to the reciprocal vibration 'imprinteth [*imprimet*]' on the 'drum of the ear' by sound,[69] and finally to the imprinting [*imprimatur*] in iron of 'an endeavor [*conatus*] towards one of the poles' by a lodestone.[70] Although Hobbes oversaw this translation, he did not execute it himself; hence, any conclusions about its continuity with *Leviathan* must necessarily be speculative. Still, a distinctive feature of the imprinting/impression metaphor in both places is that it draws attention to the permeability of the boundary between the inward and outward realms—of men, as well as lodestones. In *Leviathan*, 'endeavour' described the 'small beginnings of Motion, within the body of Man, before they appear in…visible actions'.[71] This suggests that while, in human beings, the force of an impression might not issue directly in

---

[61] Pierre Bayle, *A Philosophical Commentary on These Words of the Gospel, Luke 14.23: 'Compel Them to Come In, That My House May Be Full'*, ed. Chandran Kukathas (Indianapolis, IN: Liberty Fund, 2005), 434, 471.
[62] Ibid., 181, cf. 356–7, 475–6.   [63] Ibid., 472.
[64] Leo Strauss, *Natural Right and History* (Chicago, IL: University of Chicago Press, 1953), 198–9.
[65] See Lessay, 'Tolerance as a Dimension of Hobbes's Absolutism'; Malcolm, *Aspects of Hobbes*, 510–11; and Owen, *Making Religion Safe*, 54.
[66] Frost, 'Faking It'.   [67] DCo, 21.4.   [68] DCo, 27.6.   [69] DCo, 29.11.
[70] DCo, 30.15.   [71] L, 6, p. 78.

something so concrete as belief, it could—and would—like all motion, 'imprint' some reciprocal 'endeavour'.

Of course, for imprinting to take in the human mind, as in any other physical medium, the 'matter [must be] prepared, or fit to receive it'.[72] But how to prepare the medium? The people's minds were as 'clean paper', to be sure—'*unless* they be tainted with dependence on the potent, or scribbled over with the opinions of their doctors'. Preparing the medium for Hobbes, it seemed, meant simply denying religious and political elites the opportunity to 'scribble' in the first place.

Here, Hobbes's shift from the agricultural metaphor for education as the cultivation ('planting and watering') of seeds, to the mechanical 'imprinting' in the context of educational reform would seem to support those who see him as a champion of (tolerant) popular enlightenment. It suggests that civil sovereigns must take education out of the hands of traditional *cultural* elites—namely, the churchmen—and put it into the hands of well-trained Hobbesian teachers and licensed printers in possession of the secular sovereign text. By taking back the universities and updating the curriculum, one might at last—as chapter 47 of the Latin *Leviathan* put it—'wipe away the democratic ink' and dispel the 'darkness of vain philosophy', replacing both with true civil doctrine.[73]

But reading Hobbesian 'imprinting' as reflecting a permanent transition from intolerance and superstition to toleration and 'independency' effected through enlightened education elides another key respect in which Hobbes's metaphor broke with its ancient predecessors.[74] Wax might harden over time, but its susceptibility to heat meant the permanence of its impressions was illusory. Thus in the *Republic*, Socrates suggested that for impressions to become 'colorfast', the material must be 'prepared beforehand' like wool for dying. The pre-treatment of citizens' souls through music was crucial for this reason—thus 'persuaded by us—they should receive the laws from us in the finest possible way like a dye...[that] could not be washed out'.[75]

Hobbes would appeal to the metaphor of 'dyeing' himself in *De Cive*. But he was not sanguine about the indelibility of imprinted ink, no matter how 'clean' the popular mind was kept.[76] One of the chief lessons taught by recent events—one he wanted in particular to digest and distil for his readers—was the *impermanence* of even the deepest and most painful impressions. 'For the continuall change of mans body, destroyes in time the parts which in sense were moved: So that distance of time, and of place, hath one and the same effect.' 'This *decaying sense* ... wee call *Imagination*', but sense that is

---

[72] Compare this with Hobbes's discussion of heat and light in 'Seven Philosophical Problems [1662]', EW 7, p. 30.

[73] The Latin reads: 'Itaque atramentum illud Democraticum, praedicando, scribendo disputando eluendum est.' Curley translates this as 'wash away' which seems closer to the Latin *eluendo*.

[74] Cf. David Johnston, *The Rhetoric of Leviathan: Thomas Hobbes and the Politics of Cultural Transformation* (Princeton, NJ: Princeton University Press, 1986); Owen, *Making Religion Safe*.

[75] *Republic*, 429d–430b.

[76] Compare this with Hobbes's discussion of 'imprinting' through tattooing or branding with a hot iron in EW 7, p. 421.

'fading, old, and past, it is called *Memory*'.[77] Even memories as traumatic as those of a civil war would fade, and sooner rather than later. Sovereigns thus let slip their control over preaching and teaching at their peril, and not simply because 'unpleasing priests' and 'democratical gentlemen' might usurp them. Without the supplement of *continual*, rigorous sovereign instruction, the inexorability of forgetting meant that the lesson simply would not stick.[78]

3.5 A Civil Catechism

His surrender of the ancient aspiration to permanence perhaps explains why Hobbes's emphasis on the need for educational reform grows stronger over the course of *Leviathan*, and stronger still in the revised and expanded Latin version of 1668. In any case, in this respect the Hobbesian metaphor of imprinting dovetails clearly and neatly with the other, unmistakably religious and sacramental, metaphors in that work—metaphors consistently overlooked by proponents of the more tolerant Hobbes. For instance, the famous description of the universities in *Leviathan*'s 'Review and Conclusion' as 'the Fountains of Civill, and Morall Doctrine, from whence the Preachers, and the Gentry...use to sprinkle the same (both from the Pulpit, and in their Conversation) upon the people' not only mocked the spittle-flecked self-importance of university-educated elites; it also deliberately evoked a baptismal font as a medium of sacramental remembrance and belonging.[79]

Thus, even while banishing the churchmen from the business of education, Hobbes shamelessly adopted their pedagogical methods. His sensitivity to the problem of memory—or, more precisely, of forgetting—explains why.

Bramhall once described *Leviathan* as a 'Rebells catechism', and although Hobbes denied it, a catechism is an apt description of the popular education it described. Perhaps Hobbes was inspired by his father, a disgraced clergyman excommunicated for, among other things, failing to catechize the young.[80] In any case, he commended the wisdom of the Hebrews on this score explicitly:

[I]n antient time, before letters were in common use, the Laws were...put into verse; that the rude people taking pleasure in singing, or reciting them, might the more easily reteine them in memory. And for the same reason *Solomon* adviseth a man, to bind the ten Commandements upon his ten fingers. And for the Law which *Moses* gave to the people of *Israel* at the renewing

[77] L, 2, p. 28.
[78] As Hobbes explained to a friend (C, p. 123): 'a man remembers best those faces whereof he has had the greatest impressions, and...impressions are the greater for the oftener seeing them, and the longer staying upon the sight of them...men look upon their own faces but for short fits, but upon their friends' faces long time together...so that a man may receive a greater impression from his friend's face in a day, than from his own in a year...besides, the sight of one's friend's face two hours together, is of greater force to imprint the image of it, than the same quantity of time by intermissions...[which] do easily deface that which is but lightly imprinted.'
[79] L, 'Review, and Conclusion', p. 1140.   [80] Malcolm, *Aspects of Hobbes*, 3.

of the Covenant, he biddeth them to teach it their Children, by discoursing of it both at home, and upon the way; at going to bed, and at rising from bed; and to write it upon the posts, and dores of their houses; and to assemble the people, man, woman, and child, to hear it read.[81]

Hobbes's own reforms sought to realize this ancient wisdom on a societal scale through what I have described elsewhere as a kind of 'civic Sunday school':[82] '[S]eeing people cannot be taught [their duty], nor when 'tis taught, remember it, nor after one generation past, so much as know in whom the Sovereign Power is placed … It is necessary that some such times be determined, wherein they may assemble together, and (after prayers and praises given to God …) hear those their Duties told them [by those that are appointed to instruct them]'.[83]

   For Hobbes, however, popular education was about more than ensuring orthodoxy with respect to doctrine. The memorable engraved images of that 'Mortal God', the Leviathan, or the secular hell of the state of nature were designed to *make an impression*. Reproduced through mass media and repeated *ad nauseum* from the pulpit, they would remind the people of their duty once the memory of civil war had faded. As the unfortunate Abderites illustrated, educational imprinting targeted the preconditions of belief and fixed dispositions—in this case, the direction of our unreflective obedience. A well-educated populace would be as 'Monks, and Friers, that are bound by Vow to … simple obedience'—but to the sovereign, not their abbot.[84]

   Here again, we are reminded of the metaphor of imprinting, which described the process whereby one receives the formative ideas and images that govern one's actions over a lifetime. Often mistaken for innate, these fundamental impressions command an unreflective obedience by structuring experience itself in ways of which we rarely become aware. Hobbes's embrace of catechistical methods suggests, therefore, that he turned to education not because he thought it possible to overthrow or arrest the imprinting process, but rather because he knew that sovereigns left it to the vagaries of contingency and others' self-interest at their peril. Wise lawgivers like Numa saw the importance of bringing imprinting under sovereign control. England, on the other hand, had adopted a dangerous policy of laissez-faire and so had let a thousand enthusiastic flowers bloom.

3.6 Teaching the *Leviathan*

Both in its form and content, then, Hobbesian education would seem to present a problem for those who would characterize *Leviathan*'s educational project as one of popular enlightenment. Far from being the liberation of man's critical capacities, sovereign 'imprinting' looks more and more like a deliberate and calculated fashioning of individuals' beliefs. But what of the passages emphasized by proponents of the

---

[81] L, 26, pp. 424–6.   [82] Bejan, 'Teaching the *Leviathan*', 611.
[83] L, 30, p. 528.   [84] L, 46, p. 1090.

tolerant Hobbes? Are we not told that 'Faith hath no relation to, nor dependence at all, upon Compulsion, or Commandement; but onely upon certainty, or probability of Arguments drawn from Reason'; hence, 'Beleef, and Unbeleef never follow mens Commands'?[85] If 'the Independency of the primitive Christians' was 'perhaps the best', was it not because 'there ought to be no power over the Consciences of men but the Word it selfe, working Faith in every one'?[86]

Many scholars have read these and other passages as proto-secular, even liberal assertions by Hobbes of the inviolable sanctity of the inward realm. But not only do these comments occur in the context of delimiting *ecclesiastical*, not *civil*, power; Hobbes's own metaphor of imprinting—as a deliberate play on Plato *and* Paul under brave new technological conditions—suggests a different interpretation. In contrast to Plato's fascination with mental insemination, Hobbes would always insist that the 'seed' of religion was 'naturall' to men.[87] In emphasizing educational contingency in the *cultivation* of that seed, however, he was on solid, Platonic ground: 'For these seeds have received culture from two sorts of men ... but both sorts have done it, with a purpose to make those men that relyed on them, the more apt to Obedience'.[88] Still for Hobbes, the spectacular failure lately in England to achieve that end meant that the contingencies of 'culture' must give way to scientific, sovereign reform. Establishing *Leviathan* as an authoritative text, one that called into question traditional epistemic authorities, particularly the divine provenance of Scripture, was essential to that project.

Here, proponents of the tolerant Hobbes might see in imprinting a programme of 'trickle-down' enlightenment through secularized public instruction, leaving men—in religion, at least—to think and fend for themselves.[89] But the proceeding analysis suggests something else. Hobbes's point seems to have been rather that the paper of men's minds never remains clean for long. Given that our peculiar beliefs about religion are generally the result of accidents and unreflective cultural influences, a conscientious sovereign *must* reflect and seek to control those exposures—and eliminate accidents—as far as he was able. If faith comes by hearing, what we hear first and under what circumstances matters quite a lot. Hence control over accidental hearing and authoritative speaking was a necessary implication of the sixth right of sovereignty 'to be Judge ... on what occasions, how farre, and what, men are to be trusted withall, in speaking to Multitudes of people', as well as 'who shall examine the Doctrines of all bookes before they be published'.[90]

Here, another aspect of the early modern transformation of imprinting—from the pressing of wax with a signet ring, to the large-scale stamping of ink onto paper with a printing press—is relevant. Unlike 'printing', *imprinting* reminds us that the development of these new technologies went hand-in-hand with the invention of new

---

[85] L, 42, pp. 782–4.   [86] L, 47, p. 1116.
[87] L, 11, p. 162; 12, pp. 164, 170.   [88] L, 12, p. 170.
[89] Malcolm, *Aspects of Hobbes*, 544. See also S. A. Lloyd, *Ideals as Interests in Hobbes's 'Leviathan': The Power of Mind over Matter* (Cambridge: Cambridge University Press, 1992), 193–4.
[90] L, 18, p. 272.

regulatory regimes to control them, including that pioneered by the Catholic Church, which required texts to be submitted to the censors in advance of publication for a license or *imprimatur* ('let it be printed', in Latin). This system was adapted by Henry VIII in England, and the so-called Star Chamber would work closely with the 'Worshipful Company of Stationers' after its incorporation in 1557 to review all submitted manuscripts for heresy and sedition.[91] Even so, it was easy enough for cheap pamphlets of the kind that would later fuel the revolution to avoid the censors. The Star Chamber was abolished in 1641, and as Hobbes would make clear in both *Leviathan* and *Behemoth*, the breakdown in licensing had already resulted in a state of war in the bosom of civil society—with Charles and Laud's attempted crackdown in 1637 too little, too late.[92]

Fully cognizant of the complex histories of 'imprinting', Hobbes's appeal to that metaphor in 1651 thus looks less like a call for liberation than for a systematic reorientation of men's natural credulity. In this, the dystopian caricatures of Hannah Arendt and Eric Voegelin, who once likened *Leviathan*'s educational project to that of a 'modern minister of propaganda', may miss the point while nevertheless hitting nearer the mark.[93] Still, the charge of 'indoctrination' often associated with this interpretation will not do.[94] Hobbesian imprinting did not seek to impose particular doctrines directly, but rather to exploit the advantage of the first-mover to fix the *preconditions* of belief and the direction of citizens' intellectual allegiances thereafter. It was not a matter of commanding or coercing belief *in foro interno*, but of establishing—and limiting—the intellectual and affective grounds of all subsequent persuasion.[95] Again, 'faith hath no relation to, nor dependence at all, upon Compulsion, or Commandement'. Yet, Hobbes continues, it *does* depend 'upon certainty, or probability of Arguments drawn from Reason, *or from something men beleeve already*'.[96] And, as he makes very clear in the following chapter, 'Of What is Necessary for a Mans Reception into the Kingdome of Heaven', *what we believe already* comes by hearing. And hearing by teaching. The forces of sovereign law and punishment could not compel belief, but they could channel it—like diverting a river or switching a train of thought, already in motion, to a different track.

The conception of civic virtue as a settled disposition to obey at which Hobbes's educational reforms aimed was a far cry from that of the ancients. In both its method

---

[91] Kevin Sharpe, *The Personal Rule of Charles I* (New Haven, CT: Yale University Press, 1992), 644–54.

[92] See Teresa M. Bejan, *Mere Civility: Disagreement and the Limits of Toleration* (Cambridge, MA: Harvard University Press, 2017), chapter 3. Of course, Hobbes would have his own run-ins with the censors after the Restoration—and indeed, before. See Jeffrey Collins, 'Silencing Thomas Hobbes: The Presbyterians and *Leviathan*', in *The Cambridge Companion to Hobbes's Leviathan*, ed. Patricia Springborg (Cambridge: Cambridge University Press, 2007), 478–500; and his 'Thomas Hobbes, Heresy, and the Theological Project of *Leviathan*', *Hobbes Studies* 26.1 (2013), 6–33.

[93] Voegelin, 'The Political Religions', 55.   [94] Tarcov, *Locke's Education for Liberty*, 48.

[95] This illustrates how even in the midst of his 'rhetoric against rhetoric', Hobbes was attuned to the political importance (and persistence) of persuasion, which must begin not from first principles, but from the beliefs people happen to hold. See Bryan Garsten, *Saving Persuasion: A Defense of Rhetoric and Judgment* (Cambridge, MA: Harvard University Press, 2006), chapter 1; Quentin Skinner, *Reason and Rhetoric in the Philosophy of Hobbes* (Cambridge: Cambridge University Press, 1996).

[96] L, 42, p. 782.

and message, the individual nature of the medium, the student (or of his regime), was immaterial. Unlike Platonic *plattein* or Rousseauvian engraving,[97] Hobbesian imprinting eliminated the place and the need for virtuosi entirely, whether as students *or* as teachers. All such irregular 'scribbling' must give way to uniformity and standardization, to an education aimed at producing endless, nearly identical reprints of the sovereign text.[98] His protestations to the contrary, the chief advantage of the modern invention of printing over writing for Hobbes was not any superiority of the medium—indeed, printing on paper was often inferior in quality to the earlier technologies of writing on parchment or vellum. Rather, it derived from the fact that the printed word could be *reproduced* more quickly—and more accurately—than it could be lost or corrupted.[99] Just as the introduction of the printing press by Caxton in 1476 led eventually to the standardization of the English language and a rise in mutual intelligibility by the seventeenth century, Hobbesian imprinting aimed at minimizing the differences between men and evening out their 'natural asperity' so as to build a more stable and lasting political edifice thereafter.[100]

While Hobbes had outdone his forebears in perfecting the message, technology thus perfected the method, making possible an educational impact and reach of which Plato had only dreamed. In adopting and adapting the ancient image of 'imprinting' in his own masterwork of civil science, Hobbes's implication was clear: if our faith in the truth of any particular doctrine depends on the precedent belief in the authenticity and authority of sacred texts imprinted upon us by our teachers, why not teach *Leviathan*? The Monster of Malmesbury, like Plato and Aristotle before him, understood quite well, one never has a second chance to make a first impression. But in teaching the *Leviathan*, sovereigns would enjoy a number of unprecedented advantages—not only a uniform message and memorable images, but the *aide memoire* of multiple, and ever cheaper, editions.

---

[97] John T. Scott, 'The Illustrative Education of Rousseau's *Emile*', *American Political Science Review* 108.3 (2014), 533–46.

[98] For the importance (as well as some of the complications) of standardization in this period, see Eisenstein, *The Printing Revolution*.

[99] See Thomas Jefferson on the laws of Virginia: 'many of them were already lost, and many more on the point of being lost...the only means of preserving those remains of our laws [is] a multiplication of printed copies'. Quoted in Eisenstein, *Printing Revolution*, 89–90.

[100] The architectural metaphor in Hobbes's discussion of the virtue of 'compleasance' as a corrective to men's 'Natural Diversity' in the fifth law of nature makes a similar point (L, 15, p. 232). See also Bejan, *Mere Civility*, 99.

4

Tolerance as a Dimension of Hobbes's Absolutism

Franck Lessay

The general theme of this volume has the great virtue of correlating two fundamental sides of Hobbes's writings, we might say the two halves of *Leviathan* (Parts 1–2 and Parts 3–4): politics and religion. This chapter is an attempt to explore that correlation by focusing on some grounds and consequences of the way Hobbes politicizes religion and thereby bolsters simultaneously his defence of the sovereign's absolute power and his plea for toleration. My guiding thread will be an interrogation of what, in Hobbes's theory, makes the sovereign's commands legitimate, or in other words, acceptable, obeyed, and therefore durable. I will try to show that, given the secular basis of Hobbes's understanding of political legitimacy, it is a logically necessary conclusion that the sovereign should be both absolute and tolerant with respect to religion, or, more accurately, that tolerance is part of the sovereign's absolutism.[1]

4.1 The Conflict of Legitimacies and the Secularization of Politics

The idea that divine right, in the twofold sense of an authority received from God and a responsibility of the sovereign to God alone, might be considered as a valid source of

[1] The acknowledgement that legitimacy is a key notion for a proper understanding of Hobbes's political theory is recent. See David Dyzenhaus, 'Hobbes and the Legitimacy of Law', *Law and Philosophy* 20.5 (2001), 461–98; David Dyzenhaus, 'The Genealogy of Legal Positivism', *Oxford Journal of Legal Studies* 24.1 (2004), 39–67; David Dyzenhaus and Thomas Poole (eds), *Hobbes and the Law* (Cambridge: Cambridge University Press, 2012). In *Hobbes and Rousseau: Nature, Free Will, and the Passions* (Oxford: Oxford University Press, 2015), 145, Robin Douglass rightly stresses both philosophers' shared concern with what made the sovereign's acts legitimate once it was recognized that 'it would be self-defeating for individuals to hold rights against the sovereign' and that 'the will of the sovereign had to be absolute'. On the notion of legitimacy more generally, see Guglielmo Ferrero, *Principles of Power: Great Political Crises of History* (Westport, CT: Greenwood Press, 1984); Lauréline Fontaine (ed.), *Droit et légitimité* (Paris: Anthémis, 2011).

political legitimacy, is clearly envisaged in Hobbes's political theory.[2] One reads in *Leviathan*:

All Pastors, except the Supreme, execute their charges in the Right, that is, by the Authority of the Civill Soveraign, that is, *Iure Civili*. But the King, and every other Soveraign, executeth his Office of Supreme Pastor by immediate Authority from God, that is to say, *in God's Right*, or *Iure Divino*. And therefore none but Kings can put into their Titles (a mark of their submission to God onely) *Dei gratiâ Rex*[3]

However, several caveats are worth keeping in mind regarding Hobbes's version of divine right theory:

1. Divine right adds nothing to the sovereign's power. While it may be regarded by some as a necessary attribute of his power, it has no practical effect on his prerogatives. In a Christian commonwealth, the sovereign has neither more nor less power than he has in God's natural kingdom (i.e. in heathen republics). Although in both cases he is accountable to God only, his rights and duties as sovereign are derived from a source other than God's explicit commands.
2. No particular creed is necessary on the part of the citizen for the completion of this process. One could even imagine that an atheist admits the sovereign's *jus divinum* (although one might find this admission difficult to reconcile with the denial of God's existence).
3. The sovereign's *jus divinum* does not increase his legitimacy: it is at best a manifestation of his full legitimacy as sovereign.
4. The recognition of a divine right of the sovereign does not imply, except in the eyes of someone who holds that belief, a divine institution of sovereignty. However, it attests the conformity of sovereignty to an order intended by God for his people and for the nations which have received that people's heritage.

In short, we may consider that *jus divinum* is one component in the characterization of the Hobbesian sovereign's status. From a historical point of view, that would argue for the persistence of divine right language in seventeenth-century political discourse. Yet the place *jus divinum* occupies in Hobbes's theory as a sign, although not as a source of the sovereign's legitimacy, illustrates its decline. It seems we are thereby invited to reexamine the grounds of political obedience and what religious dimensions they include.

As Hobbes repeatedly asserts, law requires obedience because it is a command of the sovereign. This, however, is not the source of its validity. When Hobbes writes that 'by CIVIL LAWES', he means 'the Lawes, that men are therefore bound to observe, because they are Members, not of this or that Common-wealth in particular, but of a

---

[2] On divine right theory, see J. P. Sommerville, 'Richard Hooker, Hadrian Saravia, and the Advent of the Divine Right of Kings', *History of Political Thought* 4.2 (1983), 229–45; Glenn Burgess, 'The Divine Right of Kings Reconsidered', *The English Historical Review* 425 (1992), 837–61; Cesare Cuttica and Glenn Burgess (eds), *Monarchism and Absolutism in Early Modern Europe* (London: Pickering & Chatto, 2015).

[3] L, 42, p. 854.

Common-wealth',[4] he makes it sufficiently clear that the subjects' obligation to obey is derived from their status as members of society. It appears as the practical application of the social pact, as confirmed when one reads that 'Law in generall is not Counsell, but Command; nor a Command of any man to any man; but only of him whose Command is addressed to one *formerly obliged to obey him*'.[5] He who issues commands does not only need the strength necessary to coerce obedience: he must have been authorized to issue commands. He who obeys is not motivated exclusively by fear: admitting his conduct originates in a selfish calculation, it appears as a reiteration of the movement by which he has opted for life in society, in the expectation of the advantages he will receive as a result of his renunciation to his natural right to all things. Fear and hope are the negative and positive denominations of a sense of obligation which is rationally constructed and understood, independently of any references to absolute ethical values, and demonstrates that political rule cannot rely on force to obtain citizens' submission. Hobbes returns to that theme in *Behemoth* when he asks: 'if men know not their duty, what is there that can force them to obey the laws? An army you'l say. But what shall force the army?'[6] It is the deliberate and habitual consent of citizens that creates the sovereign's right of domination, and the obedience that gives practical expression to this consent is what empowers the sovereign. Some years earlier, in his controversy with Bishop Bramhall, Hobbes had strikingly asserted that 'no *law* can possibly be *unjust*, inasmuch as every man maketh, by his consent, the law he is bound to keep, and which consequently must be just, unless a man can be unjust to himself'.[7]

The sovereign's laws apply universally insofar as they originate in the will of a ruler who exists by virtue of the consent of those he commands. Their effectiveness testifies to the legitimacy of the sovereign who has produced them, i.e. to the capacity people assume he possesses to protect them. Thus, the concept of obedience which is at the heart of Hobbes's contractarianism appears inseparable from a theory of consent which forms the basis of the philosopher's doctrine of political legitimacy. The reason for this can be found in the very nature of the consent from which the sovereign draws his right to rule, as suggested by the passage in *Leviathan* in which Hobbes defines the extent of the authorization process (a passage Bramhall stigmatized as a 'rebel's catechism'):

Again, the Consent of a Subject to Sovereign Power, is contained in these words, *I Authorise, or take upon me, all his actions*; in which there is no restriction at all, of his own former naturall

---

[4] L, 26, p. 414.

[5] Ibid. (my emphasis). This is a crucial statement for at least two reasons: it appears to ruin the case for Hobbes's political theory as a variety of *de factoism* (a long interpretive tradition from Edward Hyde and John Bramhall down to contemporary commentators); it is an invitation to qualify substantially (as recently and convincingly done by David Dyzenhaus) the categorization of Hobbes's legal thinking as an early form of legal positivism. For a modern version of the *de factoism* thesis, see Kinch Hoekstra, 'The *de facto* Turn in Hobbes's Political Philosophy', in *Leviathan After 350 Years*, ed. Tom Sorrell and Luc Foisneau (Oxford: Oxford University Press, 2004), 33–74.

[6] B, p. 183.   [7] EW 4, pp. 252–3.

Liberty: For by allowing him to *kill me*, I am not bound to kill my selfe when he commands me. 'Tis one thing to say, *Kill me, or my fellow, if you please*; another thing to say, *I will kill my selfe, or my fellow*. It followeth, therefore, that

No man is bound by the words themselves, either to kill himselfe, or any other man; And consequently, that the Obligation a man may sometimes have, upon the Command of the Soveraign to execute any dangerous, or dishonourable Office, dependeth not on the Words of our Submission; but on the Intention; which is to be understood by the End thereof. When therefore our refusall to obey, frustrates the End for which the Soveraignty was ordained; then there is no Liberty to refuse: otherwise there is.[8]

Hobbes posits here the necessity that the sovereign's commands be legitimate (in other words consistent with the objective of the original contract) in order to become binding. He thus outlines the real power left by this contract to each subject.[9] Above all, he appears to suggest that the covenant on which the commonwealth rests is bound to be repeatedly questioned. In any situation involving his condition as a member of society, every subject is led to decide freely, according to what he sees as necessary to his preservation, the appropriateness of a new adhesion to the social pact.

The social pact is made up of an infinite number of acts of consent to the commands of the public will. It is not a historical event identifiable to the ritual foundation of a city, as in antiquity. It cannot be reduced to an oath.[10] It does not imply an unconditional and definitive renunciation of a person's original rights ('not all rights are alienable', as any reader of *Leviathan* knows).[11] Hobbes's contractual theory of legitimacy signals a marginalization of religion in the genetics of the state, in which secular factors prevail.

4.2 Hobbes's Discourse of Christian Liberty and the Privatization of Religion

Investing the sovereign with unlimited authority, including in religious matters, is a logical consequence of Hobbes's understanding of the mechanics of politics. The existence of inalienable rights, however, points to the particular nature of this supposedly 'absolute' power. The situation of religion in the commonwealth helps to delineate the extent of such rights. In this respect, several points made in *Leviathan* are even more explicit in the Bramhall controversy. In his *Answer to the Catching of Leviathan*,

---

[8] L, 21, p. 338.

[9] In this respect, I broadly agree with Susanne Sreedhar's thesis about the legitimacy of some forms of rebellion; see *Hobbes on Resistance: Defying the Leviathan* (Cambridge: Cambridge University Press, 2010). As will become apparent, I question what I take to be her over-restrictive understanding of the social contract.

[10] Concerning the value of oaths (a modest one, according to Hobbes), see the statement: 'a Covenant, if lawfull, binds in the sight of God, without the Oath, as much as with it: if unlawfull, bindeth not at all, though it be confirmed with an Oath', L, 14, p. 218.

[11] L, 14, p. 202.

Hobbes argues that the sovereign's exalted status does not mean that he is, in matters of faith, a source of truth and that, consequently, what is true in one commonwealth can be false in another, or that two contradictory doctrines can be simultaneously valid. That would be absurd:

Oh, but, says he, if two kings interpret a place of Scripture in contrary senses, it will follow that both senses are true. It does not follow. For the interpretation, though it be made by just authority, must not therefore always be true. If the doctrine in the one sense be necessary to salvation, then they that hold the other must die in their sins, and be damned. But if the doctrine in neither sense be necessary to salvation, then all is well, except perhaps that they will call one another atheists, and fight about it.[12]

Besides, one can hardly imagine that a Christian sovereign, whatever his particular persuasion, might try to force his subjects to reject the fundamental article of all forms of Christian religion, namely the article which is true for all Christian believers and the key to their salvation, the *unum necessarium* according to which 'Jesus is the Christ', the saviour promised to Israel and later to the peoples of the new alliance. That point is so essential that it is the only one about which any Church can claim infallibility.[13] No sovereign calling himself Christian could reasonably deny the validity of this article. In fact, any attempt to compel his subjects to share his position would be doomed to failure, quite simply because it is impossible to bind authoritatively or force consciences, which are always free in the sense that they are not susceptible to the mechanisms of obedience, which regard actions and not beliefs.[14] Once formed as a result of an inward discourse,[15] a belief escapes the dominion of the public authority, whose commands cannot apply beyond what is perceptible. Only God can know and judge the content of a belief. The sovereign's power of coercion stops where the *forum internum* begins. That is why, in the first place, the Anglican doctrine of passive obedience appears both preposterous and dangerous. By preaching unconditional submission to the sovereign while allowing insubordination in certain unspecified circumstances in which the commands received clash with one's conscience, that doctrine proves to be based on a radical misinterpretation of the nature of obedience and opens the way to a justification of rebellion, which is self-contradictory. It is always wrong and sinful to disobey, Hobbes argues, but disobeying has no more influence

---

[12] EW 4, pp. 340–1.

[13] '...about what points are *necessary to salvation*, he [Bishop Bramhall] and I differ. For I, in the forty-third chapter of my *Leviathan*, have proved that this article, *Jesus is the Christ*, is the *unum necessarium*, *the only article necessary to salvation*; to which his Lordship hath not offered any objection. And he, it seems, would have necessary to salvation every doctrine he himself thought so. Doubtless in this article, *Jesus is the Christ*, every church is infallible; for else it were no church', EW 4, p. 345. Cf. L, 43, p. 938. The sense in which the word 'salvation' is used by Hobbes must be understood is quite another matter.

[14] '...to obey is one thing, to believe is another', Hobbes objects to Bramhall (EW 4, p. 339), thus pursuing a line of thought already followed in *Leviathan*, where he had claimed that 'mens beliefe, and interiour cogitations, are not subject to the commands, but only to the operation of God, ordinary, or extraordinary', L, 26, p. 444.

[15] L, 7, p. 98.

than obeying, on what one thinks or believes inwardly, which may not be in conformity with one's outward behaviour.

Only those whose declared vocation is to preach a definite religion, like Christian ministers, must choose torture and possible death rather than renege on their belief. This sarcastic and somewhat cynical reservation, however, does not modify the implied understanding of conscience. Hobbes's position on this issue is apparently innovative. It seems to take the form of a reduction of conscience to the status of a mere opinion. The doctrine according to which '*whatsoever a man does against his Conscience, is Sinne*' must be rejected because 'it dependeth on the presumption of making himself judge of Good and Evill'. It would be acceptable in the context of the state of nature: 'he that is subject to no Civill Law, sinneth in all he does against his Conscience, because he has no other rule to follow but his own reason'; but it cannot be so in a commonwealth where the sovereign is judge of good and evil. The law there 'is the publique Conscience', which must prevail over individual judgements: '[O]therwise in such diversity, as there is of private Consciences, which are but private opinions, the Common-wealth must needs be distracted, and no man dare to obey the Soveraign Power, farther than it shall seem good in his own eyes'.[16] The primacy of private conscience seems to be denied here. Yet, what is at issue is not the primacy of God's instructions. It is the validity of the claim that one has received such instructions.

It is thereby confirmed that when Hobbes writes that a 'doctrine repugnant to Civill Society, is, that *whatsoever a man does against his Conscience, is Sinne*',[17] he does not condemn the principle of following the dictates of one's conscience, and therefore of complying with God's commands if one believes conscience to be God's voice. What he stigmatizes is the conviction that private conscience can *never* err, which is wrong and may lead to dramatic political decisions. That is the whole extent of Hobbes's redefinition of conscience.[18] Although described as a private judgement or opinion, it remains a faculty of discerning good and evil.[19] Although it is deprived of its constant and universal primacy and must give way, in many circumstances, to the 'public conscience' embodied in the laws, it is still a potentially acceptable source of duties and one can understand (although not approvingly) that, in certain conditions, the obligations it creates receive priority over other obligations in the eyes of sincere believers. The fact that it takes the form of rational deliberation is of no effect on this essential point, which is its inaccessibility to coercion. It is with good reason, therefore, that one can see in Hobbes one of those philosophers—probably the main one—who made religious

---

[16] L, 29, p. 502.   [17] Ibid.

[18] For a rich source of information on the subject of conscience, see Richard Sorabji, *Moral Conscience Through the Ages: Fifth Century* BCE *to the Present* (Oxford: Oxford University Press, 2014). For Hobbes's treatment of private conscience, see also S. A. Lloyd's contribution to this volume, 'Hobbes on the Duty Not to Act on Conscience'.

[19] That is the sense in which the word is used in most of its forty-one occurrences in *Leviathan*.

toleration thinkable and practicable.[20] By demonstrating that one's private conscience (or belief, or judgement) is not the product of will but the result of a reflection sustained by what one hears or reads, Hobbes anticipated Locke's and Bayles' doctrines of the radical inefficacy of intolerance and persecution. By making the care of civil peace the criterion by which public doctrines must be appraised, instead of intrinsic truth or the souls' salvation, he restricted the sovereign's mission in the field of religion to a secular preoccupation, thus legitimizing a policy of non-interference with spiritual or theological debates. Because no man can force me 'to think any otherwise than my reason perswades me',[21]

it is unreasonable in them, who teach there is such danger in every little Errour, to require of a man endued with Reason of his own, to follow the Reason of any other man, or of the most voices of many other men; Which is little better, than to venture his Salvation at crosse and pile.[22]

It was wholly logical for Hobbes to declare, on the basis of those statements, that 'there ought to be no Power over the Consciences of men, but the Word it selfe, working Faith in every one, not always according to the purpose of them that Plant and Water, but of God himself, that giveth the Increase'.[23]

Emperor Constantine, according to Hobbes, provided the best illustration of a sovereign's legitimate attitude to religion. He 'authorized' Christianity in the sense that he made it the religion of the empire, thus achieving a unity that is preferable for reasons of public concord; he consolidated Episcopal church governance under his authority; and he put an end to theological disputes by convening an ecumenical council at Nicea in order to arbitrate between the doctrines of Alexander and those of Arius.[24] This last initiative, however, he undertook for practical reasons not inspired by theological concerns or personal preference. Rather, the dispute between the two bishops and their followers over Jesus's equality of status with God 'became heated' and 'generated discord and slaughter in the city of Alexandria'. The emperor intervened 'to preserve the peace'.[25] That this was his sole preoccupation, Hobbes makes even clearer in what

---

[20] For a discussion of the issue of toleration in Hobbes, see Alan Ryan, 'Hobbes, Toleration and the Inner Life', in *The Nature of Political Theory*, ed. David Miller and Larry Siedentop (Oxford: Clarendon Press, 1983), 197–218; Edwin Curley, 'Hobbes and the Cause of Religious Toleration', in *The Cambridge Companion to Hobbes's Leviathan*, ed. Patricia Springborg (Cambridge: Cambridge University Press, 2007), 309–34. I agree with these two commentators' broad conclusions.

[21] L, 32, p. 578.   [22] L, 47, p. 1116.

[23] Ibid. The metaphor of faith as a plant is a paraphrase of Paul in 1 Cor. 3:5–8. I should stress here that my interpretation in no way precludes the possibility that the sovereign manages by various means to influence the subjects' beliefs. See, on that point, Teresa M. Bejan's chapter in this volume, 'First Impressions: Hobbes on Religion, Education, and the Metaphor of Imprinting', although we draw different conclusions from our analyses. For the defence of a position close to Bejan's, see also Glen Newey, *The Routledge Guidebook to Hobbes' Leviathan*, 2nd edition (London: Routledge, 2014), especially chapter 9.

[24] On the political implications of the Arian controversy and its crucial importance in the history of Christian political theology, see Robert Dagron, 'Orient-Occident: Césaro-papisme et théorie des deux pouvoirs face à la modernité', *Revue d'éthique et de théologie morale* 227 (2004), 143–57.

[25] LLA, pp. 1196–8. One might argue that Hobbes's position, at least in principle, permits intolerance if it will lead to positive consequences. The whole point of his argument is that historical experience suggests intolerance never produces such positive consequences.

appears as his most explicit plea in favour of toleration in the *Historia Ecclesiastica*. Referring to Constantine's exemplary action in that treatise in Latin verse, Hobbes argues that the sovereign should not interfere with doctrines for at least two reasons. First, if people are infected with pernicious opinions, laws will be powerless to reverse such a trend, so that it is best not to exercise any censorship ('*Nihil est resecandum*').[26] Second, in a situation of civil concord, the voice of those who speak clearly and sincerely will necessarily prevail.[27] It is consequently more reasonable to grant freedom to pen and tongue ('*sit calamus liber, sit libera lingua*').[28]

Particularly significant, as regards Hobbes's open-mindedness in religious matters is his treatment of atheism.[29] Once again with good reason, John Bramhall points to the most ambiguous character of several remarks on the subject in *De Cive*. By stating in his discussion of the origins of religion that '*superstition proceedeth from fear without right reason, and atheism from an opinion of reason without fear*', Hobbes presents atheism as 'more reasonable than superstition', argues Bramhall.[30] Hobbes makes matters worse by adding that '*atheism itself, though it be an erroneous opinion, and therefore a sin, yet it ought to be numbered among the sins of imprudence or ignorance*': 'if nature dictate to us that there is a God', according to the bishop, 'and that this God is to be worshipped in such and such manner, it is not possible that atheism should be a sin of mere ignorance'.[31] Hobbes's reply skilfully evades the issue raised by Bramhall, and leaves his argument untouched:

It is agreed between us, that right reason dictates there is a God. Does it not follow, that denying of God is a sin proceeding from misreasoning? If it be not a sin of ignorance, it must be a sin of malice. Can a man malice that which he thinks has no being? But may not one think there is a God, and yet maliciously deny him? If he think there is a God, he is no atheist; and so the question is changed into this, whether any man that thinks there is a God, dares deliberately deny it? For my part, I think not. For upon what confidence dares any man, deliberately I say, oppose the Omnipotent?[32]

While superstition is only preposterous, atheism is both irrational and reckless.[33] It is a sin insofar as it results from a fault against reason, which one cannot consider as being a crime at all.[34]

One may thus regard as purely rhetorical Hobbes's apparent concession that 'if words spoken in passion signify a denial of God, no punishment preordained by law,

---

[26]   HE, line 1170, p. 446.   [27]   HE, lines 1179–82, p. 446.   [28]   HE, line 1177, p. 446.

[29]   On the subject of Hobbes's treatment of atheism, see Patricia Springborg, 'Hobbes the Atheist and his Deist Reception', in *I filosofi e la società senza religione*, ed. Marco Geuna and Gianbattista Gori (Bologna: Il Mulino, 2011), 145–63.

[30]   EW 4, p. 289. Cf. DCv, 3.1.   [31]   EW 4, p. 290; DCv, 14.19.   [32]   EW 4, p. 293.

[33]   From that viewpoint, there is an obvious kinship between the atheist and the fool who says in his heart 'there is no such thing as justice'. See Hobbes's discussion of the fool's wrong judgement and dangerously unrealistic assessment of the consequences of a disloyal attitude; L, 15, p. 222.

[34]   'To err, to be deceived, to have a wrong opinion, is not a crime in itself', Hobbes writes in LLA, p. 1202.

can be too great for such an insolence; because there is no living in a commonwealth with men, to whose oaths we cannot reasonably give credit'.[35] As we have seen, Hobbes's trust in the value of oaths is very limited. Above all, this condemnation of atheists is in outright contradiction with what Hobbes writes in the appendix to the Latin *Leviathan*, where the justification for the punishment of atheists (and so-called heretics) is considerably qualified by three distinct arguments. Wrong beliefs, it is said in that text, are dangerous (assuming they are by themselves) only for those who hold them, so that 'it seems inequitable that a man who embraces a faith, at his own peril, and his alone, should be punished on the grounds that it is erroneous, especially by those who are not harmed by another person's error'. No error can become a crime 'so long as it is confined to a person's heart'.[36] There is no evidence that even an absurd form of belief like atheism will necessarily lead to punishable acts. About the atheist who will be punished, perhaps for valid reasons (which is uncertain), Hobbes writes:

...first he must be accused, heard, and condemned. And nothing can be made the object of an accusation other than something said or something done. But what deeds will serve as evidence of atheism? For what deed have you ever heard of so wicked or impious that a similar deed has not been committed at some time by people who not only are not regarded as atheists, but are even professed Christians? So no one can be judged an atheist on the basis of his deeds. Nor in any way can stand accused on the basis of something he has said, whether in speech or in writing, unless he has directly denied that God exists.[37]

Religious beliefs are indeed private matters, until they are made public. Even the atheist can take part in the social pact without endangering it.

4.3 A Christian Commonwealth without Christ?

The crucial importance for Hobbes of defining the exact nature of a Christian commonwealth has already been suggested, as that type of state rests on two distinct pacts (concluded between God and his peoples in the two successive alliances), with all the risks of possibly having to choose between the two.[38] However, does this particular situation confer a fundamentally specific status on Christian commonwealths in Hobbes's political theology? One may entertain strong doubts on that point.

---

[35] EW 4, p. 294. This statement strikingly anticipates John Locke's *Letter on Toleration*.

[36] LLA, p. 1202.

[37] LLA, p. 1204. Hobbes's statement is the logical deduction of a general principle applying to all sins that do not have outward effects.

[38] This obviously makes Hobbes's denial that there can be any pact with God except through a representative somewhat problematic, on which see Edwin Curley, 'The Covenant with God in *Leviathan*', in *Leviathan After 350 Years*, 199–216.

Hobbes's theology is paradoxical insofar as it is both Christocentric[39] and anti-Trinitarian.[40] The *unum necessarium* represents the essence of the Christian faith by being the only article of faith necessary to salvation.[41] It also provides a key for understanding Christian history by underlining the strictly human and secular nature of the church and the necessity that the sovereign should have full authority in religious matters, thus completing the marginalization of religion in politics. Among the arguments advanced by Bellarmine to advocate papal power are the words addressed by Jesus to Peter, '*Thou art Peter, and upon this rock I will build my Church*'.[42] To the classical Catholic conclusion that those words validate the Pope's claim to a universal and permanent mandate, Hobbes opposes the *unum necessarium* as proof that what was at issue in the exchange between Jesus and Peter was not the institution of the church, but the object of Christian belief. Having cited Jesus's next words ('*And I will give thee the keyes of Heaven; whatsoever thou shalt bind on Earth, shall be bound in Heaven, and whatsoever thou shalt loose on Earth, shall be loosed in Heaven*'), he comments:

Which place, well considered, proveth no more, but that the Church of Christ hath for foundation one onely Article; namely, that which Peter in the name of all the Apostles professing, gave occasion to our Saviour to speak the words here cited; which that wee may cleerly understand, we are to consider, that our Saviour preached by himself, by John Baptist, and by his Apostles, nothing but this Article of Faith, *that he was the Christ*; all other Articles requiring faith no otherwise, than as founded on that.[43]

According to Hobbes's interpretation, 'it is manifest, that by the Foundation-Stone of the Church, was meant the Fundamentall Article of the Churches Faith'.[44] It was not Peter alone who received the power of the keys, but all the disciples of Jesus, as shown by a later passage in the same Gospel where Jesus declares: 'whatsoever ye shall bind on earth, shall be bound in heaven, and whatsoever ye shall loose on earth, shall be loosed in heaven'.[45] Now, insofar as this capacity implies the power to teach and convert, it must of necessity belong to sovereigns as the supreme pastors of their nations:

...howsoever this be interpreted, there is no doubt but the Power here granted belongs to all Supreme Pastors; such as are all Christian Civill Soveraignes in their own Dominions. In so much, as if St. Peter, or our Saviour himself had converted any of them to beleeve him, and to

---

[39] Pocock's original interpretation of Hobbesian theology as essentially messianic is based on the acknowledgement of this fact. See J. G. A. Pocock, 'Time, History and Eschatology in the Thought of Thomas Hobbes', in his *Politics, Language and Time: Essays on Political Thought and History* (New York: Athenaeum, 1971), 148–201.

[40] On the subject of Hobbes's treatment of the Trinity, see my 'Le vocabulaire de la personne', in *Hobbes et son vocabulaire: Études de lexicographie philosophique*, ed. Yves Charles Zarka (Paris: Vrin, 1992), 155–86; George Wright, 'Hobbes and the Economic Trinity', in his *Religion, Politics and Thomas Hobbes* (Dordrecht: Springer, 2006), 175–210; Philippe Crignon, 'L'altération du christianisme. Hobbes et la trinité', *Les études philosophiques* 81.2 (2007), 235–63; Dominique Weber, *Histoire du salut: Ce que le Christ fait au Léviathan de Hobbes* (Paris: Presses de l'Université Paris-Sorbonne, 2008).

[41] On the subject of salvation, see Roberto Farneti, 'Hobbes on Salvation', in *Cambridge Companion to Hobbes's Leviathan*, 291–308.

[42] Matt. 16:18; L, 42, p. 870. [43] L, 42, p. 870. [44] L, 42, pp. 870–2. [45] Matt. 18:18.

acknowledge his Kingdome; yet because his Kingdome is not of this world, he had left the supreme care of converting his subjects to none but him; or else hee must have deprived him of the Soveraignty, to which the Right of Teaching is inseparably annexed. And thus much in refutation of his [Bellarmine's] first Book, wherein he would prove St. Peter to have been the Monarch Universall of the Church, that is to say, of all the Christians in the world.[46]

Two logics are joined together here which in fact seem to be hardly separable: that of sovereignty, which implies the extension of the sovereign's power to the spiritual domain, and that of a Christocentric doctrine, according to which Christ's action is located in a purely secular history. In a very singular way, Hobbes's Christology put into relief a twofold exteriority of Christ: on the one hand to the process of creation and development of the Church, which has always depended on strictly secular historical factors; and on the other hand to the contents of the idea of a Christian commonwealth, whose meaning is reduced to an accidental coincidence of political and religious identities. The sovereign must be the sole interpreter of God's Word because no human power can claim a transcendent origin to legitimize its assuming that prerogative. He is the sole intermediary between God and his subjects because Christ, who fulfilled that function in 'orthodox' Christian doctrines, is not, in Hobbes's eyes, the mediator who can achieve men's salvation owing to his double nature, human and divine. The pact on which God's prophetic kingdom rests, which was concluded with Abraham and renewed with Isaac, Jacob, Moses, and Jesus, remains in force, as far as Christians are concerned, only because Jesus was last in a line of prophets.

Against this interpretation of Hobbes's conception of history as non-providential, with all the consequences one may deduce from it in respect of politics, one might argue that the hand of God is in fact perceptible behind historical developments, insofar as God is the first cause of all possible developments. That, however, would point to a mode of presence in history altogether different from the providential one, which implies the decisive, purposeful interference of a will unveiling itself in the process. Should one consider that the Advent of Christ signifies one such intervention, according to Hobbes? I think not, for several reasons which emerge with particular clarity in the *Historia Ecclesiastica*.

Christ's message is but a restatement of truths already formulated in the Old Testament. That is why Christ commands us to return to the prophets ('*Antiquos Dominus nos jussit adire Prophetas*': l. 637). We remain, however, completely free to follow or to reject that injunction. Apart from the extension of the number of men concerned by the new call to self-correction, nothing is altered by Advent in human destinies. The event which ought to be viewed in a providential light is thus reduced to nearly ordinary status. Instead of history being divided into a 'before' and an 'after' disclosing *one* critical intervention of God, human affairs go on at their usual pace. At no stage can the 'fulness of time' of Christian historiography be felt or foreboded. The

---

[46] L, 42, p. 872.

Advent is just a subchapter among others in a long and tormented story read through the categories of natural and civil philosophy.

Hobbes's Christology seems impossible to dissociate from an ecclesiology which transforms the church into a mere function of the state. 'From [the] consolidation of the Right Politique, and Ecclesiastique in Christian Soveraigns', he argues, 'it is evident, they have all manner of Power over their Subjects, that can be given to man, for the government of mens externall actions, both in Policy, and Religion'.[47] True, it is not customary for sovereigns to exercise the pastoral functions which belong to them (just as they seldom sit in courts of justice or teach in universities, which they might do), but that is only because they lack time for such involvement and it is more practical for them to delegate those activities to subordinates.[48] It could even be imagined that one of them commit the care of religion to the Pope, although that would necessarily imply that the Pope recognize his supremacy, obviously an unlikely event.[49] The Pope is just a bishop among others and enjoys no particular primacy. The ecclesiastical jurisdiction of bishops is entirely derived from the sovereign's will. Supposing it can be described as *jure divino*, it is *jure divino mediato*:[50] Christ entrusted no one with such jurisdiction, and only sovereigns (as has been seen) may claim a *jure divino* power. It is therefore more accurate to say that bishops entertain with their sovereigns the same type of relationship as pastors, city magistrates, judges and army officers. They are, in other words, 'but Ministers of him that is the Magistrate of the whole Common-wealth, Judge of all Causes, and Commander of the whole Militia, which is alwaies the Civill Soveraign', as well as 'Supreme Pastor'.[51] Like '[a]ll Pastors, except the Supreme, [they] execute their charges in the Right, that is, by the Authority of the Civill Soveraign, that is, *Iure Civili*'.[52]

Hobbes's doctrine on the subject scandalized Bramhall.[53] The bishop held that the only difference between Catholics and Anglicans was that, for Catholics, the Pope alone derived his jurisdiction 'immediately from Christ', while Anglicans believed all bishops did.[54] The opposition between the two men could hardly illustrate more clearly the two versions of Erastian ecclesiology that their conceptions represented, Hobbes's appearing so radical that one wonders whether it still deserves to be called Erastian. With Richard Hooker, an acknowledged exponent of the Anglican doctrine, Hobbes shares the general principle of the sovereign's religious supremacy and the affirmation of the unitary character of the *respublica christiana*, meaning that state and church must form a single body, or a single *polity* on the model of Israel.[55] However, Hooker fully acknowledges the validity of the distinction between the temporal and the spiritual power. He endorses the refusal to recognize the sovereign's

---

[47] L, 42, p. 864.   [48] L, 42, pp. 856–62.   [49] L, 42, p. 866.   [50] L, 42, pp. 898–900.
[51] L, 42, p. 852.   [52] L, 42, p. 854.   [53] EW 4, p. 344.

[54] John Bramhall, *Schism Guarded and Beaten Back upon the Right Owners* (London, 1658), reprinted in his *Works* (Oxford: Library of Anglo-Catholic Theology, 1842–5), ii, 453.

[55] On Hooker's doctrine, see W. J. Torrance Kirby, *Richard Hooker's Doctrine of the Royal Supremacy* (Leiden: Brill, 1990).

right to preach, to minister sacraments, to ordain ministers, to have ecclesiastical jurisdiction and to excommunicate. He holds that to that extent, the sovereign's power cannot be considered as unrestricted, being limited by the laws of God, the laws of nature, and also positive laws (customs and statutes), which apply to spiritual and temporal matters as well.[56]

According to its definition in *Leviathan*, the Church has no substance other than legal. It is nothing but a civil institution which cannot exist but under the government of the sovereign who is necessarily its head in the full sense of the word. Insofar as it can be described as 'a Congregation assembled, of professors of Christianity, whether their profession be true, or counterfeit',[57] it appears as '*A company of men professing Christian Religion, united in the person of one Sovereign; at whose command they ought to assemble, and without whose authority they ought not to assemble*'.[58] To that extent, the Christian commonwealth is nothing more than a commonwealth which happens to be composed of Christians, the denominations 'Church' and 'State' serving to designate the same strictly temporal reality envisaged under two countenances:

And therefore a Church, such a one as is capable to Command, to Judge, Absolve, Condemn, or do any other act, is the same thing with a Civil Common-wealth, consisting of Christian men; and is called a *Civill State*, for that the subjects of it are *Men*; and a *Church*, for that the subjects thereof are *Christians*. *Temporall* and *Spirituall* Government, are but two words brought into the world, to make men see double, and mistake their *Lawfull Soveraign*. It is true, that the bodies of the faithfull, after the Resurrection, shall be not onely Spirituall, but Eternall: but in this life they are grosse, and corruptible. There is therefore no other Government in this life, neither of State, nor Religion, but Temporall[59]

Bramhall was again scandalized, observing that '[a]ll other men distinguish between the church and the commonwealth' and that, '[u]pon [Hobbes's] account, there was no Christian Church in these parts of the world, for some hundreds of years after Christ, because there was no Christian sovereign'.[60] Not surprisingly, the Anglican bishop was echoing one of the motives for which *De Cive* (in 1654) and *Leviathan* (in 1703) were put on the Index, the Roman censors condemning Hobbes for investing the sovereign with full spiritual power and, in the name of the principle '*una est Ecclesia et Civitas christiana*', for erasing the difference of essence between church and state.[61]

Hobbes's anti-clericalism has drawn deserved attention among commentators. It may explain what looks like an endorsement, on the philosopher's part, of congregationalism (or Independency, to give it its political name) as an acceptable form of Church organization. Independency would make clerical influence in social life discreet

[56] See book eight of Richard Hooker, *Of the Laws of Ecclesiastical Polity*, ed. Arthur Stephen McGrade (Cambridge: Cambridge University Press, 1989), especially 8.1.7, 8.2.16–17.
[57] L, 39, p. 730.   [58] L, 39, p. 732.   [59] L, 39, pp. 732–4.
[60] Quoted by Hobbes, EW 4, pp. 336–7.
[61] See Artemio Enzo Baldini, 'Censures de l'Eglise romaine contre Hobbes: *De Cive* et *Léviathan*', *Bulletin Hobbes XIII, Archives de Philosophie* 64.2 (2001), 2–7.

enough to be relatively acceptable and ecclesiastical authorities satisfactorily pliable to political rule. The thesis of Hobbes's proximity to the Independents,[62] who had their heyday during the Interregnum and in particular when Cromwell was in power, can draw arguments from more or less open statements in his writings. The best-known one occurs when Hobbes evokes present times in *Leviathan* and writes:

And so we are reduced to the Independency of the Primitive Christians to follow Paul, or Cephas, or Apollos, every man as he liketh best: Which, if it be without contention, and without measuring the Doctrine of Christ, by our affection to the Person of his Minister, (the fault which the Apostle reprehended in the Corinthians,) is perhaps the best[63]

It is tempting to correlate this passage with facts like Hobbes's long and protracted quarrels with Anglican bishops, his constant hostility to Presbyterians, and his repeated denunciation of all ecclesiastical establishments as greedy, politically ambitious, and intellectually intolerant. It invites suspicion about his attachment to the royalist cause and might suggest a possible collusion with Cromwell's Independent friends. Yet, this reading of Hobbes's apparent nostalgia for 'the independency of the primitive Christians' clashes with incontrovertible facts.[64] Independents ascribed absolute primacy to individual conscience in the interpretation of Scripture, which little agrees with Hobbes's views on the subject. They opposed uniformity of public worship, which Hobbes advocated, and denied the magistrate's right to set the form of religious ceremonies. They regarded the 'saints' as individually linked to God by a pact, while Hobbes rejected this idea, as we have seen. They stigmatized the Pope as the Antichrist, which Hobbes refused to do.[65] They denounced as tyrannical any infringement on so-called natural property rights, while Hobbes saw in property a revocable piece of legal fiction.[66] They detected the hand of Providence in Cromwell's military victories, a belief Hobbes mocked as a dangerous illusion.[67] One could also

---

[62] See Richard Tuck, *Hobbes: A Very Short Introduction* (Oxford: Oxford University Press, 2002); Tuck, *Philosophy and Government 1572–1651* (Cambridge: Cambridge University Press, 1993); Jeffrey Collins, *The Allegiance of Thomas Hobbes* (Oxford: Oxford University Press, 2005), especially 159–241. Jon Parkin offers a more balanced view of the relationship between Hobbes and the Independents in *Taming the Leviathan: The Reception of the Political and Religious Ideas of Thomas Hobbes in England, 1640–1700* (Cambridge: Cambridge University Press, 2007).

[63] L, 47, p. 1116. The biblical allusion is to 1 Cor. 1:12, 3:4, 22. Retrospective allusions to those times when Hobbes could express his views without restraint from any ecclesiastical or political authorities can be found in the short autobiographical work *Mr Hobbes Considered in his Loyalty, Religion, Reputation and Manners* (1662) and in the *Answer to the Catching of Leviathan*, where Hobbes seems pleased to recall the period of composition of *Leviathan*; see especially EW 4, p. 355.

[64] See J. P. Sommerville, 'Hobbes and Independency', in *Nuove prospettive critiche sul Leviatano di Hobbes nel 350° anniversario di pubblicazione/New Critical Perspectives on Hobbes's Leviathan upon the 350th Anniversary of its Publication*, ed. Luc Foisneau and George Wright (Milan: Franco Angeli, 2004), 155–73; Noel Malcolm, 'General Introduction' to his edition of *Leviathan* (Oxford: Clarendon Press, 2012), i, 61–5; Arash Abizadeh, 'Publicity, Privacy, and Religious Toleration in Hobbes's *Leviathan*', *Modern Intellectual History* 10.2 (2013), 261–91; Teresa M. Bejan, 'Difference without Disagreement: Rethinking Hobbes on "Independency" and Toleration', *The Review of Politics* 78.1 (2016), 1–25.

[65] L, 42, pp. 874–6.   [66] L, 24, p. 388; 29, p. 504.   [67] L, 36, pp. 678–80.

mention the fact that Hobbes attacked Independents, in *Behemoth*, for having caused the civil wars together with Presbyterians, Anabaptists, Quakers, Adamites, and other 'seducers' whose religious and political notions corrupted the people's minds.[68] Independents, in turn, displayed comparative indifference to Hobbes, and at times outright hostility, like John Owen, the vice-chancellor of Oxford University, who did his best to deter Henry Stubbe, Hobbes's friend, from translating *Leviathan* into Latin.[69] No doubt Hobbes's virulent anticlericalism also played its part in the estrangement of that faction which, after all, had its own clergy.

4.4   Conclusions

It would seem that just as he was indifferent, on the whole, to constitutional forms, Hobbes had no special preference for any one of the various religions of his time. Expediency was the safest standard to assess the adequacy of the various types of government, although monarchy seemed to have the greatest number of advantages in terms of efficiency and stability.[70] The same preoccupation with practical solutions applied to religion. The Anglican settlement looked preferable as being the most capable of achieving the coincidence of church and state and the singleness of representation of both structures in the person of the sovereign. A comprehensive 'system' (in the Hobbesian sense of the word) like the Church of England was probably also the most adept for allowing maximum individual autonomy in terms of thought and belief without undermining civil order, especially if the sovereign had both the wisdom and the authority necessary to pursue that end with success. The basically secular legitimation of the state tended to justify its religious neutrality, although it did not make it necessary to embody such neutrality in law. In a large measure, Hobbes thus announced an historical evolution which was later to take place in England and elsewhere. It was as 'supreme pastor' that the sovereign could assume his full independence from the dominant churches and achieve peace between contending faiths. Paradoxically, what divine right was left to strengthen his legitimacy served to emancipate his power from religion. From that viewpoint, Hobbes carried one essential step further the process of secularization of the state to which divine right theories had contributed by attempting to ensure the domination of prince over church.[71]

---

[68] B, p. 109.   [69] Sommerville, 'Hobbes and Independency'.   [70] L, 29, *passim.*
[71] See Bernard Bourdin, *La genèse théologico-politique de l'Etat moderne: La controverse de Jacques Ier d'Angleterre avec le cardinal Bellarmin* (Paris: Presses Universitaires de France, 2004). As convincingly demonstrated in that book, the controversy between James 1st and Robert Bellarmine over the 1606 Oath of Allegiance was a key moment in that process. In order to enable English Catholics to acknowledge his political legitimacy, while maintaining their fidelity to the Pope's spiritual leadership, James Stuart developed a theory which also dissociated political considerations of authority from questions of saving truth, thus paving the way for the autonomy of the political sphere and, simultaneously, the recognition of a subject existing in his own right.

In all commonwealths, whether Christian or not, religion is an essential dimension of social life and, as such, falls within the province of the state. On the other hand, that what makes religion a vital matter for many (most, in Hobbes's day), belongs to a strictly private sphere and is beyond the reach of any ruler. As a consequence, the sovereign's authority must go hand in hand with broad tolerance by reason of the specific nature of religion, which makes it both central to politics and a purely individual matter. One might be inclined to think that the terms of that problematic have kept their relevance.

5

Hobbes on the Motives of Martyrs

Alexandra Chadwick

Hobbes acknowledges that a desire to gain eternal life—or to avoid the torments of hell—can motivate someone to seriously risk or even willingly forfeit his temporal life by disobeying his sovereign.[1] Furthermore, he claims that prioritizing salvation is the action of one who is 'in his right mind'.[2] Reconciling the commands of God with civil obedience is accordingly a major aim of Hobbes's political writings, to which he devotes increasing attention in each iteration of his theory.[3] Yet Hobbes is notorious for positing a psychology in which bodily self-preservation is the primary motive of all human beings, or at least of all sane human beings.[4] If that is an accurate interpretation of Hobbes's position, it is not clear how he can account for the motives of martyrs, who have chosen to disobey the sovereign on religious grounds, much less believe them to be *compos mentis*.

This tension is particularly pronounced in readings of Hobbes which have grounded his theory of motivation in (what is taken to be) his mechanistic-materialist account of human psychology. On such a reading, Hobbes portrays human beings as—in David Gauthier's memorable phrase—'self-maintaining engines', which means that 'each

---

[1] See, for example, EL, 25.5: 'why should a man incur the danger of a temporal death, by displeasing of his superior, if it were not for fear of eternal death hereafter?', and DCv, 17.25: 'For *Christ* said, and in fact, nature herself also dictates: *Do not fear those who kill the body, but cannot kill the soul; but rather fear him who can destroy both soul and body in Gehenna*'. I refer to the Hobbesian individual as male in accordance with Hobbes's language.

[2] DCv, 18.14: 'For anyone in his right mind [*mentis compos*] will obey absolutely in all things a person by whose judgement, he believes, he is to be saved or damned'.

[3] Two chapters in *The Elements of Law*, the third part of *De Cive*, Parts Three and Four of *Leviathan*, and the Appendix added to the Latin *Leviathan*.

[4] Thus Johan Olsthoorn refers to the claim that 'Sane Hobbesian agents universally consider death the greatest possible evil' as the 'orthodox' interpretation, and S. A. Lloyd designates 'an overriding fear of death' as a central pillar of the 'standard philosophical interpretation' of Hobbes's theory. See Johan Olsthoorn, 'Worse than Death: The Non-Preservationist Foundations of Hobbes's Moral Philosophy', *Hobbes Studies* 27.2 (2014), 150; S. A. Lloyd, *Ideals as Interests in Hobbes's 'Leviathan': The Power of Mind over Matter* (Cambridge: Cambridge University Press, 1992), 6. Both Olsthoorn and Lloyd reject this orthodox or standard reading. A discussion of some different versions of this position can be found in Olsthoorn, 'Worse than Death', 152–4. See also Mark Murphy, 'Hobbes on the Evil of Death', *Archiv für Geschichte der Philosophie* 82.1 (2000), 36–61.

man seeks, and seeks only, to preserve and to strengthen himself'.[5] In cases where a man knowingly and voluntarily acts against his self-preservation, Gauthier argues, 'Hobbes must suppose that the functioning of the self-maintaining engine is in some manner impaired'.[6] As S. A. Lloyd makes clear, however, the emphasis Hobbes places on the potential of religious motives to conflict with the desire to obey the sovereign, and the amount of attention he gives to theology and ecclesiology in an attempt to ensure that they do not, gives the lie to the claim that Hobbes considers bodily preservation to be the fundamental human motive. Lloyd therefore rejects the view of the Hobbesian individual as motivated only by a 'narrow bodily interest' in 'keeping one's current body alive'.[7] In rescuing Parts Three and Four of *Leviathan*, however, Lloyd downplays at least half of Part One, in which Hobbes sets out his mechanistic explanations of man's mental operations, claiming that Hobbes did not intend to derive an account of human nature from these 'scattered physical scientific remarks'. [8] Hobbes's mechanistic materialism is considered to be, at best, in tension with or, at worst, incompatible with his claim that human beings often prioritize eternal over temporal life, and it is therefore denied a role in his account of motivation.

The interpretation I outline in this chapter rejects, with Lloyd, the view of Hobbesian man as a 'self-maintaining engine'. However, I do not consider this to involve rejecting the relevance of Hobbes's mechanistic materialism for his treatment of human nature. In accordance with more nuanced readings of his materialism, I argue that there is no inconsistency or tension between the assumptions of Hobbes's mechanistic account of motivation and his claim that salvation can be prioritized by an individual who is *compos mentis*. Further, I suggest that Hobbes's materialist psychology is not only compatible with his treatment of martyrdom, but also contributes to his aim of reconciling salvation with obedience. For Hobbes, those who choose martyrdom are mistaken about what is required for their salvation, and they are also mistaken about their own nature as human beings. Hobbes addresses the former in his theology, but to correct the latter requires his materialist psychology.

The first section of the chapter considers Hobbes's theological discussion of martyrdom, examining how he severely restricts the circumstances in which disobedience to a sovereign's commands is a soteriological necessity. I then turn to show that the motives of martyrs can be explained within Hobbes's mechanistic account of motivation. The third section looks at Hobbes's materialist psychology in the context of seventeenth-century claims about the soul, in order to establish how he intended to change men's views of their powers and purpose as human beings. In this way, I argue that Hobbes's materialist account of motivation contributes to his arguments for

---

[5] David Gauthier, *The Logic of Leviathan* (Oxford: Oxford University Press, 1969), 7. See also J. W. N. Watkins, *Hobbes's System of Ideas* (London: Hutchinson & Co., 1965), 115–17.

[6] Gauthier, *Logic of Leviathan*, 24.

[7] S. A. Lloyd, *Morality in the Philosophy of Thomas Hobbes: Cases in the Law of Nature* (Cambridge: Cambridge University Press, 2009), 68.

[8] Lloyd, *Ideals as Interests*, 370, n. 12.

reconciling duty to God and to man, and hence supports his belief that 'justice towards God, and peace amongst men...stand together'.[9]

5.1 Hobbes's Theological Treatment of Martyrdom

The 'martyrs' with whom Hobbes is concerned are individuals who wilfully put themselves in the position of being put to death, by disobeying their sovereign's command on the grounds that it is against the command of God.[10] In some parts of his work, Hobbes casts doubt on whether the desire to obey God is the real reason for such disobedience. Instead, one possible explanation is that those who claim to be acting out of religious conviction have seditious intent. For example, the 'difficulty...of obeying at once, both God, and Man...when their Commandements are one contrary to the other' is called 'The most frequent *praetext* of Sedition, and Civill Warre', suggesting that it is merely a mask for traitorous behaviour.[11] Alternatively, would-be martyrs might be motivated by a desire for honour and glory, albeit one which could be fulfilled only by posthumous reputation. Referring to the canonization of saints, Hobbes writes that 'he who can attract other people's subjects with such a reward can induce those who are avid for such glory to dare and do anything', before making a comparison between aspiring saints and the *Decii* who sought 'honour in the eyes of posterity'.[12] Nevertheless, Hobbes does not deny the sincerity of all those who claim to be prioritizing God's law over their current existence, but rather recognizes it as a valid motive for action: 'seeing *Eternall life* is a greater reward, than the *life present*; and *Eternall torment* a greater punishment than the *death of Nature*', he writes, '[i]t is a thing worthy to be well considered, of all men that desire...to avoid the calamities of Confusion, and Civill war...for what offences, and against whom committed, men are to be *Eternally tormented*; and for what actions, they are to obtain *Eternall life*'.[13]

---

[9] EL, 25.4.

[10] Brad S. Gregory notes that early modern Christians 'drew a sharp distinction between people being killed for actions consistent with religious commitment—which might involve considerable danger or even deliberate provocation—and people who took their own lives'. Only the former group could be called martyrs. See Brad S. Gregory, *Salvation at Stake: Christian Martyrdom in Early Modern Europe* (Cambridge, MA: Harvard University Press, 1999), 104–5.

[11] L, 43, p. 928 (emphasis added). This was not an unusual claim: the portrayal of Catholic 'martyrs' as traitors had long been a strategy of Protestant polemicists. See Susannah Brietz Monta, 'Rendering unto Caesar: The Rhetorics of Divided Loyalties in Tudor England', in *Martyrdom and Terrorism: Pre-Modern to Contemporary Perspectives*, ed. Dominic Janes and Alex Houen (Oxford: Oxford University Press, 2014), 59–86.

[12] DCv, 18.14. This point is discussed by Laurie M. Johnson Bagby, *Thomas Hobbes: Turning Point for Honour* (Plymouth: Lexington Books, 2009), 85–9, who presents martyrdom as a particular case of the 'heroic ideal' which Hobbes sought to undermine.

[13] L, 38, p. 698. Lloyd argues that religious motives should not be reduced to a desire for salvation: there can also be 'the desire to fulfill one's duty to God'. It is the latter, she claims, with which 'Hobbes's readers were primarily concerned...they were concerned to do this even though they were predestinarians and did not believe they could affect their own salvation', *Ideas as Interests*, 151–3. However, it is not clear how a desire for salvation and a desire to do one's duty can be separated, even in the case of one who believes in predestination: such a person might accept that one cannot know if they are a member of the elect, but

Hobbes's theology and ecclesiology are geared towards neutralizing the threat of religious disagreement to civil order. A significant strand of his argument is aimed at convincing subjects that obedience to their sovereign is a requirement for, rather than a threat to, obtaining eternal life. It is important to emphasize that this focus on the worldly benefit of his position need not suggest that Hobbes's theological positions were insincere, and that he was concerned only with temporal affairs. Instead, the reconciliation of religion and civil order can be interpreted as the action of one who believes that no true interpretation of his religion could be incompatible with earthly peace. This is indeed exactly how Hobbes portrays his project: in *The Elements*, for example, he lists scriptural passages which he claims teach us that '*justice and peace should kiss each other*', before concluding that 'it seemeth strange to me, that any man in a Christian commonwealth should have any occasion to deny his obedience to public authority, upon this ground, that *it is better to obey God than man*'.[14] Later, as we shall see, Hobbes goes so far as to suggest that there might be no occasion for an ordinary subject to be martyred even in a commonwealth that is *not* Christian.

In all three of his major political works Hobbes claims that entry to the 'kingdom of God' requires faith and obedience.[15] There is only one article of faith necessary for salvation: that Jesus is the Christ.[16] The 'obedience' requirement might sometimes oblige subjects to profess the truth of other articles of religion with which they disagree, but Hobbes claims that this outward conformity is different from internal belief in the eyes of God.[17] On the question of whom Christians should obey in matters of religion, however, Hobbes changes his position between *The Elements* and *De Cive* on the one hand, and *Leviathan* on the other. In the earlier works, Hobbes argues that a subject owes obedience to a Christian sovereign in all things spiritual as well as temporal. Where the sovereign is *not* Christian, however, obedience in spiritual matters should be given to 'some *Church of Christians*'.[18] This concession coheres with Hobbes's claim in *De Cive* that a sovereign is obliged to interpret questions of faith 'by means of duly ordained *Ecclesiastics*'.[19] If a subject is forced to choose between following the church and following the non-Christian sovereign, he should 'Go to Christ through

---

believe that a member of the elect would act to glorify God and fulfil His commandments, which might even mean martyrdom. Thus Gregory notes that 'Perseverance in the face of death [i.e. enduring the pains of death and temptation by the devil] seems to have been promoted and sometimes understood as a sign of election, despite the unverifiability of predestination to eternal life…Martyrdom was the final, and absolute, test of fidelity', *Salvation at Stake*, 162.

[14] EL, 25.4.   [15] EL, 25.10; DCv, 18.2; L, 43, p. 930.

[16] EL, 25.7; DCv, 18.6; L, 43, p. 938.   [17] DCv, 18.6 and 18.11; L, 42, p. 784.

[18] DCv, 18.13. See also EL, 25.14.

[19] DC, 17.28. Richard Tuck suggests that here Hobbes 'compromised the unity of his theory' by allowing 'a crucial role to the Church in the formation of public doctrine', and that this makes his position 'extremely close to orthodox Anglicanism'. See Richard Tuck, *Hobbes* (Oxford: Oxford University Press, 1989), 85; and his 'Hobbes, Conscience, and Christianity', in *The Oxford Handbook of Hobbes*, ed. A. P. Martinich and Kinch Hoekstra (Oxford: Oxford University Press, 2016), 495–8. J. P. Sommerville, however, argues that the Anglicanism of *De Cive* was 'skin-deep', since the obligation for sovereigns to interpret Scripture through ecclesiastics 'does not cohere with the rest of what Hobbes says in *De cive*'. See J. P. Sommerville, *Thomas Hobbes: Political Ideas in Historical Context* (Basingstoke: Macmillan Press, 1992), 127.

Martyrdom'. If martyrdom does not seem the better option in such cases, then it is clear that the subject was only 'using a pretence of Christian *faith* to try to slip out of his Agreement to obey the commonwealth'.[20] Nevertheless, in the early 1640s Hobbes drastically limits the circumstances in which obedience to the sovereign and the requirements of salvation might legitimately conflict, restricting the possibility to cases in which a Christian man lives under an infidel sovereign, and is forbidden to act in accordance with the Christian church he has chosen to follow.

In *Leviathan*, Hobbes no longer considers there to be any conflict between earthly obedience and salvation, even when the sovereign is not Christian. In such cases, he now claims, 'a Christian, holding firmly in his heart the Faith of Christ, hath the same liberty which the Prophet Elisha allowed to Naaman the Syrian', namely, to perform external acts of worship to an idol when commanded to do so. Even the denial that 'Jesus is the Christ' is now permitted, presented as a consequence of the argument that it is internal faith that matters for salvation, not 'Profession with the tongue'.[21] Tuck touches on the question of why Hobbes's position changes, claiming that '[i]n the earlier works he had a good reason for supposing that Christian martyrdom was a special case; in *Leviathan* he no longer had such a reason'.[22] This 'good reason' was that in *De Cive* a sovereign was said to need ordained ecclesiastics to interpret Scripture, whereas in *Leviathan* he does not. Tuck attributes this extension of the rights of the sovereign partly to Hobbes's opposition to Presbyterianism, and partly to his 'increasing awareness of the real implications of his general philosophical position'.[23] It is indeed the case that by further restricting the grounds for martyrdom between *De Cive* and *Leviathan* Hobbes ensures consistency between the conclusions of reason concerning the rights of sovereigns and duties of subjects, outlined in his civil science, and his claims about the Christian religion. This is demonstrated by the argument he provides to defend his assertion that worshipping a false idol is permissible for Christians when commanded by their sovereign. Hobbes asks whether a subject of a Christian commonwealth who is 'of the Mahometan Religion' should be present at a Christian service if his sovereign commands, or whether he is 'obliged in conscience to suffer death'. To say that the Muslim should choose death, Hobbes writes, would be to '[authorize] all private men, to disobey their Princes, in maintenance of their Religion, true, or false'. But to say that he ought to be obedient, whilst allowing Christians to disobey if the situation were reversed, is against the law of nature, which tells us '*Do not to another, that which thou wouldest not he should doe unto thee*'.[24] It is striking that Hobbes will not even allow an exception to this rule on the grounds that Christianity is the true religion and the hypothetical Mahometan is wrong. The extremes to which he will go to combine God's

---

[20] DCv, 18.13.   [21] L, 42, p. 784.

[22] Tuck, *Hobbes*, 61. More recently, Tuck writes that in *Leviathan* Hobbes was 'still saying the same kind of thing' as in *De Cive*, 'Hobbes, Conscience, and Christianity', 494.

[23] Tuck, *Hobbes*, 86. See also Johan Olsthoorn's contribution to this volume, 'The Theocratic *Leviathan*: Hobbes's Arguments for the Identity of Church and State'.

[24] L, 42, p. 786.

revealed religion with what he takes to be God's rules for establishing earthly peace (accessible through natural reason) are perhaps nowhere more apparent than here.

If disobedience is not required for salvation, the question is raised—as Hobbes acknowledges—whether all those who have been praised as martyrs 'have needlessely cast away their lives?'[25] To answer this, he distinguishes between those who 'have received a Calling to preach' and those who have not; only the former group, Hobbes claims, had cause to choose disobedience to their earthly ruler. What is more, since the word 'martyr' means 'witness', he writes, and only Christ's 'originall Disciples' were witnesses to the resurrection, they only could be 'true Martyrs'. Those who came later were merely 'Witnesses of other mens testimony' and 'are but second Martyrs'.[26] The only men who can be martyrs in the second degree are those who are 'sent to the conversion of Infidels', since there is no need of 'a Witnesse to him that already beleeveth'.[27] Allowing martyrdom to witnesses, understood in this way, not only means that Hobbes is able to accept that there have been martyrs in the past, but also ensures the survival of the Christian message that 'Jesus is the Christ'.

Later in *Leviathan*, Hobbes seemingly complicates things by suggesting that in the case of a subject ordered by an idolatrous king to worship an idol he 'doth well' to obey, if he believes in Christ in his heart, but 'he should doe better' to 'suffer death, rather than worship it'.[28] This passage, which is omitted in the Latin *Leviathan*, suggests that Hobbes considers the actions of those who choose to die in this case to be praiseworthy, but that nevertheless God would not have condemned them to eternal death for doing otherwise. It is unclear on what grounds Hobbes can justify this praise if it makes no difference in the eyes of God, and indeed his contemporary critic Bishop John Bramhall assumed that this must have been said 'in jest'.[29] But regardless of Hobbes's sincerity here, it is clear that he is only willing to sound even this cautious note of support for disobedience because he does not regard martyrdom in these limited circumstances as a serious threat to civil order, even suggesting that no 'Infidel King' would be 'so unreasonable' as to 'put to death, or to persecute' a subject whose religion teaches obedience to his laws.[30]

Bramhall relates a story that he 'heard from a gentleman of quality, well deserving credit', who when talking to Hobbes 'of self-preservation...pressed Mr. Hobbes with this argument drawn from the holy martyrs, to which Mr. Hobbes gave answer, "they were all fools"'.[31] While we have cause to doubt the anecdotes of so hostile a critic as Bramhall, Hobbes's few concessions to the possibility of martyrdom imply that many of those praised as martyrs did not merit the name, and were mistaken to consider themselves to be following God's commands. He reduces the possibilities for martyrdom

---

[25] L, 42, p. 786.   [26] L, 42, pp. 786–8.
[27] L, 42, p. 788.   [28] L, 45, p. 1038.
[29] John Bramhall, *The Works of the Most Reverend Father in God, John Bramhall* (Oxford, 1854), iv, 543.
[30] L, 43, p. 954.
[31] Bramhall, *Works*, 330. The gentleman in question is given the initials 'R. H.' in a marginal note to *Castigations of Mr Hobbes*. The editor of Bramhall's *Works* suggests a Mr Richard Harding.

to such a small number of people in such a small number of circumstances, all of which apply outside a Christian commonwealth, that if Hobbes's theology is believed there is no reason for matters of religious conscience to pose a threat to civil order.[32] Yet whether or not Hobbes thought the holy martyrs fools, he does not seem to have regarded them—and others who might be disposed to follow their example—as malfunctioning machines, as Gauthier would have it. Instead, Hobbes treated the desire for eternal life as a valid motive for action, and sought to reconcile this desire with earthly obedience. I turn now to consider how this desire can be squared with Hobbes's mechanistic-materialist view of human psychology.

5.2 Mechanistic Materialism in Hobbes's Account of Motivation

The term 'mechanistic-materialist' or simply 'mechanistic' is often used as a convenient shorthand to refer to the fact that Hobbes makes the local motion of bodies the fundamental explanatory principle of natural philosophy. Unlike his contemporaries— most notably, Descartes—Hobbes was willing to extend this principle to all the activities of the human mind, denying the existence of an 'immaterial substance' which could operate independently of the interactions of matter. Hobbes was less interested in the precise details of the anatomical mechanisms involved in mental activity than in excluding the immaterial from any plausible explanation.[33] He provided an account of what he calls the motive power of the mind, according to which all voluntary actions are caused by appetites and aversions, understood as internal physical movements (or 'endeavour') towards or away from an object that is, or was, perceived by the senses.[34] Sense itself is described as 'Motion in the organs and interiour parts of mans body', caused by the reaction of the motions of external objects with the sense organs.[35] When the object which gave rise to sense is no longer present, 'Imagination' is the name given to the motions that remain in the body.[36] Appetites and aversions are generated by the interaction of sense or imagination with the body's 'vital motion' at the heart. When the vital motion is helped, we have an appetite for the perceived object. When it is hindered, we have an aversion.[37]

---

[32] It is worth noting that, as in the rest of Hobbes's political theory, peace depends not only on the actions of subjects, but also on the actions of the sovereign. For example, if an infidel sovereign *is* 'so unreasonable' as to persecute or put to death those called to preach the Christian religion, despite that religion (on Hobbes's interpretation) teaching obedience to his laws, it is possible that he would provoke greater numbers to rally in place of the martyred preachers, posing a threat to peace.

[33] Conclusions in physics, according to Hobbes, are hypotheses: our knowledge of the causes of natural phenomena must remain hypothetical, confined to setting out 'some ways and means by which they may be, I do not say they are, generated', DCo, 25.1.

[34] For the term 'motive' power of the mind, see EL, 1.6, 6.9, 13.1.

[35] L, 6, p. 78.   [36] EL, 3.1; L, 2, pp. 26–8; DCo, 25.7–8.

[37] EL, 7.1–2; L, 6, p. 82; DCo, 25.12. Hobbes gives different definitions of vital motion. In *The Elements* the term is not explained; at L, 6, p. 78 it is applied to those motions 'continued without interruption through [an animal's] whole life', of which 'the *course* of the *Bloud*, the *Pulse*, the *Breathing*, the *Concoction*, *Nutrition*,

Before going any further, it is worth clarifying how the concept of a 'motive' can fit within this system. In an Aristotelian account of action, the Latin *motivum* could be used to refer to both final and efficient causes.[38] Hobbes's philosophy, which allows final causes in 'such things as have sense and will', can also be said to accommodate both these senses of 'motive'.[39] Thus a motive will be both the endeavour which moves the body (the efficient cause) and the object of sense or imagination towards which it is moved (the final cause). However, the distinction between final and efficient causes here is really only a distinction between two kinds of description.[40] When we describe our actions in terms of our aims or goals, we use the language of final causes, but in the language of science our actions are the effects of local motion in the body.[41] When Hobbes uses the term 'motive' himself, it is interchangeable with 'end'; therefore a motive is an imagined states of affairs which we seek to achieve.[42] But according to his theory this imagination must be understood to refer at the same time to an internal physical motion that propels the body.

According to Lloyd, Hobbes's attempt to understand motivation in physical terms 'invites the kind of overly simple psychology some of his modern commentators have attributed to him'.[43] It is primarily commentators from the 1950s and 1960s who provide the best examples of the derivation of this sort of psychology from his mechanistic-materialism: in addition to Gauthier's claim about 'self-maintaining engines', J. W. N. Watkins reads Hobbes as suggesting that 'self-preservation or the avoidance of wounds and destruction' is 'an egocentric end dictated by a man's biological-cum-psychological make-up'.[44] Specifically, it is Hobbes's account of appetite and aversion as based on alterations to vital motion that, for Watkins as for Gauthier, leads to the conclusion that 'since aversion is aroused when the vital motions are hindered, the

---

Excretion' are examples. In *De Corpore*, however, Hobbes limits vital motion to 'the motion of the blood, perpetually circulating (as hath been shown from many infallible signs and marks by Doctor Harvey, the first observer of it) in the veins and arteries'.

[38] Joseph Pilsner shows that this was the case for Aquinas, *The Specification of Human Actions in St Thomas Aquinas* (Oxford: Oxford University Press, 2006), 201–2.

[39] DCo, 10.7. See also EL, 7.5: 'As appetite is the beginning of animal motion toward something which pleaseth us; so is the attaining thereof, the END of that motion, which we also call the scope, and aim, and final cause of the same'.

[40] Thus F. S. McNeilly, notes that 'When Hobbes describes behaviour in mechanical terms, this does not of itself exclude motives', since 'what he does is to distinguish two categories of language'. See F. S. McNeilly, 'Egoism in Hobbes', *The Philosophical Quarterly* 16 (1966), 196.

[41] Thus Amy Schmitter notes that, 'Hobbes undermines the applicability of final causes even to our volitions, introducing the passions as a way to reduce voluntary action to the forward-driving motion of efficient causation'. See Amy Schmitter, 'Passions and Affections', in *The Oxford Handbook of British Philosophy of the 17th Century*, ed. Peter R. Anstey (Oxford: Oxford University Press, 2013), 456.

[42] For instance, L, 14, p. 202: 'security of a mans person' is 'the motive, and end for which [the] renouncing, and transferring of Right is introduced'; in the Latin only one term (*finis*) is used for 'motive and end'. See also L, 30, p. 542: 'The Perspicuity, consisteth not so much in the words of the Law it selfe, as in a Declaration of the Causes, and Motives, for which it was made'. The Latin has only *causa*.

[43] Lloyd, *Morality*, 57.

[44] Watkins, *System of Ideas*, 83. Or, as he later describes it, by 'Hobbes's mechanistic-cum-biological account of men', 114–15.

prospect of their stoppage, i.e. of death, will arouse the most violent aversion of all'.[45] The Hobbesian man must, on this reading, desire to preserve his body above all other things.

Some have tried to square this view with Hobbes's recognition of martyrdom by arguing that due to his materialist eschatology—according to which salvation is understood as the eternal life of the resurrected body—to desire salvation is the same as to desire preservation of the body. Thus Eric Brandon asks, 'what could be more consistent with Hobbesian egoism than for a true believer to sacrifice his or her body now in order to attain the perpetual preservation of that body in the future'?[46] However, this interpretation remains problematic if one thinks that explaining motivation in terms of the preservation of vital motion makes an appetite for death impossible; that the body is to be revived later does not change the fact of the prior cessation of motion. It is perhaps with this problem in mind that Lloyd claims that there is an 'obvious tension' between understanding Parts Three and Four of *Leviathan* as 'about a longest-run self-interest in salvation,' and mechanistic materialism.[47]

However, even if we grant that linking appetite and aversion with vital motion ensures that man will always experience an aversion to death, until the point of death itself we are dealing only with the *imagination* of death. When we deliberate about the best course of action—a process understood by Hobbes to involve the alternation of appetites and aversions as we imagine the consequences of our actions—the imagination of another outcome might produce a greater aversion than the imagination of death.[48] To think otherwise assumes that the reactions of Hobbesian man are fixed at birth, and remain constant throughout life. Such a view ignores the role that Hobbes gives to experience in shaping an individual's appetites. The very first endeavour of all men, and all creatures, is directed towards the preservation of his life, and away from death: 'the embryo . . . while it is in the womb, moveth its limbs with voluntary motion,

---

[45] J. W. N. Watkins 'Philosophy and Politics in Hobbes', *The Philosophical Quarterly* 5 (1955), 137. See also Watkins, *System of Ideas*, 115–16 for his account of the implications of Hobbes's 'physiological theory of pleasure and pain'. Similarly, Gauthier argues that it is from Hobbes's account of 'vital and voluntary motion', that 'it follows that each man seeks, and seeks only, to preserve and to strengthen himself', *Logic of Leviathan*, 7. McNeilly has argued that Hobbes's link between motivation and vital motion is not present in *Leviathan*, 'Egoism in Hobbes', 195–200. For example, he draws attention to Hobbes's claim in that text that appetite 'seemeth to be, a corroboration of vital motion' (emphasis added), whereas in *The Elements* and *De corpore* he shows no doubt about the relationship. The more cautious formulation, however, need only reflect Hobbes's conviction that the physiological details of his account can only be regarded as hypotheses. I shall not consider McNeilly's argument in more detail, however, since the fact that Hobbes states the role of vital motion in *The Elements* and reasserts it four years after *Leviathan* in *De corpore* suggests that we should not dismiss it from Hobbes's thinking about motivation.

[46] Eric Brandon, *The Coherence of Hobbes's 'Leviathan': Civil and Religious Authority Combined* (London: Continuum, 2007), 73. See also Jean Hampton, *Hobbes and the Social Contract Tradition* (Cambridge: Cambridge University Press, 1986), 96.

[47] Lloyd, *Morality*, 382.

[48] This other outcome weighed against death could be the torments of hell, but it might also be something more trivial such as social ostracism. See DCv, 6.13 where Hobbes allows that someone may 'prefer to die rather than live in infamy and loathing'.

for the avoiding of whatsoever troubleth it, or for the pursuing of what pleaseth it'.[49] But Hobbes is very clear that from this point on, bodies do not respond in the same way to the same things: 'Appetites of particular things, proceed from Experience, and triall of their effects upon themselves, or other men'.[50] Because 'the constitution of a mans Body, is in continuall mutuation', he continues, 'it is impossible that all the same things should always cause in him the same Appetites, and Aversions: much lesse can all men consent, in the Desire of almost any one and the same object'.[51] In this way Hobbes suggests that experience forges associations between objects and pleasure and pain, such that our response to the imaginations of objects changes over time. The point has been brought out well by Samantha Frost, who argues that Hobbesian bodies are not ahistorical lumps of matter, but that they 'retain the effects of [their] history'.[52] A Hobbesian man is the product of the interactions between the motions of the external world, and the internal motions which constitute his own cognitive processes. Since his internal motions retain the effects of previous collisions, the human being is changed by his passage through the world. Furthermore, the experience which shapes human motivation is not limited to the first-hand: in the quotation from *Leviathan* above, it is not only the 'triall of . . . effects upon themselves' that shapes men's desires, but experience of their effects upon 'other men'. This suggests that seeing, hearing, or reading about the harmful or beneficial consequences of an action can affect our own motives.[53]

So far I have claimed that Hobbes's materialism can accommodate the choice to prioritize eternal life over obedience. Furthermore, this choice is not due to the 'malfunction' of a system which under normal conditions maintains itself, but a consequence of the fact that (in Hobbes's view) bodies are motivated by beliefs formed through experience. In this way, we may accept that a would-be martyr is 'in his right mind' when he chooses eternal life over his present existence. It is another question, however, whether Hobbes's theory has the resources to justify some motives as belonging to one who is sane, and others as belonging to one who is not.[54] For example, Hobbes's use of the phrase *mentis compos* in *De Cive* invites comparison with a later statement in his *Dialogue between a Philosopher and a Student, of the Common Laws of England*. In the latter text, Hobbes writes that in the case of a suicide 'it is to be presumed that he is not

---

[49] DCo, 25.12. It is in this sense that we might interpret Hobbes's claims that men seek to preserve their bodies by 'necessity of nature': for example, DCv, 2.3 and L, 15, p. 232.

[50] L, 6, p. 80.

[51] The phrase 'almost any' is omitted in the Latin *Leviathan*. The same position is expressed in EL, 10.2: 'men differ much in constitution of body, whereby, that which helpeth and furthereth vital constitution in one, and is therefore delightful, hindereth and crosseth it in another, and causeth grief'.

[52] Samantha Frost, *Lessons from a Materialist Thinker: Hobbesian Reflections on Ethics and Politics* (Stanford: Stanford University Press, 2008), 82.

[53] See Robin Douglass, 'The Body Politic "is a fictitious body": Hobbes on Imagination and Fiction', *Hobbes Studies* 27.2 (2014), 126–47, on how Hobbes hopes to remodel men's imaginations through philosophical argument and therefore direct their actions towards peace.

[54] See Jean Hampton, 'Hobbes and Ethical Naturalism', *Philosophical Perspectives* 6 (1992), 340–6, for a related discussion concerning problems distinguishing irrational and rational desires in Hobbes's theory.

compos mentis, but by some inward torment or apprehension of somewhat worse than death, distracted'.[55] Quite how Hobbes can distinguish between one who is mad and one who is merely mistaken about the consequences of his actions (as it seems must be the case for would-be martyrs) is a question that cannot be considered here, since it would require engaging with the vexed question of Hobbes's understanding of rationality, taking us far from the present purpose. However, I do wish to emphasize that while Hobbes does not consider would-be martyrs to be insane, he does consider them to be mistaken not only about Scripture, but about human nature. As I shall go on to suggest, it is by correcting the latter errors that Hobbes's materialist account of human psychology contributes to his argument for the compatibility of salvation and earthly obedience.

5.3 The God-Like Immaterial Soul and the Limited Motives of Bodies

I turn now to consider Hobbes's materialist account of motivation in the context of the Aristotelian psychology he sought to replace, in order to draw out the ways in which his materialism is intended to change man's view of himself. Hobbes was a significant figure in seventeenth-century attempts to reformulate the relationship between body and soul in the face of the disintegration of the Aristotelian worldview.[56] The synthesis of an Aristotelian tripartite soul with Christian theology had long groaned under the weight of doctrinal requirements, with fifteenth- and sixteenth-century scholars struggling with the problem of guaranteeing the bodily independence of the intellect, which was thought to be necessary to establish the continued existence of the soul after death.[57] Yet the idea that man's *anima rationalis* was defined by the incorporeal faculties of intellect and will remained the standard model of human nature during the period in which Hobbes developed his political theory. In Aquinas's terms, man's rational soul was to be considered as 'the principle of intellectual operation' (*principium intellectualis operationis*), as well as the spiritual substance (*spiritualis substantia*) which, joined with body, makes a man.[58]

Hobbes's contemporary critics thought that by dismissing immaterial substance Hobbes severed the rational faculties, leaving man with only the powers of the corporeal

---

[55] DPS, p. 85. For a discussion of the *Dialogue* passage on suicide, and its compatibility with Hobbes's claims that death can be perceived as a good, see Brian Stoffell, 'Hobbes on Self-Preservation and Suicide', *Hobbes Studies* 4 (1991), 26–33.

[56] For an overview of early modern debates on the soul which considers Hobbes's position, see R. W. Serjeantson, 'The Soul', in *The Oxford Handbook of Philosophy in Early Modern Europe*, ed. Desmond Clarke and Catherine Wilson (Oxford: Oxford University Press, 2011), 119–41.

[57] On these debates over the (in)dependence of the intellect see Emily Michael, 'Renaissance Theories of Body, Soul, and Mind', in *Psyche and Soma: Physicians and Metaphysicians on the Mind–Body Problem from Antiquity to Enlightenment*, ed. John P. Wright and Paul Potter (Oxford: Clarendon Press, 2000), 147–72.

[58] Thomas Aquinas, *Summa Theologica*, trans. Fathers of the English Dominican Province (New York: Benziger Brothers, 1947), 1a. Q. 75.

sensitive soul attributed to beasts.[59] It was inconceivable that we could jettison *spiritualis substantia* while retaining *principium intellectualis operationis*. Stripped of these rational powers, men's motives could not differ from the bodily interest in self-preservation ascribed to other animals. Thus Richard Cumberland's claim that 'the *Mind* has much *greater* Powers, and is created for much *nobler Purposes*, than only to *preserve the Life of one inconsiderable Animal*' is, as Jon Parkin notes, 'something of a common-place in [seventeenth-century] Hobbes criticism'.[60] These '*greater* powers' and '*nobler* Purposes' were premised on what Cumberland calls the soul's '*spiritual, incorporeal, and God-like Nature*'.[61] If we consider what was thought to be granted to man by this nature, we can see what Hobbes's material model of man is intended to exclude. It becomes apparent that although Hobbes did not reduce men to beasts—as recent scholarship has emphasized—he nevertheless imposed a sharp distinction between the human and the '*God-like*'. In doing so, I shall argue, he undermined the view of human nature according to which man might be required to renounce his earthly pri-orities for the sake of salvation.

Edward Reynolds, whose *A Treatise of the Passions and Faculties of the Soule of Man* was published in the same year as Hobbes circulated *The Elements*, lists a number of 'naturall reasons to prove the *spirituality* of the Soule', based on abilities or characteris-tics of the rational soul that were thought to require immateriality.[62] First among these was the cognition of universals. In Hobbes's corporeal model of the mind, however, the ability to think beyond particulars is given by language, which enables us to impose 'universal name[s]' to classify our imaginations.[63] The use of language also allows human beings the capacity to carry out another intellectual act which was widely held to distinguish man from beasts: the ability to think beyond immediate needs. We can find this feature of human mental activity used by Calvin to prove that the soul has 'some divine thing [*divinum aliquid*] engraven [in] it'.

For that sense which is in brute beastes, goeth not out of the body, or at least extendeth no fur-ther than to thyngs presently set before it. But the nimblenesse of the minde of man which veweth the heaven and earth and secretes of nature, and comprehending all ages in understan-dying and memory, digeseth every thing in order and gathereth thynges to come by thinges past, doth playnly shewe that there lyeth hydden in man a certayne thing severall from the body.[64]

---

[59] See, for example, Bramhall's criticism that Hobbes has not respected the hierarchy of the powers of the human soul: 'Far be it from a reasonable man, so far to dishonour his own nature, as to equal fancy with understanding, or the sensitive appetite with the reasonable will', *Works*, 139.

[60] Jon Parkin, *Science, Religion and Politics in Restoration England: Richard Cumberland's 'De legibus naturae'* (Woodbridge: The Boydell Press, 1999), 103.

[61] Richard Cumberland, *A Treatise of the Laws of Nature*, ed. Jon Parkin, trans. John Maxwell (Indianapolis, IN: Liberty Fund, 2005), 2.4, p. 371.

[62] Edward Reynolds, *A Treatise on the Passions and Faculties of the Soule of Man* (London, 1640), 403.

[63] L, 4, p. 52. See Cees Leijenhorst, *The Mechanisation of Aristotelianism* (Leiden: Brill, 2002), 94–6.

[64] Calvin, *The Institution of Christian Religion,* trans. Thomas Norton (London, 1561), 1.15.2. While Calvin was not, of course, Hobbes's contemporary, we may nevertheless consider his *Institutes* for its status as an authoritative theological text amongst those who were.

As Philip Pettit has put it, language enables Hobbesian man to think 'beyond life in the present'.[65] Hobbes argues that any sequence of imaginations, or 'trayne of thoughts', depends on an association established by experience.[66] Beasts, without language, cannot think very far ahead because they lack the capacity to remember long sequences. Therefore 'there is no other Felicity of Beasts, but the enjoying of their quotidian Food, Ease, and Lusts; as having little, or no foresight of the time to come, for want of observation, and memory of the order, consequence, and dependance of the things they see'.[67] Men, on the other hand, can use words to 'register their Thoughts [and] recall them when they are past', enabling them to 'Register ... the cause of any thing, present or past; and what...things present or past may produce, or effect'.[68] Because of language, then, human minds are capable of 'digest[ing] everything in order and gather[ing] thynges to come by thinges past', despite being corporeal.

While those who thought that Hobbes made man into a beast went too far, they were nevertheless right to think that he was refuting widely held beliefs about man's motive power by dismissing an immaterial, divine element to his nature. There are two ways in which this is so that are particularly relevant to the discussion of the motives of martyrs. The first concerns natural knowledge of God's law, the second the *summum bonum*. To the rational soul, Reynolds writes, God 'fastened a perfect knowledge of his law and will'.[69] In this way, God gave man 'a spirituall resemblance of his owne goodnesse and sanctity'. The act of conscience, Reynolds goes on to explain, can direct men's actions by 'gathering Morall or Divine Conclusions...either from the reliques of our Originall Knowledge naturally imprest, or by concurrence of Religion and Theologicall Precepts spiritually inspired into the Practique Judgement or hearts of men'.[70] The undermining of the latter option—that knowledge can be 'spiritually inspired'—was undoubtedly an important aim for Hobbes, and indeed one in which his materialist metaphysics had a role to play.[71] But it is the former option—original knowledge—which is undermined by his materialist psychology.[72] For Reynolds, this

---

[65] Philip Pettit, *Made with Words: Hobbes on Language, Mind, and Politics* (Princeton, NJ: Princeton University Press, 2008), 91.

[66] L, 3, p. 38: 'as wee have no Imagination, whereof we have not formely had Sense, in whole, or in parts; so we have no Transition from one Imagination to another, whereof we never had the like before in our Senses.' See also EL, 4.2: 'The cause of the coherence or consequence of one conception to another, is their first coherence, or consequence at that time when they were produced by sense.'

[67] L, 12, p. 164.

[68] L, 4, pp. 48–52. See Leijenhorst, *Mechanisation of Aristotelianism*, 96.

[69] Reynolds, *Treatise*, 401.   [70] Ibid., 531–2.

[71] See L, 29, pp. 502–4 on the 'Pretence of Inspiration' as one of things that threatens the commonwealth. Hobbes's materialist metaphysics is relevant because of the explanation of 'spirit' as either something corporeal or a fiction of the mind. See L, 34, p. 630: 'On the signification of the word *Spirit*, dependeth that of the word INSPIRATION; which must either be taken properly; and then it is nothing but the blowing into a man some thin and subtile aire, or wind, in such manner as a man filleth a bladder with his breath; or if Spirits be not corporeall, but have their existence only in the fancy, it is nothing but the blowing in of a Phantasme; which is improper to say, and impossible; for Phantasmes are not, but only seem to be somewhat.'

[72] It is important to emphasize the difference between examining the significance of Hobbes's materialist metaphysics in general, and his materialist psychology in particular.

original knowledge has been obscured or corrupted by the Fall, though 'reliques' remain; for Calvin too man retains some remnants of this knowledge in regard to earthly matters.[73] But regardless of what remains now, man was created to know God's 'law and will'.

The capacity for moral and divine knowledge bestowed on man by the immaterial soul is not to be found in Hobbes's materialist mind, which is composed entirely of the variable and subjective products of bodily perception. No ideas of truth or falsity, good or evil, can come to us from 'outside' this system to provide a standard of certainty. Man's motives are limited to motions within himself, which first arose from the interactions between the body and sensible objects. Hobbes therefore does not present the lack of this knowledge as a failure of human judgement, a consequence of man's corruption, but rather as a necessary limit on the capacities of a material being. This is a highly significant conclusion in terms of Hobbes's goal to remove what he calls the 'scruple of conscience' among those who think they know God's law, since it suggests that God did not make human beings to be capable of accessing knowledge of this sort.[74]

Another proof of the immateriality of the soul, according to Reynolds, is that unlike the 'bodily cognoscitive faculties' which are damaged by 'the too great excellency of their objects, as the eye from the brightnesse of the Sunne' the immaterial intellect:

is perfected by the worthiest contemplations...And therefore *Aristotle* in his *Ethicks*, placeth the most compleat happinesse of man, in those heavenly intuitions of the minde, which are fastned on the divinest and most remote objects; which in Religion is nothing else, but a fruition of that beatificall vision...and an eternall satiating the soule with beholding the Nature, Essence, and glory of God.[75]

This point reflects what Aquinas had referred to as the *capax summi boni* conveyed by the image of God in man's immaterial soul.[76] According to scholastic faculty psychology, man's 'rational appetite' sought satisfaction in God, whereas the corporeal 'sensitive appetite' sought the satisfaction of bodily needs. It was therefore in man's nature to seek God, the greatest good, or *summum bonum*, above the bodily needs of this life. The teleological account of desire underlying this view, according to which the appetitive powers strive for perfection or completion, is ruled out by Hobbes's mechanistic

---

[73] Reynolds, *Treatise*, 532; Calvin, *Institution of Christian Religion*, 2.2.12–13.

[74] EL, 25.3, 25.14. See also Hobbes's deflationary account of conscience in EL, 6.8 and particularly in L, 7, p. 100. Of course, Hobbes thinks we have natural knowledge of the law of nature, which he presents as God's law, but this law—to the shock of his contemporaries—pertains only to earthly life and not to religion. See Bramhall's criticism of Hobbes on this point, *Works*, 520: 'reckoning up all the laws of nature at large, even twenty in number, he hath not one word that concerneth religion, or hath the least relation in the world to God...Thus, in describing the laws of nature, this great clerk forgetteth the God of nature, and the main and principal laws of nature, which contain a man's duty to his God, and the principal end of his creation'.

[75] Reynolds, *Treatise*, 404.

[76] Aquinas, *Summa Theologica*, Ia, Q. 93, A.2 '*similitudo divinae perfectionis magis invenitur in intellectuali creatura, quae est capax summi boni*'.

view of nature. He argues against the concept of a *summum bonum* on the grounds that 'felicity' cannot be a static state of satiation, but rather 'a continuall progresse of the desire, from one object to another'.[77] The non-teleological, mechanical motion which characterizes man as much as any other part of creation propels us aimlessly forward, rather than pulling us towards God. Hence man does not live in accordance with his nature by turning away from earthly goals, but rather man is made to continue living.

The type of creature that emerges from Hobbes's materialism is therefore not one that can have knowledge of a divine truth, nor one that is intended to renounce his body to realize his nature. Encouraging men to accept this new psychology, rather than to believe themselves to have '*greater* powers' and to be created for '*nobler* purposes', contributes to Hobbes's project of persuading them that God has made civil peace and salvation compatible. While acknowledging that Hobbes's materialism does not make men beasts, as his contemporaries would have it, nor turn them into the 'self-maintaining engines' of more recent scholarship, we should not lose sight of the extent to which his view of human psychology was at odds with the way in which the motives of those who prioritized eternal over temporal life were understood. Would-be martyrs are not fulfilling their nature as intellectual beings by acting on the remnants of original knowledge, and by eschewing the body in search of complete happiness. Instead, they are mistaken about what their nature is.

5.4 Conclusion

Far from being at odds with his recognition that men are prepared to prioritize eternal life over temporal, Hobbes's mechanistic-materialist psychology adds to his argument against disobeying the sovereign on religious grounds. That Hobbes condemns the pride of those who think their judgement is correct to the extent that they are prepared to sacrifice their own life and civil order is frequently noted.[78] I have sought to emphasize the role of Hobbes's materialist account of mental operations in giving man a new conception of his nature, in order to reorient him towards the prioritization of peace. The belief that salvation might require death in the name of conscience is, on Hobbes's account, based on false beliefs about our capabilities and purpose, which arise from a distorted idea of what it is to be a human being.

If a Christian subject holds fast to those false beliefs, he is more likely to reject Hobbes's theology and ecclesiology than to accept that the commands of God and the commands of sovereigns can be reconciled. The powers and purpose of the immaterial part of man's nature therefore stood in opposition to the earthly obedience required of

---

[77] L, 11, p. 150. The equation of 'Felicity' with the *summum bonum* did not imply a particular view of what the greatest good was: see, for example, Richard Barckley, *A Discourse of the Felicitie of Man, or his 'Summum bonum'* (London, 1603), which surveys different views of the *summum bonum*, concluding that the real *summum bonum* is God.

[78] See, for example, Julie E. Cooper, *Secular Powers: Humility in Modern Political Thought* (Chicago, IL: Chicago University Press, 2013), 55. This is also emphasized by Lloyd, *Ideals as Interests*, 46–7.

the Hobbesian subject. But through his mechanistic-materialist psychology, Hobbes presents man as a creature who was not made to have natural knowledge of God's law and will, and who, by rejecting bodily existence, finds not felicity but oblivion. Such a creature cannot be expected to die for religion. The argument that 'justice towards God, and peace amongst men...stand together' required Hobbes's psychology, as well as his theology.

6

Hobbes, Calvinism, and Determinism

Alan Cromartie

Hobbes's lifetime coincided with two consequential shifts in the development of English culture. The first, of which he disapproved, changed England's parliament from an occasional event into an institution through which the monarch was obliged to govern. The second transformed its religion. An Englishman of Hobbes's generation—that is, somebody whose formal education took place in the two decades either side of 1600—could assume that the country's religion was securely Protestant and that its Protestantism was in essence Calvinist. In spite of its episcopalian institutional structure and the residual ceremonies of its liturgy, the Church of England shared its basic teachings about faith, grace, and human agency with its own internal critics, the English Puritans, and with the Reformed (as opposed to the Lutheran) churches: the country was 'doctrinally a part of Calvinist Europe'.[1] Among other things, this meant that English theologians virtually all subscribed to a consensus that God had quite gratuitously predestined His elect without the slightest reference to any fact about them; more liberal-minded theories to the effect that this divine election was in some way contingent on His foresight of their faith were usually then known as 'Lutheran'.[2]

In the course of the next generation, this consensus was abandoned. In 1622, King James I formulated 'Directions for Preachers' by which non-academics (below the rank of Dean) were prohibited from dealing with predestinarian topics;[3] from 1628 onwards, disputation on such questions was a serious offence even in strictly academic settings.[4] Although these interventions were officially presented as even-handed in their character, they had the effect of transforming Calvinist theories of predestination from an unquestioned national orthodoxy into (at most) an intellectual option. In the

I am grateful to the editors, Al Martinich, and two anonymous readers for comments upon an earlier draft of this chapter.

[1] Nicholas Tyacke, 'Puritanism, Calvinism, and Counter-Revolution', in *The Origins of the English Revolution,* ed. Conrad Russell (London: Macmillan, 1973), 129.

[2] Ibid., 130.

[3] Nicholas Tyacke, *Anti-Calvinists: The Rise of English Arminianism c.1590–1640* (Oxford: Clarendon Press, 1987), 102–3.

[4] Peter Heylyn, *Cyprianus Anglicus* (London, 1668), 189.

absence of state support and university instruction, the more commonsensical 'Lutheran' views (now generally referred to as being 'Arminian') had an understandable tendency to triumph by default. Moreover, the upheavals of the English revolution considerably hastened this established tendency. The real or imagined excesses of antinomians encouraged a new suspicion of a theology that seemed to sever grace from normal standards of behaviour. The upshot, in some quarters, was a new understanding of Christianity that emphasized ethical teachings that were, at least in principle, accessible to reason at the expense of dogma and of the sacraments.

On most theological questions, Hobbes looks like a supporter of this shift in attitudes. There are some marked affinities with William Chillingworth,[5] a liberal theologian suspected of Socinianism by most Calvinists.[6] But even in questions bordering upon predestination, Hobbes's apparent sympathies were with the modernizers. At the heart of Calvinism as mainstream theologians understood it was a theology of imputation insisting that 'justification'—the pivotal transition that makes the fallen soul regenerate—is God's response to *Christ's* works as imputed to the sinner.[7] In each of his three great political works, Hobbes treated 'justification' as God's response to *human* 'faith and justice (meaning still by justice, not absence of guilt, but the good intentions of the mind, which is called righteousness by God, that taketh the will for the deed)'.[8] In *The Elements*, he argued that passages in Scripture where 'works' are criticized are actually directed against 'external' works, but 'if the will be taken for the deed, or internal for external righteousness, then do works contribute to salvation'.[9] The more this view is scrutinized, the less Calvinistic it seems. Most Calvinists admittedly defended their position by stressing that faith is in practice inseparable from works: 'justification' was the start of the process of 'sanctification' by which a vivifying faith expressed itself in action. But the Hobbesian view inverted this whole process: all three of his discussions of the subject imply that the will to act justly is an achievement *prior* to the faith that brings salvation. Good intentions set the sinner 'in an estate or capacity of salvation, whensoever he shall have faith'.[10] An unwise flourish in *Leviathan* ignores a fundamental Reformation shibboleth by suggesting—with the Catholics—that there exists a sense in which a fallen human being can 'merit' his salvation[11] (thus rejecting, among other authorities, the Church of England's Article XI:

---

[5] A. P. Martinich, *The Two Gods of Leviathan: Thomas Hobbes on Religion and Politics* (Cambridge: Cambridge University Press, 1992), 214–15, 216–17.

[6] Chillingworth's reputation was founded on one book—*The Religion of Protestants* (London, 1638)—on which see Francis Cheynell, *The Rise, Growth and Danger of Socinianisme* (London, 1643), esp. 28. Cheynell believed that Chillingworth's 'Arminian principles' were 'manifest to any man that hath but peeped into [his] book' (35).

[7] The technical points at issue are well explained in C. F. Allison's classic *The Rise of Moralism: The Proclamation of the Gospel from Hooker to Baxter* (London: SPCK, 1966).

[8] EL, 25.10, DCv, 18.12; L, 43, p. 950.   [9] EL, 25.10.

[10] EL, 25.10. Cf. DCv, 18.12; L, 43, p. 950.

[11] In what seems to be a tacit omission of error, it is omitted from the Latin version (L, 14, p. 208). For another view, see Martinich, *Two Gods*, 139–42.

'we are accounted righteous before God, only for the merit of our Lord and Saviour Jesus Christ by Faith, and not for our own works and deservings').

Underlying this essentially unProtestant position was an utterly unCalvinistic anthropology. All Calvinists believe in 'original or birth-sin' (to use the expression adopted in the heading to Article IX). Hobbes acknowledged that the Bible states that human beings are evil, but insisted that it 'cannot be conceded without impiety that men are evil by nature', if 'by nature' means 'from birth itself (*ab ipsa nativitate*)'.[12] It is impossible to reconcile his view of human passions as essentially innocent with the much more severe official doctrine that 'concupiscence and lust hath have in themselves the nature of sin' (Article IX) and even that 'we do not doubt but [works done before justification] have the nature of sin' (Article XIII). As the eighteenth-century Calvinist John Gill was to complain, in the context of a catalogue of such divergences, 'it is notorious, that in many things there's a plain and manifest agreement between him and the Socinians and Arminians'.[13]

It is hardly too much to say, then, that the only area in which Hobbesian theology concurred with Calvinism was over the complex question of the relationship between 'free will' and God's omnipotence. In the debate about free will conducted with John Bramhall, Hobbes went out of his way to identify his own determinism with the positions defended by traditional Protestants, especially their insistence that 'liberty' can be consistent with 'necessity'. He advanced the arresting thesis that 'free will' was unknown to the ancients, who recognized only 'necessity' and 'chance', while St Paul

deriveth all actions from the irresistible Will of God, and nothing from the will of him that runneth or willeth. But for some ages past, the Doctors of the Roman Church have exempted from this dominion of Gods Will, the Will of Man; and brought in a Doctrine that not onely Man, but also his Will is Free, and determined to this or that action, not by the Will of God, nor necessary causes, but by the power of the Will it Self. And though by the reformed Churches instructed by Luther, Calvin, and others, this opinion was cast out, yet not many years since it began again to be reduced by Arminius and his followers and became the readiest way to Ecclesiastical promotion...[14]

It was in this specialized context that he made the startling claim that though he despised such writers as Suarez and Duns Scotus, 'other Doctors of the Church (as Martin Luther, Philip Melancthon, John Calvin, William Perkins, and others) that did write their sense clearly, I never slighted, but alwayes very much reverenced, and admired'.[15]

Those biographically minded scholars who have been willing to accept such statements at face value have recently had a choice of two approaches. Al Martinich's straightforward and lucidly argued position has been that Hobbes was loyal to 'English Calvinism', at least if 'Calvinism' is narrowly defined as a belief about predestination. On this view, 'Calvinism' was a personal commitment: 'Hobbes is especially

---

[12] DCv, Preface, §12.   [13] John Gill, *The Cause of God and Truth*, 4 vols (London, 1737), iii, 181.
[14] QLNC, pp. 1–2.   [15] QLNC, p. 212.

committed to the thought of Calvin and of Puritan theologians such as William Perkins. Hobbes's determinism ... is not merely a part of his mechanistic materialism; it is logically tied to Calvin's doctrines of predestination and belief in the omnipotence of God.'[16] Though Calvinists might well believe 'in the ability to act from some internal principle such as the soul', they were, however, deterministic with respect to God: they did not believe that 'a human being could initiate an action that does not have God as its ultimate source'.[17] The necessity God imposes on all actions was thus seen as compatible with a weak sense of freedom. Jürgen Overhoff, by contrast, sees the determinism as wholly secular. Hobbes may of course have been sincere in appealing to the major sixteenth-century Reformers, but he did so only relatively late in his career and their theology functioned as a means of defending some doctrines that he adopted for quite different reasons. In Overhoff's view, the 'mechanistic-materialist' character of Hobbes's thinking in fact casts a degree of doubt on his sincerity, but 'judged by the ... epistemic standards of his contemporaries, Hobbes's theological doctrine of the freedom of the will was ... a recognizable and, above all, credible seventeenth century theological defense of his scientific determinism'.[18]

On both views, Hobbesian determinism could reasonably draw support from Calvinistic thinking, and Hobbes's stance in his debate with Bramhall could reasonably be taken for a Calvinist position. As we shall see, however, both views face serious problems. Noel Malcolm long ago remarked that 'the more thoroughly one supposes [Hobbes] to have been grounded in the principles of Calvinism, the more likely it seems that he would have recognized the fact that Calvinists regarded divine Providence as utterly different from causal determination'.[19] This chapter documents the truth of Malcolm's observation by showing, first, that Calvinists were not determinist and, secondly, that Hobbes revealed a striking ignorance of fairly basic features of their theology. But it also raises further, perhaps more important, questions about the *motivation* of his philosophy.

6.1   Protestantism and Determinism

During the sixteenth century, mainstream Western theology was Augustinian; both Protestants and Catholics thought it important to present their theories about grace as being compatible with St Augustine's. But Augustine's views notoriously required him to give an account of 'liberty' in two quite different contexts. His early work *De libero*

---

[16]   Martinich, *Two Gods*, 3; see also p. 273.

[17]   A. P. Martinich, 'On Hobbes's English Calvinism: Necessity, Omnipotence, and Goodness', *Philosophical Readings* 4.1 (2012), 24–5.

[18]   Jürgen Overhoff, *Hobbes's Theory of the Will* (Lanham, MD: Rowman & Littlefield, 2000), 160. For a similar view, see Leopold Damrosch, Jr, 'Hobbes as Reformation Theologian: Implications of the Free-Will Controversy', *Journal of the History of Ideas* 40.3 (1979), 339–52.

[19]   Noel Malcolm, 'Thomas Hobbes and Voluntarist Theology', PhD thesis, University of Cambridge, Cambridge (1982), 204n.

arbitrio voluntatis—'on the free choice of the will'—begins with the question 'Please tell me whether God is not the author of evil?'[20] The point of the idea of *liberum arbitrium* was to locate the origin of evil in creation in such a way as to avoid the Manichaean error of making evil equal and opposite to God and the fatalistic error of making God responsible for every evil action. By the end of his life, however, Augustine's attention had turned to his polemical battles against Pelagians: heretics who objectionably maintained that the divine election of certain human beings to salvation was contingent upon something that those human beings did. His theory of evil thus involved him in picking out a moment of free choice as the locus of evil; his anti-Pelagian polemics required him to deny that it was possible to use that freedom in such a way as to deserve salvation.

The debate of which Hobbes claimed a knowledge was Augustinian in that all (except perhaps the first) of its participants believed that their positions were non-determinist. It began in 1520, when Martin Luther provocatively endorsed John Wycliffe's thesis that every human action is 'absolutely necessary'. This rash statement gave an opening to Erasmus, who made it the occasion of his attack on Luther: *De libero arbitrio diatribe* (1523). Luther's intensely felt reply, *De servo arbitrio* (1525), could not be said to shy away from polemical overstatement, but nonetheless remained within Augustine's paradigm. He noted (which may have struck Hobbes) that secular philosophy has not yet finally settled whether anything can set itself in motion.[21] There is, however, evidence that his own view of the matter was libertarian: 'for we are not discussing being by nature, but being by grace (to put it in current terms). We know there are things *liberum arbitrium* does by nature, such as eating, drinking, begetting, ruling'.[22] Five years later, the eighteenth article of the Confession of Augsburg (1530) was to settle the point by pronouncing that 'they teach that the human will has some liberty to bring about civil justice and choose things subjected to reason'. If a determinist is somebody who thinks that human actions are externally determined in exactly the same way as other physical events, Luther was not, then, a determinist. So far from seeing the bondage of the will as an instantiation of deterministic order, he saw it as a way that postlapsarian human beings were limited in certain spheres of their activities. It was intelligible to say that that we are 'free' in ordinary secular concerns in a way that we are not free in those areas of life that have a direct bearing on our chances of salvation, and also (which, in his view, amounts to the same thing) that '*liberum arbitrium* avails only for sinning'.[23]

It may be thought that his position was nonetheless 'deterministic' with respect to God, on the grounds (to take a characteristic statement) that 'man apart from the face of God remains nonetheless under the general omnipotence of God, who does, moves,

[20] Augustine, *On the Free Choice of the Will, On Grace and Free Choice, and Other Writings*, ed. and trans. Peter King (Cambridge: Cambridge University Press, 2010), 3.

[21] Luther, *De servo arbitrio*, in *Luther and Erasmus: Free Will and Salvation*, ed. and trans. Philip S. Watson (London: SCM, 1969), 173.

[22] Ibid., 286.   [23] Ibid., 286–7.

and carries along all things in a necessary and infallible course'.[24] No one would ser-iously dispute the existence of such statements. Equally, no one would dispute that Luther believed that rational theodicy was futile. He did not appeal solely to God's omnipotence to justify the existence of evil in the world: he felt confident that God has a good reason both for permitting evil to exist and also for inscrutably deciding not to elect the vast majority of human beings. But the reason was one that will only be known with the assistance of the 'light of glory'.[25] In any case, he was loyal to the unvarnished text: the plain sense of the Bible was not to be subverted by scholastic subtleties (with an entertaining impudence Hobbes would have found amusing, scholastics were referred to as 'sophistae'). It was clear that God wills everything that happens. It was not for human beings to evade this plain biblical truth by distinguishing absolute necessity—necessitas consequentis—from a merely hypothetical necessitas consequentiae (necessity contingent on some created fact).[26] When Scripture clearly stated that God 'hardened' Pharaoh's heart, the hardening should be taken at face value: God acted on the tyrant's will to cause him to do evil.[27]

It is easy, then, to see why competent interpreters have often concluded that Luther was indeed determinist. It should, however, be noted that evidence of this sort is power-less to decide the point at issue: precisely because such passages are meant to emphasize the limitations upon human reason, they offer wide scope for acceptance of the non-Hobbesian view that the relationship between necessity and freedom is something ultimately mysterious (there is, to be sure, some mystery in the Hobbesian position, but it is located elsewhere: in the nature of God). It is also well worth noting that Luther believed his theory to be Augustinian: he certainly accepted Augustine's principle that evil is located in the wills on which God acts, rather than in the motion by which He acts upon them.[28] Like virtually all of the thinkers discussed in this chapter, he could assume an Aristotelian physics in which the fact of motion (owed to God as final cause) can in principle be severed from the direction it is given by another agent. God thus resembles somebody who rides on a lame horse: he accounts for the animal's motion but not for its stumbles.[29] By contrast, Hobbes despised the claim that 'the general power to act is from God, but the specification to do this act upon Uriah [his murder], is not from God but from Free-will . . . As if there were a power, that were not the power to do some particular act'.[30] This contrast should be borne in mind when reading the tradition that was to run from Calvin down to Perkins.

Calvin's thought resembles Luther's in its reluctance to explain away the plain sense of the scriptural revelation; like Luther, he insisted that 'hardening' meant what it said.[31] He claimed that he was loyal to the substance of Augustine, but thought that the

---

[24] Ibid. A good exposition of this kind of view is Overhoff, Theory of the Will, 146–7.
[25] Luther, De servo arbitrio, 331–2.   [26] Ibid., 120–2.   [27] Ibid., 237.   [28] Ibid., 235–6.
[29] Ibid., 232. For a later example, see William Perkins, A Golden Chaine (Cambridge, 1595), chapter 6, p. 16.
[30] QLNC, p. 108.
[31] John Calvin, Institutes of the Christian Religion (Geneva, 1559), 1.18.2, 2.4.3–4.

expression *liberum arbitrium* encouraged dangerous misunderstandings.[32] His most revealing statements, for present purposes, are not found in the *Institutes* (the great theological textbook that everyone learned had read), but in the debate he conducted with the Catholic polemicist Albertus Pighius. Pighius taxed the Lutherans with inconsistency on the grounds that 'they [now] attribute some liberty to the human will in those things which belong to civil justice and concern the outward face of things.'[33] Calvin's reply to this was interesting: he flatly denied the existence of inconsistency, while admitting that the later formulations had had the effect of altering the doctrine's exposition. He added that:

[Melancthon in his capacity as principal author of the Confession of Augsburg] wished to dwell only on that teaching which alone is proper to the church and necessary to know for salvation: that is, that the strength of nature in itself avails nothing to the conception of faith, to obedience to divine law, and to full spiritual righteousness. What it can do in civil and external affairs he did not want to dispute too curiously, because it does not have much to do with faith.[34]

His central point here is illuminating: the earliest Reformers were committed missionaries whose overriding purpose was to rescue threatened souls. Even if they had in fact believed that God controls the world in a deterministic fashion, they had no *religious* reason to emphasize the fact.

Calvin is also helpful in carefully distinguishing two different concerns that press towards determinism with respect to God. He tackled the subject of freedom in two quite different contexts within the *Institutes*: not only in the famous treatment of predestination, but also in the chapter about God's providence. In a passage of the latter that was to be appealed to by John Bramhall, his stress was on God's power to *override* the will. As Bramhall acutely remarked,

Calvine, who is the least disfavourable to [Hobbes of six authorities that Hobbes had cited], saith no more but this, *Deum quoties viam facere vult suae providentiae, etiam in rebus externis hominum voluntates flectere & versare, nec ita liberam esse ipsorum electionem, quin eius libertati Dei arbitrium dominetur.* That God (not allwayes but) as often as he will make way for his providence, even in external things, doth bow and turn the wills of men, neither is their election so free, but that the good pleasure of God hath a dominion over their liberty.

It followed that 'Calvine did know no universall determination of all externall acts by God, but onely in some extraordinary cases.'[35] This seems exactly right. Nobody who reads Calvin can fail to note his interest in *special* divine interventions. Not surprisingly, he was loyal to Augustine in wishing to stop short of 'Stoicism': 'Good luck to the Stoics with their fate', as he told Pighius, 'let the free will of God be for us the controller (*moderatrix*) of all things. But it seems absurd that contingency should be taken from

---

[32] Ibid., 2.2.8.
[33] Albertus Pighius, *De libero hominis arbitrio et divina gratia* (Cologne, 1542), fo. 6v.
[34] John Calvin, *Opuscula omnia in unum volumen collecta* (Geneva, 1552), 231.
[35] John Bramhall, *Castigations of Mr Hobbes His Last Animadversions* (London, 1658), 281–2, quoting *Institutes*, 2.4.7. The quotation transposes 'liberam' and 'esse', but is otherwise completely accurate.

the world.'[36] Unlike Luther, he accepted the distinction between *necessitas consequentiae* and *necessitas consequentis*.[37]

Thereafter, the development of Calvinist belief was in a generally libertarian direction. It was usually granted that Adam had been free (in a sense of the word 'free' that even Catholics accepted). Thus the fair-minded Cardinal Bellarmine felt safe in asserting that man 'absolutely considered' possesses *liberum arbitrium*, 'for the heretics do not contend about this matter, but only about man cast down from his condition through the sin of his first parent'.[38] He also knew that many moderate Protestants believed that fallen human beings retain some liberty; unlike the Calvinists, Melancthon and Luther had once denied that human beings have freedom in what he referred to as 'civil and external actions', but had afterwards retracted their position.[39] By the time that he was writing, however, some English Calvinists were demonstrably ready to make similar concessions.

One reason that this point has not been widely understood has been the understandable assumption that 'supralapsarian double predestination'—the belief that the decrees of reprobation and election were logically prior to God's knowledge of the Fall—implies divine determinism with respect to Adam. But the supralapsarian thinkers mentioned with respect by Hobbes—Theodore Beza[40] and his English popularizer William Perkins—in fact avoided drawing this conclusion. As the greatest living scholar of these matters has explained, 'both Beza and Perkins assume... a category of divine permission, and the existence, as well, of contingent events and free will in the world. There is not even a tendency toward metaphysical determinism'.[41] Analysis of what Perkins wrote strongly supports this verdict. Perkins refused to palliate the basic principle that the divine decree of reprobation 'ariseth of God's meere good pleasure, no respect had of good or evil in the creature.'[42] But his discussion of the fall of Adam did not assert that Adam's freedom was 'compatible' with the necessity imposed upon it. He retreated to a baffled string of reverent negations: 'we must not thinke, that man's fall was either by chaunce, or God not knowing it, or barely winking at it, or by his bare permission, or against his will: but rather *miraculously*, not without the will of God, but yet without all approbation of it.'[43] The 'hardening' that Luther and Calvin had been reluctant to explain away was treated with conspicuous

[36] 'Valeant igitur cum suo fato Stoici: nobis libera Dei voluntas omnium sit moderatrix. Sed contingentiam tolli a mundo, videtur absurdum' (Calvin, *Opuscula*, 940).
[37] Ibid. The acceptance of the two kinds of necessity was taken over, virtually unaltered, in *Institutes*, 1.16.9; the statement about the absurdity of Stoicism was not.
[38] Robert Bellarmine, *Disputationum... de controversiis Christianae fidei, adversus huius temporis hereticos*, 4 vols (Ingolstadt, 1601), iv, col. 690.
[39] Ibid., col. 714–16.
[40] Beza is not mentioned in QLNC, but his biblical commentaries are cited at L, 44, p. 978 (where Hobbes is critical) and L, 44, p. 1010 (where Hobbes is favourable).
[41] Richard A. Muller, *Post-Reformation Reformed Dogmatics: The Rise and Development of Reformed Orthodoxy, ca.1520 to ca.1725* (Grand Rapids, MI: Eerdmans, 2005), i, 128.
[42] William Perkins, *A Christian and Plaine Treatise of the Manner and Order of Predestination*, trans. Francis Cacot and Thomas Tuke (London, 1606), 25.
[43] Perkins, *Golden Chaine*, chapter 11, p. 25 (my emphasis).

moderation: it involved a combination of 'permitting', 'occasioning', and 'disposing' (so ordering things that good comes out of evil); it did not involve specific direct action on the will.[44] Though God imposed necessity upon the universe, he did so in a fashion that:

doth not take away freedome in election, or the nature and propertie of second causes, but onely brings them into a certaine order, that is, it directeth them [to] the[ir] determinate end: whereupon the effects and events of thinges are contingent or necessarie, as the nature of the second cause is.[45]

In a work that began by stating common ground with Catholics, he held that 'we joyne with the papists' in asserting liberty 'even since the fall of Adam by a naturall power of the mind'. This liberty extended to 'outward performance of civill and ecclesiasticall duties'. Perkins cautioned that 'man's will is weake and feeble, and his understanding dim and darke', and also that 'the will of man is under the will of God', but the dutiful qualifications confirm the principle that the human will is free in just the sense of the word 'free' that ordinary Catholics accepted.[46]

So far as we know, this position was quite conventional. No one had better Calvinist credentials than the rigorous supralapsarian William Twisse (later the prolocutor of the Westminster Assembly that would produce the Calvinistic Westminster Confession). But a Calvinistic pamphlet attributed to Twisse approvingly recalled that:

In the time of my minoritie in the Universitie [Twisse had matriculated in 1596, received his MA in 1604, and disputed for his BD in 1612], in divinitie disputations we heard concerning free will such a distinction as this of common course. The actions of men are eyther naturall or morall, or spirituall; the resolution of the truth, as touching free will, according to the foresayde distinction, was this; we have not lost our free will, in actions naturall, nor in actions morall, but only in actions spirituall.[47]

Elsewhere, Twisse definitely pointed out that Calvinistic writers were actually more careful than some Augustinian Catholics to steer clear of deterministic language: 'to necessitate the will or determine the will are noe phrases of our Divines'.[48] Moreover, 'we know God is the first cause, and all other are but second causes in comparison to him. Yet we willingly confesse that the providence of God is wonderfull and of a mysterious nature in this.'[49] It goes without saying that God determines everything that happens, but he 'moves every creature to worke agreeably to its nature, necessary things necessarily, contingent things contingently, free Agents freely'.[50]

[44] Perkins, *Predestination*, 61–6.   [45] Perkins, *Golden Chaine*, chapter 6, pp. 14–15.

[46] William Perkins, *A Reformed Catholike* (Cambridge, 1598), 11–13. For a very similar statement, again noting that free will exists but is 'verie weake', see Perkins, *Golden Chaine*, chapter 12, p. 30.

[47] William Twisse, *The Doctrine of the Synod of Dort and Arles Reduced to the Practise. With a consideration thereof* (Amsterdam, 1631), 17.

[48] [William Twisse], *The Riches of Gods Love unto the Vessells of Mercy* (Oxford, 1653), book 2, 74.

[49] Ibid., 75.

[50] Ibid, 80. This is uncontroversial: for a similar example, see Martinich, 'Hobbes's English Calvinism', 24–5. The point that is at issue is whether 'predestination' that is sensitive to the modes of 'freedom' and 'contingency' can usefully be associated with Hobbes's style of determinism.

The church's official pronouncements were equally cautious. The canons of the synod of Dort conceded that 'there are still in lapsed man some remains of the light of nature', implying not just some knowledge of 'the difference betweene good and evill', but even 'some care (*studium*) of vertue, and of outward discipline'. Needless to say, 'hee doth not make right use thereof in naturall things, and civill affairs: nay, that which it is, he many ways defileth it' all.[51] But the careful qualifications do not by any means exclude—and arguably imply—some traces of survival of Adamic liberty. The English delegation went much further, stating baldly that 'it is in every man's power to rule his moving faculty; and experience proves it, because wee see, in outward things, men, as they will themselves, doe this or that, or omit both.'[52] In the absence of qualifications, the commonsensical tone of the appeal to 'experience' seems to demand a libertarian reading. But here as elsewhere, the decisive point is the presence of the notion that men enjoy *more freedom* in some spheres of life than others and that the level of their freedom varies. Even at the high-water mark of English Calvinism, there seems to be no evidence that any of its leaders were in a modern sense deterministic.

6.2 Hobbes, Calvinism, and Determinism

My argument so far has been that mainstream Calvinism was not deterministic—even with respect to God—and that suggestions that it was were typically made by outsiders. There is good reason to believe that Hobbes was just such an outsider. But there is also one suggestive detail that might be thought to point in a quite different direction. Hobbes spent five years at Magdalen Hall in Oxford (from 1602 or 1603 to February 1608). As an undergraduate studying the Arts course, he had, of course, no formal academic obligation to take an interest in theology; nor can it be assumed that theological instruction would have said much about predestination. The great theologian Richard Field (1561–1616), who had delivered well-regarded 'catechism lectures' at Magdalen Hall in the early 1590s, is said to have disapproved of disputations on the subject.[53] But from 1605 onwards, the Hall was controlled by John Wilkinson, an ardent Calvinist who had or developed an interest in doctrinal education; William Pemble's *Vindiciae fidei* (1625)—a clear and forceful statement of the Calvinist understanding of the theology of justification—was written, at Wilkinson's request, as a Magdalen Hall lecture series.[54] As Wilkinson recommended Hobbes for the attractive post of tutor and companion to a rich nobleman, it is unlikely that he doubted Hobbes's orthodoxy.[55] It is,

---

[51] *The Judgement of the Synode holden at Dort* (London: John Bill, 1619), 33.

[52] *The Collegiat Suffrage of the Divines of Great Britaine* (London, 1629), 68.

[53] Nathaniel Field, *Some Short Memorials Concerning the Life of that Reverend Divine Richard Field* (London, 1717), 3–4, 21–2.

[54] Pemble died young (at 29) in 1623. The lectures were probably written in the early 1620s.

[55] Thomas Hobbes, *Thomae Hobbesii Malmesburiensis Vita* (London, 1679), 3. In the prose autobiography, Hobbes says he was recommended by 'amici'; the plural suggests that Wilkinson was advised by some third parties. See *Thomae Hobbes Angli Philosophi Vita* (London, 1681), 1.

however, clear that Hobbes's Oxford education had not included anything resembling Pemble's lectures; in the absence of an open challenge to the Reformed position, perhaps no such instruction was considered necessary.[56] If Hobbes had been grounded in orthodox Calvinist doctrine, he would, for example, have realized that his view of human 'merit' resembled the traditional Roman Catholic position.[57]

In any case, his early works yield little evidence that he identified with Calvinism. In a 1630 letter from Geneva, he praised a minister as 'a very wise and honest man and not of the Geneva print, more then is necessary for an inhabitant and minister of the place'.[58] Perhaps the expression 'the Geneva print' refers primarily to social and political attitudes as opposed to fundamental theological commitments, but it does seem to suggest a certain detachment. His later works suggested that he saw 'the Calvinists' as upholders of a basically scientific thesis. In *The Elements of Law*, he wrote that 'this whole controversy, concerning the predestination of God, and the free-will of man, is not peculiar to Christian men', supporting this claim by referring, suspiciously vaguely, to 'huge volumes of this subject, under the name of fate and contingency, disputed between the Epicureans and the Stoics'.[59] The same detachment is observable in the 'Objections' he produced to Descartes' *Meditations* (1641), where he questioned the philosopher's conventional remark that 'my errors depend on two concurrent causes, that is, the faculty of coming to know that is in me and the faculty of choosing (*facultas eligendi*) or freedom of the will (*arbitrii libertas*)'. Hobbes noted that '*arbitrii libertas* is assumed without proof, against the opinion of the Calvinists'.[60]

If we turn to his first expression of his own philosophy—the so-called 'Short Tract on First Principles'[61]—we find that his determinism developed very early, but that his line of argument involved no reference to theological considerations. In the thirteenth and fourteenth 'Principles' of the Short Tract's Section One, he set out definitions that his later works adhered to:

12. Necessary is that which cannot be otherwise.
13. A Necessary cause is that, which cannot but produce the effect.
14. A sufficient cause is that, which hath all things requisite to produce the effect.[62]

---

[56] According to Nicholas Tyacke, open anti-Calvinism did not emerge in Oxford before 1607, that is, Hobbes's final year in residence, *Anti-Calvinists*, 62–3.
[57] William Pemble, *Vindiciae fidei* (Oxford, 1625), 229–31.   [58] C, p. 10.
[59] EL, 25.9. Cf. DCv, 18.14.   [60] Hobbes, *Opera Latina*, v, 269.
[61] The argument presented here would not be much affected if, as many think, the Short Tract is actually a work by Hobbes's close friend Robert Payne. It is common ground that the impressive verbal and substantive parallels between the Tract and Hobbes's later writings include his accounts of 'necessary' and 'sufficient' causes, as well as the (logically faulty) transition to asserting that the Molinist definition of a 'Free Agent…implies a contradiction'. If the author was Payne, he must either have borrowed these ideas or else (which seems fantastic) devised a deep, original, and dangerously heterodox theory, then somehow induced Hobbes to take it over. In other words, the argument—and possibly its phrasing—is surely Hobbesian, even if the Short Tract as a whole was written by another. For the parallels, see Karl Schuhmann, '*Le Short Tract*, première oeuvre philosophique de Hobbes', in his *Selected Papers on Renaissance Philosophy and on Thomas Hobbes*, ed. P. Steenbakkers and C. Leijenhorst (Dordrecht: Kluwer, 2004), 239–40; for an acknowledgement of their force, see Noel Malcolm, *Aspects of Hobbes* (Oxford: Clarendon Press, 2002), 128–9.
[62] 'Short Tract', British Library, Harley MS 6796, fo. 297, §1 princ. 12–14.

In the eleventh 'Conclusion' of that Section, he deduced that 'A Sufficient Cause is a Necessary Cause' on the grounds that:

That cause which cannot but produce the effect, is a Necessary Cause (by the 13. prin:) but a sufficient cause cannot but produce the effect. because it hath all things requisite to produce it (by the 14. prin:) For if it produces it not, somewhat els is wanting to the production of it, and so the cause is not a sufficient cause, which is contrary to the supposition.

Corollary.

Hence appears that the definition of a Free Agent, to be that *Which, all things requisite to worke being putt, may worke, or not worke,* implyes a Contradiction.[63]

In an implicit rejection of the *necessitas consequentiae/necessitas consequentis* distinction, he went on to maintain (in Conclusion 14) that 'Necessity hath no degrees', on the grounds that 'that which is necessary is impossible to be otherwise (by the 12. Prin.) and that which is impossible is Non-ens; and one Non-ens cannot be more Non-ens than another'.[64] This argument is of interest because it seems to show that he was already committed to the extreme position that all events are 'necessary' or 'impossible' (that is, there is no middle ground of 'possibility'; as in his later writings, non-entity maps onto non-possibility).[65] Even at this early stage, then, Hobbes went beyond the thinking of Calvin and Perkins, both of whom went out of their way to leave space for possibility: as Calvin explained, 'that which God has ordained necessarily comes to pass in such a way that it is not, however, precisely or in its own nature necessary'. A prophecy made it certain that Christ's bones would not be broken, but it would still make sense to say that they were breakable.[66]

There is no sign, then, that the Tract's position owes much to any form of Calvinism. It is, however, possible to find a *Catholic* source. The definition of a 'Free Agent' that Hobbes criticized is a word-for-word translation of a formulation offered in two widely read works by the Jesuit Francisco Suarez: *Metaphysicae Disputationes* (1597) and 'De concursu, motione, et auxiliis Dei' (the latter printed in successive editions of *Varia Opuscula Theologica*, 1600).[67] The Short Tract's understanding was shaped by the former, which is a work of secular metaphysics (at least in the sense that its argument is said not to rely on premises disclosed by revelation). At some point, however, Hobbes

---

[63] Ibid., §1, conc. 11. The words printed in italics are written in a fractionally different lettering presumably meant to signal a quotation.

[64] Ibid., §1, conc. 14.   [65] DCo, 10.4; AW, 37.5.

[66] Calvin, *Institutes*, 1.16.9. Cf. Perkins, *Golden Chaine*, chapter 6, p. 15: 'if we respect the temperature of Christs body, he might have prolonged his life'.

[67] Suarez, *Metaphysicarum Disputationum Tomi Duo* (Moguntiae, 1614), 19.4.1; 'De concursu Dei', 1.3.2 in Francesco Suarez, *Varia opuscula theologica* (Moguntiae, 1600), 13. On the relationship with Suarez, see Schuhmannn, 'Le Short Tract', 250–7. Suarez in turn drew his definition from Molina: Thomas Hobbes and John Bramhall, *Hobbes and Bramhall on Liberty and Necessity*, ed. Vere Chappell (Cambridge: Cambridge University Press, 1999), 39n. *Pace* Schuhmann (p. 256), Hobbes's later admission that he did not know who invented it (AW, 33.1) is not a sign that he had forgotten Suarez, but only that he was aware that many writers used this formulation.

also acquired some knowledge of the latter, which was a theological discussion of the relationship between the Catholic Christian God and human *liberum arbitrium*.[68]

In his capacity as a metaphysician, Suarez contrasted 'causes necessarily acting, if all things requisite to action are present' and 'causes that work without necessity and with liberty'.[69] For Suarez a 'cause' was an 'agent', and 'things requisite to action' included the proximity of another entity with characteristics requisite to being acted on. A cause necessarily acting would invariably act when brought into proximity with a suitably disposed patient. There were, however, agents that could refrain from acting even in such conditions. Suarez gave Hobbes the germ of an important argument by admitting that a cause that worked without necessity would require a 'faculty or power that has the strength to restrain its own working (*vim continendi operationem suam*), even when all things requisite to working have been put'.[70] In the Short Tract, Hobbes accepted the essentials of this theory: he too believed that agents work if and only if they are combined with 'patients' that are suitably located and appropriately disposed (although he insisted on contact, not just proximity). But he thought that a 'power to suspend' an act upon a patient would always operate unless it was itself suspended by a second-order power to suspend 'and so in infinitum, which is absurd'.[71]

The Suarezian framing of Hobbes's theory has large and interesting implications.[72] For present purposes, though, its salient feature is that the Hobbesian view of *Protestant* theology is noticeably Suarezian in character. In a full and helpful discussion of the possible range of senses of the liberty–necessity distinction, Suarez points out that if 'necessary' means 'involuntary', then liberty does not exclude

determination to one with an incapacity of restraining action, but excludes only violence and coercion; in which sense it is evident that there are actions that are not necessary not only in human beings but also in brutes, although those actions are more completely free in human beings to the extent that the basis of the voluntary [which Suarez believed to be the intellect] is more completely found in them. On which grounds some, especially heretics, have taken occasion to say that human actions are free on no other grounds than that they are completely voluntary...[73]

Suarez seems not to have thought that all these heretics believed in physical determinism: he mentioned that 'some denied liberty in all actions, internal and external, good and bad, but others only in moral or worthy actions, but not in civil or indifferent ones'.[74] But on the one occasion that he referred to 'Calvin and his followers', he accused them of defending an outright fatalism in which necessity was imposed 'not only by the influence of the stars, but by the higher influence of God moving and setting to

[68] L, 8, p. 122; QLNC, p. 9.   [69] Suarez, *Metaphysicae Disputationes*, 19.1 and 2.

[70] Ibid., 19.2.4.   [71] 'Short Tract', §1 conc. 8.

[72] For a helpful account of contrasts between their views of agency, see Thomas Pink, 'Suarez, Hobbes and the Scholastic Tradition in Action Theory', in *The Will and Human Action: From Antiquity to the Present Day*, ed. Thomas Pink and M. W. F. Stone (London and New York: Routledge, 2004), 127–53.

[73] Suarez, *Metaphysicae Disputationes*, 19.2.9.   [74] Ibid., 19.2.10.

work all the second causes in such a way that they do by necessity that to which they are impelled and nothing else'.[75]

The thinker who did most to shape the Hobbesian theory was thus a Roman Catholic who seems to have believed that Calvinism *was* determinist. It is not clear when, if ever, Hobbes obtained a first-hand knowledge of mainstream Protestant theology. There is, however, one passage of his critique of Thomas White (a work composed in 1642–3) suggesting he had read a little further. In that work, Hobbes notes that some people believe in an absolute power of doing or not doing, while others maintain (as he did) that liberty is simply power to do what one happens to will. But he also notes the existence of a third opinion: that 'men have *liberum arbitrum ad malum* in such a way that they can absolutely do or not do an evil that is presented to them, but not *liberum arbitrium ad bonum*, and therefore that men are in such a condition with respect to choice of the good that they are as it were dead.' In discussing this opinion, he objected, among other things, to the simile of death.[76] In doing so, he was objecting to Calvinist language: William Perkins, for example, held 'that Man not regenerate hath free-will to do onely that which is evill, none to doe good', on the scriptural grounds that 'Man is not said to be weak, or sicke, but dead in sinnes'.[77] But Hobbes thought that this was the 'opinion of few men and one that perhaps furthers their other opinions'.[78] This baffled remark suggests that he had failed to recognize that this 'opinion of few men' was quite conventional. The same surprising ignorance affected his performance when he embarked on his debate with Bramhall.

6.3 Hobbes and Bramhall

The Hobbes–Bramhall debate was really not one but two debates. The first, which took place in 1645–6, was a three-part written exchange (Bramhall—Hobbes—Bramhall) arising from an earlier, oral discussion in the presence of their patron, the earl of Newcastle.[79] As numerous features of his stance reveal, John Bramhall, the bishop of Derry, was an Arminian. There is no doubt, however, that his intellectual training had left him with a grasp of Calvinism. His Cambridge education had been received at Sidney Sussex College, a Puritan foundation and a Calvinistic stronghold whose famous Master, Samuel Ward, attended the Synod of Dort. As we shall see, a striking feature of the episode was that a competent thinker with a background of this type was unaware of anyone who seriously defended Hobbes's extreme determinist position.

At Newcastle's suggestion, Bramhall drafted a brief paper that set out the case for 'free will' as he then understood it. One interesting point that emerges from this statement is

---

[75] Ibid., 19.11.3.   [76] AW, 37.7.

[77] Perkins, *Golden Chaine*, chapter 51, p. 250.   [78] AW, 37.7.

[79] On the chronology and other circumstantial detail, see Nicholas D. Jackson, *Hobbes, Bramhall and the Politics of Liberty and Necessity: A Quarrel of the Civil Wars and Interregnum* (Cambridge: Cambridge University Press, 2007).

that the opponents that Bramhall found it easiest to imagine were not, in any ordinary sense, determinist. They were people, to begin with, who objected to being called 'Stoic', unless their Stoicism was identified as 'Christian'. A *Christian* Stoic asserted 'that the Stoicks did take away liberty and contingence, but [we] admit it' and that 'in respect of the second causes many things are free, but in respect of the first cause, all things are necessary'.[80] As later allusions confirm,[81] his most important target here was Justus Lipsius, who made the points attributed to these Christianized Stoics within a single chapter of his *De Constantia*.[82] But the Lipsian position was an undemanding one; as Bramhall later remarked, Lipsius was 'no such friend of any sort of destiny, as to abandon the liberty of the will. The Stoics themselves came short of T.H. his universal necessity'.[83] The Lipsian text confirms this particular claim: Lipsius invoked traditional distinctions between necessitation and foreknowledge that Hobbes was subsequently to scorn as meaningless:

God by the power of destiny draweth al things, but taketh not away the peculiar facultie or motion of any thing. He would that trees and corn should grow. So do they, without any force of their owne nature. Hee would that men should use deliberation and choyse. So do they, without force, of their free-will. For God that created all things useth the same without any corruption of them. And yet, whatsoever they were in mind to make choyse of, God foresaw from all eternitie: He fore-saw it (I say) not forced it: hee knewe it, but constrained not: he fore-tolde it, but not prescribed it.[84]

Some of Bramhall's other targets were, however, 'Calvinist'. From a Calvinist perspective, his most offensive view was his complete rejection of the legitimacy of the *non-violent* manipulation that Calvinists routinely attributed to God:

If a strong man holding the hand of a weaker, should therewith kill a third person, *haec quidem vis est*, this is violence, the weaker did not willingly perpetrate the fact, because he was compelled. But now suppose this strong man had the will of the weaker in his power as well as the hand, and should not onely incline, but determine it secretly and insensibly to commit this act, is not the case the same?

In a curious illustration of what he was trying to say, Bramhall compared the ravishing of Lucretia to the approach of someone who made subtle use of magic to 'incline her effectually, and draw her inevitably, and irresistibly to follow him spontaneously'. Both lines of conduct were deplorable,

but the latter person is more guilty, and deserves greater punishment, who endeavours also so much as in him lies, to make Lucretia irresistibly partake of his crime. I dare not apply it, but thus only: take; heed how we defend those secret and invincible necessitations to evil, though spontaneous and free from coaction.[85]

---

[80] QLNC, p. 193.   [81] QLNC, pp. 195, 197; Bramhall, *Castigations*, 244.

[82] Justus Lipsius, *Two Books of Constancie*, ed. Rudolf Kirk, trans. Sir John Stradling (New Brunswick, NJ: Rutgers University Press, 1939), 121–3.

[83] Bramhall, *Castigations*, 244.   [84] Lipsius, *Constancie*, 122.   [85] QLNC, p. 216.

The obvious application of this general principle was that the Calvinists had made the Almighty the author of sin. But Bramhall's evident distaste for Calvinistic theories did not impel him to misrepresent them. He took it for granted that 'the greatest opposers of our liberty, are as earnest maintainers of the liberty of Adam'.[86]

In his reply to Bramhall, Hobbes crossed the territory of Calvinist/Arminian disagreements without, however, presenting himself as Calvinist. Moreover, he made an extraordinary tactical blunder that somebody familiar with Calvinist ideas might reasonably have hoped to have avoided. As Bramhall implied when speaking of Lucretia, Calvinists from Calvin onwards had characterized sinful actions as being 'spontaneous' (Latin: *spontaneus*). Calvin himself defined the will as being 'spontaneous' if it 'turns itself of its own accord wherever it is led, but is not wrested or drawn unwillingly'.[87] On a page Hobbes later quoted, the theologian Girolamo Zanchi (1516–90) explained that 'the spontaneous is not opposed to the necessary, but to the violent'. Zanchi went on to argue that human actions were spontaneous, even if they were moved by an 'external principle', if they were also approved by an 'internal principle' (his example was somebody led by the hand to a banquet in his honour).[88] Hobbes might have been expected, then, to appropriate the word by reserving it for cases in which the causal chain ran through a person's appetite, in other words *equating* the term spontaneous with 'voluntary'. But when he came to write about the word 'spontaneous', he opted instead to *distinguish* the two concepts, denying the term 'spontaneous' to actions performed out of fear (though he admitted that such acts were 'willing'), and denying the term 'voluntary' to actions that were done without some precedent deliberation. In doing so, he set off a fruitless wrangle in which he regretted the use of 'this strange word Spontaneous' and asked (rhetorically) 'Why did the School-men bring it in, if not meerly to shift off the difficulty of maintaining their tenet of Free-Will'.[89] It seems to have escaped him that the use of the strange word was actually characteristic of the Calvinist position.

Hobbes's self-presentation in this first phase of debate thus tells against the theory that he was motivated by any real Calvinist commitment. In the later phase, however, some reference to the Calvinist/Arminian disputes was practically unavoidable. The occasion of the later publications was the emergence into print of Hobbes's little treatise (without the piece by Bramhall to which it was an answer). To make things worse, the book was given a shrill anticlerical preface (which was clearly not by Hobbes) and

---

[86] QLNC, p. 79.

[87] 'Spontaneam dicimus, quae ultro se flectit, quocumque ducitur, non autem rapitur, aut trahitur invita' (Calvin, *Opuscula*, 252).

[88] 'Neque spontaneum opponitur necessario, sed violento'. Girolamo Zanchi, *Hieronymi Zanchii Tractationum theologicarum volumen* (Neostadii Palatinatus, 1603), 117. The citation ('Tract Theol. Cap.6. Thes. 1') is found at QLNC, p. 235. To complicate matters, there was no agreement about what counted as *spontaneus*. In Zanchi's view, the term could be extended to cover the fall of a stone, that is, a response to natural final causation (*Tractationes*, 118). Bramhall, by contrast required 'an inward principle (that is the will) with some knowledge of the end', *Castigations*, 74.

[89] QLNC, p. 69.

the misleading title: *Of Liberty and Necessity A Treatise, Wherein all Controversie concerning Predestination, Election, Free-will, Grace, Merits, Reprobation &c is fully decided and cleared, in answer to a Treatise written by the Bishop of London-derry on the same subject* (1654). At this point, Bramhall published *A Defence of True Liberty from Antecedent and Extrinsecall Necessity* (1655), which reproduced all three of the earlier treatises with a very brief explanatory preface. Beyond deploring the ridiculous title, he made no attempt to divert the debate to discuss theological questions. It was Hobbes's riposte (the fourth of the five contributions), *The Questions Concerning Liberty, Necessity, and Chance* (1656), that insisted on connecting his ideas with Calvinism, in doing so giving Arminians an opportunity to tar their enemies with the brush of Hobbist heresy.

One passage in *The Questions* is particularly important. Hobbes was contesting Bramhall's claim that 'he who doth necessitate the Wil to evil is the true cause of evil', by which, Hobbes said, 'he thinks he shall force me to say, that God is the cause of sin'.[90] He commented that 'to use so unseemly a Phrase as to say that God is the cause of sin, because it soundeth so like to saying that God sinneth, I can never be forced by so weak an argument as this of his.'[91] He then went on to quote six Protestant sources who shared his view that liberty, though it excludes 'constraint', is quite consistent with 'necessity'. He went on to remark that 'all the famous Doctors of the Reformed Churches, and with them St Augustine are of the same opinion. None of these denied that God is the cause of al Motion & Action, or that God is the cause of al Lawes, and yet they were never forced to say that God is the cause of sin.'[92] Hobbes was on firm ground here. It is, however, worth noting that he was arguing *ad hominem*: he was arguing that thinkers that Bramhall had a duty to respect had not been obliged by the premise that Bramhall criticized to '*say*' something '*so like to*' the statement that 'God sinneth'. The Latin version of *Leviathan* denies the conventional claim that God is not the 'cause' of sin, while agreeing with the Calvinists that God is not its 'author'.[93] He was borrowing one feature of a theology with which he had virtually nothing else in common.

When they were faced with Hobbes's appeal to Calvinism, Arminians had a choice between two possible responses. The first to emerge, by Thomas Pierce, made use of Hobbes's statements to attack the Calvinists. He set out to insinuate that Hobbesian ideas had close affinities with Calvinism: 'I have many reflexions on Mr Hobbs, because

---

[90] QLNC, p. 234.   [91] QLNC, p. 235.   [92] QLNC, p. 235.

[93] LL, 46, p. 1093. A. P. Martinich, in his helpful essay, 'L'auteur du péché et les démoniaques', in *Jean Calvin et Thomas Hobbes: Naissance de la modernité politique*, ed. Oliver Abel, Pierre-François Moreau, and Dominique Weber (Geneva: Labor et Fides, 2013), 50, notes that Hobbes was critical of the Calvinist position that God can cause the action without also causing the sin, but sees Hobbes's position on the authorship of sin as an argument defending Calvinism. Hobbes offers three arguments (53–4) against God's authorship, two of which were certainly also employed by Calvinists. What is non-Calvinist about his thinking is that these arguments omit a reference to 'freedom'. Hobbesian freedom (absence of obstruction) has no conceivable bearing upon theodicy: in other words, it does not play the part assigned to freedom in the tradition founded by Augustine to which all mainstream Calvinists belonged.

he jumps so often with my Assailants.'[94] This line of attack had potential, but the confla-tion of the two positions was really a polemical Arminian construction. Bramhall's approach was different and perhaps more damaging. It seems to have been *The Questions* that made him realize how little Hobbes knew about Calvinism, at least as it was understood in academic circles. In his final contribution, this ignorance in itself became one of his major targets. Bramhall's answer to *The Questions*, his vigorous *Castigations of Mr Hobbes his last Animadversions* (1658), is amongst other things a defence of the whole enterprise of university theology. His defence of scholastic learn-ing was ecumenical: Hobbes was unfair to Catholics 'as if they exemted the will of man from the dominion of God's will';[95] he was unfair to the Reformed in holding that their positions were deterministic. As an Arminian, Bramhall had an obvious interest in claiming (like Pierce) that Calvinists were really Hobbesian. But he opted not to do so. Hobbes had professed himself puzzled by Bramhall's statement that 'the conversion of a sinner concerns not the Question'.[96] Bramhall commented:

He saith, *He understands not these words* [the conversion of a sinner concernes not the ques-tion]. I do really believe him...Let him study better what is the different power of the will, in naturall or civill actions, which is the subject of our discourse, and morall or supernaturall acts, which concernes not this question; and the necessity of adding those words, will clearly appear to him.[97]

At this point, of course, one should pause. Many modern accounts of pre-modern theological debates reproduce the most tiresome feature of their material: its tendency to endless selective proof-texting. It was only to be expected that a rather hasty reading of some rather abstract works that tried to hold apparently conflicting truths in tension should yield a hasty reader the results he was expecting: these works undoubtedly con-tain a plethora of statements that seem, in isolation, to be determinist. Moreover, it was a feature of the Hobbesian position that he agreed that 'Men are Free to *Do* as they *Will*, and to *Forbear* as they *Will*';[98] his objection was to language involving a regress in which the will was something 'free' distinct from the action of willing. But it is difficult to see how a philosopher who was in some sense *motivated* by his 'Calvinism' could have been, and remained, so ignorant of the libertarian side of books that he was anx-ious to imply that he had read. For example, he was happy to excerpt the misquotation 'Witness the devils who are necessarily wicked, and yet sin freely without constraint' from the conclusion of the following passage:

We intend not to take from the corrupt and unregenerate man, all freedome of will: we know well, that in naturall actions, which are ruled by the will, as to eate and to go...man freely chuseth among many objects...we say more, that is, that man hath his free will in good and honest actions, belonging to civill honesty: as the actions of pagans, which helpe a man up that

[94] Thomas Pierce, *Autokatakrisis, or Self-Condemnation Exemplified* (London, 1658), 'To the reader'.
[95] Bramhall, *Castigations*, 4.   [96] QLNC, p. 3.
[97] Bramhall, *Castigations*, 7. See also pp. 30, 69.   [98] QLNC, sig.a.

is fallen downe…And which is more, we say that the unregenerate man sinneth very freely, and without constraint, and betweene two evils chooseth very freely. And this is the same liberty, which imposeth on him the necessity to sinne, because he is naturally subject to his will, naturally evill. Therein consists his mischiefe, that he is too free to do evill, so that his freedome is the cause of his servitude. Now this necessity to sinne is not repugnant to the freedome of the will. Witness the devils, which are necessarily and naturally wicked, and yet sinne most freely and without constraint[99]

Even if all this language about freedom is taken to refer to merely Hobbesian liberty—the freedom to do what one wills—it remains the case that whether or not an act is free depends upon the *sphere* that it belongs to. Either Hobbes was uninstructed in some fairly basic features of actual Jacobean orthodoxy or his contempt for it was so complete that he cared little how he tortured it. In either case, his radically deterministic vision was not, in any important sense, the fruit of Calvinism.

6.4 Conclusion

This chapter's main conclusions have been rather negative; it seems worth emphasizing they are also limited. If the arguments brought forward are basically sound, they show that Hobbes's thinking about necessity and liberty was neither derived from early doctrinal instruction nor from a subsequent study of the writers he referred to. It is, however, possible that there were Calvinists who were becoming open to deterministic views. The example well known to Hobbes scholars is Edward Bagshaw, an erratic young man of unquestionable Calvinist credentials who wrote to Hobbes requesting clarification about the question of divine foreknowledge.[100] It is at least imaginable that somebody who started from a Calvinist position might have been driven by interest in mechanistic physics towards a Hobbesian determinism resembling, perhaps, the ideas of Jonathan Edwards.[101]

As we have seen, however, it is implausible that someone who knew as little as Hobbes about elementary details of Calvinist ideas of justification could possibly have had a Calvinistic starting point. This raises an interesting question. If 'Calvinism' was irrelevant—and if determinism was virtually unknown—it is natural to wonder what features of his outlook could possibly have *motivated* his extreme position. The conventional explanation is that he was responding to the works of Galileo, but it was possible to admire the recent advances in physics without feeling driven to such extreme conclusions. Moreover, his convictions were developed very early. As we have seen, the Short Tract includes the argument that 'that which is impossible is Non-ens;

---

[99] Peter du Moulin, *The Buckler of the Faith* (London, 1620), 81–2. This work was first published in French as *Le bouclier du foi*, but Hobbes quotes the title in English.

[100] C, pp. 497–9, 782–5.

[101] A point about which Edwards himself was sensitive. See James A. Harris, *Of Liberty and Necessity: The Free Will Debate in Eighteenth-Century British Philosophy* (Cambridge: Cambridge University Press, 2005), 14.

and one Non-ens cannot be more Non-ens then another', implying, against Suarez,[102] that events are either necessary or impossible.[103] It is, then, worth considering another explanation in which religious feeling plays a more significant role.

It goes without saying that one pressure on Hobbes comes from 'Philosophy', a discourse shaped by what can be 'imagined'. For Hobbes, imagination deals with bodies and their motions. It thus excludes theology, which deals with the 'doctrine of God, eternal, ingenerable, incomprehensible and in whom there is nothing to divide nor compound, nor any generation to be conceived'.[104] A major unsolved problem facing Hobbes scholarship is the precise relationship between Philosophy (which must have meaning) and talk about God (which is really 'worship': that is, which gives expression to opinions of His power).[105] It is relevant to this problem that the boundaries of philosophy are surprisingly extensive: as we have seen, both 'free will' and the Eucharistic presence are thought to fall within its jurisdiction. So, much more questionably, does the idea of God's 'foreknowledge', which cannot, Hobbes alleges, be merely 'intuitive', that is, divorced from physical causation.[106] Foreknowledge lay at the heart of a revealing disagreement arising from one of Bramhall's strongest debating points. Bramhall acutely stated that 'he will not deny, but if it had been the good pleasure of God, he might have made some causes free from necessity, seeing that it neither argues any imperfection, nor implies any contradiction'.[107] Hobbes tacitly conceded this involves no contradiction, but replied 'that if God had made either causes or effects free from necessity, he had made them free from his own Praescience, which had been imperfection'.[108] There are two ideas at work here: one, which is philosophical, is an analysis of prescience that utterly refuses to divorce it from causation; the other, which is religious, is that God would be 'imperfect' if (as He might do) He released control.

It was the interaction between these two ideas that gave Hobbes's determinism plausibility. The latter was admittedly a Calvinist conception (this is the constructive truth within the Calvinism thesis), but there was no need to derive it from Calvinist sources: all Calvinists were determined to uphold God's sovereignty, but so, in their own sense, were virtually all scholastic theologians. As Bramhall had said, 'he wrongs the Doctours of the Roman Church, as if they exemted the will of man from the dominion of God's will'.[109] Without abandoning the claim that God is in control, the Augustinian paradigm that still shaped Calvinism had the resources to describe a textured universe in which *liberum arbitrium* played an essential role in giving God just enough distance from his creatures' sinful actions. But Hobbesian philosophy did away with those resources. Within his flattened universe, imagined as bodies in motion, the physical 'concourse of causes' *is* the 'decree of God'.[110] The God-free agent nexus is in all respects the same as God's connection with all other unobstructed motions. Somebody who

---

[102] Suarez, *Metaphysicae Disputationes*, 19.2.8.   [103] 'Short Tract', s. 1 conc. 14.   [104] DCo, 1.8.
[105] L, 31, p. 560.   [106] QLNC, p. 346   [107] QLNC, p. 320.   [108] QLNC, pp. 325–6.
[109] Bramhall, *Castigations*, 4.   [110] QLNC, p. 80.

thinks of the world in this way is bound to be affronted by 'the Doctrine of Free-Will', understood (as it must be within this radically simplified system) as 'a Will of man, not subject to the Will of God'.[111] It was quite understandable that Hobbes should have scorned as evasions both the concept of permission and the idea that God can cause the act but not the sin.[112] The point he did not grasp was that these Arminian evasions were actually evasions that were shared with Calvinists.

It is, however, important that this biographical finding about Hobbes's Calvinism does not decide the question about his theism. If near the heart of Hobbes's thought was a religious vision requiring that God have the *same kind* of necessary relation to every event and action within the universe, it would explain how he arrived at his determinism at such an early moment of his development—and why he was so loyal to what his contemporaries in general regarded as a ludicrous position. If it was religious excitement that played at least some role in shaping Hobbes's theory, there would also be a further, more political implication: the proper response—'honour'—to divine omnipotence would surely include individual and collective acts of worship.

---

[111] L, 46, p. 1090. Cf. QNLC, p. 111.   [112] QLNC, p. 89.

7

Mosaic Leviathan
Religion and Rhetoric in Hobbes's Political Thought

Alison McQueen

... the interpretation of a verse in the Hebrew, Greek, or Latine Bible, is often-times the cause of Civill Warre, and the deposing and assassinating [of] Gods anointed... It is not the Right of the Soveraigne, though granted to him by every mans expresse consent, that can enable him to do his Office, it is the obedience of the subject which must do that. For what good is it to promise allegiance, and by and by to cry out (as some Ministers did in the pulpit) to your tents O Israell.[1]

There were virtually no Jews in mid-seventeenth-century England.[2] Yet the history of biblical Israel was at the heart of the charged political and religious debates of the English Civil War (1642–50) (see Figure 7.1). This fact was not lost on Thomas Hobbes. Looking back from the comparative calm of the Restoration, Hobbes implicated both the learning of Hebrew and the history of biblical Israel in England's recent political upheavals. There is a small but growing literature on the 'Hebraic Hobbes' which seeks to understand and interpret his references to the Old Testament within his political and religious writings.[3] However, there are few sustained attempts to read Hobbes's

This chapter has benefited from feedback from Joshua Cohen, Robin Douglass, Dan Edelstein, Ryan Harding, Burke Hendrix, Kinch Hoekstra, David Laitin, Melissa Lane, Eric Nelson, Philip Pettit, Arlene Saxonhouse, Quentin Skinner, Nigel Smith, Sarah Song, Anna Stilz, Laurens van Apeldoorn, Paul Weithman, Leif Wenar, and Yves Winter, as well as audiences at UC-Berkeley, Princeton University, the 2015 meeting of the American Political Science Association, and the 2016 meeting of the Western Political Science Association.

[1] B, p. 302.

[2] Jews were expelled from England in 1290. While some Jews remained in England after this, their numbers were likely small. Oliver Cromwell tacitly readmitted Jews in 1656. The readmission was de facto, not de jure.

[3] See, for instance: Ronald Beiner, *Civil Religion: A Dialogue in the History of Political Philosophy* (Cambridge and New York: Cambridge University Press, 2010); Frank M. Coleman, 'Thomas Hobbes and the Hebreic Bible', *History of Political Thought* 25.4 (2004), 642–69; Daniel J. Elazar, 'Hobbes Confronts Scripture', *Jewish Political Studies* 4.2 (1992), 3–24; Meirav Jones, '"My Highest Priority Was to Absolve the

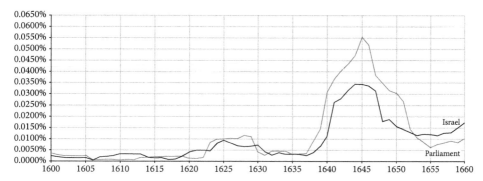

Figure 7.1 Frequency of 'Israel' (black line) in British English texts published between 1600 and 1660 (measured as a percentage of all unigrams, or single words, contained in Google's sample of books from this period). Note the steep increase during the first half of the English Civil War. To put this information in context, I have also included the frequency of 'Parliament' (grey line) during the same period. Google Books Ngram Viewer.

discussions of the figures and narratives of biblical Israel as polemical interventions in the political debates of his day.[4]

Hobbes's engagements with the Old Testament became more pronounced in the early 1640s. While only 16 per cent of the scriptural citations in *Elements of Law* are drawn from the Old Testament, this proportion increases to 52 per cent in *De Cive* and declines only somewhat to 44 per cent in *Leviathan*. As the civil war raged on, Hobbes came to focus on the early history of the Mosaic polity in the book of Exodus and substantial portions of *Leviathan* deal with this period.[5] This focus coincides with his elevation of Moses as the scriptural exemplar of a Leviathan sovereign.

My aim in this chapter is to defend three connected claims. In the first section, I argue that biblical Israel occupied a central place in the political and religious debates of seventeenth-century England. The polity of the Israelites came to be seen as an authoritative expression of God's political preferences and therefore as a model for England. Defenders of monarchical power and royal supremacy over the church looked

Divine Laws": The Theory and Politics of Hobbes' *Leviathan* in a War of Religion', *Political Studies* 65.1 (2017), 248–63; Joshua Mitchell, 'Luther and Hobbes on the Question: Who Was Moses, Who Was Christ?', *The Journal of Politics* 53.3 (1991), 676–700; Eric Nelson, *The Hebrew Republic: Jewish Sources and the Transformation of European Political Thought* (Cambridge, MA: Harvard University Press, 2010); Joel Schwartz, 'Hobbes and the Two Kingdoms of God', *Polity* 18.1 (1985), 7–24; J. P. Sommerville, 'Hobbes, Selden, Erastianism, and the History of the Jews', in *Hobbes and History*, ed. G. A. J. Rogers and Tom Sorell (London: Routledge, 2000), 160–88.

[4] An important recent exception is Jones, 'My Highest Priority'.

[5] While the top three books of the Old Testament cited in *De Cive* are to Proverbs, Deuteronomy, and Genesis (which make up 14, 12, and 10 percent of total citations to the Old Testament, respectively), the top three books cited in *Leviathan* are Exodus, Deuteronomy, and Genesis (which make up 14, 12, and 11 percent of total citations to the Old Testament, respectively). These figures are based on a count that comprises those citations included by Hobbes as well as the biblical passages that Hobbes quotes directly (even if he doesn't provide a citation).

to the period of the Davidic kings to ground their claims. However, as the political and religious conflict of the seventeenth century intensified, parliamentarians and republicans would increasingly turn to the polity of the Israelites under Moses for enticing alternatives to a powerful monarchy. While many interpreters of Hobbes have used these parliamentarian and republican discourses to contextualize his philosophical arguments, there has been comparatively less attention paid to the political theological dimensions of these discourses.[6]

In the second section, I argue that when read against these developments in the English political and rhetorical context, Hobbes's interest in the Mosaic polity and his attempt to position Moses as a Leviathan sovereign is puzzling. It is puzzling as a contextual matter because appeals to the Davidic kings had been used to ground arguments for monarchical authority and civil supremacy over the church for some time. They would have presented Hobbes with a ready store of scriptural narratives and images to support his political arguments. As a textual matter, Hobbes's own accounts of the Mosaic polity and the period of Davidic kingship suggest that the latter fit much better with his philosophical account of the basis of sovereign authority.

I argue in the third section that Hobbes's use of Moses is best seen as a rhetorical and polemical move that appropriates the images and narratives of parliamentarians and republicans and subversively redirects them in the service of absolutism. I suggest that this is both an interpretively radical and politically risky strategy. It is radical because it demands a thoroughgoing (and perhaps implausible) reinterpretation of the locus, basis, and scope of political authority in the Mosaic polity. It is a politically risky strategy because the powerful arguments, narratives, and imagery that result from it are themselves subject to redirection by those with more reformist or revolutionary aims. In part for these reasons, the strategy opened Hobbes's argument to criticisms that it might otherwise have been able to avoid from those who might otherwise have been allies. I present suggestive textual evidence that these risks made Hobbes somewhat uneasy.

7.1 God's Pattern, England's Politics

The roots of seventeenth-century England's Hebraic politics lie in Reformation theology and the political and religious changes wrought by the country's break from Rome. A Protestant culture of scriptural reading and translation encouraged literate believers to read the Old Testament for themselves. Instruction in biblical Hebrew blossomed in England, as it did in other Protestant states. Hebrew grammars became more readily available and the study of the language became part of the humanist curriculum at Oxford and Cambridge.[7] The Reformation also prompted a shift in the way in which

[6] Important exceptions include Jeffrey Collins, *The Allegiance of Thomas Hobbes* (Oxford: Oxford University Press, 2005); Jones, 'My Highest Priority'; Nelson, *Hebrew Republic*, 23–56.
[7] G. Lloyd Jones, *The Discovery of Hebrew in Tudor England: A Third Language* (Manchester: Manchester University Press, 1983), 180–220.

the figures and narratives of the Old Testament were read and interpreted. The church fathers and medieval Catholic interpreters tended to read the figures and events of the Old Testament typologically, as shadowy prefigurations of the fuller reality of Christ.[8] On this interpretive approach, the Old Testament had been superseded and 'hence made "old" by the New Testament or Gospel'.[9] While the Reformation did not do away with typological interpretations,[10] it did transform them. Suspicious of Catholic allegorizing, reformers read the narratives of the Old Testament as a historical record of an actual people—a people uncorrupted by the ceremonies and doctrines of a fallen church. Eager to make sense of their own collective identity, reformers also read the Old Testament as a prefiguration of the contemporary Protestant experience—the experience of a chosen people battling persistent challenges to their faith and to their obedience to God.[11]

The Reformation also raised urgent questions of political and ecclesiastical legitimacy. After England's break from Rome in 1534 and Elizabeth I's excommunication in 1570, these questions became particularly pressing. Many of the efforts to answer them approached the Old Testament not only as a prefiguration of the challenges faced by contemporary Protestants but also as an authoritative statement of God's political preferences. But what were these preferences? The biblical Israelites had a long and complex history during which they adopted or endured a variety of institutional arrangements. They had been ruled more or less directly by God, by priests and judges, by kings, and by conquerors. Which among these alternatives did God prefer?

For those seeking to defend royal authority and supremacy, these answers were clear. In order to ground their case for obedience to monarchical authority, many thinkers turned to the moment in the Old Testament when the Israelites ask Samuel to 'make us a king to judge us like all the nations'.[12] As Eric Nelson has shown, this passage proved central to early modern debates about the best regime.[13] God instructs Samuel to heed the Israelites' request but also to issue a warning to 'shew them the manner of the king that shall reign over them'.[14] The warning Samuel conveys is harrowing and worth quoting at length:

This will be the manner [מִשְׁפַּט] of the king that shall reign over you: He will take your sons, and appoint them for himself, for his chariots, and to be his horsemen ... And he will appoint him captains over thousands, and captains over fifties; and will set them to ear his ground, and to reap his harvest, and to make his instruments of war, and instruments of his chariots. And he

---

[8]   For instance, Jonah's three days and three nights in the belly of a whale prefigure Christ's 'three days and three nights in the heart of the earth' (Matthew 12:40).

[9]   Achsah Guibbory, *Christian Identity, Jews, and Israel in Seventeenth-Century England* (Oxford: Oxford University Press, 2010), 9.

[10]   Cf. Nelson, *Hebrew Republic*, 13–14.

[11]   Barbara K. Lewalski, *Protestant Poetics and the Seventeenth-Century Religious Lyric* (Princeton, NJ: Princeton University Press, 1979).

[12]   1 Samuel 8:5. Unless otherwise noted, all citations to the Old Testament are from the King James Version.

[13]   Nelson, *Hebrew Republic*, 23–56.   [14]   1 Samuel 8:9.

will take your daughters to be confectionaries, and to be cooks, and to be bakers. And he will take your fields, and your vineyards, and your oliveyards, even the best of them, and give them to his servants. And he will take the tenth of your seed, and of your vineyards, and give to his officers, and to his servants. And he will take your menservants, and your maidservants, and your goodliest young men, and your asses, and put them to his work. He will take the tenth of your sheep: and ye shall be his servants. And ye shall cry out in that day because of your king which ye shall have chosen you; and the LORD will not hear you in that day.[15]

John Calvin had argued that this speech was a warning to the Israelites that they must not resist even bad rulers. Translating מִשְׁפַּט in the opening line of the passage as 'right', rather than 'manner', Calvin notes that the kings could not behave in these ways by virtue of a *legal* right since 'the law trained them to all restraint'.[16] However, 'it was called a right in relation to the people, for they had to obey it and were not allowed to resist'.[17] This reading was later adopted and deployed by others seeking to make a case for non-resistance, including Hugo Grotius and Charles I's Chaplain Extraordinary Henry Ferne.[18] James I offers a similar reading, interpreting the speech as a warning meant to 'prepare their hearts... [for] the due obedience of that King, which God was to give unto them'.[19] That God consents to this arrangement is proof that he embraces a doctrine of non-resistance. That the Israelites consent to it is evidence that they have forever renounced their rights against their kings. As Robert Filmer would later put it after citing James's interpretation with approval, the Israelites 'never shrank at these conditions proposed by Samuel, but accepted of them as such as all other nations were bound unto'.[20] James concludes that since this 'Kingdom and Monarchy of the Jews' was 'founded by God himself', it 'ought to be a pattern for all Christian and well founded Monarchies'. And, if this is the case, 'what liberty can broiling spirits, and rebellious minds claim justly to against any Christian Monarchy[?]'.[21]

Similarly, in his defence of the Elizabethan Religious Settlement and royal supremacy over the church, Richard Hooker invokes the example of the Israelite kings as a pattern for England. 'It was not thought fit', he writes, 'in the Jews' Commonwealth that the exercise of Supremacy Ecclesiastical should be denied unto him, to whom the exercise of Chiefty Civil did appertain, and therefore their kings were invested with both.' It was precisely because the Davidic kings enjoyed not only civil but also ecclesiastical authority that they were able to rightly make 'those laws and orders,

---

[15] 1 Samuel 8:11–18.   [16] Calvin refers here to Deuteronomy 17:14–20.

[17] John Calvin, *Institutes of the Christian Religion*, ed. John T. McNeill, trans. Ford Lewis Battles (Philadelphia, PA: Westminster Press, 1960), ii, 1514.

[18] Hugo Grotius, *De Imperio Summarum Potestatum Circa Sacra*, trans. Harm-Jan Van Dam (Leiden: Brill, 2001), i, 213–15; Henry Ferne, *A Reply unto Severall Treatises Pleading for the Armes Now Taken up by Subjects in the Pretended Defence of Religion and Liberty* (Oxford, 1643), 56.

[19] James VI and I, *The Trew Law of Free Monarchies*, in *King James VI and I: Political Writings*, ed. J. P. Sommerville (Cambridge: Cambridge University Press, 1994), 67.

[20] Robert Filmer, *Patriarcha*, in *Patriarcha and Other Writings*, ed. J. P. Sommerville (Cambridge: Cambridge University Press, 1991), 37.

[21] James VI and I, *Trew Law*, 70.

which the Sacred History speaketh of concerning the matter of mere religion, the affairs of the Temple and Service of God'.[22] For Hooker, as for James I, the fact that such an arrangement prevailed among 'God's chosen people' and persisted with 'approbation from heaven' lends it divine authority and makes it an exemplary model for England.[23] Because the Elizabethan settlement is itself 'according to the pattern of God's own ancient elect people', it has a powerful and divinely sanctioned legitimacy that should protect it against arguments for the independence or separation of civil and ecclesiastical authority.[24]

However, these associations of England with Israel and English monarchs with the Davidic kings extended far beyond the realm of intellectual argument. Both political and popular representations of monarchical power repeatedly affirmed these Hebraic connections. During a visit to Norwich as part of Elizabeth I's 1578 royal progress through the English countryside, the city's mayor spoke of the people's great joy in receiving their Queen: 'the spirit and lively blood tickle in our arteries and small veins, in beholding thee the light of this Realm (as David was in Israel)'.[25] After the failed invasion of England by the Spanish Armada in 1588, James VI of Scotland (shortly to become James I of England) compared the 'defeat' to David's triumph over the Philistines. This proved an apt Hebraic connection for James, who would eventually cast himself as a modern-day Solomon—David's successor, who ruled over a peaceful, united kingdom and built the first Temple.[26] Many others would affirm this association both during James's life and after his death. Bishop John Williams's sermon at the king's funeral, *Great Britains Salomon*, imagined James interred in Solomon's 'glorious tomb', along with the other great kings of Judah.[27] Less than a decade later, at the beginning of England's civil war, Charles I ordered the publication of a series of devotions drawn from 'King David's Psalms' and selected to console and encourage the king's supporters.[28] As parliamentarians and radicals were fanning the flames of war and revolution, these devotions 'represented Charles as David, who had also faced the rebellion of his subjects. The analogy asserted Charles's sacred authority. It also implied that the kingdom was not at the point of dissolution, despite appearances.[29] England's monarchs understood themselves and were understood by many of their people in Davidic terms.

While challengers of royal supremacy and absolute sovereignty also saw the Old Testament as an authoritative statement of God's political preferences, they resisted the monarchist interpretation of these preferences. For example, in the midst of the religious and ecclesiastical debates of the English Civil War, Presbyterian theologian

---

[22] Richard Hooker, *Of the Laws of Ecclesiastical Polity*, ed. Arthur Stephen McGrade (Cambridge: Cambridge University Press, 1989), 128–9.

[23] Ibid., 153.   [24] Ibid., 138.

[25] John Nichols, *The Progresses and Public Processions of Queen Elizabeth* (London: John Nichols and Son, 1823), ii, 140.

[26] Guibbory, *Christian Identity*, 33–55.

[27] John Williams, *Great Britains Salomon* (London, 1625), 7.

[28] [Anon.], *Mercurius Davidicus, or A Patterne of Loyall Devotion* (Oxford, 1643), 1.

[29] Guibbory, *Christian Identity*, 124.

George Gillespie wrote a pamphlet that staged a dialogue between a 'civilian' and a 'divine' about the proper relationship between church and state. He uses the example of biblical Israel to counter an argument not only for royal but for *civil* supremacy over the church. The civilian notes that he has 'heard it asserted by some learned men, that among the Jews, there was no government nor discipline in the Church distinct from the government of the State . . . but that the Jewish Church was the Jewish State, and the Jewish State the Jewish Church.' Echoing Gillespie's own views, the divine resists this conclusion. First, he notes, while 'the Jewish Church and Commonwealth were for the most part not different materially, the same men being members of both', they were nonetheless still distinct as a matter of institutional design and ordinary practice. Second, he observes that the government of the polity changed over time. The Israelites adopted or endured different political and constitutional arrangements 'under the Judges, under the Kings, and after the captivity: shall we therefore say the Church was altered and new moulded, as oft as the Civil government was changed[?]'[30] As the divine ultimately concludes, the association of political and ecclesiastical authority is historically contingent and variable. An appeal to the example of the biblical Israelites cannot therefore ground an argument for civil supremacy.

In the midst of these debates about church and state, English parliamentarians were turning to the Old Testament to resist Charles I and to make the case for war. After a series of successful ad hoc Fast Day sermons beginning in 1640, the House of Commons began a regular programme of them in 1641 and printed those of which it particularly approved. These sermons are marked by their Hebraic preoccupations.[31] Many Parliamentary preachers drew their audience's attention to the less savory kings in the Davidic line. Preaching in 1643, Arthur Salwey spoke of Ahab, king of Israel and husband to the foreign Jezebel. Ahab, Salwey argued, had urged his people into the idolatrous service of Baal, likely at Jezebel's behest. The implicit political parallels would have been clear to Salwey's audience—the 'popish' ceremonialism of the Church of England under Archbishop Laud was akin to serving Baal. Ahab 'was Charles, seduced to idolatry by his Catholic wife, Henrietta Maria'.[32] Salwey urged the parliamentarians to play the zealous prophet Elijah to Charles's idolatrous Ahab— 'down with Baal's altars, down with Baal's priests'.[33] These Hebraic parallels would have been ominous ones for Charles's royalist supporters. Both Ahab and Jezebel met

---

[30] George Gillespie, *A Late Dialogue Betwixt a Civilian and a Divine Concerning the Present Condition of the Church of England* (London, 1644), 18–19. See also Charles W. A. Prior, 'Hebraism and the Problem of Church and State in England, 1642–1660', *The Seventeenth Century* 28.1 (2013), 37–61.

[31] Christopher Hill notes that 'of 240 sermons which got into print, the texts of 181 were drawn from the Old Testament, 59 from the New: a ratio of 3 to 1 . . . From November 1640 to October 1645, the preponderance of the Old Testament is even more remarkable: 123 texts to the New Testament's 26, a ratio of 4 ¾ to 1.' Christopher Hill, *The English Bible and the Seventeenth-Century Revolution* (London: Penguin Press, 1993), 83.

[32] Guibbory, *Christian Identity*, 99.

[33] Arthur Salwey, *Halting Stigmatiz'd in a Sermon Preached to the Honorable House of Commons* (London, 1644), 19.

with the violent and gruesome ends foretold by Elijah.[34] Ahab was hit by a stray arrow in battle and bled to death in a chariot. A few years later, Jezebel was defenestrated and eaten by dogs.

Other preachers turned to an earlier time in Israelite history—one uncorrupted by the rule of human kings. Addressing Parliament after a series of royalist military victories in 1643, William Greenhill invited its members to be 'the worthies of our Israel, to repair her breaches, and settle her foundations'. He concluded by calling upon them to intercede with an angry God: 'You that are the Mosesses that sit at the stern, and know all passages, hasten to the Lord, pour out your hearts before him, your sighs, tears, prayers may... secure the kingdom.'[35] Not long after, Henry Scudder echoed this call, casting parliamentarians as the 'repairers of our breaches' and urging them to be 'Mosesses and Phineasses to our Israel'.[36] For these preachers and for their audience, the Davidic kings offered lessons in the dangers of idolatry and corruption, while the Mosaic period offered an enticing model of political founding and new beginnings. Parliamentarians differed, of course, about what such new beginnings might look like. Many envisioned a constitutional monarchy, others advocated more robust forms of parliamentary supremacy, while an increasing number of more radical members pursued republican alternatives.

Like these Fast Day preachers, English republicans would turn to the Mosaic period, finding in it the model for a divine polity with no earthly king.[37] These republican interpretations would only begin to receive their fullest articulations in the Interregnum. However, these later interpretations give us some idea of what Parliament's republicans might have had in mind. For James Harrington, as well as for many of his seventeenth-century republican contemporaries, the Mosaic polity was a 'commonwealth' of the sort he advocated for England. On Harrington's account, the crucial political moment for the Israelites comes not with their covenant with God at Sinai, but when a weary and frustrated Moses cries out, 'I cannot carry all this people by myself, for it is too much for me.'[38] In response, God instructs him to appoint seventy elders (in Harrington's reading, a 'senate' of sorts) for assistance. From this point onward, Harrington argues, Israel had a mixed constitution of the kind favoured by republicans. Moses stood 'no more alone', but was now 'prince of the senate, which God appointed to stand with him'.[39] While God, Moses, or the senate might *propose* laws, the power of *resolution* or decision

[34] 1 Kings 22:29–40; 2 Kings 9:30–7.
[35] William Greenhill, *The Axe at the Root, a Sermon Preached before the Honorable House of Commons* (London, 1643), epistle, p. 50.
[36] Henry Scudder, *Gods Warning to England by the Voyce of His Rod... A Sermon Preached... before the Honourable House of Commons* (London, 1644), epistle.
[37] Graham Hammill, *The Mosaic Constitution: Political Theology and Imagination from Machiavelli to Milton* (Chicago, IL: University of Chicago Press, 2012), 208–42; Nelson, *Hebrew Republic*, 37–56.
[38] Numbers 11:14.
[39] James Harrington, *Pian Piano*, in *The Political Works of James Harrington*, ed. J. G. A. Pocock (Cambridge: Cambridge University Press, 1977), 376.

on these propositions rested with the people as the ultimate source of legal and political authority.[40] In Harrington's hands, the Mosaic polity became a Roman commonwealth.

Just as the Mosaic polity provided a pattern worthy of imitation, so its ultimate fate offered a cautionary example for England. After the death of Moses's successor, Joshua, the Israelites, 'mindless of the excellent orders of their commonwealth', allowed their institutions to decay. In the anarchy that ensued, the Israelites appointed judges or, in Harrington's Roman reading, 'dictators'. The failure of these leaders to guarantee a stable order prompted the popular demand for a king and the transition to monarchical rule, 'under which [Israel] fared worse'.[41] For Harrington and his fellow republicans, Samuel's harrowing warning about kingly rule was not, as defenders of monarchical authority had maintained, a list of kingly behaviours against which subjects must not resist. Echoing early monarchomach arguments, republicans read the passage as a prophetic caution that would ultimately be vindicated in the profound moral failures of the bad Davidic kings and the idolatrous missteps of the good ones.[42] As his republican contemporaries John Milton and Algernon Sidney argued in even clearer terms, the Israelites had sinned against God by asking for a king. Their yearning for monarchy, their desire to have a king 'like all other nations', was itself a form of idolatry that ought to have been resisted.[43] No longer safe in the hands of absolutists and defenders of royal supremacy, the Old Testament proved as powerful and authoritative a tool for parliamentarians and republicans as it had for monarchists.

7.2 The Road Not Taken: Davidic Kingship

Given the core commitments of his political philosophy, as well as his diagnosis of the causes of civil war, it is hardly surprising that Thomas Hobbes thought that the *content* of these challenges to absolute sovereignty and civil control of the church demanded a response. However, he was also increasingly concerned by these challengers' scriptural *modes* of argument as well. In order to see why, consider what Hobbes himself tells us about the circumstances in which he came to write *Leviathan*.[44] Despite having fled

---

[40] James Harrington, *The Prerogative of Popular Government*, in *Political Works of James Harrington*, 421.

[41] Harrington, *Pian Piano*, 378.

[42] James Harrington, *The Art of Lawgiving*, in *Political Works of James Harrington*, 599–704; Ronald Beiner, 'James Harrington on the Hebrew Commonwealth', *The Review of Politics* 76.2 (2014), 169–93. For earlier monarchomach readings of the passage, see George Buchanan, *A Dialogue on the Law of Kingship among the Scots*, ed. and trans. Roger A. Mason and Martin S. Smith (Aldershot: Ashgate, 2004), 109–11; [Anon.], *Vindiciae, Contra Tyrannos*, ed. and trans. George Garnett (Cambridge: Cambridge University Press, 1994), 128–9. Indeed, it is Buchanan and others to whom James VI/I's reading of the passage is responding.

[43] John Milton, *A Defence of the People of England*, in *Complete Prose Works of John Milton*, ed. Don M. Wolfe, trans. Donald C. Mackenzie (New Haven, CT: Yale University Press, 1966), iv, 301–537; Algernon Sidney, *Discourses Concerning Government*, ed. Thomas G. West (Indianapolis, IN: Liberty Fund, 1996); Algernon Sidney, *Court Maxims*, ed. Hans W. Blom, Eco Haitsma-Mulier, and Ronald Janse (Cambridge: Cambridge University Press, 1996); Nelson, *Hebrew Republic*, 37–55.

[44] Hobbes's description of these circumstances echoes the one he gives in the preface to the second edition of *De Cive*.

to Paris in November or December of 1640, he monitored events in England quite closely. It was the spring of 1646.[45] He had immersed himself in the development of his systematic philosophy, resuming work on *De Corpore*. However, in July, the young prince Charles and his entourage arrived in Paris with fresh news of royalist defeats, which the king's enemies were interpreting as evidence of God's support for the parliamentarian cause. Hobbes writes that he 'could not bear to hear such terrible crimes attributed to the commands of God'. He set *De Corpore* aside and, determined 'to write something that would absolve the divine laws', turned his attention to the work that would become *Leviathan*.[46] Hobbes's alarmed response not only to the rebellious doctrines circulating in England but also to their scriptural modes of expression suggest one explanation for his increasing use of biblical argument in his political philosophy. And, as biblical Israel had assumed such a central and authoritative place in the scriptural politics of the civil war, it is hardly surprising that Hobbes focused substantial attention on the Old Testament.

What is more puzzling, however, is the period of Israelite history on which Hobbes comes to focus his attention in *Leviathan*. As we saw at the outset, his patterns of scriptural citation suggest that he focuses a substantial amount of this attention on the Mosaic period, especially compared to that which he gives to the era of the Davidic kings. Indeed, in *Leviathan* Hobbes devotes much of his scriptural argument to showing that Moses is a paradigmatic Leviathan sovereign. Having concluded the work's philosophical argument, he acknowledges that there may be some who reject it. However, he goes on, 'supposing that these of mine are not such Principles of Reason; yet I am sure they are Principles from Authority of Scripture; as I shall make it appear, when I shall come to speak of the Kingdome of God, (administered by *Moses*,) over the Jewes, his peculiar people by Covenant'.[47] Hobbes repeatedly refers to the sovereign as he who sits in 'Moses seat' or holds 'the place of Moses' and thus continues a pattern set by this exemplary figure.[48] However, as we shall see, the interpretive challenges of appropriating Moses as a Leviathan sovereign are much more pronounced than they would have been in the case of the Davidic kings. What is more, there was a robust contextual precedent for justifying both absolute sovereignty and civil supremacy over religion by appeal to the Davidic kings. Given these interpretive challenges and contextual

---

[45] Hobbes's own dating of the start of his work on *Leviathan* is contested because his account was written after the Restoration and he may have had cause to cast his motivations in a pro-Stuart light. That Hobbes might, writing years later, have been somewhat muddled about the precise chronology of his work on *Leviathan* seems plausible. That his account of his motivations was significantly distorted by a desire to establish his royalist credentials with the restored Stuarts is less so. And it is the question of motivations, rather than dating, that is important for my argument here. The preface to the revised edition of *De Cive*, along with several of the arguments in that work and an even greater number of those in *Leviathan*, show that Hobbes was deeply concerned with refuting arguments that God's laws justified rebellion against any established sovereign.

[46] As quoted in Quentin Skinner, *Reason and Rhetoric in the Philosophy of Hobbes* (Cambridge: Cambridge University Press, 1996), 330–1. These are Skinner's own translations of Hobbes's Latin verse autobiography.

[47] L, 30, p. 522.   [48] E.g. L, 41, p. 766; 40, p. 744.

precedents, I suggest, we need an account of why it is that Hobbes decided to engage the Hebraic debates of his time in overwhelmingly Mosaic terms. Such an account, I will ultimately argue, tells us something important about Hobbes's rhetorical strategy.

The biblical Moses is a famously reluctant prophet. He claims that a speech impediment renders him unqualified to serve as a representative of God and the Israelites.[49] While these worries turn out to have been unfounded, what does seem clear is that Moses lacks some of the most basic qualifications to serve as an exemplar of Hobbes's Leviathan sovereign. To see why, we need to consider Hobbes's account of the history of biblical Israel. For Hobbes, the kingdom of God over the Israelites 'is a reall, not a metaphoricall Kingdome'.[50] God did not just rule over the Israelites *naturally* by his might', as he did over all men, but also as a civil sovereign over his *'peculiar* Subjects'.[51] As their king and civil sovereign, God governed the Israelites 'and none but them, not onely by naturall Reason, but by Positive Lawes, which he gave them by the mouths of his holy Prophets'.[52] Moses and his successors served as God's 'Lieutenants, or Vicars', conveying His commands to the Israelites.[53] In this important sense, their authority was the product of 'divine right', which Hobbes thought was a profoundly unstable basis for political obligation.[54] To the extent that they ruled, they did so as God's instruments, 'by Authority immediate from God'.[55] Because Moses and his successors were merely intermediaries, it is possible for Hobbes to say that the polity of the Israelites was 'an utterly free regime' whose people were not 'subject to any human power'.[56] When questions arose about who had the authority to serve as a divine intermediary and instrument, God would occasionally intervene directly. When Corah, Dathan, and Abiram gathered 'two hundred and fifty Princes of the assembly' to accuse Moses and Aaron of unjustly elevating themselves above the rest of His holy people, 'God caused the Earth to swallow' the three leaders 'with their wives and children alive, and consumed those two hundred and fifty Princes with fire'.[57]

This system of divine sovereignty came to an end when the Israelites, frustrated by the anarchy of private judgement and corruption during the period of the Judges, asked Samuel for 'a king to judge us like all the nations'.[58] For Hobbes, much hinges on the fact that Davidic kingship is the product of a popular request to be ruled 'like all the nations'. As Michael Walzer has pointed out with reference to the biblical text, there is an important sense in which this request is impossible. For Israel's neighbours in the ancient Near East, monarchy would have been seen as 'the divine and natural form of government'. The fact that the Israelites 'imagine a king being made at their instance means that he can't be a king like the kings of all other nations'.[59] Yet the very thing that makes the request impossible makes it a boon for Hobbes's purposes. Like

---

[49] E.g. Exodus 4:10, 6:12, 6:30.   [50] L, 35, p. 642.   [51] L, 35, p. 634.   [52] L, 31, p. 556.
[53] L, 35, p. 644.   [54] I discuss the reasons for this in section 7.3.   [55] L, 40, p. 748.
[56] DCv, 17.7. Hobbes removes this language about the freedom of the polity of the Israelites in *Leviathan*.
[57] L, 40, p. 744. See also Numbers 16:1–35.   [58] 1 Samuel 8:5.
[59] Michael Walzer, *In God's Shadow: Politics in the Hebrew Bible* (New Haven, CT: Yale University Press, 2012), 54.

the Leviathan sovereign, the authority of the Davidic kings is artificial—the product of human will. That the Israelites choose to subject themselves to monarchical authority even after hearing Samuel's harrowing litany of kingly abuses is, for Hobbes, evidence of an especially robust and informed consent.[60] While his monarchist forerunners and contemporaries had appropriated members of the Davidic line to ground arguments for divine right, Hobbes shows that their authority can plausibly be read as the product of popular consent.

Hobbes argues that the Israelites' request for a king amounted to a rejection of 'that peculiar Government of God'.[61] When God granted this request, he ceased to be the Israelites' civil sovereign and, from then on, ruled them as he did all other people—by natural reason alone. The Davidic kings then exercised rightful jurisdiction over both civil and spiritual affairs, 'for there was no other Word of God in that time by which to regulate Religion, but the Law of Moses, which was their Civill Law'.[62] These kings were thus in a situation tightly analogous to contemporary civil sovereigns, whose authority is grounded in a social contract borne of an acute awareness of the inconveniences and dangers of anarchy. In the succeeding period, which will endure until the restoration of divine rule with the Second Coming of Christ, argues Hobbes, the political and ecclesiastical authority of civil sovereigns is grounded in consent, rather than divine right. God no longer intervenes directly to make his will known. In the absence of miraculous manifestations of divine will, we can rely only on Scripture and by right it falls to the civil sovereign to interpret its commands for his people.[63] Thus, in contrast to Moses, who occupies a different stage of sacred history and stands in a markedly different relationship to divine authority, Hobbes's *own* account of the Davidic kings suggests that they shared the primary attributes of the Leviathan sovereign. Given his own textual account of the history and development of the polity of the Israelites, Hobbes's decision to appeal to Moses and not one or more of the Davidic kings as the central biblical exemplar of sovereign power remains a puzzling one.

While there are no clear textual grounds for Hobbes to avoid selecting a biblical sovereign exemplar from among the Davidic kings, perhaps there were contextual reasons for the decision. One strikes me as at least potentially plausible. Parliamentarians and republicans had found in the history of the Davidic line a catalogue of monarchical abuses. As we have seen, these abuses offered compelling fodder for parliamentary fast sermons, which tended to emphasize the idolatrous and despotic habits of the biblical kings. Perhaps Hobbes was eager to choose a biblical exemplar less tainted by these tyrannical associations. The problem with this suggestion is that the appalling behaviour of several of the Davidic kings was an asset for Hobbes's line of argument.

---

[60] L, 20, p. 316; DCv, 11.6. Hobbes's reasoning here echoes an argument more fully laid out in James VI and I, *Trew Law*, 70. Where Hobbes differs from James and other earlier thinkers who relied on the passage to ground claims about non-resistance is that Hobbes reads the passage as one that unambiguously describes the rights of the king. See DCv, 11.6; L, 20, p. 316.

[61] L, 40, p. 750; see also Nelson, *Hebrew Republic*, 23–6, 53–6.

[62] L, 40, p. 752.   [63] L, 32, p. 584.

Consider the brief use he makes of Saul—a jealous, deceptive, and murderous king and therefore hardly a paragon of monarchical virtue. Saul was a brute, Hobbes acknowledges. Yet David, the king's primary rival and ultimate successor, refused to slay him and likewise forbade his servants from doing so. This, for Hobbes, serves as scriptural proof that the power of sovereigns is absolute and that 'Kings cannot be punished by their subjects'.[64] That Saul was every bit as tyrannical as parliamentarians and republicans alleged is essential for Hobbes's argument. No matter how terrible their kings, the Israelites had no legitimate right to revolution and regicide.[65] And they knew it. As for Israel, so too for England. Far from wanting to avoid the tyrannical associations of the Davidic kings, Hobbes had good reason to embrace them. We must, then, look elsewhere for an explanation of Hobbes's Mosaic turn.

7.3 Subversive Integration: Mosaic Leviathan

I suggest that the best way to make sense of Hobbes's Mosaic turn is to see it as an instance of a broader strategy of 'subversive integration'.[66] This strategy begins by accepting the basic premises of parliamentarians and republicans but ends by showing how these premises can support substantially less radical conclusions. As Quentin Skinner has shown, this is precisely what Hobbes does in his account of the social contract. Parliamentarian propagandists like Henry Parker had sought to resist divine right arguments by arguing that the rule of kings is neither natural nor instituted by God. The natural state is one of perfect freedom in which men possess complete powers of self-government. Any legitimate form of political authority, then, must be grounded in the 'common consent and agreement' of all those subject to it and expressed in the form of 'Pactions and agreements'.[67] Free and equal people would hardly yield all of their natural liberty to a king. They would institute a form of limited government in which the king held his authority conditionally as a trust.[68]

Rather than attempting a point-by-point criticism and rejection of this account, Hobbes seeks to discredit the parliamentarian argument 'by demonstrating that it is possible to accept the basic structure of their theory without in the least endorsing any of the radical implications they had drawn from it'.[69] He affirms the foundational premises of the argument—that political authority is artificial, that the natural state of man is one of perfect freedom, and that any legitimate political authority must be grounded in consent expressed in the form of a social contract. Hobbes's innovation is

---

[64] DCv, 11.3.

[65] Once again, Hobbes's reasoning here closely tracks an argument in James VI and I, *Trew Law*, 70.

[66] I borrow this term from Franck Lessay, who uses it to characterize Hobbes's approach to covenant theology. Franck Lessay, 'Hobbes's Covenant Theology and Its Political Implications', in *The Cambridge Companion to Hobbes's Leviathan*, ed. Patricia Springborg (Cambridge: Cambridge University Press, 2007), 258.

[67] Henry Parker, *Observations upon Some of His Majesties Late Answers and Expresses* (London, 1642), 1.

[68] Ibid., 4.

[69] Quentin Skinner, 'Hobbes on Representation', *European Journal of Philosophy*, 13.2 (2005), 169.

to show that with an appropriately frightening account of man's natural state and a proper appreciation for the instability of limited government, these parliamentarian premises can easily ground absolutist conclusions. But Hobbes's use of the strategy came at a high cost. Those who would otherwise have been friendly to the work's political conclusions saw in its premises the seeds of rebellion. Bishop Bramhall, for instance, suggested that *Leviathan* might have been better titled the *Rebel's Catechism*.[70]

Given that Hobbes uses a strategy of subversive integration in the philosophical arguments, it seems reasonable to think that such a strategy is at work in his scriptural argument. And this may explain why he turns increasingly to the history of the Mosaic polity and, despite all the interpretive difficulties of doing so, seeks to elevate Moses—the Hebraic hero of his parliamentarian and republican contemporaries—to the position of paradigmatic Leviathan sovereign. However, in order for Moses to serve as an exemplar in this way, Hobbes must embark on a radical reinterpretation of the locus, basis, and scope of political authority in the Mosaic polity. The Israelite Kingdom of God, Hobbes explains, was a civil kingdom. God ruled over the Israelites as their civil sovereign and chose Moses alone to serve as his 'Lieutenant' or 'Viceregent'.[71] On this account, the ultimate locus of political authority was God. Moses exercised political authority merely on God's behalf. This fact seems to pose a serious problem for any attempt to use Moses as an exemplar of Leviathan sovereignty, which, as Hobbes is at pains to insist, must be both unified and supreme.

Hobbes's unorthodox solution to this problem is to cast God as a *silent* sovereign. Frightened of his awesome power, the Israelites ask to be protected from immediate access to God: 'And all the people saw the thunderings, and the lightnings, and the noise of the trumpet, and the mountain smoking: and when the people saw it, they removed, and stood afar off. And they said unto Moses, Speak though with us, and we will hear: but let not God speak with us, lest we die.'[72] At their own behest, God did not speak to the Israelites directly, but rather 'by the mediation of Moses'.[73] As Bryan Garsten puts it, 'God was effectively silent from the perspective of the people.'[74] Moses is the only authoritative interpreter of God's will. His authority to render this will law and to enforce it is therefore, from the perspective of the Israelites, as unified and supreme as that of any Leviathan sovereign.

However, God's silence raises an important question about the basis of Moses's authority. If God did not speak to the Israelites directly and if Moses's authority derived solely from the fact that God spoke *only* to him, 'it appeareth not as yet, that the people were obliged to take him for God's Lieutenant, longer than they beleeved that God spake unto him'. This, for Hobbes, is one problem with any form of political authority

---

[70] John Bramhall, *Castigations of Mr. Hobbes His Last Animadversions in the Case Concerning Liberty and Universal Necessity Wherein All His Exceptions About That Controversie Are Fully Satisfied* (London, 1657), 515.

[71] L, 40, pp. 738–40; 41, p. 331.   [72] Exodus 20:18–19.   [73] L, 40, p. 740.

[74] Bryan Garsten, 'Religion and Representation in Hobbes', in *Leviathan*, ed. Ian Shapiro (New Haven, CT: Yale University Press, 2010), 536.

grounded in divine right. Such an account of the basis for political authority only works to secure obedience as long as subjects continue to believe that their sovereign is chosen by God. When belief fails, the grounds of obedience dissolve and subjects are no longer 'obliged to take any thing for the law of God, which [their sovereign] propounded to them in God's name'.[75] In order for this belief to remain stable in perpetuity, subjects will require repeated supernatural signs of the divine favour of their sovereign. It is for this reason that the subjects of sovereigns who rule by divine right are, on Hobbes's view, miracle-hungry. The experience of the Israelite polity under Moses illustrates the problem well. Despite the many miracles performed during the exodus from Egypt, the absence of Moses and his attendant miracles for a mere forty days caused the Israelites to relapse 'into the Idolatry of the Egyptians'.[76] While belief can certainly ease the path of obedience, sovereign authority that rests on belief alone is always vulnerable to the whimsy of subjects.

It is therefore important for Hobbes that the authority of Moses not be seen to rest only (or even primarily) on his status as God's chosen instrument. It is crucial that his authority, 'as the authority of all other princes, must be grounded on the consent of the people and their promise to obey him'.[77] Here again, the Israelites' terrified request that Moses speak to God on their behalf is central to Hobbes's account. Hobbes finds in this request their moment of consent and their promise of 'absolute obedience to *Moses*'.[78] It was by this request that 'they obliged themselves to obey whatsoever [Moses] should deliver unto them for the Commandment of God'.[79] And though their consent is, in typical Hobbesian fashion, born of fear, it is not undertaken hastily. As Hobbes reminds us, the Israelites were not only 'wholly free' when they consented 'but also totally hostile to human subjection because of their recent experience of Egyptian slavery'.[80] The Israelites, like the subjects of the Leviathan state, assumed the burdens of the law fearfully but willingly.

The vision of political authority that emerges against the backdrop of a silent God and a consenting people is one whose scope encompasses both civil and religious questions. Here again, a consideration of the weakness of political authority founded on divine right is essential. Even if subjects do manage to maintain a stable belief that their sovereign rules by divine right, this basis for political authority is a dangerously promiscuous one. As Kinch Hoekstra puts the problem, 'just as belief in the divine inspiration of the sovereign would further his authority, so belief in the inspiration of a subject would further his authority, at the expense of the sovereign's. If divinity or special access to divinity confers authority, then it is difficult to restrict the author-ity to the sovereign, as nothing can stop God from entering into or communicating with whomever he chooses.'[81] Without God's public affirmation of his own will, this

[75] L, 40, p. 740.   [76] L, 12, p. 184.   [77] L, 40, p. 740.
[78] L, 20, p. 316.   [79] L, 40, p. 740.   [80] DCv, 16.8.
[81] Kinch Hoekstra, 'Disarming the Prophets: Thomas Hobbes and Predictive Power', *Rivista di Storia della Filosofia* 59.1 (2004), 128.

proliferation of claims to divine authority could continue almost indefinitely. This, on Hobbes's reading, was precisely what had happened in the lead-up to the English Civil War. Self-styled prophets claimed divine inspiration in order to authorize their challenges to civil sovereignty.[82] Hobbes's response to this problem was, at least in part, to insist again on the effective silence of God. While it is possible that God speaks directly to particular individuals, he does not confirm his will publicly to the rest of us. Divine inspiration cannot therefore ground any claim of political or religious authority. The only authoritative public expression of God's will is Scripture, which is subject to competing interpretations. In order to stabilize this interpretive anarchy and to avert the threat it poses for civil peace, we must vest our civil sovereign with the sole authority to interpret Scripture.[83]

Similarly, in the Mosaic polity, the consent of the Israelites to the sovereignty of Moses amounted to an agreement that he would be the sole legitimate interpreter of God's commands. While Israel had prophets of its own in the form of the seventy elders appointed by Moses to help him in the difficult work of government, God had endowed them 'with a mind conformable and subordinate to that of Moses, that they might Prophecy, that is to say, speak to the people in Gods name, in such manner, as to set forward (as Ministers of Moses, and by his authority) such doctrine as was agreeable to Moses his doctrine.'[84] Their prophetic authority came not from divine right but was rather derivative of and subordinate to the sovereign and interpretive authority of Moses. In order for this interpretive authority to remain unchallenged, the bounds of Mount Sinai were strictly policed. God instructs Moses to 'set bounds unto the people' around the mountain and to tell them: 'Take heed to yourselves, that ye go not up into the mount, or touch the border of it: whosoever toucheth the mount shall be surely put to death.'[85] In one of the greatest Hebraic analogies of *Leviathan*, Hobbes then continues:

Out of which we may conclude, that whosoever in a Christian Common-wealth holdeth the place of Moses, is the sole Messenger of God, and Interpreter of his Commandments. And according hereunto, no man ought in the interpretation of the Scripture to proceed further than the bounds which are set by their severall sovereigns. For the Scriptures since God now speaketh in them, are the Mount Sinai; the bounds whereof are the Laws of them that represent Gods Person on Earth. To look upon them, and therein to behold the wondrous works of God, and learn to fear him is allowed; but to interpret them, that is, to pry into what God saith to him whom he appointeth to govern under him, and make themselves Judges whether he govern as God commandeth him, or not, is to transgresse the bounds God hath set us, and to gaze upon God irreverently.[86]

Faced with a God who is publicly silent, Moses and the Leviathan sovereign must represent his will on earth. By reinterpreting the locus, basis, and scope of political authority in the Mosaic polity, Hobbes has attempted to take one of the most powerful

---

[82] B, p. 138.   [83] L, 32, p. 584; 40, pp. 742–6.   [84] L, 40, p. 746.
[85] Exodus 19:12; L, 40, p. 744.   [86] L, 40, pp. 744–6.

narratives of parliamentarians, republicans, and radicals and subversively integrate it into a scriptural justification of the Leviathan state.

The argument that I have offered here may strike some as implausible. After all, as much as Hobbes insists on the *exemplarity* of the Israelite kingdom of God under Moses, he is also sometimes at pains to stress its *exceptionalism*.[87] The Israelites, he repeatedly emphasizes, were God's special people or 'peculiar subjects'.[88] The particular experiences of the Israelites and their relationship to God must not, Hobbes suggests, shape the politics of the present too much. He would have wanted, for instance, to resist in the strongest possible terms the suggestion made by some of his more radical contemporaries that England should reinstate the entire legal code of the Mosaic polity.[89] Another reason for his insistence on Israelite exceptionalism is that some political and religious radicals in Hobbes's time had believed that the Kingdom of God was at hand and had, on the basis of this belief, licensed rebellion against their earthly sovereign.[90] By insisting that the kingdom of God was a civil kingdom of God's 'peculiar subjects' that came to an end with the election of Saul and would not be restored until the Second Coming of Christ, Hobbes attempts to close off this licence for rebellion by stressing the exceptionalism of the polity of the Israelites and fixing it in a securely historical past.[91]

I would suggest that this uneasy tacking back and forth between Israelite exemplarity and exceptionalism might also reflect a certain anxiety about his chosen rhetorical strategy. I have argued that Hobbes's decision to turn to the early history of the Israelite polity and to the figure of Moses in particular is part of a strategy of subversive reintegration. Recognizing that the scriptural account of the Mosaic commonwealth was especially authoritative for his parliamentarian and republican contemporaries, he sought to subversively integrate it into a defence of absolute sovereignty. As we have seen, subversive integration is both a demanding and a risky rhetorical strategy. It is demanding because it requires a radical (and perhaps often implausible) reinterpretation of the argument, imagery, or narrative one is trying to integrate. In Hobbes's hands, Moses becomes not only (or even primarily) a lieutenant of God who rules by divine right but a Leviathan sovereign who is God's sole representative on earth. This is no small feat and the two visions of the Mosaic polity ultimately rest uneasily with one another.

Subversive integration is a risky strategy because it exposes one's argument to criticisms that it might otherwise have been able to avoid. In the case of Hobbes's

---

[87] David Nirenberg, *Anti-Judaism: The Western Tradition* (New York: W. W. Norton & Co., 2013), 312–17.

[88] L, 35, 634 ff.

[89] Hobbes therefore insists on distinguishing those laws that obligated the Israelites by nature and were therefore universally applicable and those that God gave as the civil sovereign of his chosen people and were therefore particular to the Israelites. See, for example, DCv, 16.10. See also Nirenberg, *Anti-Judaism*, 300–24; Guibbory, *Christian Identity*, 21–120.

[90] L, 44, p. 960.

[91] L, 35, p. 642. Indeed, the place in *Leviathan* where Hobbes most stresses the Israelites' identity as God's 'peculiar' subjects is in chapter 35, 'Of the Signification of Kingdom of God'.

philosophical arguments, these criticisms often came from those like Bishop Bramhall and Robert Filmer who might otherwise have been sympathetic to some of the work's political conclusions. At least part of the concern in both of these cases is that, whatever conclusions Hobbes uses them to reach, parliamentarian premises and language are so suggestive and fertile that they can easily be reappropriated for more radical ends. By giving these arguments and language such systematic and persuasive expression, Hobbes may have, in spite of himself, helped rather than hindered the cause of future rebellion. We might read the uneasy tension between Israelite exemplarity and exceptionalism as a reflection of a similar anxiety on Hobbes's part. Because the polity of the Israelites under Moses was seen by Hobbes's more radical contemporaries as an especially authoritative source for political argument, it made polemical and rhetorical sense for Hobbes to redeploy it. But for the same reason, it was very difficult to control the results of that redeployment once it had been made, as Bramhall and Filmer would have been all too aware.

As it turns out, Hobbes had grounds for such concerns. While there is not, to my knowledge, evidence that his account of the Mosaic polity was taken up and redeployed by parliamentarian or republican contemporaries, other aspects of his Hebraic arguments may well have been. This is clearest in the case of his reading of the Israelites' request for a human king.[92] For Hobbes, in making this request, the Israelites reject, refuse, and depose God as their king.[93] The radical possibilities of such an argument were not lost on Hobbes's absolutist critics, who were eager to contain them. Filmer was quick to claim that the request had been borne of short-term prudential concerns, rather than a considered decision in favour of regime change: 'The people did not totally reject the Lord... they did not desire an alteration of government, and to cast off God's laws, but hoped for a certainer and speedier deliverance from danger in time of war.'[94]

Filmer was right to have been worried. The republican theorist James Harrington, who had attended closely to Hobbes's account of the polity of the Israelites and shared his Erastian commitments, seized on this reading of the request for a king as evidence that the Mosaic polity had been a popular commonwealth.[95] To reject God, Harrington reasons, 'that he should not reign over them, was as civil magistrate to depose him. The power therefore which the people had to depose even God himself as he was civil magistrate, leaveth little doubt, but that they had the power to have rejected any of those laws confirmed by them throughout the Scripture.'[96] That the Israelites had the authority to 'depose even God himself' was proof that (contra Hobbes) the Mosaic polity was an exemplary instance of popular sovereignty. Hobbes's account of the

[92] 1 Samuel 8:7.   [93] L, 12, p. 184; 29, p. 506; 35, p. 640; 40, p. 750.
[94] Robert Filmer, *Observations Concerning the Originall of Government*, in *Patriarcha and Other Writings*, 196.
[95] Harrington frequently cites Hobbes and aspects of the former's ecclesiological arguments track those of the latter quite closely. These connections were not lost on several of Harrington's contemporary critics. For detailed analysis of these connections, see J. G. A. Pocock, 'Historical Introduction', in *Political Works of James Harrington*, 77–99; Collins, *Allegiance*, 185–91; Beiner, 'Harrington on the Hebrew Commonwealth'.
[96] James Harrington, *The Commonwealth of Oceana*, in *Political Works of James Harrington*, 175.

polity of the Israelites, it would seem, was itself subject to a strategy of subversive integration.[97] A certain anxiety about this possibility may explain Hobbes's decision in the Latin *Leviathan* to remove or soften the language of several passages dealing with the Israelites' request for a king.[98] Once loosed, this politically explosive narrative of God's chosen people had proven impossible to contain.

7.4 Conclusion

I have argued that Hobbes's attention to the Old Testament can be explained by appealing to the polemical work that biblical Israel was doing in seventeenth-century England. Because it was thought to express God's political preferences, the Old Testament was authoritative. It seems plausible that Hobbes realized this and, for this reason, sought to engage extensively with it in *De Cive* and *Leviathan*. His decision to focus particularly on the Mosaic polity in *Leviathan*, I have argued, is part of a demanding and risky rhetorical strategy of subversive integration. In his extensive use of this strategy, Hobbes may well have been—if one can forgive the anachronism—'the first counter-revolutionary'.[99] More modestly, we might say that the account offered in this chapter confirms a picture of a Hobbes who, despite his exile in Paris, was deeply attuned to the political discourse in his native England. He was clearly troubled not only by the content of the political arguments that were being made by parliamentarians, republicans, and radicals, but also by their scriptural and Hebraic modes of expression. However, he also recognized the rhetorical and polemical power of Hebraic narratives and was willing to radically reinterpret them and risk the support of his political allies, in order to redeploy them.

---

[97] In response to a suggestion by the clergyman and scholar Matthew Wren that 'Mr Harrington...does silently swallow down such Notions as Mr Hobs hath chewed for him', Harrington responded that his interpretation of the Israelite request for a king can be traced back to the Roman-Jewish historian Josephus, a source 'more ancient than Hobbes'. See Harrington, *Prerogative*, 423. He does not, however, go so far as to deny that Hobbes was the proximate source of the interpretation.

[98] Cf. Nelson, *Hebrew Republic*, 25.

[99] Corey Robin, *The Reactionary Mind: Conservatism from Edmund Burke to Sarah Palin* (New York: Oxford University Press, 2011), 61.

8

Devil in the Details

Hobbes's Use and Abuse of Scripture

Paul B. Davis

As the other essays in this volume clearly demonstrate, the examination of Hobbes's religious views has been a growth industry in Hobbes studies over the past few decades. The analyses of numerous scholars, including F. C. Hood, Howard Warrender, J. G. A. Pocock, A. P. Martinich, Richard Tuck, Noel Malcolm, Eric Nelson, and Jeffrey Collins, have all been invaluable in tracing Hobbes's complex and shifting religious positions.[1] From their excavation, it is now evident that many of the most original and controversial claims in *Leviathan* were located squarely in its treatment of religion. Hobbes's theories of sense perception, the state of nature, and the duties of subjects had already been aired in *The Elements of Law* and *De Cive*, but it was only in *Leviathan* that Hobbes put forth his most radical views on revelation, prophecy, angels, demons, and the composition of the Bible itself. Indeed, in the dedicatory epistle to *Leviathan* Hobbes himself acknowledged 'That which perhaps may most offend, are certain Texts of Holy Scripture, alledged by me to other purpose than ordinarily they use to be by others.'[2]

For their comments on earlier iterations of this project and chapter, I am indebted to Eric Nelson, Richard Tuck, David Armitage, Mark Kishlansky, Mark Somos, Ada Palmer, Monica Poole, Peter Gordon, Adam Beaver, Tony Grafton, and Adrian Blau. I am also indebted to the participants of Princeton's Early Modern History Workshop, the 2013 conference of the Association for Political Theory in Nashville, Tennessee, and the 2015 meeting of the European Hobbes Society in London.

[1] Some of the most prominent works include Howard Warrender, 'The Place of God in Hobbes's Philosophy', *Political Studies* 8 (1960), 48–57; Samuel I. Mintz, *The Hunting of Leviathan* (Cambridge: Cambridge University Press, 1962); J. G. A. Pocock, 'Time, History, and Eschatology in the Thought of Thomas Hobbes', in his *Politics, Language, and Time* (New York: Athenaeum, 1971), 148–201; A. P. Martinich, *The Two Gods of Leviathan: Thomas Hobbes on Religion and Politics* (Cambridge: Cambridge University Press, 1992); Richard Tuck, 'Hobbes and Locke on Toleration', in *Thomas Hobbes and Political Theory*, ed. Mary Dietz (Lawrence, KS: University of Kansas Press, 1990), 153–71; Noel Malcolm, 'Leviathan and Biblical Criticism', *Leviathan After 350 Years*, ed. Tom Sorell and Luc Foisneau (Oxford: Oxford University Press, 2004), 241–64; Jeffrey Collins, *The Allegiance of Thomas Hobbes* (Oxford: Oxford University Press, 2005); Eric Nelson, *The Hebrew Republic: Jewish Sources and the Transformation of European Political Thought* (Cambridge, MA: Harvard University Press, 2010); and Noel Malcolm, 'General Introduction', to his edition of *Leviathan*, i (Oxford: Clarendon Press, 2012).

[2] L, 'Epistle Dedicatory', pp. 5–6.

In this chapter I will focus on those 'texts of Holy Scripture' as texts, with an eye to divergences between Hobbes's biblical quotations and the language of contemporary translations. While Hobbes's more general religious views have been studied in great detail, his use of Scripture largely remains terra incognita.[3] This is a shame because an examination of Hobbes's modifications of Scripture helps to shed light on what issues Hobbes cared about, how he composed particular sections of *Leviathan*, and whose ideas he borrowed without attribution. Hobbes's alterations were of great interest to contemporary critics like Edward Hyde and Alexander Ross and they should be of interest to modern critics as well. As Hobbes wrote in *Behemoth*, 'the interpretation of a verse in the Hebrew, Greek, or Latine Bible, is oftentimes the cause of a Civill Warre and the deposing and assassinating Gods anointed.'[4] The interpretation of Scripture was no idle hobby in the seventeenth century: Hobbes understood the stakes and so should we.

8.1   Choice and (Mis)use of Biblical Texts

The first thing to note about Hobbes's alterations to biblical language is that they are very much the exception, not the rule. Hobbes was no Hebraist, but he possessed an extensive knowledge of Greek. Indeed, his publishing career was bookended by translations of Thucydides in 1629 and Homer in the 1670s. Hobbes could have easily brought that expertise to bear on explicating biblical passages, but in actuality such interventions are exceedingly rare for the New Testament and almost non-existent for the Old.[5] Instead, his modus operandi was to adhere more or less faithfully to a single biblical translation. However, those translations differed from work to work. When Hobbes composed *De Cive* and his Latin *Critique of Thomas White's 'De Mundo'* in the 1640s, his base text was the Clementine edition of the Latin Vulgate—the standard edition for Catholics in the wake of the Counter-Reformation.[6] In Hobbes's English treatises, the story is a bit more complex. While he quoted from the Geneva Bible in the *Elements of Law*, he transitioned to using the 1611 Authorized Version (AV) commissioned by James I as his primary base text for quotations in *Leviathan*. Arrigo Pacchi's assertion, echoed by Tuck in his edition of *Leviathan*, that Hobbes's biblical quotations

---

[3] Hobbes's use of Scripture is woefully understudied, but there have been a few recent articles on the topic. See, e.g., Arrigo Pacchi, 'Hobbes and Biblical Philology in Service of the State', *Topoi* 7.3 (1988), 231–9; James Farr, 'Atomes of Scripture: Hobbes and the Politics of Biblical Interpretation', in *Thomas Hobbes and Political Theory*, 172–96; Cameron Wybrow, 'Hobbes as an Interpreter of Biblical Political Thought', in *Liberal Democracy and the Bible*, ed. Kim Ian Parker (Lewiston, NY: The Edwin Mellen Press, 1992), 39–71; Tracy B. Strong, 'How to Write Scripture: Words, Authorities, and Politics in Thomas Hobbes', *Critical Inquiry* 20.1 (1993), 128–59; Frank M. Coleman, 'Thomas Hobbes and the Hebraic Bible', *History of Political Thought* 25.4 (2004), 642–69.

[4] B, p. 302.

[5] Hobbes discussed the creation of the Septuagint in *Leviathan* and noted Cardinal Bellarmine's utilization of it, but there is no evidence that Hobbes made use of it himself. LL, 14, p. 199; 19, p. 305. For Hobbes's Hebrew (or lack thereof), see Noel Malcolm, *Aspects of Hobbes* (Oxford: Oxford University Press, 2002), 413 n. 103.

[6] Hobbes's critique of White is frequently termed 'Anti-White'. As we will see, Hobbes used a combination of the Vulgate, the Tremellius–Junius translation of the Hebrew Bible, and Beza's translation of the New Testament when composing the Latin *Leviathan*.

'were not, except occasionally, taken from contemporary translations, but from Hobbes's own rendering of what one must suppose to have been the Latin of the Vulgate' is incorrect.[7] In fact, only a tiny fraction of Hobbes's quotations were his own translations.

Hobbes's turn to the AV may have been insignificant, a mere by-product of what books he happened to have on hand in Paris, but there are reasons to think that the shift may have been more deliberate. The Geneva Bible, translated by English exiles in Calvin's theocracy who fled the reinstitution of Catholicism by Queen Mary in the 1550s, was filled with marginal notes denouncing tyranny and advocating civil disobedience on the part of the godly.[8] Both Elizabeth and her successor James I were keenly aware that its explicit support for monarchomachy posed a threat to their own authority and sought to replace the Geneva edition with more politically palatable alternatives. Despite their best efforts, however, the translation remained popular with the English people, serving as the bible of choice for so-called Puritans with 144 editions printed before 1640.

Given his views on the legitimacy of rebellion, it is easy to see why Hobbes came to prefer King James's Authorized Version, which eliminated the Geneva Bible's subversive notes. The AV also had the added virtue for Hobbes of being officially authorized by a sovereign power.[9] Whereas in *De Cive* and the *Elements of Law* Hobbes had made the conventional claim that the Bible received its authority from the testimony of the visible church, in *Leviathan* Hobbes maintained that the Bible received its canonicity from the authority of the sovereign alone.[10] For Hobbes, the question of how we know that Scripture is the word of God was incoherent: we cannot 'know' it to be so, we can only believe that it is and 'some are moved to beleeve for one, and others for other reasons'.[11] From this fideistic stance, the critical question became 'By what Authority they are made Law' to which Hobbes's predictable answer was the authority of the sovereign. As Edward Hyde, the first Earl of Clarendon, shrewdly noted, Hobbes's Erastianism placed the Bible on 'the same scale with the *Alcoran*, which hath as much autority by the stamp which the Grand *Signior* puts upon it in all his Dominion'.[12] Thomas Tenison had a similar critique, writing of Hobbes, 'He hath subjected the

---

[7] Pacchi, 'Hobbes and Biblical Philology', 231.

[8] David Daniell, *The Bible in English* (New Haven, CT: Yale University Press, 2003), 291–319; Christopher Hill, *The English Bible and the Seventeenth-Century Revolution* (London: Penguin Press, 1993), 56–9.

[9] Kinch Hoekstra, 'The *de facto* Turn in Hobbes's Political Philosophy', in *Leviathan After 350 Years*, 54.

[10] An example of that fact for Hobbes was the differing use of the Apocrypha from country to country, both between Protestantism and Catholicism and within Protestantism itself. In his response to Bramhall, Hobbes wrote: 'If it be not from the king's authority that the Scripture is law, what other authority makes it law? Here some man being of his Lordship's judgment, will perhaps laugh and say, it is the authority of God that makes them Law. I grant that. But my question is, on what authority they believe that God is the author of them?... If it be said we are to believe the Scripture upon the authority of the universal church, why are not the books we call Apocrypha the word of God as well as the rest?', EW 4, pp. 339–40.

[11] L, 33, p. 604. For *Leviathan*, I will follow Malcolm in quoting from the so-called 'Head' edition, which is widely acknowledged to be the first edition, with the similar 'Bear' and '25 Ornaments' editions viewed as later reprints. For more on these editions, see Malcolm, 'General Introduction', 197–271.

[12] Edward Hyde, *A Brief View and Survey of the Dangerous and Pernicious Errors to Church and State, in Mr. Hobbes's Book, entitled Leviathan* (Oxford, 1676), 198.

Canon of Scripture to the Civil Powers, and taught them the way of turning the Alcoran into Gospel.'[13] Hobbes was well aware of the problems his theory posed for Christians living under non-Christian rulers, but he viewed this approach as the only way to avoid both the anarchy of private interpretation and the perils of divided rule through the power of independent prelates, foreign or domestic.[14]

Authorized or not, the AV still posed problems for Hobbes's political project. One example can be found in chapter 34 of *Leviathan*, wherein Hobbes attempted to show that evidence for the existence of incorporeal spirits was absent from the Bible. Hobbes suggested that one cause of confusion on the part of incautious readers was the use of the word 'ghost' in biblical translations like the AV. After quoting from Luke 4:1, which states that Jesus was 'full of the Holy Ghost', Hobbes pointed out that in their accounts of the same event, Matthew and Mark describe Jesus as being led by 'the Holy Spirit' instead. Hobbes argued that in this context, being full of the Holy Spirit simply meant that Christ had 'Zeal to doe the work for which hee was sent'. As he put it:

to interpret it of a Ghost, is to say, that God himselfe (for so our Saviour was,) was filled with God; which is very unproper, and unsignificant. How we came to translate *Spirits,* by the word *Ghosts,* which signifieth nothing, neither in heaven, nor earth, but the Imaginary inhabitants of mans brain, I examine not: but this I say, the word *Spirit* in the text signifieth no such thing; but either properly a reall *substance,* or Metaphorically, some extraordinary *ability* or *affection* of the Mind, or of the Body.[15]

One of Hobbes's primary aims in *Leviathan* was to overturn belief in incorporeal beings through the articulation of a materialist ontology. For Hobbes, belief in ghosts was a tool of priestcraft that threatened subjects' loyalty to their sovereigns by driving them into the arms of whatever clergymen seemed to offer protection from supernatural forces. As he stated early on in *Leviathan*:

If this superstitious fear of Spirits were taken away, and with it, Prognostiques from Dreams, false Prophecies, and many other things depending thereon, by which, crafty ambitious persons abuse the simple people, men would be much more fitted than they are for civill Obedience.[16]

To remove that fear, Hobbes spent much of chapter 34 arguing that the word 'spirit' was used in the Bible to mean a variety of perfectly natural things including an inclination

---

[13] Thomas Tenison, 'Epistle Dedicatory', in *The Creed of Mr. Hobbes Examined* (London, 1670), A4 verso. This was an era of increased interest in the Qur'an; Alexander Ross's 1649 translation of Du Ryer's *L'Alcoran de Mahomet* was the first English version of the text and Hobbes's friend Henry Stubbe disseminated his sympathetic *Account of the Rise and Progress of Mahometanism* in the 1670s.

[14] Hobbes reconciled this tension by arguing that mere belief is necessary for salvation, and dissimulation is permissible if living under a regime where Christianity is forbidden. He cites one of the biblical passages favoured by advocates of Nicodemism: Naaman's decision to accompany his master to the pagan temple of Rimmon in 2 Kings 5:17. L, 42, p. 784. For other uses of this passage by Nicodemists, see Perez Zagorin's problematic but suggestive study *Ways of Lying: Dissimulation, Persecution and Conformity in Early Modern Europe* (Cambridge, MA: Harvard University Press, 1990).

[15] L, 34, p. 618.   [16] L, 2, p. 34.

to godliness, exemplary understanding, and proper obedience.[17] Since the word 'ghost' in English possessed a more supernatural connotation, Hobbes periodically emended the language of the AV to remove the troublesome term. These changes include silent revisions of 'Holy Ghost' to 'Holy Spirit' in otherwise straightforward AV quotations from 2 Esdras 14 in chapter 33, John 20:22 in chapters 34 and 42, Acts 15:28 in chapter 42, 1 John 5:7 in chapters 33 and 42, and 2 Peter 1:21 in chapter 34.[18]

However, revising the conventional meaning of spirits was not as simple as Hobbes might have hoped: in seeking to cast doubt upon supposed prophecy, Hobbes came across an additional stumbling block in 1 Samuel 18. Arguing that prophecy in the Bible often denoted 'incoherent speech' indicative of madness, Hobbes wrote: 'In the Scripture I find it also so taken [1 Sam. 18.10] in these words, *And the Evill spirit came upon Saul, and he Prophecyed in the midst of the house*.'[19] The problem with Hobbes's naturalistic account of Saul's erratic behaviour is that the AV actually says 'And it came to passe on the morrow, that the evil spirit *from God* came upon Saul, and he prophesied in the midst of the house.' Supernatural spiritual intervention on the part of God to facilitate Saul's raving would have rendered this supposed example of 'incoherent speech' more complicated, and the corresponding demystification of prophecy debatable. Instead of addressing that challenge, Hobbes simply omitted the problematic clause.[20]

When it came to descriptions of God speaking to individuals in their dreams, Hobbes demonstrated similar tendencies. For Hobbes, claims about supernatural visitations in dreams were inherently dubious: 'if a man pretend to me, that God hath spoken to him supernaturally, and immediately, and I make doubt of it, I cannot easily perceive what argument he can produce, to oblige me to beleeve it.'[21] As he put it, for a man to say that God 'hath spoken to him in a Dream, is no more then to say he dreamed that God spake to him', and Hobbes had already discussed the irrational nature of dreams in chapter 2.[22] With that in mind, it is curious to note that Hobbes rewrote Jacob's account of one such vision in Genesis 31:11 ever so slightly, claiming that 'Jacob saith thus, *The Angel of the Lord appeared to mee in my sleep*.'[23] The language of apparition is Hobbes's addition: the AV, following the Hebrew, is more definite in its claim that 'The Angel of God spake unto me in a dream'.

---

[17] L, 34, pp. 614–20.   [18] L, 33, p. 598; 34, p. 632; 42, pp. 774, 776, 890.   [19] L, 36, p. 660.

[20] In the Latin edition of *Leviathan*, this sleight of hand is absent because Hobbes omitted the verse entirely. LL, 36, p. 661. As it happens, Hobbes was not alone in finding this passage bothersome: in his edition of the Bible, the LDS prophet Joseph Smith altered the verse to read 'the evil spirit which was *not* of God'.

[21] L, 32, p. 578.   [22] L, 2, pp. 30–4.

[23] L, 34, p. 624. As Malcolm notes, Hobbes altered the quotation in the Latin *Leviathan* as well, writing '*Angelus Domini apparuit mihi in somno*' instead of the Vulgate's '*dixitque angelus Dei ad me in somnis*'. Fifteen pages later, in speaking of a similar account in Genesis 28:12, Hobbes wrote 'that is to say (as are the words of the text) *Iacob dreamed that he saw a ladder, &c.*' But once again, those are not in fact 'the words of the text': the language of the passage in the AV, the Geneva, and the original Hebrew does not indicate that the existence of the ladder is conditional on Jacob dreaming it. L, 36, p. 664.

A desire to paper over troublesome descriptions of supernatural phenomena may have led Hobbes to elide another clause in chapter 42 involving the relationship between Joshua and Israel's high priest, Eleazar. In contrast to Robert Filmer, who viewed Joshua as the sovereign successor of Moses, Hobbes maintained that it was Eleazar who served as God's viceroy after Moses's death. That distinction provided justification for Hobbes's central claim that secular and religious authority ought to be inseparable, and a passage in Numbers assisted in that effort by indicating Eleazar's primacy over Joshua. Hobbes observed that it was said of Joshua in Numbers 27 that 'He shall stand before Eleazar the Priest, who shall ask counsell for him, before the Lord, at his word shall they goe out, and at his word they shall come in, both he, and all the Children of Israel with him.'[24] From this passage, it would appear that Eleazar acted as an intermediary between Israel and God, and his word was authoritative.

However, in the AV this was not the whole story: Eleazar would 'ask counsel' for Joshua, but it was 'after the judgment of Urim before the LORD'. As John Selden had argued, the Urim and Thummim mentioned in the Bible were tools of divination that the high priest used to ascertain God's will.[25] Unfortunately for Hobbes, such divination was exactly the sort of practice he sought to discredit in his chapter on prophecy, which may explain its convenient disappearance from his quotation about Eleazar's authority.

On the topic of Eleazar's authority, another interesting change occurs in the same chapter when Hobbes discusses the establishment of the Commonwealth of Israel with Moses as its vice-regent. Hobbes was keen to show that the 'Kingdom of God' mentioned so frequently in the Bible was simply a historical entity: it existed from Moses to Samuel, ended when the Israelites chose to change their form of government to a monarchy under Saul, and would not exist again until the eventual return of Christ.[26] In Hobbes's view, belief in the contemporary existence of a spiritual 'kingdom of God' was a pernicious error that dissolved bonds of loyalty to human rulers, and could only be dismantled by showing that there had once been an actual kingdom ruled indirectly by God. In describing the 'Generation of a Commonwealth' in chapter 17 of *Leviathan*, Hobbes wrote that it was necessary for individuals in the state of nature to submit their wills and 'conferre all their power and strength upon one Man, or upon one Assembly of men', and Hobbes thought that he had found one such moment in Exodus when the children of Israel authorized Moses to exercise sovereign power on God's behalf.[27] Hobbes argued that the Israelites 'had obliged themselves... to obey Moses, in these

---

[24] L, 40, p. 748.

[25] Interestingly, Selden is the only contemporary writer that Hobbes cites approvingly in all of *Leviathan*, mentioning 'Mr. *Seldens* most excellent Treatise' on titles of honour, a work published in 1614. L, 10, p. 148.

[26] The definitive account of this argument can be found in Eric Nelson's *The Hebrew Republic*. On this point, it is worth mentioning that on several occasions Hobbes changed biblical references to the 'Kingdom of Heaven' to the 'Kingdom of God' (e.g. for Matthew 3:23). L, 42, p. 870. This was likely due to his belief that the future Kingdom of God would be a terrestrial kingdom on earth, merely ruled by a celestial sovereign. L, 38, pp. 704–6.

[27] L, 17, p. 260.

words (*Exod.* 20.19) *Speak thou to us, and we will hear thee; but let not God speak to us, lest we dye.*'[28]

Yet if one inspects this text carefully, one finds again that Hobbes had subtly altered the text in question, which in fact reads 'Speak thou *with* us, and we will hear: but let not God speak *with* us, lest we die.' Hobbes's alteration had the effect of presenting an image of explicit submission and obedience to Moses. This illustrated Hobbes's theory of state formation very nicely, but reflected the language of the Bible less well. Hobbes made identical substitutions when quoting from the same passage in chapter 20.[29]

8.2 Habits of Transcription and the Latin *Leviathan*

From the moment *Leviathan* appeared in print it was a sensation, eliciting both admiration and animosity. Hobbes's friends on the Continent clamoured for him to make a Latin translation as soon as possible, and an acquaintance in England even tried his own hand at it.[30] Hobbes initially resisted this demand, but eventually acquiesced in the 1660s. A letter from the son of his Dutch printer on 9 December 1667 reveals Hobbes's work habits: he devoted two hours a day to translation, dictating to an amanuensis on account of the weakness in his arms (likely his 'shaking palsy').[31] Unfortunately, his scribe did not understand Latin, so Hobbes gave his copy to someone else for corrections. The work was eventually published in Amsterdam in 1668.[32]

While the chronological relationship between the Latin and English *Leviathan*s would seem apparent, a handful of scholars, including Zbigniew Lubienski, F. C. Hood, and François Tricaud, have maintained that all or part of the Latin text preceded the English.[33] Their arguments for Latin anteriority have included its shorter length, less developed arguments, apparent backpedalling on certain issues, and references to the Civil War as ongoing. These claims have been plausibly countered by their opponents, and the theory remains a minority view.[34] While Noel Malcolm has done a great deal to refute the theory of Latin anteriority, Hobbes's biblical citations and quotations provide additional evidence by serving as embedded proof of the language in which he composed various sections.[35]

---

[28] L, 42, p. 814.   [29] L, 20, p. 316.   [30] C, p. 431.   [31] C, p. 693.

[32] The differences between the English and 1668 Latin versions are considerable, the net effect of which is difficult to gauge—in some places the anti-Catholicism is toned down, in others it is amplified. Quentin Skinner, *Reason and Rhetoric in the Philosophy of Hobbes* (Cambridge: Cambridge University Press, 1996), 403. For the fullest treatment of these differences, see Malcolm, 'General Introduction', 175–96.

[33] George Wright, *Religion, Politics and Thomas Hobbes* (Dordrecht: Springer, 2006), 3. For the arguments in favour of Latin anteriority, see Zbigniew Lubienski, *Die Grundlagen des ethisch-politischen System von Hobbes* (Munich: E. Reingardt, 1932), 253–73; F. C. Hood, *The Divine Politics of Thomas Hobbes: An Interpretation of Leviathan* (Oxford: Clarendon Press, 1964), 54–6; François Tricaud, 'Introduction', in Thomas Hobbes, *Léviathan*, trans. François Tricaud (Paris: Sirey, 1971), pp. xvi–xxviii; Edwin Curley, 'Purposes and Features of this Edition', in Thomas Hobbes, *Leviathan: With Selected Variants from the Latin Edition of* 1688, ed. Edwin Curley (Indianapolis, IN: Hackett, 1994), pp. lxxiii–lxxiv.

[34] The most thorough refutation of this hypothesis can be found in Malcolm, 'General Introduction', 165–95.

[35] Malcolm gestures toward this sort of analysis, ibid., 171–2 and 189–91.

There is always the possibility that a decision to opt for a particular phrasing over another was based upon careful study and consideration rather than mere copying from another text. Hobbes might have done serious research in various languages and each alteration reflected a deliberate, scholarly decision. In that case, alterations would fail to say anything useful about the language of composition—only Hobbes's unwillingness to justify his editorial decisions. Fortunately, that does not seem to be the case. By looking at instances where he was clearly copying from another source, Hobbes's habits of transcription become quite apparent.

For example, take these three quotations from chapter 31: '*God is King, let the Earth rejoice* [Psal. 96. 1.]', '*God is King though the Nations be angry; and he that sitteth on the Cherubins, though the earth be moved* [Psal. 98. 1.]', '*How Good* (saith *David*) *is the God of Israel to those that are Upright in Heart; and yet my feet were almost gone, my treadings had well-nigh slipt; for I was grieved at the Wicked, when I saw the Ungodly in such Prosperity* [Psal. 72. ver. 1, 2, 3].'[36] All three passages differ from the language of the AV and every other English translation: 'The Lord reigneth; let the earth rejoice', 'The Lord reigneth; let the people tremble: he sitteth between the cherubims; let the earth be moved', 'Truly God is good to Israel, even to such as are of a clean heart. But as for me, my feet were almost gone; my steps had well nigh slipped. For I was envious of the foolish, when I saw the prosperity of the wicked.' Above and beyond any differences in language, the numerical citations for all three quotations are inaccurate: if English readers attempted to look them up, they would have been extremely perplexed since the relevant passages are found in Psalms 97, 99, and 73, respectively.

To understand why Hobbes depicts God sitting on the cherubim instead of between them, one need only look up the original citations in the Vulgate: 'Dominus regnavit, exultet terra', 'Dominus regnavit, irascantur populi: qui sedet super cherubim, moveatur terra', 'Quam bonus Israel Deus his, qui recto sunt corde. Mei autem pene moti sunt pedes: pene effusi sunt gressus mei. Quia zelavi super iniquos, pacem peccatorum videns.' Hobbes evidently made his own translations of these passages and copied over the corresponding citations without realizing that the Vulgate differed from English bibles in its numbering of the Psalms.

This would seem to suggest that these passages in *Leviathan* had been copied from a previous Latin text, and indeed, they likely were, but unfortunately for the proponents of Latin *Leviathan* anteriority there is a simpler explanation that accords with the chronology of publication: these quotations and citations are found in chapter 15 of *De Cive*, which closely mirrors *Leviathan*'s chapter 31. Similarly, Latinate quotations in chapter 20 of *Leviathan* were also evidently copied over from chapter 11 of *De Cive*. While the changes in language and errors in citation do point to an original Latin source, it is not the Latin *Leviathan*. In fact, the divergent Psalm numbering proves problematic for the Latin *Leviathan* theory insomuch as the reversal of the same error occurs in chapter 33, where references to Psalms 137 and 126 in *Leviathan*, which are

---

[36] L, 31, pp. 554, 558.

properly aligned with the AV, are copied over as 'Psalmus 137 & Psalmus 126' in the Latin *Leviathan* even though those citations are inaccurate in the Vulgate.[37] The same error also occurs in a later discussion of Psalm 105 in the Latin *Leviathan*.[38] In these cases, it would appear that the relevant research had been done in English and then copied into Latin in accordance with the order of publication.

Similar issues with the numbering of biblical books offer indications of shifts between English and Latin: for example, 1, 2, 3, and 4 Esdras in the Vulgate correspond to the books of Ezra, Nehemiah, and 1 and 2 Esdras in the AV. While attempting to compose a French translation of *Leviathan*, François du Verdus was unable to locate a passage Hobbes cited as the second book of Esdras, asking in a 1656 letter to Hobbes, 'in which part of the Vulgate edition of the Bible I can find the passage which you cite from 2 Esdras 14 ('this law is burnt...'). For in the Vulgate, the second book of Esdras has only thirteen chapters.'[39] The problem, of course, was that Du Verdus should have been looking in the Vulgate's 4 Esdras. Hobbes does refer inaccurately to 3 and 4 Esdras in chapter 33 of the English *Leviathan*, but there is a simple explanation for that example: the references occur in a list extracted from the writings of St Jerome.[40]

Another example of discordant numbering is the fact that in the Vulgate, 1 and 2 Samuel are labelled as 1 and 2 Regum (i.e. Kings), with the English books of 1 and 2 Kings numbered as 3 and 4 Regum. When Hobbes makes a passing reference to 'the Fasting of *David* for *Saul* and *Jonathan*, mentioned (2 *Kings*, 1. 12.)' in chapter 44, his English readers would have been lost insomuch as the story in question actually occurs in 2 Samuel. Hobbes appears to have copied this reference to fasting out of a Latin source without verifying its presence in English bibles. Once again, however, his source for this particular verse citation was not the Latin *Leviathan*; instead, it was the writings of Cardinal Bellarmine, whom he cites explicitly in the passage.[41] Indeed, the biblical quotations in Hobbes's extended refutation of Bellarmine provide perhaps the strongest evidence that the English *Leviathan* preceded the Latin: whereas the English version demonstrates serious engagement with Bellarmine's examples of papal authority drawn from the Vulgate, in the Latin *Leviathan* the passages are confusingly presented in the language of Beza's Latin New Testament.

For example, one of Bellarmine's proofs for ecclesiastical discipline came from 1 Corinthians 11: 'Laudo vos, quod praeceptamea tenetis.'[42] Bellarmine viewed this as evidence of initial authority on the part of St Paul. Hobbes fielded this challenge by presenting Bellarmine's quotation from the Vulgate as '*I commend you for keeping my Precepts as I delivered them to you*' and then proceeding to argue that the passage ought to have been translated '*I commend you for keeping those things I delivered to you, as I delivered them. Which is far from signifying that they were Laws, or any thing else, but*

---

[37] L, 33, p. 596. Cf. LL, 33, p. 597.   [38] LL, 36, p. 655.   [39] C, p. 327.

[40] L, 33, p. 588. The same passage contains other signs of copying in its use of Latin names like 'Tobias' instead of the Anglicized 'Tobit'.

[41] L, 44, p. 994.

[42] Robert Bellarmine, *Opera Omnia*, 6 vols (Naples: Josephum Giuliano, 1856–62), i, 312.

good Counsell.'[43] Instead of performing a similar rhetorical move in the Latin *Leviathan*, Hobbes merely copies over the verse from Beza's edition, '*Laudo verò vos, fraters, quod omnia meministis, & sicut tradidi vobis traditiones retinetis*' and lets the absence of any reference to 'precepts' speak for itself.[44] This section of the English *Leviathan* contains material copied from a Latin text, but that text is quite clearly Bellarmine, not the Latin *Leviathan*. In sum, the arguments for Latin *Leviathan* anteriority, improbable to begin with, are even less probable once one carefully examines Hobbes's use of Scripture.

8.3 Biblical Exegesis and Joseph Mede

A final example of the utility of examining Hobbes's verses can be found in chapter 38 of *Leviathan* wherein Hobbes presents a host of radical ideas about the afterlife.[45] Hobbes rejected the idea of eternal torment: instead of burning eternally in hell, Hobbes argued that the reprobate would merely suffer for a brief period of time before dying again.[46] On a very precise linguistic level, this view did not contradict the Thirty-Nine Articles, or any of the three creeds accepted by the Church of England. The Athanasius Creed declared that the wicked will go into 'everlasting fire', but Hobbes shrewdly observed that simply because the fire would last forever (or until the end of the world), 'it cannot thence be inferred, that hee who shall be cast into that fire, or be tormented with those torments, shall endure, and resist them so, as to be eternally burnt, and tortured, and yet never be destroyed, nor die.'[47]

In making the case against the existence of a literal hell, Hobbes listed the various contradictory descriptions of hell in the Bible—a bottomless pit, a bituminous lake, etc.—arguing that these accounts could not all be true, and thus that they were 'spoken metaphorically'.[48] In the course of that effort, Hobbes quoted three passages from the Bible that described hell as an underwater realm filled with giants. The first of his quotations came from Proverbs 21:16: 'The man that wandreth out of the way of understanding, shall remain in the congregation of the Giants.' The second from Job 26:5 reads 'Behold the Giants groan under water, and they that dwell with them.' The third from Isaiah 14:9 was a prophecy directed towards the Babylonian king: 'Hell is

[43] L, 42, p. 896.

[44] For a discussion of Hobbes's use of the Beza New Testament and Tremellius–Junius Old Testament when translating *Leviathan* into Latin, see Malcolm, 'General Introduction', 189–91.

[45] Tuck has called this chapter 'the core' of Hobbes's 'new theology'. Richard Tuck, 'The Civil Religion of Thomas Hobbes', in *Political Discourse in Early Modern Britain*, ed. Nicholas Phillipson and Quentin Skinner (Cambridge: Cambridge University Press, 1992), 128.

[46] L, 38, pp. 716, 718.

[47] L, 38, p. 718. Two passages indicating that the fire would burn 'for ever' in the 'Head' edition of *Leviathan* were changed to 'as long as the World stands [or lasts]' in the 'Bear' and '25 Ornaments' editions, making this theory fit better with Hobbes's eschatology. Needless to say, Hobbes encountered plenty of criticism for these views. See, e.g., John Bramhall, *The Catching of Leviathan* (London, 1657), 256.

[48] L, 38, p. 714.

troubled how to meet thee…and will displace the Giants for thee.'[49] None of these descriptions accords with the text of the AV, which instead mentions 'the congregation of the dead', 'dead things' under the water, and hell stirring up 'the dead' to make room for the aforementioned king. One must instead look to the Vulgate to find the relevant references: 'in coetu Gigantum commorabitur', 'Ecce Gigantes gemunt sub aquis', 'suscitavit tibi Gigantes'. The reason for this discrepancy between the two versions is the late introduction of vowel points in Hebrew. The absence of vowels provides uncertainty about whether the singular of the relevant noun is *raphah* ('giant': the word used to describe Goliath), or *rapheh* ('one who is powerless' or 'a shade').

Hobbes suggested that these descriptions of a watery hell were intended to remind readers metaphorically of 'those mighty men of the Earth, that lived in the time of Noah, before the floud, (which the Greeks called *Heroes*, and the Scripture *Giants*, and both say, were begotten, by copulation of the children of God, with the children of men,)' and who were 'for their wicked life destroyed by the generall deluge'.[50] Given the necessity of the Vulgate for this argument, this would seem like a strong candidate for Latin anteriority. However, there is another more probable possibility: Hobbes borrowed the evidence for this section from the Cambridge theologian Joseph Mede without acknowledging his source.

It is an understatement to say that Hobbes was stingy in acknowledging intellectual debts. The names of other authors appear rarely in Hobbes's works, and when they do occur it is almost always in reference to their errors. In taking aim at opponents Hobbes set his sights high; the list of writers criticized in *Leviathan* includes Plato, Aristotle, Livy, Beda, Francisco de Suarez, Theodore Beza, and Edward Coke. Hobbes did not mince his words either. The language he used to describe the ideas of these individuals— 'useless', 'absurd'—was far from polite. He was particularly unkind to scholastics, denouncing the 'frivolous Distinctions, barbarous Terms, and obscure Language of the Schoolmen'.[51] After translating from a passage by Suarez filled with opaque terminology, Hobbes queried: 'When men write whole volumes of such stuffe, are they not Mad, or intend to make others so?'[52]

Hobbes frequently mocked those who appealed to the authority of respected authors instead of evaluating arguments themselves, likening their logic to the casting up of 'many little summs into a greater, without considering whether those little summes were rightly cast up or not'.[53] In a celebrated line, Hobbes declared that 'words are wise mens counters, they do but reckon by them: but they are the mony of fooles, that value them by the authority of an Aristotle, a Cicero, or a Thomas, or any other

---

[49] L, 38, p. 712.

[50] L, 38, p. 712. Hobbes was referring here to the *nephilim* mentioned in Genesis 6:4.

[51] L, 47, p. 1110.

[52] L, 8, p. 122. Hobbes inclined toward the latter hypothesis, arguing that the ideas of the scholastics about the soul and demons and the afterlife facilitated papal domination by instilling irrational fear in the laity.

[53] L, 4, p. 56.

Doctor whatsoever, if but a man'.[54] With those views in mind, it is surprising to see Hobbes in his published response to John Bramhall referencing another author as support for a biblical argument in *Leviathan*. In defending his belief that the 'Daemoniacks' mentioned in Scripture were simply madmen, Hobbes wrote '*I see nothing at all in the Scripture that requireth a belief* to the contrary, adding 'this is also made very probable out of Scripture, by a worthy Divine Mr. Meade'.[55]

The worthy divine in question, Joseph Mede, has generated a fair amount of attention in recent years.[56] Mede was born in Essex to parents of 'honest rank' in 1586 and attended Christ's College, Cambridge, at the same time that Hobbes was enrolled at Oxford.[57] Mede stayed on as a tutor at his alma mater and served in that capacity until his death in 1638.[58] Mede was an accomplished scholar of both Greek and Hebrew, and it is very likely that John Milton studied Hebrew under him.[59] Mede argued that the demoniacs mentioned in Scripture were madmen in a collected volume of discourses published posthumously in 1642 as *Diatribae: Discourses on Divers Texts of Scripture*.[60]

The evidence that Hobbes read this work and borrowed its ideas when writing *Leviathan* is extensive. The section of *Diatribae* immediately following the discussion of demoniacs contains all of the passages about giants that Hobbes used in *Leviathan*, with Mede quoting them in Latin and making the same connection that Hobbes makes between the giants dwelling underwater and the *nephilim* killed in the Flood. Mede also showed that the name for hell of 'Gehenna' came from the Valley of Hinnom where infants were sacrificed to the god Moloch: a fact also mentioned by Hobbes in *Leviathan*.[61] In making sense of these different accounts, Mede concluded that 'all the expressions almost in Scripture, whereby this place of eternall punishment is represented, relate and allude to some places or Stories remarkable for Gods exemplary vengeance executed upon sinners'—the same belief advocated by Hobbes.[62]

In all probability, Hobbes borrowed other biblical ideas from Mede. It is likely, for example, that Hobbes's argument that the term 'prophets' was used in the Bible to describe mere musicians who praised God in holy songs was also derived from Mede's writings given the similarity of their evidence.[63] There are additional similarities in the accounts that both men provide of baptism.[64] Scholars have long known that Hobbes's biblical exegesis did not emerge *de novo*, but the task of tracking down his critical sources has proved daunting. Fortunately, Hobbes's use and alteration of biblical verses serve as helpful clues linking *Leviathan* to its sources.

---

[54]   L, 4, p. 58.   [55]   EW 4, p. 327.

[56]   Jeffrey K. Jue, *Heaven Upon Earth: Joseph Mede (1586–1638) and the Legacy of Millenarianism* (Dordrecht: Springer, 2006).

[57]   Jue, *Heaven Upon Earth*, 8–10.

[58]   Given the long-running debate about Hobbes's scepticism, it is interesting to note that Mede supposedly came across an open copy of Sextus Empiricus in 1603 and struggled with scepticism himself. Richard Popkin, *The History of Skepticism*, revised edition (Oxford: Oxford University Press, 2003), 64–5.

[59]   Barbara K. Lewalski, *The Life of John Milton: A Critical Biography*, revised edition (Oxford: Blackwell Publishing, 2003), 18–20.

[60]   Joseph Mede, *Diatribae: Discourses on Divers Texts of Scripture* (London, 1642), 83–90.

[61]   Ibid., 91; L, 38, p. 714.   [62]   Mede, *Diatribae*, 96.

[63]   Ibid., 173–9; L, 36, p. 658.   [64]   Mede, *Diatribae*, 188–91; L, 41, p. 772.

8.4 Contemporary Responses

While Hobbes's cavalier attitude to the text of the Bible is an aspect of *Leviathan* that has gone largely unnoticed by modern commentators, his initial readers were more astute. For example, the Scottish critic Alexander Ross highlighted a passage wherein Hobbes suggested that 'spirit' could simply mean wind, citing Genesis 8:1: '*I will bring my Spirit upon the Earth, and the waters shall be diminished.*' Hobbes was drawing upon the Vulgate's 'Adduxit spiritum super terram', but as Ross saw it, Hobbes 'misalledgeth the words; for thus it is written, *And God made a winde to pass over the Earth*; for winde in Scripture is never called the Spirit of God.'[65] Edward Hyde likewise noticed that the aforementioned example from 1 Kings 18 did not line up with his Bible, writing caustically of the 'unnecessary Learning and curiosity' which Hobbes 'seems to recreate himself upon all the Texts of Scripture, which he thinks fit to apply to his use, and in which he takes much pains to mend many expressions in Scripture, for the impropriety of Speech, without accusing the translation'.[66]

At the end of the third section of *Leviathan*, 'Of a Christian Commonwealth', Hobbes presented a defence of the approach he had taken to the Bible in the preceding chapters, writing:

in the allegation of Scripture, I have endeavoured to avoid such texts as are of obscure, or controverted Interpretation; and to alledge none, but in such sense as is most plain, and agreeable to the harmony and scope of the whole Bible; which was written for the re-establishment of the Kingdome of God in Christ. For it is not the bare Words, but the Scope of the writer that giveth the true light, by which any writing is to bee interpreted; and they that insist upon single Texts, without considering the main Designe, can derive no thing from them cleerly; but rather by casting atomes of Scripture, as dust before mens eyes, make every thing more obscure than it is; an ordinary artifice of those that seek not the truth, but their own advantage.[67]

In actuality, Hobbes quoted from many biblical texts in *Leviathan* that were 'of obscure, or controverted Interpretation' and parsed some of the most controversial passages in the entire Bible, from the rights of kingship in 1 Samuel 8 to the powers granted to St Peter in Luke 22.[68]

---

[65] Alexander Ross, *Leviathan Drawn out with a Hook* (London, 1653), 37.

[66] Hyde, *A Brief View*, 201.   [67] L, 43, p. 954.

[68] In his quotation of 1 Samuel 8, copied from a corresponding section of *De Cive*, Hobbes followed the Vulgate in declaring that the oppressive monarchical actions Samuel warned the Israelites about were the '*Right of the King you will have to reigne over you*'. There is no language of 'right' in any English translation. L, 20, p. 316. In his Latin *First Defense* of the English regicide, Milton employed his knowledge of Hebrew to argue that very point. He noted that the word in question is used just six chapters earlier to describe the impious manner of Eli's sons who served as priests and defrauded the people. Since it was their behaviour that prompted the people to depose Samuel and choose a king in the first place, Milton reasoned that it could not be an unquestionable 'right', and subjects were free to unseat kings who behaved in similarly unjust ways. While Hobbes exhibited no deference to prior biblical commentators, Milton drew upon the writings of the Church Father Sulpitius Severus, as well as Jewish commentators. John Milton, *Pro Populo Anglicano Defensio* (London, 1651), 45–7.

While Hobbes may have viewed his exegeses as both modest and logical, contemporaries disagreed. To demonstrate that the Scriptures received their authority from the sovereign alone, Hobbes argued that the earliest books of the Old Testament had been compiled at a much later date than the events they depicted—in all likelihood by Ezra after the return of the Israelites from captivity. While contemporary Christians believed that Moses had personally authored the books of the Pentateuch, Hobbes saw this as implausible, noting that the last chapter of Deuteronomy mentions of Moses's tomb *'that no man knoweth of his sepulcher to this day'*—a day presumably after Moses's death.[69] He pointed out that expressions like *'the Canaanite was then in the land'* in Genesis 12 suggested that the text was composed after the Canaanite was no longer in the land (i.e. long after Moses's death). Hobbes made similar arguments about other books, and suggested that the New Testament was not rendered canonical until the Council of Laodicea in 364 AD, after the conversion of Constantine had allowed for the reunion of civil and religious authority.

John Bramhall likened such arguments to digging a hole of doubt which unsuspecting believers might fall into, and then failing to cover it up again. In an allusion to the Mosaic law, Bramhall wrote:

I know not whether he [Hobbes] do this on purpose to weaken the authority of holy Scripture, or not. Let God and his own conscience be his Triers: But I am sure he hath digged a pit for an oxe or an asse, without covering it again, and if they chance to stumble blindfold into it, their blood will be required at his hands. If a Turke had said so much of the Alchoran at Constantinople, he were in some danger.[70]

Given the foreseeable consequences, it seems highly probable that Hobbes did not put forth these views lightly: he considered his theological positions essential to the success of his philosophical programme. As long as men believed in a fate worse than death, they could not be restrained by prudential calculations when making decisions about allegiance and rebellion in this life. To break this cycle of fear, Hobbes argued against ecclesiastical power, supernatural inspiration, demonic possession, and eternal torments. By reducing the essence of Christianity to personal faith and obedience to civil authority, Hobbes sought to ensure that men would no longer face the false choice of serving God or Caesar and if it took a bit of textual emendation to achieve that aim he saw that as a small price to pay.

In Hobbes's view, the individuals most unsuited to be trusted with the reading and interpretation of Scripture were those who have 'studied the Greek or Latine, or both tongues, and that are withall such as love knowledge, and consequently take delight in finding out the meaning of the most hard Texts, or in thinking they have found it, in case it be new, and not found out by others.'[71] He knew whereof he spoke. In his

---

[69] For a discussion of Hobbes's Ezran hypothesis and similar claims by Spinoza, see Malcolm, *Aspects of Hobbes*, 383–431.

[70] John Bramhall, *Castigations of Mr. Hobbs His Last Animadversions* (London, 1657), 174.

[71] B, p. 178.

Dialogue of the Laws of England, written near the end of his life, Hobbes acknowledged that perpetual peace in the international realm was almost certainly impossible, but claimed that 'Peace at home' would be 'durable' if:

the common people shall be made to see the benefit they shall receive by their Obedience and Adhaesion to their own Soveraign, and the harm they must suffer by taking part with them, who by promises of Reformation, or change of Government deceive them. And this is properly to be done by Divines, and from Arguments not only from Reason, but also from the Holy Scripture.[72]

Leviathan was Hobbes's attempt to erect a suitable political theology, and scriptural citations were the nails which held it aloft. The work of inspecting those nails has only just begun.

[72] DPS, p. 12.

9

The Politics of Hobbes's *Historia Ecclesiastica*

Patricia Springborg

9.1 Contextualizing Hobbes's *Historia Ecclesiastica*

Hobbes's long, 2242 line, iambic pentameter Latin poem, the *Historia Ecclesiastica*, published posthumously in 1688, remains somewhat of a mystery to this day.[1] It takes the name of the great ecclesiastical histories from the fourth century on by Eusebius, Rufinus, Socrates of Constantinople, by Sozomen and Evagrius, by the Arian Philostorgius and the Nestorian Theodoret. Hobbes's choice of title could not have been accidental, even if his reasons for writing it are not entirely clear. It is really a mixed-genre piece as well as being a display of erudition expected of Renaissance humanists, of whom Hobbes was one, so that from at least Erasmus of Rotterdam to Hobbes's contemporary, William Petty, the capacity to write Latin poetry was a test of their credentials. As expected, Hobbes's poem opens by paying deference to classical Latin poetry. Preliminaries set the scene between the interlocutors, Primus and Secundus, reminiscent of the singing shepherds of Theocritus, Horace's *Odes*, Virgil's *Eclogues* and especially his *Aeneid*, which opens with them singing of 'arms and the man'.

---

[1] Grateful thanks to my publisher Honoré Champion, and for my co-editors for the right to quote from Thomas Hobbes, *Historia Ecclesiastica*, ed. Patricia Springborg, Patricia Stablein, and Paul Wilson (Paris, 2008) and, in particular, from my lengthy Introduction. Citations are to lines and page numbers in this edition. The first modern translation of Hobbes's *Historia Ecclesiastica* was the pioneering Italian edition, *Storia Ecclesiastica, narrata in forma di carmine elegiaca*, trans. G. Invernizzi and A. Lupoli, in Thomas Hobbes, *Scritti teologici* (Milan: Franco Angeli, 1988), while Springborg et al. is the first English translation. For recent essays on the *Historia Ecclesiastica*, see Springborg, 'Hobbes, Heresy and the *Historia Ecclesiastica*', *Journal of the History of Ideas* 55.4 (1994), 553–71, which was, I think, the first article on the poem in English; Springborg, 'Hobbes's Theory of Civil Religion: The *Historia Ecclesiastica*', in *Pluralismo e religione civile*, ed. Gianni Paganini and Edoardo Tortarolo (Milano: Bruno Mondadori, 2003), 61–98; Springborg, 'Hobbes and the Word', in *Obbedienza religiosa e resistenza politica nella prima età moderna. Filosofi ebrei, cristiani e islamici di fronte alla Bibbia*, ed. Luisa Simonutti (Turnhout, Belgium: Brepols Publishers, 2015), 183–212; Franck Lessay, 'Hobbes and Sacred History', in *Hobbes and History*, ed. G. A. J. Rogers and Tom Sorell (London: Routledge, 2000), 147–59; J. P. Sommerville, 'Hobbes, Selden, Erastianism, and the History of the Jews', in *Hobbes and History*, 160–87; Jeffrey Collins, 'Thomas Hobbes's Ecclesiastical History', in *The Oxford Handbook of Hobbes*, ed. A. P. Martinich and Kinch Hoekstra (Oxford: Oxford University Press, 2016), 520–44.

This is no mere pastoral flourish, for Hobbes intends the audience to understand that his subject is civil war, and the disruption to the peace caused by religion and priestcraft. Paraphrasing Thucydides 3.82 on the power of war to corrupt discourse, he observes that the problem now is 'that religion is shaped into some impossible system, theology'.[2] He turns to the Church Doctors, each shouting to his own sect, ' "Follow me to the Kingdom of Heaven" ',[3] and the procession of Shades and Spectres they invoke to frighten men into submission, which 'the laws of kings are incapable of preventing'.[4]

Hobbes goes on to catalogue the simultaneous rise of astrology and the state where, 'for the sake of their own safety, many small men united so there could be one great man',[5] a strong man to 'rout the common enemy with all of their resources, conserve peace and maintain justice at home'.[6] Thereafter a standard Epicurean account of the rise of civilization and of the arts in priest-ridden Egypt follows,[7] heavily reliant on Diodorus Siculus, but with references to Ovid, Lucretius, Lucian, and Homer. From the Ethiopians (synonym for Egypt) and the Egyptians (so-named), Hobbes moves to the Assyrian and Chaldean soothsayers peddling their wares in Rome,[8] and finally to the Greek philosophers who replaced them when those reprobates were thrown out,[9] including Socrates, the bad citizen, of whom he wishes: 'If only he had met his death earlier, struck on his ugly head with a [chamber] pot by his mad wife [Xanthippe]'.[10] Aristotle is included in the catalogue of philosophers who preached against kings, and were therefore indirectly responsible for the English Civil War, a catalogue that extends to all the 'democratic authorities' of the time, namely those Greek 'sects' who by inciting the clergy encouraged the regicide.[11]

Hobbes's account of the mendacity of the 'Greek sects' continues to the time of the apostle Paul,[12] at which point it morphs into church history. A scathing account follows of the 'Greekification' of the primitive Christian church out of which sectarianism and 'the names heretic and Catholic were born'.[13] For, 'when a judgment of the Council ended the dispute, to win was Catholic, to lose was heretical'.[14] But 'the pagan', for whom Hobbes seems to have had great sympathy, 'believed both sides and fled the sweet yoke of Christ'.[15] Along comes Constantine, the first Christian Emperor 'who bathed the earth in the blood [of unbelievers]',[16] but established thereafter a period of peace and prosperity for the church. Constantine's reign marks a turning point for Hobbes. What follows is a remarkably detailed account of the first four ecumenical councils of the fourth century, including the defining Nicene Council,[17]

---

[2] HE, line 17, pp. 304–5.   [3] HE, line 57, pp. 308–9.   [4] HE, line 90, pp. 312–13.
[5] HE, lines 115–16, pp. 316–17.   [6] HE, lines 117–18, pp. 316–17.
[7] HE, lines 140–280, pp. 317–33.   [8] HE, lines 290–324, pp. 332–9.
[9] HE, lines 325–50, pp. 338–43.   [10] HE, lines 359–60, pp. 342–43.
[11] HE, lines 372–80, pp. 344–5.   [12] HE, lines 381–470, pp. 344–55.
[13] 'Greekification' was the term pioneered by Erasmus for the contamination of primitive Christianity by Greek philosophy. See HE, line 512, pp. 365–7.
[14] HE, lines 514–15, pp. 360–1.   [15] HE, line 510, pp. 360–1.
[16] HE, lines 519–20, pp. 362–3.   [17] HE, lines 560–670, pp. 366–81.

which made enemies of a long list of 'heretics' in the ongoing battles over Arianism,[18] and provided permitting conditions for the papal ascendancy,[19] the rise of universities as papal foundations, the invasions of the Goths, sectarian persecutions, and the subjugation of kings;[20] all of which bundled together constitute the prehistory of the English Civil War.

How did Hobbes's *Historia Ecclesiastica* become such a pastiche of genres, and what were his motivations in writing it? We know from the book list of the Hardwick Hall Library that he had access to a wide range of patristic sources, including most of the Greek Fathers, as well as a considerable range of Jesuit and Protestant commentaries. Hobbes's preoccupation with heresy was a principal motivation for the burst of creative activity on that subject in the 1660s, which included his *Ecclesiastical History*, and it is true that from Eusebius on, Christian historiographers were obsessed with heresy. But there is an alternative and not unrelated hypothesis, which is that Hobbes, who had condoned Cromwellian Independency and was an Erastian at heart, was appealing to the relative tolerance of the early Christian historiographers against the rabid sectarianism of heresiologists of the 1640s such as Ephraim Pagitt, Thomas Edwards, and Alexander Ross. It follows that the Restoration Hobbes might have wanted to establish the credentials of a more inclusive Anglicanism as a civil religion, appealing to its catholicity as a panacea for schism and dissent, in the same way that the ecclesiastical historians had appealed to Catholicity as one of the marks of early Christian orthodoxy. It is perhaps this feature of Hobbes's strategy that some readers have mistaken for toleration.[21] But before making such a judgement it is necessary to review the Christian historiographic tradition pioneered by the ecclesiastical historians, with whom Hobbes appears to be well acquainted, to see how such a highly satirical work could fly this banner.

It is my claim that the *Historia Ecclesiastica* fits into the schema of Hobbes's works in a hitherto unexplained way, as a missing link between the English and the Latin versions of *Leviathan*. The twentieth-century revival of Hobbes scholarship was focused on establishing the integrity of *Leviathan* by restoring the last two books on religion, missing from some modern editions and largely ignored. Recent revisionist Hobbes scholarship has shown that it was precisely his religious doctrine, and specifically, the Erastian doctrine that the state is supreme over the church in ecclesiastical matters, that flouted the religious sensibilities of his contemporaries, causing wave after wave of hostile reaction and concerted efforts at censorship of his heretical views, first from Presbyterians and then by Anglicans at home;[22] and by critics on the Continent to the point where the

---

[18]   HE, lines 671–870, pp. 380–407.   [19]   HE, lines 871–1290, pp. 406–7.
[20]   HE, lines 1291–2242, pp. 466–581.
[21]   For a defence of Hobbes as a theorist of toleration see Franck Lessay's chapter, 'Tolerance as a Dimension of Hobbes's Absolutism', in this volume.
[22]   Jeffrey Collins, *The Allegiance of Thomas Hobbes* (Oxford: Oxford University Press, 2005), provides the first systematic analysis of Hobbes's ecclesiology in terms of the Interregnum and post-Interregnum struggles in which he was engaged.

Elector of Saxony, Friedrich Augustus, stepped in to prevent the republication of the *Opera Philosophica*.[23] The Latin *Leviathan* took back some of the most controversial doctrines and inflammatory rhetoric of the English, but it added more, in particular the rehearsal of Hobbes's credo of disbelief, his analysis of the Nicene Creed.[24] The *Historia Ecclesiastica* not only anticipates, but more fully develops some of this new material, known to us hitherto—and then not widely known—only from the Appendix to the Latin *Leviathan*, and incidental material in *Behemoth* and the *Dialogue Concerning the Common Laws*, works roughly contemporaneous with the poem.

Contextualizing the *Historia Ecclesiastica* casts important light on the circumstances in which Hobbes found himself in the early 1660s. For the *Historia Ecclesiastica* belongs to a stream of Hobbes's works on heresy that gathers force around the years 1666 to 1670. Of these works, seven, including the *Historia Ecclesiastica*, deal with heresy: Hobbes's *Response to Bramhall's 'The Catching of Leviathan'*, written in 1666–7; the Chatsworth MS on Heresy of 1673; his *Historical Narration Concerning Heresy* of 1668; *De Haeresi*, his Appendix to the Latin *Leviathan* of the same year; the *Dialogue Concerning the Common Laws*, written after 1668, the section on heresy relating to the Scargill affair of 1669; and *Behemoth*, written between 1668 and 1670. It is my hypothesis that the *Historia Ecclesiastica*, although recorded as completed only in 1671, may stand earlier in this series. There are several clues in its preoccupations. For instance, Hobbes casts the central power struggle between Arius and Alexander as that between an Elder (*Presbyter*) and a Bishop (*Ephor*),[25] playing on terms that are never innocent, Presbyterians and Bishops being his nemeses in the 1650s and 1660s. It demonstrates a level of interest in the early church councils and subtleties of scholastic doctrine also to be found in the companion works, the *Historical Narration Concerning Heresy* and the 1668 Appendix to the Latin *Leviathan*, but missing from the English *Leviathan*; while Hobbes's engagement with Bellarmine and seventeenth-century scholastics, so evident in the English *Leviathan*, is missing from the *Historia Ecclesiastica* and his other works of the 1660s.[26]

9.2 The *Historia Ecclesiastica*: Form, Content, and Genre

In form the Latin poem, comprising 2242 lines of iambic pentameter, and announced in the 1688 printed edition as *A Church History in the form of an Elegiac Poem*, the *Historia Ecclesiastica*, is of mixed genre, moving between pastoral, satire, and poetic

---

[23] See Noel Malcolm, *Aspects of Hobbes* (Oxford: Clarendon Press, 2002), 461.
[24] See Glen Newey's chapter, 'A Profile in Cowardice? Hobbes, Personation, and the Trinity', in this volume.
[25] HE, lines 550–5, pp. 365–7.
[26] On *Leviathan* and Bellarmine, see Patricia Springborg, 'Thomas Hobbes and Cardinal Bellarmine: Leviathan and the Ghost of the Roman Empire', *History of Political Thought* 16.4 (1995), 503–31; Springborg, 'Hobbes on Religion', in *The Cambridge Companion to Hobbes,* ed. Tom Sorell (Cambridge, Cambridge University Press, 1995), 346–80.

history. Set as a dialogue between two interlocutors, it shares a format in common with three of Hobbes's seven works of the 1660s: the *Dialogue Concerning the Common Laws*, the Appendix to the Latin *Leviathan*, and *Behemoth*, but in the *Historia Ecclesiastica*, unlike the other works, the interlocutors require some dramatic introduction and engage in some pastoral preliminaries. After reflecting upon the pleasures of the countryside, compared with the perils of the city in time of war, the topic turns to the question of the causes of war and especially civil war. Hobbes takes up the principal theme of *Behemoth*, written as much as ten years later, that religion is the primary cause of civil conflict; followed in this case by an account of the nature and purpose of religion as a palliative for fear of death; an Epicurean account heavily indebted to Lucretius and Diodorus Siculus, whom he constantly cites, reminiscent of chapter 12 of *Leviathan*. He portrays primitive Christianity as a simple and pacific religion satisfying the requirements of a civil religion, up to its encounter with, and contamination by, the Greek philosophical sects and the rise of Arianism.[27] Secundus's remark at lines 643–4, 'I really want to know what happened because it is relevant to the history of heresies',[28] more or less sums up the purpose of the poem as we finally have it, the bulk of which concerns doctrinal developments that permitted the rise of clericalism and its most extreme form, the papal ascendancy.

Franck Lessay in an excellent essay on the *Historia Ecclesiastica* has analysed the structure of the poem in similar terms.[29] But to speak of structure risks overschematizing a work that is shaped untidily, giving the impression of having been picked up and put down many times, themes breaking off, only to be picked up again later, for no obvious reason—perhaps it had even been reconstructed or at least partially rewritten. The haphazard structure of the poem suggests a work of private reflection, almost a memoir, to which Hobbes could retreat under duress from campaigns being waged against him, his Epicurean garden. The *Historia Ecclesiastica* is more than that of course, but what more precisely? To answer this question we must first look at its complicated textual history. In addition to the 1688 printed edition and the witty 1722 paraphrase, which is anonymous, we have three manuscripts of the *Historia Ecclesiastica*. The first MS, (A), although undated, must have been transcribed some time before the printed edition appeared in 1688, because it is corrected in heavy black ink to that edition. It is held in the British Library as BL Harl. 1844, its title page reading: *Historia Ecclesiastica Romana. Autore Pereximio Viro THOMA. HOBBESIO Malmesburiensi* (*History of the Roman Church by that very famous author, Thomas Hobbes of Malmesbury*). The other two MSS are of continental provenance; the second MS, (B), is the Royal Copenhagen Library MS Thotts Sml., 4o Nr. 213. Its title page reads: *HISTORIA ECCLESIASTICA ROMANA. consignata à THOMA HOBBESIO. Ex Bibliotheca My Lord Vaugan. exscripsit Londini, Georgius Grund Ad 1685* (*History of the Roman Church, copied by George Grund from the one signed by Hobbes in Lord Vaughan's Library*). It appears to be a better copy of the same original as MS A before it

[27] HE, lines 70–870, pp. 310–407.   [28] HE, lines 643–4, pp. 376–7.
[29] Lessay, 'Hobbes and Sacred History'.

was corrected to the 1688 edition, thus allowing us to date both MSS as contemporaneous and prior to the printed book. The third MS, (C), the Vienna MS, replicates the title page of the 1688 printed edition, of which it is a more or less exact copy, including the epigram from Ovid, but gives the date as 1678.

Apart from the printed book, the manuscripts, and the eighteenth-century paraphrase, we have five important pieces of circumstantial evidence for the dating of Hobbes's poem, the first four of which are well known:

1. John Aubrey, Hobbes's biographer, reports:

In 1659, his lord was and some years before—at Little Salisbury House (now turned to the Middle Exchange), where he wrote, among other things, a poem in Latin hexameter and pentameter, of the encroachment of the clergy (both Roman and reformed) on the civil power. I remember I saw then over five hundred verses (for he numbered every tenth as he wrote). I remember he did read Cluverius's Historia universalis, and made up his poem from this.[30]

Aubrey adds: 'His amanuensis remembers this poeme, for he wrote them out, but knows [not what became of it]'. Aubrey speaks as if the copy he sighted was written by Hobbes 'for he numbred every tenth as he wrote', and recopied by Wheldon. But we have his own testimony that Hobbes's hand was palsied by 1650 and illegible by 1665–6.[31] Was it Hobbes's or his amanuensis James Wheldon's copy that he sighted around 1659? And what happened to these manuscripts? The contemporary manuscripts extant, Harley 1844 (A) and Royal Copenhagen Thott MS (B), do not number the lines, which are however numbered in the Vienna MSS (C), but copied from the 1688 printed edition. Aubrey's report goes on to speculate about the fate of the verses, suggesting that Hobbes may have burned them:

There was a report, (and surely true) that in Parliament, not long after the king was setled, some of the bishops made a motion, to have the good old gentleman burn't for a Heretique; which he hearing, feared that his papers might be search't by their order, and he told me he had burn't part of them.[32]

2. We have a second, and slightly different, report from Aubrey, this time in an undated antiquarian work mostly compiled between 1659 and 1670, although this item probably dates to 1674, where he records:

About the time of the Kings Returne, he [Hobbes] was makeing of a very good Poëme in Latin hexameters: it was the *History of the Encroachment of the clergie (both Roman and Reformed) on the Civil Power*. I sawe at least 300 verses (they were mark't). At what time there was a report the Bishops would have him burn't for a Heretique. So he then feared the search of his papers, and burned the greatest part of these verses.[33]

---

[30] John Aubrey, *Brief Lives, Chiefly of Contemporaries*, ed. Andrew Clark (Oxford: Oxford University Press, 1898), i, 338–9. Cluverius was a major source for Hobbes, see Patricia Springborg, 'Writing to Redundancy: Hobbes and Cluverius', *The Historical Journal* 39.4 (1996), 1075–8.

[31] Aubrey, *Brief Lives*, 165.   [32] Ibid., 339.

[33] Aubrey, *An Essay towards a Description of the North Division of Wiltshire*, cited by Philip Milton, 'Hobbes, Heresy and Lord Arlington', *History of Political Thought* 14.4 (1993), 510. Milton speculates on the

3. The account book of James Wheldon's personal finances, dated September–October 1671, 'At Chatsworth', records: 'Given me by Mr. Hobbes for writing a book, *Historia Ecclesiastica Romana*, one pound';[34] and

4. William Crooke's catalogue of Hobbes's various manuscripts, published in June 1675 as *A Supplement of Mr Hobbes his Workes printed by Blaeu at Amsterdam*, includes the *Historia Ecclesiastica Romana*.[35]

A fifth fact has not been previously taken into account and may cast some light on the nature of the poem, when and why Hobbes wrote it:

5. A letter from François du Verdus to Hobbes, dated [24 July] 3 August 1664, reported to Hobbes news from M. du Prat, that 'you were putting your entire philosophical system into Latin verse, in a style somewhat similar to that of Hesiod, with whose works you had closely familiarized yourself for that purpose'.[36]

Important for the dating of the HE, Du Verdus' 1664 letter has been overlooked because it seems to suggest a different genre of poem. 'As soon as I heard mention of a philosophical poem, I conceived the plan of translating it, as soon as it appeared, into Italian *versi sciolti*, like the ones Annibale Caro used in his translation of the *Aeneid*', Du Verdus claims, offering Hobbes an English translation of an opera he wrote in Italian called 'Iris in Love with Phoenix' as a sample of his style, while informing him of his plan to have his own translation of all Hobbes's works printed—he did in fact publish a French translation of *De Cive*. Personally engaged in property disputes with the church in Bordeaux, Du Verdus was an ardent Erastian anti-clericalist and knew Hobbes's mind.[37] He read *Leviathan* as a bible for the Cromwellian commonwealth, marvelling that, as the very model of a bishopless Erastian state, it was surprising that the Commonwealth had not 'heaped the highest rewards' on Hobbes for showing 'that the authority of the state is absolute and indivisible'.[38] Du Verdus even proposed in 1654 removing himself to England as a 'safe haven' in which he could pursue his study of Bacon and Hobbes in peace;[39] whereupon Hobbes offered advice on how to ingratiate himself with the Protectorate,[40] extending to him repeated invitations to come, in response to which Du Verdus enthused:[41]

What a pleasure it would give me, Sir, to be supported by Protestants; to try to become known to the Lord Protector; to dedicate my translation of your book to him; and to beg him, in my

---

basis of interpolations in this part of Aubrey's text which mention the composition of Hobbes's 'life [*Vita*] last year viz 1673 in Latin-verse', that this particular entry was made around 1674.

[34] Miriam Reik, *The Golden Lands of Thomas Hobbes* (Detroit: Wayne State University Press, 1977), 225 n. 3.

[35] Karl Schuhmann, *Hobbes. Une chronique* (Paris: Vrin, 1998). I thank Professor Franck Lessay for pointing this out to me.

[36] C, p. 625.   [37] C, pp. 299, 325, 367–74, 454.

[38] C, p. 228, cited by Collins in *Allegiance*, 174, to whom I am indebted for this account of du Verdus' relation to Hobbes.

[39] C, pp. 196–7.   [40] C, pp. 263, 285.   [41] C, p. 414.

dedication, to send a copy to the [French] King and invite him to read it, to learn from it about the rights of the sovereign which were stolen from him by the priests!

Du Verdus was not alone among Hobbes's French associates in his estimate that *Leviathan* was targeted at Cromwell as a sovereign who was not shackled by bishops and priests.[42] Du Verdus' mention of Annibale Caro (1507–66) throws us off the scent in terms of the *Historia Ecclesiastica*'s genre. But Caro, a writer of burlesques and satires in blank verse (*versi sciolti*), beginning with his *Ecloga* (1534) and including *Eneide di Virgilio, tradotta in versi sciolti* (1581), may nevertheless be a clue to the style of Hobbes's poem in one of its incarnations; and the reason why Thomas Rymer, editor of the 1688 printed edition, gave it the subtitle: *carmine elegiaco concinnata* (if in fact it was Rymer who gave it). I have no doubt that Du Verdus' reference is to the *Historia Ecclesiastica*, despite Malcolm dismissing it in favour of the astronomical poem *De motibus solis, aetheris et telluris*.[43] The long poem fits Du Verdu's description, while the brief astronomical poem does not. It is true that the Chatsworth account book corroborates a date of 1671 for the copying of the *Historia Ecclesiastica* by Wheldon, but this does not mean that it was only written in 1671 and indeed we have Aubrey's reports that it was under way from as early as 1659. Du Verdus' 1664 description of the poem as a translation of Hobbes's entire philosophical system into Latin verse suggests a work already substantially completed and corroborates Rymer's assessment of the poem's purpose. Why the gap of almost seven years between the poem's substantial completion, in 1664, and the making of a fair copy, in 1671? If, in fact, one set of verses went missing or was burned, as we have Aubrey's report to suggest, Du Verdus' account might refer to an earlier version of the poem, as being between 300 and 500+ verses that were later burned.

Aubrey's report suggests two copies, as already noted: Hobbes's which he saw, and Wheldon's which he heard about (from Wheldon). The poem that Wheldon remembers copying might have been a later and longer reconstruction, made by Hobbes when he felt the coast was clear. Possibly the shorter poem was more Hesiodic in tone than the version that was ultimately printed. That it was at the same time a fit candidate for translation by someone who specialized in burlesques and satires, is also plausible. Although the theogony with which Hobbes begins his poem is clearly taken from Diodorus Siculus, it parodies Hesiod's own *Theogony*, its story of the creation of the world, and genealogies of the gods and heroes from the pagan cosmologies.[44] One can see remnants of Hesiodic themes from *Works and Days* in Hobbes's account of the calendar of Christian feasts as a co-optation of earlier pagan festivals, such as the feast of Chronos, or Saturnalia, which becomes Carnivale, the celebration of Priapus and the May pole, the feasts of Ceres Bacchus and the Ambarvalia.[45] The poem even

---

[42] For example, see Hobbes's correspondence with Thomas de Martel (C, p. 464) and John Evelyn's remarks about Samuel Sorbière: Evelyn to Sprat, 31 October 1664, British Library Evelyn MS 39a, fo. 128.

[43] C, p. 628 n.

[44] HE, lines 80–350, pp. 310–43.   [45] HE, lines 1338–54, pp. 472–5.

contains a relic of the myth of Iris as a rainbow,[46] the subject of du Verdus' sample of poetry from his opera, 'Iris in love with Phoenix', that he presents as evidence of his translation skills.

In sum, since Hobbes's poem, as we have it in final printed form, begins as an imitation of a classical Greek or Latin poem in the tradition of the idylls of Theocritus and Horace's epodes,[47] it is not at all implausible that, seen in progress in 1664, it could be characterized as Hesiodic. That it was material for burlesque, we know from the English paraphrase, *A True Ecclesiastical History from Moses to the Time of Martin Luther*, which is in the tradition of Scarron's *Le Virgile Travestie*, a notorious work much imitated in Hobbes's day. This was a tradition with many layers, for Lucian himself, a poet much celebrated by Hobbes, in his *Satires*, especially in his *Dialogues of the Gods*, had lampooned Hesiod's *Theogony* and Ovid's *Metamorphoses*.[48] But none of the seventeenth-century Scarronesque Travesties referred much to Virgil or Ovid. They were rather burlesques, irreverent works of political and social commentary designed to get past the censor, which is probably what Hobbes, like Du Verdus, had in mind.

9.3 Hobbes and the Ecclesiastical Historians

The *Historia Ecclesiastica* may present a genre problem, but in the last instance Hobbes did decide to name his poem in the venerable tradition of ecclesiastical histories of the past, as all our evidence suggests. Thomas Rymer in his Preface mentions only Eusebius's *Life of Constantine* and the writings of the Blessed Hillary as among Hobbes's sources, but by this mention gives us a possible clue to the editions of *Historiae Ecclesiasticae* Hobbes might have consulted. The seventeenth century was a golden age for patristics—in particular, commentary on the Greek Fathers—and Hobbes's poem is a display of ecclesiological erudition probably based on the Latin translations of their works. The early Greek *Ecclesiastical Histories* had been accessible in Latin since Epiphanius Scholasticus, at the suggestion of Cassiodorus, undertook the translation of Theodoret, Socrates, and Sozomen, which Cassiodorus edited and selected for his *Historia Ecclesiastica Tripartita*. A work frequently reprinted, the first edition, published in Paris and Basle in 1523, became the basis for subsequent and enlarged anthologies. In the Hardwick Hall book list, we have two possible Latin candidates for Hobbes's sources for the patristic *Historiae Ecclesiasticae*, one of which we can be almost certain about because it contains the work by that title of St Dorotheus of Tyre, cross-referenced. This is the *Eusebii. Pamph. Historia Ecclesiastica cum Sozomeno et Socrate, Theod. Lect., Evag., et Dorothei Tyri vitis Prophetarum et Apostolorum ex ejusdem Musculi interpretatione et Theodoreti H. E. ex versione Joach. Camerarii* (Basle, 1544, fol.; 2nd edition Basle, 1557, fol., frequently reprinted). The second candidate, the *Historiae ecclesiasticae scriptores Graeci*, edited by John Christopherson,

---

[46] HE, line 1403, pp. 478–9.   [47] HE, lines 1–10, pp. 304–5 and notes.
[48] See Lucian, *Works*, ed. M. D. Macleod (London: Heinemann, 1961), vii, 262–349.

Bishop of Chichester (Cologne, 1570, also frequently reprinted) includes the *Historiae Ecclesiasticae* of Eusebius (10 books), Evagrius (6 books), Socrates of Constantinople (7 books), Theodoret (5 books), and Sozomen (9 books), as well as Eusebius's *De vita Constantini Magni* (3 books), and the Blessed Hilary's *De Trinitate*, both mentioned in Rymer's Preface as sources. Eusebius's *Life of Constantine* is not separately listed, although the works of Hilary are, which suggests that the library may well have had the Christopherson edition, which includes it, or that Hobbes found a copy elsewhere. But the Christopherson edition does not include Dorotheus of Tyre's *Historia Ecclesiastica*, which means that the anthology listed in the Hardwick Hall collection with the shelf-mark W.3.19 must have been another which did include it, probably the Basel 1544 anthology, or a later edition of it.

To defend my thesis that Hobbes's poem was intended to appeal to the relative humanism of the Christian historiographers against the rabid sectarianism of the heresiologists of his day it is necessary briefly to review the Christian historiographic tradition pioneered by the ecclesiastical historians.[49] It took some time for the Christian tradition of universal history to develop. If Luke the evangelist had exhibited a strong historiographic sense, there was nevertheless a long gap in the Judeo-Christian historiographical tradition between the gospels and the first church histories, a gap mostly filled with extra-canonical *Acta Apostolorum* and other apocryphal New Testament material. Christian historiography as such first arose in response to the challenge of Greek and Roman historians claiming that the decline of the Roman Empire was due to the vengeance of the gods against Christianization—a thesis revived in modified form by Edward Gibbon, for which Hobbes's poem might be seen as an anticipation.[50] It was the provocative hypothesis of Christianity as a destructive force that the Latin Fathers, the North African lawyer, Quintus Tertullian (*c*.160–225), and the North African Church Fathers, Bishop Cyprian (d.258), Arnobius of Sicca (from 303), Origen of Alexandria (*c*.185–*c*.254), and Firmianus Lactantius (*c*.240–*c*.320) were intent on overturning; a challenge which the universal historians Orosius (*c*.385–420) and Augustine of Hippo (354–430) sought again to meet. But when universal history, the epitome of antique high culture and its values, came to be written again, now in the form of church history, it was the Greek Fathers, challenged by the resurgence of paganism and its infection of the church in the form of heresy, who wrote it. The striking feature of *koine historia*, or universal history, at the hands of its greatest exemplars, the Hellenistic Polybius and Diodorus, had been its capacity to domesticate the foreign. Catholicity and continuity were its trademarks in the pre-Christian era and, not

---

[49] My use of the term 'humanism' denotes respect for the individual and relative diversity of opinion, which is widely acknowledged as a feature of early Christian, as well as Stoic Christian, traditions, and not simply a monopoly of Renaissance humanists.

[50] J. G. A. Pocock, author of the magisterial six-volume work on Gibbon, *Barbarism and Religion* (Cambridge: Cambridge University Press, 1999–2015), communicated to me that he looked for evidence that Gibbon might have read Hobbes's HE but found none.

surprisingly, at the hands of its Christian practitioners.[51] Aristotle's intuition in the *Poetics* that, while history remains fragmented, poetry universalizes because it reproduces the pathos of the human condition, had become axiomatic. But Aristotle's defence of poetics as the bearer of universal truths, and history as particularizing, was reversed by the universal historians, and the long centuries of their labour succeeded in reversing it for posterity as well.

Much ink has been spilt on this important reversal, but it is now generally agreed that a change in way of life produced a change in emphasis, registered in terminological change.[52] The multi-ethnic Hellenistic *oekoumene* encouraged emphasis on catholicity (*kathalon*), rather than pathos. Characterology, derived from fragments of the Peripatetics,[53] was critical for holistic history and its focus on behaviour. Aristotle himself had discerned two causes of *praxis*, thought (*dianoia*) and character (*ethos*). Diogenes Laertius and Posidonius advanced the Peripatetic theory of history by seeing the study of *praxeis* as a branch of ethics and acts as representing the symptomology of the soul. *Praxeis* to Theopompus comprehended the acts of barbarians as well as of Greeks,[54] and both he and Dionysius of Hallicarnassus understood the study of *praxeis* in terms of discerning motives, feelings, apparent virtues and unsuspected vices,[55] a methodology paradigmatic for Hobbes. Diodorus, Ephorus, and Theopompus were considered by the Church Fathers major philosophers of the Hellenistic world, to which Christianity belonged.[56] Like Polybius, Josephus, and Plutarch, they practised *pragmatike historia*, assuming that acts or deeds, *koinas praxeis*, or *res gestae*, were the appropriate subject of history.[57] *Res gestae* comprised the *Acts of Divine Augustus*, but also the *Acts of the Apostles*.[58]

In the grand tradition of the Roman exemplary historians, Lucian, Appian, and Dio Cassius, who wrote in the service of old virtues and old gods, the Christian historiographers wrote in the service of new virtues and a new God, exhibiting a strong sense of the church's institutional strength, its new and powerful *ethos*, and melded these to the tropes of ancient historiography.[59] Among the most important of these was the notion of 'the critical moment' or *kairos*, the preoccupation of pagan Graeco-Roman historiography, which sought in the decision of a singular individual, or a single event, the small beginnings of a momentous historical departure, the Stoic Fate or Polybius's Fortune.[60] Eusebius himself, the first of the great Christian historiographers, reworked this trope, reverting to Aristotelian language to recast Christianized pagan *Fortuna* as *symbebêkota*, the 'accidents' of history, while subsequent historians used different terms. Theodoret used a whole series of Fortune words, such as *symphora, euklêria,*

[51] See Raoul Mortley, *The Idea of Universal History from Hellenistic Philosophy to Early Christian Historiography* (Lewiston, NY: Edwin Mellen Press, 1996), 9.

[52] Ibid., 10–15.   [53] Ibid., 54–5.   [54] Ibid., 36–7.   [55] Ibid., 39.   [56] Ibid., 40.
[57] Ibid., 41–2.   [58] Ibid., 42.

[59] Garry W. Trompf, *Early Christian Historiography: Narratives of Retributive Historiography* (London: Continuum, 2000), 134.

[60] Glenn F. Chestnut, *The First Christian Histories: Eusebius, Socrates, Sozomen, Theodoret and Evagrius* (Paris: Editions Beauchesne, 1986), 182.

and *dysklêria*, while Socrates and Evagrius referred to *kairos*. We see classical models clearly at work in Socrates Scholasticus of Constantinople, for instance, when in the introduction to his *Historia Ecclesiastica* he introduces *kairos,* echoing Thucydides 1.23.1–3 on the proof of the importance of the Peloponnesian Wars as expressed in earthquakes, droughts, eclipses, etc. that took place during its course: 'having set forth to write ecclesiastical history, we mix in with it also those wars which took place at critical moments (κατα καιρόν)…this we do…before all else so that it might be known how, when state affairs have been troubled, the affairs of the churches have been troubled out of sympathy also'. Nor was this sympathetic linkage unidirectional: 'Sometimes the affairs in the churches lead the way; then affairs of state follow in turn; and sometimes the reverse'. Socrates explicitly states that 'the nexus connecting troubles in the church with troubles in the state…is a *kairos*', events in church and state paralleling cosmic events such as earthquakes, etc.[61] For instance, he connects the Council of the Dedication at Antioch in 341, which tried to put up the first counter-creed to the Nicene declaration, with raids by the Franks into Gaul and earthquakes in the East.[62] Evagrius Scholasticus provided a more down-to-earth characterization of *kairos* as 'the opportune moment', personified, and to be 'grasped by the forelock'.[63]

One would be remiss to overstate the humanism of the universal historians and present the conception of *kairos* as a kind of objectivity on their part. Evagrius's observation nicely captures the personalism which imbued their work. Their relentless pursuit of 'retributive justice' (Garry Trompf's rather euphemistic term) is expressed in the shrill voice of partisanship and doctrinal controversy. This was Hobbes's chief complaint against them, as Rymer notes in his clever preface. Not one of the church histories, from Eusebius on, fails to stake out an adversarial position, and defend it to the teeth: Eusebius as the glorifier of Constantine, and Rufinus as his continuator; Athanasius as the vilifier of Arius and Eusebius, the latter mildly Arian-leaning; Philostorgius as the vilifier of Athanasius and defender of Arius; Socrates of Constantinople, a triumphalist in the tradition of Eusebius; Sozomen more sceptical; Theodoret more balanced, but celebrating the Great Theodosius as Eusebius had celebrated Constantine; and so on. The Church did not enjoy a pacific universality, as the historians freely admitted, nor was its continuity that of a benign orthodoxy. It was threatened by tyrants from without and heretics from within, all of them judged by portents and the punishments the wrath of God rained down upon them, from pest and plague to miracles, showers of stones, and sudden death.[64] Nor is it contradictory to argue for the relative humanism of the ecclesiastical historians, on the one hand, who see the church as a grand institutional edifice after the model of the Roman Empire, a work of artifice in Hobbesian

---

[61] Ibid., 184, citing Socrates Scholasticus, *Historia Ecclesiastica*, book 5, introduction; and books 2.25–26 and 6.6.

[62] Ibid., 186 n. 89, citing Socrates Scholasticus, *Historia Ecclesiastica*, book 2.10.

[63] Evagrius, *Historia Ecclesiastica*, book 3.26, cf. 6.12, cited by Chestnut, *First Christian Histories*, 183.

[64] HE, line 1338, pp. 470–1, for instance, uses the idiom 'drenched by a shower of stones', to be found in Pliny, *Natural History*, 2.38.

terms; and their tendentiousness and tendency to demonize, on the other, as crusading ideologues determined to maintain their battle positions. Such ambivalence characterizes social movements to this day, from crusading Marxists to defenders and detractors of Brexit and the dream of the European Union.

Hobbes, preoccupied by the threats and counter-threats of heresy in his own day, recaptures the idiom of the early church histories, one of biting invective and perpetual wrangling even if, in their eyes, it is the story of the progressive growth of a majestic parastatal institution. From the time of Constantine, who in 313 declared Christianity *religio licita*, a religion recognized by the Roman authorities,[65] the histories of Church and Empire are incestuously entwined. Eusebius glorified Constantine in comparison with his co-ruler, the tyrant Licinius, and defended his rule in terms of the promise that piety and propitiation of the appropriate God offer as security against plague and pestilence.[66] Rome, as the last Empire of the prophecies of the Book of Daniel, was a preparation for God's 'final triumph' and, in his *Life of Constantine*, Eusebius foreshadows an afterlife of beatitude for Christian martyrs who promote it, and the work of the devil in those who frustrate it, chief among them being heretics.[67] Eusebius is the first to chronicle the rise of heresy from Simon Magus to Arius. He is not afraid to criticize Christian pride, sloth, hypocrisy, and factionalism as provocations to persecution;[68] and if he is more restrained than his successors in cataloguing doctrinal wrangling, he lived to see less of it than they did. Philostorgius (*c.*368–*c.*439), whose work was preserved by the bibliophile Photius, was the first of the famous line of post-Eusebian ecclesiastical historians from the Greek East, which included Socrates Scholasticus (*c.*380–*c.*450), Salaminius Hermias Sozomen (*c.*400–*c.*450), and Theodoret of Cyrrhus (*c.*393–*c.*458). But while the latter three were orthodox, Philostorgius was an Arian. Meanwhile, Athanasius, Eusebius's nemesis, had completed his *Historia contra Arianorum* sometime in the 360s, excoriating the Arian heresy as 'some great monster' rending the Christian body, and the Arian bishop Gregory, installed at Alexandria after the Council of Antioch, 337–8, as 'an outrageous robber of mendicants',[69] language familiar to us from Hobbes.[70] Athanasius is not above exploiting the ignominious end to Arius, who died from copious bowel haemorrhaging in Constantinople,[71] and Hobbes's evocation of the Arian Goths as a pustule that spawned many diseases is also not uncharacteristic of Athanasian rhetoric,[72] although his unsympathetic characterization of Athanasius, forced into exile, owes more to Eusebius.[73] It is to this sort of

[65] Trompf, *Historiography*, 118.
[66] Ibid., 123, citing Eusebius, *Historia Ecclesiastica*, book 9, 7.8, 7.11, and 7.14.
[67] Ibid., 129, 133, citing Eusebius, *De Vita Constatini*, book 2.26.
[68] Ibid., 132, citing Eusebius, *Historia Ecclesiastica*, book 8, 1.7–8, cf. 6; and book 8, 2.4–5.
[69] Ibid., 187–8.
[70] See HE, lines 297–302, pp. 334–5, for a typical Hobbesian catalogue of abuse.
[71] Trompf, *Historiography*, 187–8.
[72] See HE, lines 931–2, pp. 414–15: 'the Goths had a common origin, many pustules come from a single disease'.
[73] See HE, lines 889–94, pp. 408–9.

crusading anti-Arianism that Philostorgius was to respond, extolling the providential role of the Arian confessor, Eusebius of Nicomedia, at Constantine's deathbed; treating the *homoousian* clause defended by Athanasius as a pollution;[74] finding miracles and divine portents aplenty in support of the Arian cause and in defiance of the Theodosian order; and possibly an analogue for Arius's grisly death in the death of Theodosius from dropsy.

9.4 The Ecclesiastical Historians and the Heresiarchs

Hobbes in the 1660s was bedevilled by the problem of heresy and must have seen that the early ecclesiastical historians, despite their flair for universal history and a fine sensibility for the rise of the church as an institution, were also perpetrators of sectarianism. The tendentiousness of the ecclesiastical histories of Athanasius and Philostorgius fed off retributive argument and promoted it.[75] All three orthodox Eastern post-Eusebian historians, Socrates Scholasticus, Sozomen, and Theodoret, responded in turn in a chorus of reproaches against those, including Philostorgius, who impugned the Great Constantine or the Great Theodosius. While Socrates Scholasticus is the more judicious and objective in his use of source material, examining imperial letters to instance Arius's treachery before his (fittingly) ignominious death, Sozomen is the first to paraphrase *in extenso* Athanasius's letter to Serapion, to show that the citizens of Constantinople in fact took the manner of Arius's death to be an expression of divine wrath.[76] Socrates Scholasticus finds signs of divine displeasure in the earthquake and Frankish invasion that follow the exclusion of the *homoousion* clause from the Antiochene Creed; Constantius's attempt to convene the synod at Nicomedia is frustrated by an earthquake and, shocked by the apostasy of his nephew Julian, he dies of apoplexy.[77]

Sozomen, like Rufinus, is impressed by miracles and more credulous than Socrates, but like Rufinus is also more quietly confident in the institutional 'progress' of the church through the cycle of peaks and troughs. 'Thus before Julian's rule the rewards of the faithful are more emphasized by Sozomen than the punishments of evil, concomitant with his picture of a slow decline from the zenith of "the Constantinian era" to the death of Constantius'.[78] Sozomen tells how Julian the Apostate was punished for defecating on a Christian altar by immediate corruption of his rectum and genitals, a story Theodoret retells more elaborately. And Sozomen is the first to provide, in the case of Julian, a Christian defence of tyrannicide; a fact that cannot have escaped Hobbes.[79]

---

[74] The term *homoousion*, 'one substance', was used by the Council of Nicaea, AD 325, to define the doctrine of the Trinity, as opposed to the term *homoiousion*, 'like substance', favoured by the Arians. See HE, line 674 and notes, p. 381.

[75] Trompf, *Historiography*, 198 ff.   [76] Ibid., 219.

[77] Ibid., 218–19, citing Socrates, *Historia Ecclesiastica*, books 2.10, 2.39, 2.47.

[78] Ibid., 220, citing Sozomen, *Historia Ecclesiastica*, books 1–4, at 1.1.

[79] Sozomen, *Historia Ecclesiastica*, book 2.1–2, cited by Trompf, *Historiography*, 227.

Theodoret is the most polemical of the three, crusading against the impiety of Arianism as work of the Devil ('o Daimon, 'o diabolos), while portraying Constantine as 'profoundly wise'.[80] The treatment of events from the untimely death of the orthodox Jovian and leading up to the reign of Theodosius I, and particularly the treatment of Christian persecutions by the Arianizing Valens, is a test case for the differences between the three. In general, they tend to show church–state relations as ones of mutual infection, rather than direct causality,[81] this infection evidenced by divine portents. So, for instance, both Socrates and Sozomen have no difficulty in explaining Valentinian's death in a fit of rage as caused by the inroads of the barbarians, while for Theodoret, the reason for Valens' death while fighting the barbarians was not open to question: it was divine retribution for 'the magnitude of his errors overthrowing the proper measure of humaneness'.[82]

Socrates closes his history with an account of the peace of the Theodosian order in the same spirit of triumphalism exhibited by Eusebius, reviewing the reign of Constantine.[83] Socrates does not suggest, however, that the problem of heresy had been finally laid to rest, while Sozomen, who takes his history further, through the barbarian invasions, contrasts the pacific rule of Theodosius II in the East with disorder in the West, culminating in the sack of Rome by Alaric, as divine retribution for the Eternal City's luxury and excess. Theodoret goes further in insisting that the resolution of matters of state is necessarily partial to piety and, where this principle does not appear to be vindicated, he is discretely silent, as in the case of contemporary theological debates and particularly the Monophysite–Nestorian controversy and the 'Robber Council' of 449–50, in which he had been so heavily implicated. He chose to ignore the wailings of the exiled Nestorius—whom he had so recently defended—against Cyril of Alexandria as 'the father of many heresies'.[84] Eschewing cosmic punishments for the wicked—he even refrains from mentioning the sack of Rome—he had his own explanation for impiety in sacred history, from which however, the lover of peace could take cold comfort: 'These wars and the unconquerability of the Church were predicted by the Lord, and this teaches us about [political] affairs that war brings more blessing than peace'.[85]

There is an uncanny likeness between the histories of Eusebius, his translator and continuator, Rufinus, the anti-Arian Athanasius and Arian Philostorgius, and later the Byzantine trio, Socrates, Sozomen, and Theodoret, as narratives of the vindications of an avenging God, and the heresiography of the Puritan sects of the 1640s. Perhaps it is this observation that drives Hobbes's *Ecclesiastical History*, or counter-history. Like the

[80] Theodoret, *Historia Ecclesiastica*, books 1.2, 4.1, 7.1, 10, 15–18, etc., cited by Trompf, *Historiography*, 220.
[81] Chestnut's 'cosmic sympathy'; see Chestnut, *First Christian Histories*, 206.
[82] Theodoret, *Historia Ecclesiastica*, book 5.1, quoted by Trompf, *Historiography*, 231.
[83] Cf. Eusebius, *Historia Ecclesiastica*, book 1.1, cited by Trompf, *Historiography*, 234.
[84] Ibid., 239, citing 'Theodoret's *Reprehen. duodec. capit. seu anathem. Cyril*'.
[85] Theodoret, *Historia Ecclesiastica*, book 39.24–26, quoted by Trompf, *Historiography*, 240–1.

Church Fathers themselves, he believes that the sickness of the sects has the power to affect the health of the realm. The Fathers, like the later heresiarchs, appeal to the Old Testament God, who speaks through portents and miracles, whose judgements are announced by flood and earthquake, a God of war and not of peace. But this, in Hobbes's view, is surely the old dispensation of sectarianism and violence that the new dispensation of Christ was born to remove. It is not improbable that he saw a parallel between the obsession with heresy of the authors of the ancient ecclesiastical histories and the fanaticism of contemporary heretic hunters. So, for instance, Ephraim Pagett in his *Heresiography: Or a Description of the Heretickes and Sectaries Sprang Up in these Latter Times*, published in 1654, gives a list of between forty and fifty heresies, including lengthy discussions of 'Brownists, Semi-separatists, Independents, Familists, Adamites, Antinomians, Arminians, Socinians, Antitrinitarians, Millenaries, Hetheringtonians, Antisabbatarians, Trafkites, Jesuits, Pelagians, Soule-sleepers, Antiscripturians, Expecters or Seekers, and Papists';[86] continuing with a comparison between Papists and yet more heretics, Catharists, etc.[87] Pagett notes that he includes Papists with 'late Hereticks', because 'there is a great difference between ancient Papists and the moderne since their Trent Conventicle'.[88] It is significant, perhaps, that he concludes his work with a postscript in defence of tythes which his 'Sectary' parishioners refuse to pay!

Pagett's work was based in turn on Daniel Featley's *The Dippers dipt or the Anabaptists d'nckt and plunged over head and ears* (1645)—a title that Hobbes perhaps hints at with his own short catalogue of sects and factions in the poem, beginning with 'Independents, Quakers, Presbyterians, Fifth Monarchy Men, Episcopalians', and finishing with Anabaptists, whom he refers to as 'twice dipped'.[89] Judged in their own time as products of a paranoid imagination, Thomas Edwards' *Gangraena, Catalogue and discovery of many of the errors, heresies, blasphemies and pernicious practices of the sectaries of this time*, 1646, is just as obsessive; while Alexander Ross's *Pansebeia: or A View of All the Religions of the World* took a more academic approach to heresy, in contrast to John Davies' *Apocalypsis: Or Revelation of Certain Notorious Advancers of Heresie*, bound together with it, but came up with just as impossibly long a list of heretics.

The patristic works on heresy were not necessarily more restrained. The *Panarion* of Epiphanius, Bishop of Salamis, in volume 2 of Denis Petau's edition of *Epiphanii opera* (held in the Hardwick Hall Library at shelfmark F.3.1), for instance, lists some eighty sects, a term Epiphanius uses flexibly to cover both formally organized groups like the Manichaeans, schools of philosophy, tendencies of thought, or more general religious or philosophical classifications, like Epicurean and Jew.[90] Alexander Ross in *Leviathan Drawn out with a Hook*, with likely reference to the *Panarion* of Eusebius,

---

[86] Ephraim Pagett, *Heresiography, or, a Description and History of the Hereticks and Sectaries Sprang Up in these Latter Times* (London, 1645), 54, 146.

[87] Ibid., 156 ff.   [88] Ibid., 146.

[89] 'Dibaphi' (from Gr. *dibaphos*), literally twice dipped. HE, line 1560, pp. 498–9.

[90] See the Forward to Epiphanius, *The Panarion of St. Epiphanius, Bishop of Salamis, Selected Passages*, ed. Philip R. Amidon (Oxford: Oxford University Press, 1990).

accused Hobbes of reviving the heresies of 'Anthropomorphists, Sabellians, Nestorians, Saduceans, Arabeans, Tacians or Eucratists, Manichies, Mahumetans and others'.[91] Hobbes himself, in the person of interlocutor B in the 1668 Appendix to the Latin *Leviathan*, §88, cites Epiphanius's *On the Trinity*, book seven, to make the important point that: 'The word of God was sufficient for all believers . . . But we are forced by the errors of the heretics and blasphemers to do that which is not permitted and speak of that which is ineffable and to fall into that error which is the contrary of theirs'. To which Interlocutor A responds, 'Epiphanius wrongly excuses himself, for, without threats or outright force, no one can be compelled by another's error to do that which is not allowed'.[92]

There are other clues that Epiphanius may have been an important source for Hobbes: in particular his use of the term *pharmakon*, indicating a cure for heresy, or poison,[93] and his discussion of 'Hellenism' (*hellenismos*) as Graecismus.[94] It seems highly likely that Hobbes would lump together heresiarchs ancient and modern in his *Ecclesiastical History*, which is both a history of gentilism and a history of (un)civil religion. It is also a long prehistory of causes of the English Civil War which he laid at the door of presbyters and priests, as well as of the condition in which he found himself, hounded by heresy hunters. But the *Historia Ecclesiastica* also targets the universities, whose provenance Hobbes traces to the papal foundations of the Middle Ages, bastions of the church's institutional structure; seats of controversy and heresy hunting of which Hobbes was a victim,[95] especially in the case of the Oxford Presbyterians, with whom he fought such long-running battles.

---

[91] See Ross's epistle 'to the reader' prefacing *Leviathan Drawn out with a Hook* (1653), cited by Collins, *Allegiance*, 269.

[92] See George Wright, 'Thomas Hobbes: The 1668 Appendix to *Leviathan*', *Interpretation* 18.4 (1991), 365, 398 n. 110, and 399 n. 124.

[93] See HE, lines 1091–2, pp. 436–7 and notes.

[94] The late François Tricaud suggests that Hobbes's discussion of 'Grecism', Hellenism, and Judaism in *Leviathan* may have been taken from Epiphanius's response to Acacius and Paul, where he addresses the Pharisees, Sadducees, and Essenes, in the manner of Hippolytus before him. See François Tricaud's editorial notes to Thomas Hobbes, *Léviathan Traité de la matière, de la forme et du pouvoir de la république ecclésiastique et civile* (Paris: Sirey, 1971), 750 n. 7; see also Wright, 'The 1668 Appendix', 399 n. 124.

[95] See HE, lines 1847–60, pp. 532–7 and notes.

10

A Profile in Cowardice? Hobbes, Personation, and the Trinity

Glen Newey

'It is no trampling on the Ashes of Mr. *Hobbs* to say, that he was a great Coward, his whole Life was govern'd by his Fears'.[1] White Kennett's non-trample, pre-echoed by Hobbes himself,[2] has shaped perceptions of his life and writings, and was already doing so before Hobbes confirmed his worst fears by dying.[3] One need not be Melanie Klein to suspect that Hobbes's crafting of a fearless sovereign might express a need to evict something bad from his psyche. The verse from the Vulgate that lends *Leviathan* its title page inscription—Job 41:33, *Non est potestas super terram quae comparetur ei*—is completed by *qui factus est ut nullum timeret*—in the Authorized Version, 'who is made without fear'. But Hobbes's political theory need not be seen as an exercise in autotherapy—not least because it serves in the economy of fear not to abolish, but only displace its object from other subjects to sovereign. One might add that people fearful of their own fearfulness are usually less open about it than Hobbes was.

L'homme est né poltron, Conrad has one of his characters say,[4] and indeed Hobbes thought fear was the passion dominating not just him, but human beings generally.[5] Nonetheless, the portrayal of Hobbes as an egregious yellow-belly was by no means universally endorsed by his contemporaries (of whom Kennett, still an undergraduate when Hobbes died, was barely one). Aubrey recorded the description of him by the German legal scholar Conringius as 'temerarius'.[6] Abraham Cowley's Pindaric ode to

---

[1] White Kennett, *A Sermon Preach'd at the Funeral of the Right Noble William Duke of Devonshire: With some memoirs of the family of Cavendish* (London, 1708), 113.

[2] E.g. in the verse autobiography, 'Atque metum tantum concepit tunc mea mater, | Ut pareret geminos, meque metumque simul'. English version, 'which struck so horribly my mother's ear | That she gave birth to twins, myself and fear'. See OL 1, p. lxxxvi.

[3] E.g. in John Wallis, *Hobbius Heauton-timoroumenos. Or a consideration of Mr. Hobbes his dialogues. In an epistolary discourse, addressed to the Hon. R. Boyle* (London, 1662).

[4] The character of the French Lieutenant, as reported by Marlow, in *Lord Jim*. See Joseph Conrad, *The Complete Works of Conrad: Lord Jim* (New York: Doubleday 1925), 147.

[5] Famously at L, 14, pp. 216, 217.

[6] John Aubrey, *Brief Lives, Chiefly of Contemporaries*, ed. Andrew Clark (Oxford: Oxford University Press 1898), i, 390; cf. Samuel I. Mintz, *The Hunting of Leviathan* (Cambridge: Cambridge University Press, 1962), 1.

Hobbes likens him to 'embolden'd snow'.[7] Hobbes famously remarked of the *Tractatus Theologico-Philosophicus* that 'I durst not write so boldly' as Spinoza had. But that is a comparative judgement: Hobbes was not saying that he did not write boldly, and had seen the censorious post-Restoration regime that aborted republication of *Leviathan* in the year the *Tractatus* appeared. Assuming Aubrey's report of Hobbes's comment is true, and contrary to Israel's portrayal of Hobbes as a conservative beside the 'radical' Spinoza, Hobbes held views that were barely distinguishable from the *Tractatus*'s author on matters like the reality of miracles.[8] Hobbes impressed many contemporaries not by his timidity, but his boldness. John Bramhall described Hobbes as being as 'bold as blind Bayard' or a child trying to drain the sea with a cockleshell.[9] Ralph Bathurst's dedicatory verses to *Human Nature* describe Hobbes as 'Consultator audax'. Wallis remarked in a letter to Thomas Tenison that Hobbes had denigrated John Selden, who when moribund had refused to see him (with the words 'No Hobbes, No atheist'), for failing at the last to have the courage of his lack of conviction. Hobbes reportedly remarked that Selden had 'lived like a wise man, and died like a fool'.[10]

Opinions about this, like many other aspects of Hobbes's life and thought, were mixed. That is hardly surprising, given that Hobbes took care to cover his tracks—a concern particularly clear in *Leviathan*, whose versions can be read in juxtaposition, and where (unlike with *De Cive*) Hobbes can confidently be credited as directly authorizing each version. Interpretative orthodoxy on Hobbes's theological stance in the 1660s, insofar as it exists, risks doublethink: even though he found the Restoration regime far more congenial to his political outlook, Hobbes had to self-censor far more than he had under the Council of State and Cromwell; so much so that he dreaded that the Anglican bishops (whom his own theory saw merely as executors of the sovereign's will) would have him executed, the several obstacles to this notwithstanding.

In this chapter, I propose that Hobbes's cowardice has been exaggerated in relation to an important area of his thought, namely the theology of his political writings. I will focus particularly on the Appendices to the Latin version of *Leviathan* (LLA).[11] There, I argue, one sees not a Hobbes cowed by the newly assertive Anglicanism of the

---

[7] Joshua Scodel draws a parallel between Cowley's audacious use of the Pindaric and Hobbes's philosophical spunk. See 'The Cowleyan Pindaric Ode and Sublime Diversions', in *A Nation Transformed: England after the Restoration*, ed. Alan Houston and Steve Pincus (Cambridge: Cambridge University Press, 2001), 189–90.

[8] Cf. Edwin Curley, 'Spinoza's Exchange with Albert Burgh', in *Spinoza's 'Theological-Political Treatise':* *A Critical Guide*, ed. Yitzhak Melamed and Michael Rosenthal (Cambridge: Cambridge University Press, 2010), 14; cf. Jonathan Israel, *Radical Enlightenment: Philosophy and the Making of Modernity 1650–1750* (Oxford: Oxford University Press, 2001), chapter 8.

[9] John Bramhall, quoted in *An Answer to a Book Published by Dr. Bramhall*, EW 4, p. 315.

[10] Aubrey, *Brief Lives*, ii, 221.

[11] For an important discussion see Mónica Brito Vieira, *The Elements of Representation in Hobbes: Aesthetics, Theatre, Law, and Theology in the Construction of Hobbes's Theory of the State* (Leiden and Boston, MA: Brill, 2009), chapter 4, which correctly emphasizes that Hobbes's political theology aims at defeating arguments for mixed monarchy via the Trinitarian analogy, as the manifestations of the Godhead are treated as emanations of a unitary divine person.

Restoration settlement, but one—perhaps despite himself—taking his theology in a bold and potentially heterodox direction.[12]

10.1 Hobbes and Heresy

It is well known that Hobbes made repeated recensions of his philosophy, and this is as true of his political theory as elsewhere. My concern is with the substance of the changes and how far they respond to the protean political and religious currents in England at the time. Contextualist approaches to the reading of historical texts have encouraged readers to see philosophical works, especially politically or theologically controversial ones, as interventions in historically localized debates rather than as contributions to a timeless seminar. The case I focus on is the religious politics of *Leviathan*, and specifically the account of personation that Hobbes applies there to Trinitarian doctrine. I will take the cut-off dates as the composition of the English *Leviathan* (L) in the late 1640s and the publication of the first Latin edition (LL) by Johannes Blaeu in Amsterdam in 1668.

During the composition of L or earlier, it occurred to Hobbes that the theory of personation set out in chapter 16 could be applied both to his formal account of political sovereignty and to the person of the Christian deity. It is not clear which application of the theory occurred to him first. Since it plays a larger role in Hobbes's theology and biblical exegesis than in the political theory, it seems quite possible that it was suggested to him by his patristic researches, notably in Tertullian's theology, and that Hobbes then applied this to the account of political representation. It is clear that Hobbes developed—or, less tendentiously, modified—the theory in subsequent recensions of his thought, the main landmarks being the remarks in L, then in chapter 13 of *De corpore* in 1655, and then the three appendices to LL.[13]

One of the main questions posed by the LLA is why Hobbes chose to add a quite substantial body of wholly new material to a text that elsewhere was quite drastically pruned from its English precursor.[14] On the best guess about the chronology of their

---

[12] In this I respectfully demur from the traditional view of Hobbes as cowed by the threat of heresy proceedings, which has recently been restated by Jon Parkin in an important article, 'Baiting the Bear: The Anglican Attack on Hobbes in the Later 1660s', *History of Political Thought* 34.3 (2013), 421–58. Parkin gives valuable information into the background of the moves in Parliament and among the episcopacy against Hobbes. But some facts recounted there tell against the view that he was concerned above all to forestall heresy proceedings, particularly his ambition, discussed in a letter to Johannes Blaeu which Parkin mentions, of getting the Latin *Leviathan* published in England (p. 438 and n. 75). Hobbes was surely concerned to defend the orthodoxy of his views but also had good reason to think that it was a quixotic enterprise to try to convince the Anglican establishment of this. Hobbes insisted on setting out these views in the hope less of persuading others than of showing how his position could be motivated from scriptural and patristic sources, notwithstanding the fact that the personation theology laid him open to charges, severally, of atheism, tritheism, Sabellianism, Unitarianism, or Arianism.

[13] In the polemics with Bramhall, Hobbes provided a summary statement of his views on personation; see EW 4, pp. 315 ff. I return to this later.

[14] There is no compelling evidence for the hypothesis, advanced by Zbigniew Lubinski in the 1930s, and François Tricaud in the 1970s, that an *ur*-version of the Latin existed in a substantial form before

composition,[15] Hobbes was working on them in late 1667 or early 1668. That chronology suggests a ready circumstantial motive. As is well known, Hobbes, like his friend Thomas White, was subject to parliamentary investigation during and immediately before this period, during proceedings under the Atheism Bill; Hobbes and White had been specifically named in House of Lords debates.[16] By Aubrey's account, Hobbes was terrified at the prospect of legal proceedings against him and the danger of being burned for heresy. He sought protection at court from Henry Bennet, since 1665 Earl of Arlington, who may have been among the 'disciples' of Hobbes at court of whom Clarendon complained.[17] Under the *Ordinance for Punishing of Blasphemies and Heresies* (1648), denying the divinity of Christ and denying the Trinity were each punishable by execution on first conviction.[18] Eric Nelson remarks, for instance, that '[t]here is...a large class of cases in which Hobbes chose to excise material from the English version in a clear attempt to mute its religious heterodoxy'.[19]

On this account, then, Hobbes, aghast at the prospect of criminal and perhaps capital liability, adopted a two-pronged strategy for self-defence: drawing on his remaining influence at court, and elucidating his philosophical theology with a view to securing its orthodoxy *modulo* Anglican formularies. Patricia Springborg, for instance, remarks that Hobbes 'came perilously close to heresy by anyone's reckoning' and 'he revised his doctrine in the appendix to the Latin *Leviathan*'.[20] Hobbes took the chance presented by the publication of the Latin version to reaffirm his orthodoxy, and head off the threat of heresy proceedings instigated by his enemies in the Anglican episcopate. Even Philip Milton, who expresses scepticism about the idea that Hobbes solicited help from the court in the person of Arlington,[21] asserts that Hobbes's overriding aim in his writings after the mid-1660s was avoiding incineration. Milton remarks that he 'wrote with one aim in mind: to establish that Thomas Hobbes could not lawfully be burnt as a heretic'.[22]

Nonetheless, this seemingly plausible account of Hobbes's intentions in writing LLA leaves questions, including the one already raised: namely, why he wrote them in the first place. This question is not laid to rest by assuming that Hobbes intended

---

the 1660s. See Noel Malcolm, 'General Introduction' to his edition of *Leviathan* (Oxford: Clarendon Press, 2012), i, 153–8.

[15] Malcolm, 'General Introduction', 167–8.

[16] Philip Milton, 'Hobbes, Heresy and Lord Arlington', *History of Political Thought* 14.4 (1993), 501–46.

[17] Edward Hyde, *A Brief View and Survey of the Dangerous and Pernicious Errors to Church and State, in Mr. Hobbes's Book, Entitled Leviathan* (Oxford, 1676), 9.

[18] Milton, 'Hobbes, Heresy and Lord Arlington', 523.

[19] Eric Nelson, 'Translation as Correction: Hobbes in the 1660s and 1670s', in *Why Concepts Matter: Translating Social and Political Thought*, ed. Martin Burke and Melvin Richter (Leiden and Boston, MA: Brill, 2012), 122.

[20] Patricia Springborg, 'Hobbes on Religion', in *The Cambridge Companion to Hobbes*, ed. Tom Sorell (Cambridge: Cambridge University Press, 1996), 365.

[21] Milton speculates that surviving correspondence from Hobbes to Arlington is most plausibly viewed not as Hobbes's petitioning of Arlington to intercede to stall heresy proceedings, but to remind him of arrears in the payment of Hobbes's pension ('Hobbes, Heresy and Lord Arlington', 528 ff.).

[22] Ibid., 532.

LLA as self-vindication: why, if Hobbes indeed found himself in a hole because of his unorthodox theological views, did he keep digging? When one's words are scrutinized intensely for signs of deviance, the better part of valour is surely reticence. Conversely, saying more than is necessary is usually ill-advised.[23] *Pace* Nelson, what needs explaining, even if many of the excisions made in transforming L to LL tend to 'mute' Hobbes's theological radicalism, is why he continued to stick his neck out in LLA—and in some respects stuck it out much further than before.[24]

After the Restoration the new regime at court, led by Edward Hyde (Earl of Clarendon from 1661) as Lord Chancellor, moved fairly quickly to re-establish Anglican orthodoxy. It did so by measures including the 1662 Act of Uniformity, a measure that led to a widespread cull of Puritan sympathizers among Church of England clergy; a prime mover in the bilking of efforts by Presbyterians like Richard Baxter to moderate the post-Restoration clerical settlement was Hobbes's old Great Tew associate Gilbert Sheldon, Bishop of London (and later Archbishop of Canterbury). This reassertive Anglican regime, and (despite *A Review and Conclusion* to L) the measures against conventicles in particular, need not be seen as specially uncongenial to Hobbes's own religious outlook, though in Samuel Pepys's celebrated phrase L was a book which after 1660 the bishops would 'not let be printed again', a view borne out by the suppression of an attempt to reprint it in 1670.[25]

By then Hobbes had had his collar felt by the authorities. The *Commons Journal* for 17 October 1666 noted the proceeding.

Ordered, That the Committee to which the Bill against Atheism and Profaneness is committed, be impowered to receive Information touching such Books as tend to Atheism, Blasphemy, or Profaneness, or against the Essence or Attributes of God; and, in particular, the Book published in the Name of one [Thomas] White; and the Book of *Mr. Hobbs*, called The *Leviathan*; and to report the Matter, with their Opinions, to the House.[26]

---

[23] As indicated in the text, Malcolm has provided the best-informed speculation about the chronology of LL's authorship. Malcolm assumes that LL was composed sequentially, and indeed circumstantial evidence indicates that this must have been Hobbes's working method with L. See Malcolm, 'General Introduction', 9–12. Maybe Hobbes adopted the same approach with LL, but with the structure already in place from L, that may have been less pressing. A fortiori, the entirely new LLA might have been composed at any stage in the composition of LL as a whole, including perhaps before the proceedings on the Atheism Bill. The argument of this chapter, though, is that the question of what Hobbes was about in LLA becomes in some ways *harder* to answer if its composition is taken as later than, and a response to, the initiation of parliamentary proceedings against Hobbes.

[24] On the content of Hobbes's theology as a vehicle for his theory of personation, see Arash Abizadeh, 'Hobbes's Conventionalist Theology, the Trinity, and God as an Artificial Person by Fiction', *The Historical Journal* 60.4 (2017), 915–41. Abizadeh takes the further step of arguing that Hobbes denied that God was a natural person but existed insofar as he was represented by divine agents. This, if true, would further reinforce the radicalism of Hobbes's position.

[25] Samuel Pepys, *The Diary of Samuel Pepys*, ed. Robert Latham and William Matthews (London: Bell and Hyman, 1970–83), ix, 298. On the suppressed printing of the putative 'Bear' edition in 1670, see Noel Malcolm, *Aspects of Hobbes* (Oxford: Clarendon Press, 2002), chapter 11.

[26] *House of Commons Journals: Volume 8, 1660-1667* (London, 1802), 636; *Calendar of State Papers, Domestic, 1666-1667* (London, 1907), 209.

A couple of weeks earlier the Commons had established a committee to examine 'former Laws against Atheism, Profaneness, Debauchery, and Swearing'.[27] This seems to lend colour to Milton's view of Hobbes's intentions. But, as we shall see, this is less plausible than attention to immediate context may make it look.

Subsequent remarks fall into two parts: first, the circumstances surrounding the appearance of LL, and in particular an attempt to gauge Hobbes's intentions in getting it published; second, an interpretation of LLA, paying attention to its use of the personation doctrine and Trinitarian orthodoxy.

10.2 Censorship, Heresy, and the Publication of LL

Noel Malcolm writes in a teleological way that the 'threat' of proceedings for heresy was one to which Hobbes 'responded... in a number of ways',[28] including the composition of LLA. Malcolm assumes sequential composition of the Latin text, so that 'it was probably in the spring of 1668' that he wrote LLA; he also cites the famous account by Aubrey that 'the good old gentleman' feared that the parliamentary investigation would lead to his 'being burn't for a heretique',[29] and thereupon settled for the lesser incineration of some of his papers. Of course, even if LLA's composition were significantly earlier, it could still post-date the Commons proceedings begun in autumn 1666, a possibility which, if true, might support the notion that LLA was conceived as a response to them. Even so, teleological extrapolation from any chronology has still to deal with the *post hoc, ergo propter hoc* objection.

Part of the problem is that Hobbes had decisive reason for doubting that L or other pre-1660 writings would leave him liable to heresy proceedings. Despite Aubrey's story, the parliamentary proceedings did not specifically mention heresy. Nor had civil tribunals jurisdiction in heresy proceedings, since they were a matter for diocesan courts, heresy being a matter of canon law. Lay authorities were deployed at the executive rather than the forensic stage, in tracking down offenders and enforcing punishment on conviction. The common-law writ *De haeretico comburendo* could be directly issued by the sovereign for the dispatch of recalcitrant offenders. It was this procedure that Kennett referred to in noting Hobbes's fear that 'Messengers would come for him, and the Earl [of Devonshire] would deliver him up, and the Two Houses commit him to the Bishops, and they decree him a Heretick, and return him to the Civil Magistrate for a Writ *de Heretico comburendo*'.[30] The probability that this chain of events would occur was, however, remote, and in fact never got as far as even the first stage. As Hobbes knew, the Court of High Commission, as a juridical junction between secular and clerical authority, had been dissolved by the Long Parliament in 1642. Above all, the Act of Oblivion[31] of 1660 granted a general amnesty for crimes committed during

[27] *House of Commons Journals: Volume 8*, 630. Cf. Malcolm, 'General Introduction', 153.
[28] Malcolm, 'General Introduction', 154.   [29] Aubrey, *Brief Lives*, i, 339.
[30] Kennett, *A Sermon Preach'd*, 109.
[31] In full, the Act of Free and General Pardon, Indemnity, and Oblivion, 2 Car. II, *c.* 11.

the Interregnum, a fact of which Hobbes was well aware, and acknowledged in the 1662 *An Apology for himself and his Writings* and in *Behemoth*.[32]

It is nonetheless clear that during the late 1660s and beyond Hobbes was actively interested in philosophical and ecclesiological issues surrounding the notion of heresy; LLA chapter 2 is given over to the subject. There is also no doubt that he went to considerable lengths in both *Leviathan*s to show that his theological views, quirky as Hobbes himself acknowledged them to be,[33] had solid scriptural warrant. This goes not just for his view of the Trinity but also his mortalism and his claim that the reprobate in Hell, far from enduring eternal torment, would pass through a strikingly worldly cycle of birth, reproduction, and death.[34] It seems plain that Hobbes's argumentative strategy in Parts Three and Four and the appendices aims to show that his views are supported by or at least consistent with Scripture and the Church Fathers, notably Tertullian, whose views were enshrined in the conciliar tradition at Nicaea.[35]

Even so, the strategy seems an odd one. Hobbes surely realized it was very unlikely, however firmly he insisted that his views enjoyed scriptural and conciliar warrant, that orthodox Anglicans would find them persuasive. The most he could have hoped to achieve was a demonstration, not of warrant, but of sincerity—that he could conscientiously derive his views from canonical sources. If his aim really was to avoid prosecution, the strategy seems risky, since what would matter for juridical purposes was not Hobbes's confessedly eccentric reading of core doctrine, but that of the legal authorities. Such a distinction, too, was one Hobbes was well placed to draw. Like *Behemoth* and the *Dialogue of the Common Law*, *Leviathan* repeatedly lambasts the exegetical state of nature unleashed in the print skirmishes of the 1640s. If anything defined the intellectual basis of reformed religion, it was solefidianism combined with devolved scriptural exegesis—and the less clerically mediated, the more radical its political implications.[36] Hobbes repeatedly inveighed at subjecting the Bible's public meaning to individuals' idiosyncratic reading. He then proceeded to do precisely that.

One pragmatic tension in Hobbes's position lay in his assertion of rights that his own political theory implied that he, an ordinary subject, lacked. Hobbes comes close to arguing that the warrant for mediated divine agency can be borne only by a sovereign.

---

[32] E.g. Hobbes remarks in the *Apology* that 'I rely upon...your Majesties most Gracious General Pardon' (in Hobbes, EW 4, p. 407).

[33] E.g. LLA, p. 1227: 'Insunt in singulis partibus Paradoxa quaedam tum Philosophica, tum Theologica'.

[34] E.g. L, 38, pp. 718–19; LLA, pp. 1160–1. Hobbes claims that there is nothing in the Bible to show that after death the reprobate will not carry on much as in their terrestrial life, and continue to eat, drink, and copulate. Hobbes slyly describes the supporting verses from Luke 20:34–36 as 'a fertile text'. L, 44, pp. 990–2. This passage is dropped in LL and in the 'Bear' and 'Ornaments' variants of L. See Milton, 'Hobbes, Heresy and Lord Arlington', 537–8.

[35] Hobbes might be thought disingenuous in not acknowledging that it was non-mortalist aspects of Tertullian's thought that influenced the formulation of the Nicene Creed.

[36] A point famously picked up by John Milton in the anti-Presbyterian 'On the New Forcers of Conscience Under the Long Parliament' of 1646: 'Men whose life, learning, faith and pure intent | Would have been held in high esteem with Paul | Must now be named and printed heretics | By shallow Edwards and Scotch what d'ye call'. *The Poetical Works of John Milton*, ed. Edward Hawkins (Oxford: J. Parker, 1824), iv, 175–6.

If it came to a dispute between Hobbes and the Anglican divines who after all bore the person of Charles II regarding doctrinal norms, there could be only one winner. In 1668 Hobbes published *An Answer to Bishop Bramhall*, a response not to Bramhall's polemics on free will, but his attack on *Leviathan* ten years earlier. Hobbes (perhaps ruefully) notes that 'nor was I forbidden, when I published my *Leviathan*, to publish anything which the Scriptures suggested. For when I wrote it, I may safely say there was no lawful church in England, that could have maintained me in, or prohibited my writing anything. There was no bishop... There was no church in England, that any man living was bound to obey'.[37] That unregulated situation no longer obtained.

Hobbes adds that the doctrine of *sola scripture* is subscribed in the twentieth of the thirty-nine articles. Bramhall had objected to the doctrine of sovereign personation: 'Upon these grounds every king hath as many *persons*, as there be justices of the peace and petty constables in his kingdom. Upon this account God Almighty hath as many *persons*, as there have been sovereign princes in the world since Adam'.[38] In reply, Hobbes disarmingly says that there are indeed as many persons as the (earthly) sovereign has officers. He then comes out with another *mea culpa* for the putative inclusion of Moses in the Trinity, though again he notes that he rather than Bramhall picked this up ('His Lordship all this while hath catched nothing').

> The fault I here made, and saw not, was this; I was to prove that it is no contradiction, as Lucian and other heathen scoffers would have it, to say of God, he was one and three. I saw the true definition of the word *person* would serve my turn in this matter; God, in his own person, both created the world, and instituted a church in Israel, using therein the ministry of Moses: the same God, in the person of his Son God and man, redeemed the same world, and the same church; the same God, in the person of the Holy Ghost, sanctified the same church, and all the faithful men in the world. Is this not a clear proof that it is no contradiction to say that God is three persons and one substance?[39]

Hobbes could safely cite Tertullian, but not Lucian, who lampoons Christianity. He notes, in a comment either ironic or disingenuous, that the Moses claim has been eliminated in the Latin version of *Leviathan* 'which by this time I think is printed beyond the seas [in Amsterdam] with this alteration, and also with the omission of some such passages as strangers [foreigners] are not concerned in'.[40]

Hobbes presumably knew that there was little hope of publishing *An Answer* in England. Nonetheless he had pressed ahead with the publication of LL, despite the advice of one of his more sympathetic episcopal readers, John Cosin, Bishop of Durham, that the personation theory (and not only the inclusion of Moses) could not be applied to the Trinity.[41] No doubt he was minded to reaffirm, by close biblical reading, the orthodoxy of his views. But it does not follow that he hoped or believed that this would persuade Anglican grandees whose opinions might figure

---

[37] EW 4, p. 355.   [38] EW 4, p. 315.   [39] EW 4, p. 316.   [40] EW 4, p. 317.
[41] In 1662 Hobbes had called upon Cosin's testimony that when close to death in Paris in 1647, Hobbes had taken the sacrament, as proof of his subscription to Christianity. EW 7, pp. 1–68.

in formal proceedings against him. So conceiving of his purpose in composing *An Apology*, for example, would have been quixotic: when Hobbes wrote it Bramhall had been dead five years.

10.3 Textual Scholarship and Divine Personation in the Latin Appendices

Hobbes's argument in LLA chapter 1 focuses on the nature of the divine being, with particular reference to the Nicene Creed, belief in which was endorsed by the Thirty-Nine Articles. As usual, Hobbes's exegetical method involves textual criticism as well as interpretation. He devotes considerable attention to what the Greek New Testament calls *hypostasis* (ὑπόστᾰσις),[42] an underlying matter or stuff ('standing under'). The upshot of this exegesis, as we shall see, is that God can be thought of as diverse personifications of a single individual, whom Scripture represents as a unitary natural person.

In reapplying the personation theory of L to the Trinity, Hobbes's key idea is that the person of God may represent himself, as a natural person, or via a proxy or proxies—a possibility that falls within the rubric of what different texts call either 'artificial' or 'fictional' personation. The question of nomenclature is significant, and Hobbes's taxonomy varies in the published versions of the theory. In L he had seemingly endorsed a tripartite schema of 'natural', 'artificial', and 'fictional' persons. The categorical boundaries are not fully clear, but Hobbes takes as a paradigm of artificial personation the representation of plaintiff by a lawyer, while cases of fictional personation (or 'persons by fiction') are natural persons who represent buildings or institutions such as churches, bridges, and hospitals.[43] As I have argued elsewhere, the question with whom, representer or represented, a person should be identified in cases of personation is a malformed question.[44] At any rate, when Hobbes turns in L Part Three to transfer this categorization to the Trinity from political representation, he seems to place representations of God by persons other than God Himself in the category of artificial personation: God's representation by Jesus Christ, for instance, as Hobbes tells it, seems to be on a par with a lawyer's representation of a client. This link is indeed reaffirmed in LLA chapter 1.[45]

---

[42] In Aristotle the term means roughly 'real underlying nature', contrasted with appearance. See *De Mundo*, 'τῶν ἐν ἀερι φαντασμάτων τά μέν ἐστι κατ᾽ ἔμφασιν, τά δέ καθ᾽ ὑπόστασιν, 19, 395{a}, 30.

[43] L, 16, pp. 246, 247.

[44] Glen Newey, *The Routledge Guidebook to Hobbes' Leviathan*, 2nd edition (London: Routledge, 2014), chapter 7. Skinner's important work on this subject suffers not only from posing the wrong question, but also in giving what is in its own terms the wrong answer to it, i.e. that Hobbes assigns the identity of artificial persons to that which is represented, rather than that which represents. This contradicts L, 41, p. 772, where Hobbes explicitly says that God is one person as represented (say) by Moses, and another as represented by Christ. On my reading, Hobbes is simply saying here that these persons are distinct. Then, of course, a question arises about the orthodoxy of his view of the Trinity. For Skinner's reading the danger for Hobbes is of endorsing Arianism. On my reading, he risks Tritheism.

[45] LLA, p. 1179.

In chapter 15 of *De Homine*, published in 1658, the second section of the *Elementorum philosophiae*, Hobbes had reformulated the taxonomy in a way that seems to streamline it.

Whereas the Greeks talked of a 'πρόσωπον', the Romans talked sometimes of the 'facies' or 'os' of a man, and sometimes of a 'persona': they would use 'facies' if they meant a real person, and 'persona' if they meant a fictional one, as they used to have with comedians and tragedians in the theatre. For in the theatre it was understood that it was not the actor himself who was speaking, but someone else, such as Agamemnon, namely by the actor's donning the fictive face [mask] of Agamemnon and becoming him for the duration [of the play]; however afterwards he could be understood without the fictive face, namely as someone acting, rather than the character to be acted. And fictions of this kind are no less necessary in the commonwealth than in the theatre, on account of commerce and contracts [in the absence of those concerned]. However, as far as the usage of civil personation goes, it may be defined as follows: *a person is one to whom the words and actions of men are attributed, whether they be his own or another's*; if they are his, he is a *natural* person; if another, he is a *fiction*[al person]. So just as the same actor may at different times assume different characters, so may any man whatever represent different men.[46]

Hobbes now seems to have adopted a bipartite taxonomy, distinguishing natural and fictive persons. The distinction rests on whether the words and actions of a given individual are attributed to that individual or someone else. However, that way of putting it short-circuits itself, as it equivocates about attribution. If the actor's words and deeds are attributed to Julius Caesar, say, one still lacks a basis for distinguishing attributions to the real-life Caesar from a dramatic impersonation of him; if one then says that in the latter case the words and deeds are the actor's, the locus of attribution has shifted. The primitive notion, not defined in terms of something else, is that of an individual object of ascription. With the fictional personation which consists in the representation of one individual A by another B, A and B are such that there is a set N of natural persons and that A and B both belong to N, and A is not identical with B; and that the words voiced and actions embodied by B are attributed to A.[47]

This taxonomy telescopes cases that the earlier one distinguished. Indeed, it conflates the previous paradigm cases of artificial and fictional personation: where a

---

[46] Hobbes, OL 2, p. 130. 'Quod Graeci πρόσωπον, Latini dicunt quandoque *faciem* sive *os* hominis, quandoque *personam*: *faciem* si de homine vero, *personam* si de fictitio intelligi volunt, qualem in theatro solebant habere comoedi et tragoedi. Intelligebatur enim in theatro loqui non ipse histrio, sed aliquis alius, puta Agamemnon, nimirum faciem fictitiam Agamemnonis induente histrione, qui pro illo tempore erat Agamemnon; quod tamen postea intelligebatur etiam sine facie ficta, nimirum profitente se actore quam personam acturus erat. Nec minus necessariae sunt in civitate fictiones hujusmodi, propter absentium commercia et contractus, quam in theatro. Quod autem ad usum personae civilem attinet, definiri potest hoc modo: *persona est, cui verba et actiones hominum attribuuntur vel suae vel alienae*: si suae, persona *naturalis* est; sil alienae, *fictitia* est. Ut ergo idem histrio potest diversas personas diversis temporibus induere, ita quilibet homo plures homines repraesentare potest.'

[47] That can be formalized notationally, but will rely on a prior definition of natural personation, with 'A = B' in place of the non-identity in the text. The formalization would rely on already having to hand a means of individuation, and then assigning to the category 'natural person' those individuals who are self-representers.

natural person on the one hand, represents another natural person, and on the other, represents something other than a natural person. One problem raised by Hobbes's application of the personation theory to the Trinity in L is that of theistic overcrowding. If the personation idea is meant to explain the Trinity, then apart from God's self-representation, orthodoxy demands exactly two further personations of him by agents other than the Almighty himself. Unfortunately, Hobbes says at the end of chapter 41 that 'One And The Same God Is The Person Represented By Moses, And By Christ',[48] which could be taken to license at least a four-persona divinity, even before other Old Testament prophets are factored in.

God's house might have many mansions, but post-Nicene orthodoxy demanded that most of them stay vacant. In the passage in LL chapter 16 corresponding to the L discussion of civic personation, Hobbes truncates the *dramatis personae* seemingly called for by the earlier theory, to include only what were previously (in *De Homine*) called 'natural' and 'fictional' personation (although LL chapter 16 dispenses with this contrastive terminology).

A person is *one who acts either in his own name or that of another*. If he acts in his own name, he is a *proper*, or *natural* person; if in that of another, the person is his in whose name a *representative* acts. The Greeks call a person '*πρόσωπον*', which signifies the natural face of a man. But 'person' is very often applied by the Romans to the fictitious face, also called a 'mask', which actors used in theatres.[49]

Hobbes carries over from L the claim that an idol, as a 'meer Figment of the brain', can nevertheless be personated. The 'true God may be Personated' also[50] in essentially the same way that any natural person may be: by appointing someone else to represent him. By contrast, an idol like Rimmon can only achieve representation, and thereby be personated, by 'the introduction of Civill Government'—that is, by the human creation of a juridical mechanism by means of which non-persons may be given a voice. Since such a mechanism is sufficient for divine personation, it follows that natural revelation is not needed to make the true God manifest. God, as a natural person, has seemingly used revelation from time to time as a means of disclosing his will.[51]

---

[48] L, 41, p. 772, marginal heading; cf. LL, 41, p. 773, which omits the concluding paragraph that begins, 'Our Saviour therefore, both in Teaching, and Reigning, representeth (as Moses did) the Person of God'.

[49] LL, 16, p. 245. My translation. 'Persona est *is qui suo vel alieno nomine Res agit*. Si suo, Persona *Propria*, sive Naturalis est; si alieno, Persona est ejus, cujus Nomine agit *Representativa*. Personam Graeci vocant πρόσωπον, quod significat Faciem hominis Naturalem. Sed à Latinis Persona frequentissimè sumitur pro Facie Fictitiâ, quae & *Larva* dicitur, quali utebantur in theatris Histriones.'

[50] L, 16, p. 248.

[51] A burlesque passage where Hobbes cites the bogus miracles of 'Egyptian conjurors' (L, 44, p. 968) comparing them with Roman Catholic priests officiating at the Eucharist to the latter's disadvantage, specifies two tricks—namely those of seeming to turn a rod into a serpent, and water into blood—which have a direct biblical precedent, and which Hobbes had already discussed. This is the episode where Moses works miracles to convince the Israelites that he is God's agent (Exod. 4:1; cf. L, 37, p. 686), via these selfsame acts, of turning a rod into a serpent, and water into blood (the latter being omitted in LL). Hobbes indicates that Moses performed these feats not to convert the Egyptians, but to promote belief among the

The upshot is that the cases of non-natural personation range from representation of one individual by another, to many–one, one–many, and many–many structures, as well as the cases identified in L as personation 'by fiction', where the represented is not a natural person at all. This raises the question in what sense the personation in question is fictive. There are at least three possibilities. First, there is the familiar case where a natural person represents another such, as in lawyer–client relationships. Second, the represented, although a person, is not natural but fictive, as with Agamemnon. Third, the represented is not regarded as a person at all, even in the *alienans*[52] sense conferred by the locution 'fictive person'. This would pull in the cases given by Hobbes in L and LL chapter 16, as well as *De Homine* chapter 15, involving bridges and suchlike. This third case might be thought no different from the second case, in that neither Agamemnon nor (say) a bridge counts as a natural person, while each may nonetheless be treated as such for certain legal purposes. The difference is that bridges are not even seen as natural persons, whereas (within the conventions of dramatic representation) Agamemnon is.

There is a further dimension of fictiveness not yet touched on. The authorization itself may be fictive, as with unauthorized autobiography, or the bogus 'Hitler diaries'. It may take in other representations of real-life figures, such as Shakespeare's *Julius Caesar*, whose original did not authorize *this* representation—unlike, say, the portrait of Caesar that readers get in *De bello gallico*. It need hardly be said that the question whether a given vatic pronouncement counts as authorized is a thorny one for theism; Hobbes pays much attention to it in Part Three of *Leviathan*.[53] Obviously the most emphatic way in which a person can authorize a representation of himself is simply by speaking and acting *in propria persona*, though clearly even here room remains for dissimulation. God's communicative interventions in the world tend to the oblique, whence the problem of authorization. But to assimilate all purported cases of divine communication to the second and third types, where the authorization itself is a fiction, rather than including some cases of the first type, where the authorization is real, would be heretical: it would amount to a blanket denial of the authority, and hence the credibility, of revelation.[54] A sizeable existential hole looms. But the hole, precipitous as it may be, shrinks beside the possibility that divine intervention should be seen as fictive not merely because it has not really been authorized by the Almighty, but also because the author is a nonentity—for example, because it is not a body, and

---

elect, i.e. the Israelites. His ulterior point is that they showed that Moses had divine warrant for exercising secular rule over them.

[52] *Alienantes* terms remove or reduce the force of the terms they qualify, e.g. 'bogus', 'imaginary', 'so-called', etc.

[53] See, e.g., L, 36, p. 666; 43, pp. 928, 944. At L, 36, p. 676, Hobbes notes that 'seeing there is so much Prophecying in the Old Testament...there were many more false then true Prophets' (in LL, 36, p. 677, 'tanta prophetatio erat sub Veteri Testamento... & quoniam major plerumque est Prophetarum falsorum, quam verorum numerus').

[54] Including, most centrally, Scripture as evidence of God's revealed will. Hobbes notes that the authority on which specific claims about God's will rests can only be supernatural revelation or the promulgation of an interpretation of it by secular authority, L, 33, pp. 604–5.

the only things that there are, are bodies. In Hobbes's talk of personation, the absence of God is the elephant not in the room.

While, as commentators have noted, LL in general reduces L—a fact put down again to Hobbes's fear of heresy proceedings—sometimes the reverse is the case, and not only in LLA.[55] For instance, LL chapter 46, 'De Tenebris ab inani Philosophiâ', contains a good deal of material without a precedent in L. This is particularly true of the chapter's handling of the Trinity and Nicene Creed. Here, so far from chopping out doctrinally controversial matter, Hobbes actively interpolates, criticizing at what seems needless length—for someone intent, come what may, on avoiding an *auto da fé*—the idea that the members of the Trinity form a single 'substance'. As Hobbes insists, '[w]here can it be read in scripture or in the Nicene Creed, that there are three "hypostases", that is, three substances, that is, three Gods, or anything equivalent to that?'[56]

In LLA Hobbes goes further, in a most uncharacteristic *mea culpa*. Via the mouthpiece of 'B', Hobbes writes that his remark in L that '[t]he person of even the true God was borne...by Moses'[57] was 'gross carelessness' (*Valde hoc negligenter*).[58] It may seem plain that Hobbes was concerned to anticipate the charge of heresy here, but how this remark serves that presumptive aim leaves room for debate. As Malcolm has noted, a startling feature of the LLA passage is that it responds to an objection that few, if any, of the numerous critics of L had actually made of the book.[59] Critics had shown themselves more inclined to charge Hobbes with Arianism than with multiplying deities beyond Trinitarian orthodoxy. That prompts the conjecture that Hobbes's retraction on Moses might simply be diversionary, letting him present himself as concessive on a comparatively minor count while sticking to radical heterodoxy in a much larger adjacent field.

That is suggested also by Hobbes's idea that divine representations can only operate by 'fiction', as understood in the *De Homine* taxonomy and in LL itself. Whether or not by Hobbes's design, the nature of divine personation is blurred. Of course there is the possibility that God is represented by a natural person, such as Jesus Christ or Moses. That invites the unwelcome inference that Moses, by divine authorization, is coequal with the other personae of the Trinity, as we have seen. But the more theologically glaring problems attend the possibility that all purported prophetic communications of the divine will are fictions, like unauthorized biographies. Since Scripture repeatedly

---

[55] LL did not face censorship by the Lord Chamberlain, since Blaeu was publishing it in Amsterdam. Copies soon found their way to England, without any known official attempt to impede their circulation, around the time when the authorities were taking direct action to suppress the reprinting of L. The English distributor of the 1668 edition of LL was the bookseller Cornelius Bee; the publisher John Thompson distributed the 1670 edition. See Jon Parkin, *Taming the Leviathan: The Reception of the Political and Religious Ideas of Thomas Hobbes in England* 1640–1700 (Cambridge: Cambridge University Press, 2007), 284.

[56] LLA, p. 1232: 'Ubi legitur in Scripturis Sacris, aut in Symbolo Niceno, tres esse *Hypostases*, id est, tres *Substantias*, id est, tres *Deos*, aut aliud quod tantundem valet?'

[57] L, 16, p. 248.   [58] LLA, p. 1233; Malcolm's translation at p. 1232.

[59] Malcolm, 'General Introduction', 157. Malcolm remarks that Moses' elevation to the Trinity was a heresy 'of which no critic had seriously accused him in print'.

has God interpolating the Hebrews by various means, the effect would be to question whether revelation had a veridical scriptural basis. But even that is less doctrinally egregious than adding to it an explanation of why authorization is fictive—whether talk is of Agamemnon or a bridge, there is nobody who really authorizes their representation in the way that a natural person can. Matters are not helped by Hobbes's remark that there can be no non-natural personation outside the commonwealth,[60] which comes close to saying that divine revelation cannot occur without a political authority to authenticate it.

Early Church Fathers developing the doctrine of the Trinity faced awkward philosophical problems, among them what kind of *stuff* secured the unity of Father, Son, and Holy Spirit. Problems were compounded by the fact that patristic writers were trying to find Latinate equivalents for Greek terms, including the words 'hypostasis' and 'ousia'. At length, the Trinitarian orthodoxy emerged that the triune deity was 'three *hypostases* in one *ousia*'.[61] Confusion was compounded by the fact that *hypostasis* could be calqued into patristic Latin as 'substantia', its etymological analogue. But in fact it was the term *ousia* that was standardly Latinized as 'substantia': for instance, in the Nicene formulation, Jesus Christ is described as 'ὁμοούσιον τῷ Πατρί, a description rendered in the Latin version as 'ejusdemque substantiae qua Pater est'. Thus the formula 'three *hypostases* in one *ousia*' might be rendered 'three *substantiae* in one *substantia*'.

That of course constitutes a less than limpid gloss on the Trinity. Hobbes's basic point, which has been echoed by some more recent scholars, is that doctrinal formation was distorted by the back-formation into Greek of ὑπόστᾰσις from 'substantia', leading to an understanding of the Trinity on which God was one individual, but comprising three 'substances'. In the Athanasian creed the Latin formula is *Unus omnino, non confusione substantiae, sed unitate personae*—'one absolutely, not by confusion of substance, but by the unity of personification', as it might be rendered. Hobbes argues in LLA that the Athanasian Creed is to be understood only as paraphrasing the Nicene.[62] Tertullian offered Hobbes a useful foil because of not only his apparent mortalism, as voiced in *Adversus Praxeam*,[63] but also to block the inference that the Nicene Creed's 'ὁμοούσιος' must connote 'coessential'—with, that is, a spiritual substance.[64]

Hobbes argues that Cardinal Bellarmine failed to understand the import of the Greek 'πρόσωπον', and that the word 'signifies nothing but the face';[65] in the *Disputationes* Bellarmine had glossed the term as 'prima substantia'. Since however post-Nicene fathers, notably Theodorus, had elected that the 'ousia' mentioned in the Nicene Creed was equivalent to 'substance', some alternative appellation was needed. *Persona* and its English and Greek equivalents answered to this need. From Hobbes's standpoint, *persona* fitted the bill precisely because it licensed, as regards

[60] L, 16, pp. 246, 247.
[61] Lloyd Geering, *Christianity Without God* (Santa Rosa, CA: Polebridge, 2002), 69–70.
[62] LLA, pp. 1180–1.   [63] LLA, pp. 1228–9; cf. p. 1063.
[64] LLA, pp. 1228–9; Hobbes ascribes this interpretation to Constantine.
[65] LLA, pp. 1180–1.

the Trinity, the well-rehearsed deflationary exegesis that read scriptural passages in purely corporeal terms.

A remaining problem was that the Athanasian Creed formed part of the Anglican liturgy, a point on which interlocutor 'A' remarks early in LLA.[66] Here again, Hobbes seems not to go out of his way to placate the guardians of orthodoxy. He cites Augustine as 'excusing' the Greek language for having no translation of Latin's 'persona', and that 'hypostasis' was gratuitously spatchcocked into the Athanasian Creed.[67] On Hobbes's reading, Tertullian anticipates modern prosopographical exegesis in understanding what would later be labelled 'hypostases' as (in English) 'persons'.[68]

Jon Parkin sees the dialectical aims of LLA as compromised from the outset by Hobbes's insistence on applying the personation theory to the Trinity.

The problem here was that Hobbes was still trying to make the religious facts fit his eccentric understanding of personation, and the theory, which conformed to the understanding of 'person' neither in the scripture nor in any other context, could never capture the meaning of the Trinity without falling unto [sic] absurdity and multiplying members of the Trinity.[69]

As we have seen, however, it seems strained to say that Hobbes in LLA was bent on dodging the pyre at all costs, while he continued to insist on a reading of the Trinity that virtually everyone thought eccentric at best.[70] Rather than having encumbered himself with a dogmatic theology that was unfit for purpose, Hobbes seems to have pressed on because he thought what he said was right, in the sense that a careful reader could conclude this from scriptural and other canonical sources.

Tertullian may have appealed to Hobbes by providing materials for a deflationary account of the Trinity. The word '$\pi\rho\acute{o}\sigma\omega\pi\sigma\nu$' and its inflections crop up quite often (sixty-five instances) in the New Testament, notably at 1 Corinthians 13:12. There, as elsewhere, it signifies the face, as Hobbes remarks in L chapter 16, while also noting its use as a counterpart to *persona*.[71] Tertullian chose to render the word in Latin as 'persona'. Perhaps Tertullian's usage led Hobbes to the idea that assuming a persona, for instance by donning a mask, offered a paradigm of the generic notion of personation—that is, the thought that God projected Himself via diverse personae was the basic idea from which Hobbes inferred other forms of prosthetic personhood. It is basic to the theory of personation set out in L and reworked thereafter that it allows, via the idea of personation by fiction, that not merely the representation, but the representability,

---

[66] LLA, pp. 1156–7.   [67] LLA, p. 1067 ('excusat').

[68] See e.g. Eric Osborn, *Tertullian: First Theologian of the West* (Cambridge: Cambridge University Press, 1997), 137–8.

[69] Parkin, *Taming the Leviathan*, 286.

[70] To this extent I agree with A. P. Martinich, *The Two Gods of Leviathan: Thomas Hobbes on Religion and Politics* (Cambridge: Cambridge University Press, 1992), 31, that '[t]here was little evidence that [Hobbes] was an intellectual coward'. I disagree, however, that this provides evidence in itself that Hobbes's personal religious convictions were theistic: even atheists can be motivated by conscience. Cf. Alan Cromartie and Quentin Skinner, 'General Introduction', to their edition of Thomas Hobbes, *Writings on Common Law and Hereditary Right* (Oxford: Clarendon Press, 2005), p. li.

[71] I.e., '$\pi\rho\acute{o}\sigma\omega\pi\sigma\nu$ $\pi\rho\grave{o}\varsigma$ $\pi\rho\acute{o}\sigma\omega\pi\sigma\nu$', 'face to face' in the Authorized Version. L, 16, p. 244.

of that which is personated can be created by the very fact of being represented. It is only thus that a being absent from the state of nature, i.e. the 'state', can be represented via the compact of civil association.

In fact, the personation theory, far from being a dogmatic straitjacket, gave Hobbes a good deal of leeway as it could be reconciled with Unitarianism at one end to polytheism at the other. It could also be squared with atheism, because of the possibility of personation 'by fiction' in both its political and theological applications. The fixed point in the political landscape of the later 1660s was Anglican hegemony, with subscription to the Thirty-Nine Articles.[72] Even the Anglican formularies, whose interpretation in Hobbes's political theology demanded sanction by the sovereign, could be tweaked with appropriate hermeneutic tools. If whatever exists must exist as a body, that left open what to say about divine instantiation: one person's *modus ponens* is another's *modus tollens*. Hobbes studiously refrains from offering his readers direct guidance with this choice.

10.4 Conclusion

Hobbes's stance in LLA and other writings from the later 1660s is hard to understand if one assumes his prime goal was avoiding combustion. Had that been his aim, and the case against him rested on L, his best bet would have been silence, rather than reopening the hole that had been sealed, as Hobbes knew, by the Act of Oblivion. His insistence on doing so could only incite influential enemies like Seth Ward and Thomas Tenison with key positions in the Restoration Anglican church. While authors are not always astute judges of their work's reception, Hobbes can hardly have thought that his radically deflationary account of the Trinity would play well in Salisbury or Lambeth. Nor, as his response to Bramhall's onslaught on *Leviathan* shows, was his main aim to win over his antagonists.

Leviathan's theory of political sovereignty has been called a 'purely artificial' form of personation.[73] Skinner's point is that in the covenant of civil government people are thought of as forming a corporate individual, the state, and that individual is represented by the sovereign; there is no natural individual (i.e. an individual in the state of nature) to which that understanding of the 'state' corresponds. If so, it seems that sovereign representation must be identified with one of the cases of what Hobbes after the publication of L came to call 'representation by fiction', where either the represented is a fictional person like Agamemnon, or a real thing which, though not a person, is treated as such. Hobbes does not seem to worry much, having

[72] In a further irony for Hobbes, his liberty to assert his views depended not (only) on the silence of the laws, but also that of the bishops, despite the fact that, as he noted, their 'praeterpoliticall' power (L, 47, p. 1114) had been dissolved by Elizabeth I. Since the bishops held office on the sovereign's authority, they could however be seen as agents authorized to implement his will.

[73] Quentin Skinner, 'Hobbes and the Purely Artificial Person of the State', *Journal of Political Philosophy* 7.1 (1999), 1–29.

distinguished these possibilities, about which applies to political personation. Maybe the state in Hobbes's sense can be thought of as agent-like in itself, as Agamemnon can, whereas walls and bridges cannot. But the wider point is that the very act of instituting juridical representation invests what is represented with the agency needed for authorization to work.[74]

To that extent the represented appears as a kind of back-formation from the advent of the representer. That is also a possible view of the self-tokening by the Almighty through manifest signs. For Hobbes, having survived a period when God had filled the ether, at least in the prognostics of men like Thomas Harrison, with manifest signs, channelling revelation via the earthly sovereign was the only way to jam the traffic in divine signals. An irony of Hobbes's intellectual course in the later 1660s is that in *Leviathan* he found himself at loggerheads with the very figure—the sovereign's deputy, in the person of Roger L'Estrange, Surveyor of the Imprimery and Licenser of the Press, leant on by the bishops—whom his own theory made the definitive judge of publishable orthodoxy.

Hobbes presumably saw the irony, and in any event as we have seen pulled out passages from the text of L that Anglican divines could brand as heterodox. Hobbes, whom Wallis[75] called '*heauton-timoroumenos*'—roughly, 'self-torturing'—during their wrangles, continued tweaking by the tail the beast that his own theory gave him reason to dread.

---

[74] As I argue in *Hobbes' Leviathan* and in 'First Politics, Second Nature: Political Representation in Hobbesish Mode' (MS), one can see the civil covenant as effecting an agreement to create a natural person, the sovereign, whose relation to the 'state' corresponds to that of representer to represented in natural personation.

[75] See n. 3. The title glances at a comedy by Menander.

11

Hobbes and the Future of Religion

Jon Parkin

Perhaps unsurprisingly, commentators have not tended to engage in detailed speculation as to how Hobbes thought that a future shaped by his ideas might develop, although readings of his texts often imply utopian or dystopian possibilities.[1] There are obviously good reasons to avoid such projects, not least the fact that Hobbes rarely articulated visions of a Hobbesian future.[2] That said, Hobbes clearly hoped that his work would be converted from the truth of speculation to the utility of practice, and this presumably entailed some thought about what the outcome would be. What makes any speculation in this direction peculiarly difficult is that although it is possible to see that Hobbes's arguments are clearly designed to have a transformative effect upon his readers (sovereigns and subjects), it is not always clear what kind of change Hobbes envisages. Hobbes typically identifies the conceptual, philosophical, political, and religious problems that presented the major threats to peace in his time. His suggested solutions point beyond the present and imply a different future, but he does not give us a very clear institutional blueprint about what that society will look like. The problem looks intractable, but the thought that I want to explore is that its very intractability may perhaps offer clues about the character of Hobbes's theory, not least about the extremely vexed question of Hobbes's religious identity. The suggestion here is that thinking a little harder about

---

[1] One might think of the various interpretations that paint Hobbes as the promoter of an enlightened rational utopia. For example, see David Johnston, *The Rhetoric of Leviathan: Thomas Hobbes and the Politics of Cultural Transformation* (Princeton, NJ: Princeton University Press, 1986); Richard Tuck, 'The Utopianism of *Leviathan*', in *Leviathan After 350 Years*, ed. Tom Sorell and Luc Foisneau, (Oxford: Oxford University Press, 2004), 125–38. Alternatively, one might think of the darker interpretations of the Hobbesian state as a kind of despotic dystopia. See, for example, Charles Tarlton 'The Despotical Doctrine of Hobbes', *History of Political Thought* 23.1 (2002), 62–89. A more subtle analytical account of the shape of the Hobbesian religious future (as a 'nonsectarian state church') can be found in Travis D. Smith's 'Forgiving Those Not Trespassing against Us', in *Civil Religion and Political Thought*, ed. R. Weed and J. von Heyking (Washington, DC: Catholic University of America Press, 2010), 93–120. I would like to thank one of the anonymous referees for drawing my attention to this work.

[2] There are, of course, moments where Hobbes does seem to look forward to a world transformed by *scientia civilis*. See particularly his comments in DCv, 'Epistle Dedicatory'.

how Hobbes's theory was designed to work on its readers may tell us something about Hobbes's practical conception of the future of religion, and that that in turn might lead us to revise some of the assumptions that commentators have tended to make about the nature of Hobbes's religious identity and its implications.

11.1 The Puzzle of Hobbes's Religious Identity

Hobbes's religious identity and the nature of his engagement with religion is a perennial problem for Hobbes scholars. It is an enquiry that goes to the heart of understanding what Hobbes's project is really about, and what he may have been up to in writing as he did. Was Hobbes a closet atheist, or some of sort of sincere believer? Was he trying to undermine Christianity, or was he attempting to save it in some way? As well as being interesting in their own right, these questions are important because the answers might help political philosophers to establish whether Hobbes might be thought of as a sort of liberal/conservative/authoritarian/libertarian (or some combination of those), or whether he was a thinker who looked forward to the Enlightenment, or perhaps back to the civic religion of the classical past. For historically minded commentators, solving the identity issue would help to situate Hobbes contextually, to establish which side he might have been on in debates of the time, and to allow us to say with more certainty what specific positions he was accepting, rejecting, satirizing, repudiating, or ignoring. The difficulty for interpreters of all kinds is that Hobbes does not supply terribly clear answers to either the analytical or historical questions about his religious identity, and the detail of Hobbes's religious faith (or lack of it) remains quite mysterious, despite considerable recent advances in terms of what we know about Hobbes's life and work.

The mystery is unusually murky because Hobbes gives us many reasons to suspect that the textual evidence upon which commentators rely could well be a misleading guide to what he actually thought. Hobbes was a writer who practised self-censorship. As Jean-Baptiste Lantin recalled, Hobbes 'used to say that he sometimes made openings, but he could not reveal his thoughts more than half-way; he said he imitated people who open the window for a few moments but then close it again immediately for fear of the storm'.[3] This suggests that Hobbes deliberately concealed his private views out of a concern for the way that his reading public might respond to them. One obvious motive for engaging in this form of concealment was self-preservation: if he had published unacceptable theological views it is highly likely that he would have faced prosecution on a capital charge like heresy. But although this was undoubtedly a powerful consideration, Hobbes's silences were not just about avoiding threats to his own preservation. We know this because he also self-censored when his personal safety was not in jeopardy and on at least one occasion explained his reasons for doing

---

[3] Quoted in Noel Malcolm, *Aspects of Hobbes* (Oxford: Clarendon Press, 2002), 524 and n. 306.

so.[4] The broader motive for engaging in self-censorship was that Hobbes's theory suggested that self-censorship was an appropriate stance, and indeed the natural duty, of a responsible citizen.[5]

Self-censorship multiplies the interpretative difficulties when considering Hobbes's views about religion. If we assume that Hobbes was an esoteric writer, this encourages the thought that lurking beneath the textual evidence there is a 'real' Hobbes, with very distinctive but hidden preferences in terms of theology and ecclesiology. How this is reconstructed tends to depend upon one's starting point, so if one is particularly drawn to the thought that Hobbes is a sort of undercover radical writing in fear of persecution, then he can be construed as a kind of proto-deist or sly atheist.[6] If one is, say, a historian conscious of the immediate contextual circumstances, one might be more inclined to find the key to Hobbes's underlying identity in his similarity to some of the options on the contemporary agenda: royalist species of Episcopalian Anglicanism, or Cromwellian magisterial Independency, perhaps influenced by a 'fundamental' allegiance to Lutheranism or Calvinism of some sort.[7]

Although these interpretative options are disconcertingly diverse, I mention them because there is plausible evidence for each one. The difficulties with the evidence make it hard to rule any of them out. I certainly do not want to do that here. Indeed, I want to suggest that many of them are in fact legitimate interpretations of how religion might go in the future under a Hobbesian scheme. This is to make a rather different sort of claim about the character of Hobbes's account of religion and his hopes for the future. I would suggest that interpretation of Hobbes's religious identity often falls into the trap of overcommitment to more or less exclusive accounts of what Hobbesian religion might entail. Although this is a natural way of thinking about Hobbes's views, what it may not capture is the complicated sense in which Hobbes sought to bring about a kind of transformation that might not be straightforwardly revelatory of a specific preference for particular theological or ecclesiological options.

---

[4] In the summer of 1645 Hobbes explained to his patron why he wanted to keep his necessitarian views on free will secret: 'I must confess, if we consider the greatest part of Mankinde, not as they should be, but as they are, that is, men, whom either the study of acquiring wealth, or preferment, or whom the appetite of sensual delights, or the impatience of meditating, or the rash embracing of wrong principles have made unapt to discuss the truth of things, I must say I confess, that the dispute of the question will rather hurt their piety…', *Of Libertie and Necessitie* (London, 1654), 35–6. The publication of this work in 1654 was not authorized by Hobbes, although by that time he had published a version of his necessitarian doctrine as part of the broader argument *Leviathan*. This suggests that the contextual circumstances of publication were a matter of some importance to Hobbes.

[5] For discussion of Hobbes and self-censorship, see Jon Parkin, 'Hobbes and the Problem of Self-Censorship', in *The Art of Veiled Speech: Self-Censorship from Aristophanes to Hobbes*, ed. Han Baltussen and Peter J. Davis (Philadelphia, PA: University of Pennsylvania Press, 2015), 293–317.

[6] For Hobbes as a sly atheist see Edwin Curley, ' "I durst not write so boldly" or, How to Read Hobbes' Theological-Political Treatise', in *Hobbes e Spinoza*, ed. D. Bostrenghi (Naples: Bibliopolis, 1992), 497–593.

[7] For Hobbes as an Anglican with orthodox Calvinist views, see A. P. Martinich, *The Two Gods of Leviathan: Thomas Hobbes on Religion and Politics* (Cambridge: Cambridge University Press, 1992), 333–7. For Hobbes's affinities with magisterial Independency, see Jeffrey Collins, *The Allegiance of Thomas Hobbes* (Oxford: Oxford University Press, 2005), chapter 6.

Indicative of the complications here is Hobbes's own self-representation as an author. His own theory of course makes the point that any public statement should operate within the terms of what is legally permissible at the time of writing, and what Kinch Hoekstra has called Hobbes's 'doctrine of doctrines' is one of the main reasons why Hobbes's multilayered self-censorship is peculiarly impenetrable.[8] But it was not just a matter of staying within the terms of the law: Hobbes's self-representation also moved about as he addressed different audiences: those transactions involved complicated narrative scripts and Hobbes adjusted his *persona* to play particular roles, often with a view to persuading particular audiences. When dealing with Anglicans, he adopted Episcopalian stances. In the mid-1650s he reinvented himself as a scripturally literate Protestant layman prone to quoting Reformers. In the early years of the Restoration he became a loyal courtier and a scourge of Presbyterians and Cromwellians. By the late 1660s he was a parliamentary Anglican appealing to the jurisdictional framework of the Henrician and Elizabethan reformations.[9] Hobbes alluded to all of these identities, and to several of them within the same text, but not necessarily with the intention of telling us anything about his own preferences. He did so because he wanted to persuade readers with similar views to endorse his transformative project.

This matters because whatever Hobbes was doing, he was not offering a straightforward institutional or theological prescription for the future of religion, or indeed its destruction. The difficulties involved in trying to derive such a model from his writings are perhaps a clue that this might be the case. Here I would like to explore this thought in a number of ways: firstly, by thinking about the way that Hobbes's presentation of his arguments led to distinctive patterns of response amongst his actual readers. It is, of course, problematic to assume that one can necessarily infer authorial intention from reception.[10] But when a variety of readers report similar responses to a text, there is a case for thinking that the author may have intended to produce those responses. I would suggest that we can see such a pattern of response in Hobbes's readers' reactions to his religious doctrine, which his readers found very difficult to pin down. The argument is that Hobbes intended to produce a distinctively ambiguous religious identity, and he did so partly with a view to engaging with a variety of different audiences through which he could attempt to promote a more stable version of Christianity for the future. This leads to a rather different way of thinking about how Hobbes saw the future of religion: a future that had less to do with generating one version of Hobbesian religion, than with generating a variety of plausible Hobbesian futures, linked not by

---

[8] Kinch Hoekstra, 'Tyrranus Rex *vs.* Leviathan', *Pacific Philosophical Quarterly* 82.3–4 (2001), 434.

[9] For the complex character of Hobbes's self-representation, see Jon Parkin, 'Hobbes and the Reception of *Leviathan*', *Journal of the History of Ideas* 76.2 (2015), 289–300.

[10] Indeed, reception evidence can simply provide evidence of deliberate misconstrual or misunderstanding. For the thought that Hobbes was often not understood by his contemporary readers, see A. P. Martinich, 'Law and Self-Preservation in *Leviathan*: On Misinterpreting Hobbes 1650–1700', in *The Persistence of the Sacred in Modern Thought*, ed. Chris L. Firestone and Nathan A. Jacobs (South Bend: University of Notre Dame Press, 2013), 38–65.

any partisan ecclesiological allegiance but rather by a set of Hobbesian background conditions that might play out in a number of different ways in practice. The suggestion is that Hobbes did not commit to one view of the future of religion because he envisaged multiple possibilities. To that extent, the fact that commentators have been able to identify many different modes of Hobbesian religion may in fact capture something important about the character of Hobbes's project, but perhaps not in the way that many of them have previously thought.

11.2   Reading Hobbesian Religion in the Seventeenth Century

The uncertainty about Hobbes's religious identity, or about what he meant by proposing the doctrines that he did, is not new. It has been a feature of Hobbes's reception since the first appearance of his work. Early readers, like modern commentators, found Hobbes's religious views impossible to pigeonhole satisfactorily and in ways that go quite a long way beyond the modern preoccupations with the denominational characteristics of his arguments. Indeed, a common early response to Hobbes's religious doctrine was that there was no particularly coherent account of religion at all. Several early commentators referred to Hobbes's religious arguments as 'rhapsodies', muddled collections of words and ideas that did not add up to a systematic position. This was the case with Hobbes's earliest published work on the subject, *De Cive*. European readers saw the discussion of religion in that text as an essentially paradoxical 'rhapsody of heresies', full of 'new and audacious ideas' that would spread confusion.[11] A similar response can be found amongst the English clergy, who were equally perplexed by what seemed to be the deposition of Christ from his 'true kingly office', suspicious about the meaning of Hobbes's unusual scriptural exegesis, and anxious about his rewriting of the roles of the clergy and the implications of his rational religion for mysteries like the Incarnation and the Trinity.[12] Although the constitutive elements of Hobbes's discussion undeniably looked familiar, the package was odd: paradoxical, provocative, troubling. *Leviathan*, of course, was worse: the early reception of that work is even more bewildered, the arguments characterized as 'Wild and unchristianly', a 'farrago of all the maddest divinity that was ever read', a 'rapsodie' of heretical and blasphemous antinomianism, 'a rhapsody of as strange Divinity, as since the dayes of Gnosticks, and their several Progenies, the Sun ever saw'.[13] Alexander Ross suggested that there was nothing structurally coherent about Hobbes's positions, which were

---

[11] Baptiste Masoyer-Deshommeaux, quoted in Malcolm, *Aspects of Hobbes*, 473; Gabriel Naudé, quoted in A. L. Schino, 'Tre lettere inedite di Gabriel Naudé', *Rivista di storia della philosophia* 4 (1987), 697–708.

[12] See the discussion in Jon Parkin, *Taming the Leviathan: The Reception of the Political and Religious Ideas of Thomas Hobbes in England, 1640–1700* (Cambridge: Cambridge University Press, 2007), 32–71.

[13] Brian Duppa, *The Correspondence of Bishop Brian Duppai*, ed. G. Isham (Northampton: Northamptonshire Record Society, 1951), 41; Henry Hammond to Matthew Wren, in [Anon.], 'Illustrations

strung together from an exotic variety of defunct heresies.[14] What many of these
early statements have in common is their authors' difficulty in identifying Hobbes's
treatment of religion as a single identifiable project, and this has been a problem that
has dogged commentary on Hobbes ever since.[15]

If Hobbes's religion was very difficult to pigeonhole, at the same time many early
readers, even those starting from a critical perspective, were willing to concede that
Hobbes did have some sort of commitment to Christianity. It was perhaps a sign that
Hobbes's work was not transparently *anti*-Christian that *Leviathan* was licensed by
the commonwealth's Puritan licenser, the divine John Downham.[16] One of the things
that made this possible was that even if one was puzzled by the theology, the very fact
of its presence made it hard to come to the conclusion that Hobbes was an unbeliever.
And relatively few people did jump to that conclusion. Although anti-atheist literature
was a recognizable genre at the time that *Leviathan* was published, Hobbes was not
targeted by it. There is no discussion, for example, of any of Hobbes's work in Charleton's
Darkness of Atheism (1652), or (perhaps more surprisingly) Henry More's *Antidote to
Atheism* (1653). The first published suggestion that Hobbes was an atheist in the
formal sense of the term had to wait until a full three years after the publication of
Leviathan, and even then its author (Seth Ward) was forced to make an embarrassing
public retraction of the claim after Hobbes objected to it.[17] At that point Hobbes was
able to crow that plenty of men read *Leviathan*, and 'yet they all find not such enmity in
them against religion'.[18] The evidence suggests that he was probably right. Heretical,
blasphemous possibly, but Hobbes was not widely viewed as an atheist until the 1660s,
and even then, there is quite a lot of evidence that the anti-Hobbesian slur about
Hobbesian atheism never convinced everyone. Even casting Hobbes as a blaspheming
heretic involved its own difficulties, particularly in the 1650s when a wide variety of
religious views were tolerated by the state. Richard Baxter and his Presbyterian associates tried to make legal issues out of Hobbes's heterodoxy on more than one occasion
during the Interregnum, but the authorities were not particularly interested in pursuing

of the State of the Church during the Great Rebellion', *The Theologian and the Ecclesiastic* 9 (1850), 294–5;
Henry Hammond, *A Letter of Resolution to Six Quaeres* (London, 1653), 384.

   [14] Alexander Ross, *Leviathan Drawn out with a Hook* (London, 1653), 121–2.

   [15] Although modern historians probably find *Leviathan* much less confusing with the benefit of various
forms of hindsight informed by several centuries of commentary designed to render Hobbes's work coherent in one way or another. Traditions of interpretation can have a screening effect. It is an argument for the
importance of studying reception that early reader response may capture something about the design of a
work like *Leviathan*. It is hard to believe that Hobbes did not realize that this was the effect that his book
would have, which in turn leads to the thought that there might have been something deliberate about the
design of the text that it produced this effect.

   [16] G. E. Ayre, C. R. Rivington, and H. R. Plomer (eds), *A Transcript of the Register of the Worshipful
Company of Stationers from 1640–1708* (London, 1913–14), i, 358. For Downham's role in licensing see
Parkin, *Taming*, 94–5.

   [17] Seth Ward, *In Thomae Hobbii Philosophiam Exercitatio Epistolica* (Oxford, 1656), 340.

   [18] EW 7, p. 350. Hobbes made a similar statement in 1662 that his doctrine showed 'no sign of Atheism'.
Hobbes, *Mr Hobbes Considered in his Loyalty, Religion, Reputation and Manners* (London, 1662), 37.

the matter, and at least twice the attempts backfired as Hobbes's Presbyterian antagonists were condemned for their intolerant bigotry.[19]

So Hobbes was not obviously an atheist, but of course that perception in itself was not likely to attract or enthuse his readers. But there were features of Hobbes's work that readers did find attractive, and this is something that is often forgotten in the light of Hobbes's later notoriety. There was something for nearly everyone in a work like *Leviathan*. This was even the case for readers who were critics. A standard feature of early criticism is that Hobbes's critics drew attention to the philosopher's learning, and the fact that he had said some good things, before they launched their attacks. Bishop Brian Duppa commented that there are 'many things said so well that I could embrace him for it'.[20] William Rand, a republican Independent, detected some 'fine cleare notions' before lamenting the state of Hobbes's paradoxes.[21] Sir Robert Filmer approved of what Hobbes said about sovereignty, and Alexander Ross commented upon Hobbes's 'excellent parts' and the fact that *Leviathan* contained much 'gold' before commenting upon some of the accompanying 'dross'.[22] Beyond the critics a surprisingly broad range of readers expressed positive views of Hobbesian ideas and formulae during the 1650s including Independent Congregationalists (William Rand, John Owen, Henry Stubbe, Edward Bagshaw), Presbyterians (Philip Tanny), Episcopalians (John Hall, Matthew Wren), and even Catholics (John Austin, Thomas White).[23] What is striking about this approval is that it comes from all points on the religious spectrum. Indeed, the only people who consistently opposed Hobbes's arguments were those who made strenuous claims about the *jure divino* authority of the clergy but, as Hobbes probably recognized, this involved a relatively small percentage of his English readership.

Thinking about Hobbes's religious arguments there was plenty to like, and even to enjoy. In *Leviathan* Hobbes's authorial *persona*, the scripturally literate layman puncturing the pretensions of crafty priests, was familiar from a rich English tradition of anticlerical writing reaching back into the sixteenth century.[24] The one clearly identifiable polemical position, anti-Catholicism, was comfortably familiar for English Protestant readers. Hobbes's overt targets, particularly the 'unpleasing priests', were often stereotypical straw men in this vein. That large sections of *Leviathan* offered an

---

[19] Parkin, *Taming*, 112–16, 176; Collins, *Allegiance*, 209–10; Noel Malcolm, 'General Introduction' to his edition of *Leviathan* (Oxford: Clarendon Press, 2012), i, 152.

[20] Duppa, *Correspondence*, 41.   [21] Rand to Hartlib, 18 July 1651, *Hartlib Papers*, 62/30/3b–4a.

[22] Robert Filmer, *Patriarcha and Other Writings*, ed. J. P. Sommerville (Cambridge: Cambridge University Press, 1991), 184–5; Ross, *Leviathan Drawn out*, 'Preface'.

[23] See the discussion in Parkin, *Taming*, and the works cited there: for Rand, see 99–101; Owen and Stubbe, 171–5; Philip Tanny, 162; Hall, 140–4; Wren, 205–7; Austin, 101–2, 129–30; White, 138–40.

[24] One might think here of the Marprelatean satirical tradition, for which see Nigel Smith, *Literature and Revolution in England 1640–1660* (New Haven, CT: Yale University Press, 1994), chapter 9, or anticlerical work by writers like Alexander Leighton and William Prynne. For discussion of the similarity between Hobbes and the latter, see the suggestive remarks in Nicholas Jackson, *Hobbes, Bramhall and the Politics of Liberty and Necessity: A Quarrel of the Civil Wars and Interregnum* (Cambridge: Cambridge University Press, 2007), 92–3.

anatomy of clerical ambition and its baleful effects ensured that these chapters could and did attract an appreciative audience. Hobbes provided an analysis that the reader could extend more or less as their interpretative fancy took them. Hobbes's deployment of ambiguous and non-specific metaphors from the notion of 'a confederacy of deceivers' through to the 'kingdom of darkness' allowed plenty of scope for these discourses to be defined by the reader to include one's least favourite clerical interest group: Hobbes's work provided useful resources for anti-Presbyterians, anti-Episcopalians, and anyone reacting to religious enthusiasm. Hobbes's deliberate under-definition of those targets saved his work from being easily labelled as supporting one position rather than another. Indeed, in 1656 this allowed him to say (without too much exaggeration) that his attack upon clergymen with magisterial ambition in *Leviathan* operated 'without any word tending to the disgrace of Episcopacy or Presbytery'. *Leviathan*'s doctrine, he noted, was 'generally received' by all of the clergy, except for those who did not see it in their interest to be subject to the civil power.[25] We might be a little sceptical that many clergymen necessarily accepted *Leviathan*'s doctrine in quite the way that Hobbes tried to claim, but there is no doubt that many of them did occasionally find Hobbes's arguments congenial, at least as someone who could be perceived to be an enemy of their enemies.

As I have noted, it is problematic to assume that we can infer too much from the way that Hobbes was read. But Hobbes's reception history does point to some distinctive features of his writing about religion. His slightly strange, non-specific, and allusive arguments do seem designed to do a number of different things. Aside from Roman Catholicism, he does not explicitly identify any particular denominations or rule any of them out. They also provide plenty for writers from different denominations to like. This was true of Hobbes's critical mode, in that he provides open-ended arguments that could be applied to one's clerical opponents. It was also true of some of his more constructive comments: so Hobbes signals some sympathy for the sort of ritual practice that appealed to higher-flying Episcopalians, but also drops hints that he might be sympathetic to the approach of Independent Congregationalists.[26] No wonder that commentators have been puzzled, then and now, as to what he actually thought. To understand what may be going on here I think that we need to consider what Hobbes might have been up to in writing about religion in this way.

11.3 Re-Engineering Christianity

An important place to start is with Hobbes's remarks about religion in chapter 12 of *Leviathan*. This is where Hobbes spells out exactly why religious belief is an inescapable feature of the human condition. The seeds of religion might lie in human ignorance

---

[25] EW 5, p. 454.
[26] Comments about the advantages of public worship that was uniform and beautiful (DCv, 15.15) proved to be attractive to a Laudian like John Cosin (see the annotations to his copy of *De cive* in Durham's Palace Green Library (shelfmark Cosin T.5.57)). Hobbes alludes to Independency in chapter 47 of *Leviathan*.

and weakness but they 'can never be so abolished out of humane nature, but that new Religions may againe be made to spring out of them, by the culture of such men, as for such purpose are in reputation'.[27] Religion is therefore inevitable and an inescapable feature of human life. But its institutional manifestation is also constantly vulnerable because of its foundation in faith—a faith also necessarily invested in the fragile credibility of human actors. If religion is founded in the faith that the multitude has in 'some one person, who they reckon to be wise and holy', then the perennial problem of religion is that 'when they that have the Government of Religion, shall come to have either the wisedome of those men, their sincerity, or their love suspected; or that they shall be unable to shew any probable token of Divine Revelation; that the Religion which they desire to uphold, must be suspected likewise; and…contradicted and rejected'.[28] Hobbes tells us how religions come to be undermined: through the tendency to require belief in contradictions, the scandalous self-interested behaviour of priests and their failure to produce the miracles necessary to underpin their authority. Sacred and secular history were full of relevant examples: the children of Israel's regular apostasy followed the pattern, as did the decline of Roman religion. Christianity, structurally no different to any other religion, showed the same frailties. Roman Catholicism was extinguished in England partly because of the corruption of the clergy and partly because of the absurdities and contradictions of scholasticism. Religions came to grief because of 'unpleasing Priests', and this was not only true of Catholicism, but also for 'that Church that hath presumed most Reformation'.[29] The alternate line in the manuscript version removed the typically misty allusion to the unspecified Protestant church (Protestant churches generally? Presbyterianism? Episcopalian Anglicanism?), but the comment there that men turn on the unpleasing priests and end up bearing down upon the civil government that sustains them, conjures up for that audience (Charles II) recent history, and links the story to the moment in time that Hobbes is writing. Chapter 47's famous account of the dissolution of the praeterpolitical knots on Christian liberty offers a similar trajectory for the more recent decline of Christendom, and seems to capture the inevitable slippage that Hobbes imputes to this natural process: popes, bishops, Presbyters, Independents. That story can suggest that Hobbes might be alluding to a religious future defined by contemporary Independency, but there are reasons to be cautious before making such an assumption. Hobbes's insistently conditional commentary on the benefits of primitive Christian Independency indicates that it might only be the best and future state if it can break free of the essential problems of natural religion.[30] As many commentators have observed, Hobbes is unlikely to have seen the religious situation in 1651 as meeting those demanding conditions.[31]

---

[27] L, 12, p. 180.   [28] L, 12, p. 180.   [29] L, 12, p. 186.

[30] L, 47, p. 1116: '…if it be without contention, and without measuring the Doctrine of Christ, by our affection to the Person of his Minister…'

[31] See, for example, Alan Cromartie 'The God of Thomas Hobbes', *Historical Journal* 51.4 (2008), 857–79, and more recently Teresa M. Bejan's comments on the passage in 'Difference without Disagreement: Rethinking Hobbes on "Independency" and Toleration', *The Review of Politics* 78.1 (2016), 1–25.

So if there was no automatic shortcut to either an unproblematic religion of nature or a priest-free world, then what was the best response? The answer supplied by Parts Three and Four of *Leviathan* appears to be that the best response was a systematic attempt to rewrite the Christian script with a view to remedying the major deficiencies and political dangers of organized religion. The components of those solutions are familiar enough to students of *Leviathan*: the critique and reconstruction of the traditional sources of ecclesiastical authority; the decisive assimilation of church and state; the systematic reinterpretation of Scripture to render it compatible with the requirements of Hobbesian sovereignty, and the materialist ontology that Hobbes believed would bring some philosophical coherence to religious discourse.

My interest here is less in the specific contents of that project than in Hobbes's presentational strategies for those arguments. Clearly the theory was important, but these strategies reveal something about how Hobbes wanted this programme to be adopted and applied by contemporary readers. Sovereigns needed to be persuaded to implement Hobbesian policies and subjects also needed to be persuaded because, as Hobbes pointed out, force by itself could never compel belief.[32] If a new kind of Christianity was to be promoted, then it would have to persuade existing users of religious language. Hobbes's presentational strategies suggest that this is what he was trying to do: present arguments that were (i) credible to a variety of religious believers, (ii) familiar to particular audiences, (iii) constituted in a provocative and challenging manner, and which (iv) allowed scope for readers to engage with them in their own ways.

There are a number of features of Hobbes's arguments that gave the religious reader cause to take Hobbes's work seriously. They were points noted even by his enemies. John Eachard commented that Hobbes's message was insinuated with all 'demureness, solemnity, quotation of Scripture, and appeals to conscience and church history'.[33] When Thomas Tenison acknowledged the possibility that Hobbes's discussion of God might deceive readers into a good opinion of his philosophy, he was implicitly acknowledging the fact Hobbes had done enough to convince readers that his presuppositions fell within the bounds of orthodoxy and Hobbes's relatively wide readership confirms this thought.[34]

There are structural features of the presentation of Hobbes's arguments that make the claim more plausible. Hobbes's minimalist approach to central features of religion, a crucial part of his attempts to simplify and rationalize ecclesiastical

---

[32] Hobbes famously notes that 'Beleef, and Unbeleef never follow mens Commands', L, 42, p. 784. Hobbes seems to have been aware of the problems involved in resting religious doctrine upon the arbitrary commands of the sovereign, which may explain why he goes to so much trouble to persuade subjects as well as sovereigns.

[33] John Eachard, *Some Opinions of Mr. Hobbs Considered* (London, 1673), Sig A5r–v.

[34] Thomas Tenison, *The Creed of Mr. Hobbes Examined* (London, 1670), 132. It is also worth noting that the distinctive process of anti-Hobbesian heterodox creed-making that was a characteristic response to this indeterminacy is also an implicit acknowledgement that Hobbes's readers generally did find it easy, at least until the anti-Hobbes industry got going, to take his religious work seriously. Hobbes's enemies had to work hard to isolate and highlight Hobbes's heterodoxy.

authority, typically involved identifying positions with which most of his audience were likely to agree. The reduction of the essentials of Christianity to the belief that Jesus was the Christ, in chapter 43, however unsatisfactory it might have been to some readers as a full account of what salvation required, was nevertheless a necessary component of such an account. Indeed, there was little in Hobbes's account of religion that was entirely unprecedented or unfamiliar and historians have done excellent work in uncovering the discussions and sources to which Hobbes, usually obliquely, alluded, often with particular audiences in mind.[35] To take one example, we might think of the way that Hobbes's account of the relationship between Scripture and natural law quite clearly evoked Grotius's work, and shared a common framework with the arguments produced by Episcopalians during the late 1640s and early 1650s.[36] The Grotian and Erastian cast of Hobbes's ecclesiology, as has been shown, also made some aspects of his state-as-church doctrine congenial to the views of 'magisterial Independents'.[37] Of course the thought that Hobbes's ecclesiology fitted into contemporary discussion in the 1650s is hardly surprising. Hobbes's theology and scriptural criticism was perhaps a rather different matter, although closer inspection of that has also suggested that even in these more controversial sections of *Leviathan*, Hobbes was adapting positions from an orthodox mainstream which might have been markedly less problematic for contemporary readers than modern interpretations of their radicalism might suggest.[38]

This is not to claim that Hobbes's arguments were passively adopted from his sources, and this brings us to another relevant structural feature of his approach: his distinctive habit of adapting existing positions for his own purposes. Often this involved the appropriation of arguments that Hobbes wished to turn against their authors. This was a distinctive 'judo-style' tactic that one finds throughout Hobbes's work, a signature move that almost defines the project of *Leviathan*.[39] It is most obvious in Hobbes's appropriation of discourses associated with sedition. In Parts One and Two of *Leviathan* Hobbes took theories of natural and civil law, contract, liberty, and representation, all of which had been used by opponents of the crown, and decisively re-engineered them in such a way that they could be made to work together to underpin political stability. Clearly Hobbes was carrying out the same general exercise in his discussion of religion. We find just about every flavour of potentially subversive religious belief (about the

---

[35] Examples are too numerous to mention but one might single out J. P. Sommerville's enviably durable *Thomas Hobbes: Political Ideas in Historical Context* (Basingstoke: Macmillan Press, 1992), which does an excellent job of identifying possible sources for Hobbesian ideas.

[36] See Sarah Mortimer, 'Christianity and Civil Religion in Hobbes's *Leviathan*', in *The Oxford Handbook of Hobbes*, ed. A. P. Martinich and Kinch Hoekstra (Oxford: Oxford University Press, 2016), 501–19.

[37] Collins, *Allegiance*.

[38] Noel Malcolm's meticulous dissection of Hobbes's account of Ezra points in this direction, *Aspects of Hobbes*, 383–431.

[39] See Malcolm's important comments about the 'complicated and opportunistic judo-like manoeuvres' characterizing the relationship between heterodox and orthodox writers (including Hobbes) during the seventeenth century. Ibid., 411.

sources of scriptural authority, the significance of key scriptural language, the notion of the kingdom of God, prophecy, miracles, the afterlife, the concept of the church, and the nature of salvation) systematically rearticulated to become compatible with the requirements of peace. Further careful attention to the oblique allusions in Parts Three and Four will undoubtedly reveal more of the same structural links to contemporary discussions of religion. But we need to be careful before we conclude that Hobbes's re-engineering of conventionally familiar terms was simply designed to disable and discredit those languages. To re-engineer a discourse is not necessarily to reject it, and just as we might be suspicious of the thought that Hobbes simply meant to eliminate what was useful in apparently subversive political theory, it is also problematic to infer that Hobbes's retelling of the Christian story was designed to discredit it altogether. Indeed, it was probably very important for Hobbes to carry out his adjustment of Christianity in a way that would *not* alienate too many of the existing users of the discourses that he was interested in colonizing. The Christian elements had to be persuasive enough for the project to work at all.

But familiarity was not enough. Hobbes did need to find an arresting way to encourage his readers to engage with his project actively. Hobbes managed this through the self-consciously paradoxical presentation of his arguments. As I have observed elsewhere, Hobbes's use of paradox is one of his most distinctive writing strategies and can be traced in all of his works from *The Elements of Law* to *De Cive*, *Leviathan*, and beyond.[40] Nearly all of Hobbes's critics identify him as a writer of paradoxes, both in the literal sense that the arguments that he made seemed to go beyond accepted opinion, but also to draw attention to the way that Hobbes appeared to take an, at times, perverse delight in surprising his readers with profoundly counter-intuitive observations from his broadly conventional and familiar premises. Hobbes himself seemed content to be characterized as a writer of paradoxes and spoke with some pride about them.[41] This was much more than a mischievous stylistic tic. In deploying paradox Hobbes was making use of a particular psychological theory about the best way to arouse curiosity. The theory was based upon the familiar classical thought that the experience of *thaumadzein*, or wonder, provoked the wonderer's desire for knowledge.[42] This usually happened when men encountered strange natural phenomena, but Hobbes noted that the same effects could be brought about by the artificial creation of wonder, a discussion of peculiar relevance to the issue of religion.

The artificial creation of wonder was clearly one of the means by which the priests (the ancient *thaumaturgi* and their spiritual successors) established their often dubious claims to authority through the use of miracles. This worked best on ordinary people whose limited knowledge, particularly of natural causes, made them easy to deceive.[43]

---

[40] Jon Parkin, 'Hobbes and Paradox', in *Oxford Handbook of Hobbes*, 624–42.

[41] LLA, p. 1227; C, p. 124.

[42] Michael Funk Deckard, 'A Sudden Surprise of the Soul: The Passion of Wonder in Hobbes and Descartes', *The Heythrop Journal* 49.6 (2008), 948–63.

[43] L, 37, pp. 682–5.

That thought seems to have driven Hobbes's interest in the artificial creation of wonder, which clearly offered a means by which man's natural response to wonders might be enlisted in the service of a new Hobbesian religion. By a neat and typically Hobbesian reversal, the very same tools deployed by the *thaumaturgi* could bring about the establishment of a very different sort of religious institution. Hobbes's wonders would be worked through words. The creation of surprising novelty, on this account, generated *admiratio*, a term that Hobbes uses interchangeably with wonder: 'for novelty causeth admiration, and admiration curiosity, which is a delightful appetite of knowledge'.[44] The figure traditionally associated with this sort of show-stopping novelty was indeed paradox, and Hobbes deployed paradox on an industrial scale in *Leviathan*, from the title of the book, to the image on the title page, to the paradoxes listed by nearly all of Hobbes's commentators, not least the provocative inversions of human and divine authority in discussion of Scripture, miracles, or prophets. Such arguments might be latent in the existing discussion of the relationship between reason and revelation, but they were pressed by Hobbes in ways that were immediately arresting and troubling for his readers. Hobbes thus positioned himself to be a miracle-working prophet of a rather different kind of religion.

Hobbes's book of wonders was troubling, but the paradoxes themselves exhibited another distinctive feature. Their resolution, the way that they were to be cashed out in practical terms, whether that was institutional arrangements or the detail of theological doctrine, was often left in the hands of the reader.[45] Just as Hobbes's readers were invited to interpret the denominational implications of Hobbes's deliberately ambiguous ecclesiological remarks, so they are often left to work out the implications of the paradoxes that structure the discussions of Hobbesian theology. The broadly Erastian principles underlying Hobbes's religious arguments are made clear enough. Hobbes explicitly and decisively excludes certain propositions that he viewed to be fundamentally incompatible with peace: those proceeding from ideas of incorporeal substance, suggestions of unmediated divine revelation, notions of the visible church that are not coextensive with the state, and so on. Such conditions constitute unambiguous 'blocking manoeuvres' designed to prevent particular subversive positions from being developed.[46] But Hobbes does not always spell out the positive implications of the blocks that he puts in place, and the reader is often left to ponder what they might be. Again the reception history supplies examples of readers confronting the interpretative gaps which do seem to be a consistent feature of Hobbes's transactions with his readership. To take one of the most infamous: in 1656 Seth Ward admitted that he could not prove that Hobbes was an atheist, but he drew attention to the

---

[44] Hobbes, in William Davenant, *A Discourse upon Gondibert* (London, 1650), 138.

[45] Clearly this could be a very important reader, for example, a sovereign (or a member of a sovereign assembly) who might be responsible for determining religious policy, but Hobbes clearly also intended his work to be read by subjects, who were also invited to consider how Hobbesian ideas might be applied.

[46] I am indebted here to Noel Malcolm's suggestion that Hobbes's work involves particular epistemological blocking moves, *Aspects of Hobbes*, 428.

paradox lurking at the heart of Hobbes's discussion of God. If everything that is, is body, is God body or is he nothing at all? It was difficult to understand how God could exist 'in the Hobbesian way of considering things'.[47] One way to explain this might be along the lines suggested by Hobbes's enemy John Wallis in 1655: that Hobbes left these things unsaid because, if the real consequences were to be spelled out, he would fall foul of the authorities.[48] Although this is undoubtedly a credible suggestion, the thought that Hobbes was simply trying to dodge legal sanction did not appear to stop him exploring more explicit arguments concerning the corporeal nature of God in 1668 at a point when he knew that heresy charges were being prepared against him.[49] It may be just as plausible to suggest that Hobbes was leaving space for his readers to work out what his positions *could* mean. Sometimes this allowed Hobbes to exploit their responses: when Alexander Ross first attempted to grapple with the problems thrown up by the Hobbesian deity, his response was to identify it with Tertullian's position in *De Carne Christi*.[50] Although there do not seem to be any signs that Hobbes had Tertullian in mind when he was writing *Leviathan*, he did subsequently cite Tertullian as a more orthodox precedent for his position in 1662, and in 1668, in the Appendix to the Latin *Leviathan*, Hobbes deployed the Church Father more extensively in support of his argument.[51] The efforts of several subsequent critics to attack Hobbes's use of Tertullian in that text speaks to some anxiety that Hobbes might in fact have found a dangerously persuasive way to develop his underdetermined case for a material God.[52]

11.4 Thinking 'Hobbesianly' about Religion

So far we have seen examples of a number of distinctive writing strategies that seem to be designed with the intention of producing particular effects. Hobbes avoids aligning himself with particular positions but alludes to several forms of Protestantism, albeit obliquely. He uses familiar materials in a paradoxical fashion that seems designed to provoke informed readers into an engaged response. He often sets out a series of fundamental conditions or principles (typically moves that block problematic positions), but he tends to leave the detail of his ecclesiological and theological positions underdeveloped, requiring the reader to work out the implications of what has been said. What Hobbes does not provide is a straightforward template for a particular or existing religious position. What he may be providing is a toolkit to enable a variety of

---

[47] Ward, *Exercitatio*, 340.

[48] John Wallis, *Elenchus Geometriae Hobbianae* (Oxford, 1655), 89–90.

[49] For the circumstances of this episode, see Jon Parkin, 'Baiting the Bear: The Anglican Attack on Hobbes in the Later 1660s', *History of Political Thought* 34.3 (2013), 421–58.

[50] Ross, *Leviathan Drawn out*, 35–6.   [51] Hobbes, *Mr Hobbes Considered*, 37; LLA, pp. 1228–31.

[52] Tenison, *Creed*, 21–2; John Templer, *Idea theologiae Leviathanis* (Cambridge, 1673), 34.

existing religious believers to work through the implications of his ideas from their own perspective. In short, Hobbes does not offer his readers a worked-out alternative model of Christianity in a detailed and determinate manner, but suggests how to rearticulate their own version of reformed Christianity in a Hobbesian manner. To borrow a formula from Michael Oakeshott, this is to make the Hobbesian project *adverbial* in its operation: designed to persuade a variety of religious actors to think 'Hobbesianly' in articulating their religious doctrine.[53] In doing so, various species of Christianity could be rendered compatible with political stability, and perhaps, potentially, with each other.[54] To carry out such a task necessarily precluded any obvious statement of religious identity from Hobbes, but also required his position to be plausible and applicable to a range of religious actors. It also required them to be sufficiently convinced by Hobbes's arguments to attempt to interpret their religious doctrine in accordance with his principles.

If this seems a little far-fetched, we do have quite a few examples of the process in action. We might think of the negotiation between Hobbes and his Episcopalian friend Robert Payne in 1649.[55] In *De Cive* and elsewhere Hobbes had typically left open the thought that his scheme could encompass a church which had an Episcopalian shape. Payne readily grasped that what mattered to Hobbes was not the labelling of the clerical office itself, but rather the distinctively Hobbesian relationship of those officers with the sovereign power. Bishops who did not make illegitimate claims about their authority potentially satisfied the conditions of Hobbes's theory, which blocked the thought that clerics could claim authority independent of the state. In correspondence Payne attempted to explain to Hobbes how an Episcopalian regime could be rede-scribed in Hobbesian terms. Payne's ingenious rewriting of Episcopalian Anglicanism involved construing the consecration and ordination of bishops as analogous to the creation of academic physicians or lawyers, office holders who are always subordinate to the civil authority.[56] Any more elevated function—for example, their role in consecrat-ing new monarchs—might be properly understood not as a mark of intrinsic authority, but as a prudent piece of stage management designed to enhance the authority of the royal office.[57] The example shows how someone like Payne, an engaged religious reader, might respond creatively to Hobbes's adverbial requirements. Hobbes's response is also interesting. Payne partly hoped that Hobbes might be persuaded to make a defence of

[53] Michael Oakeshott, *On History and Other Essays* (Indianapolis, IN: Liberty Fund, 1999), 137.

[54] This might be the (futuristic) thought underpinning the allusion to Independency in chapter 47. Once individuals subscribe to Hobbes's adverbial requirements there would be no need for the sovereign to regulate or proscribe religious doctrine. This would not be toleration (a word not used at all in the Independency passage) so much as indifference. For Hobbes's theory as an attempt to eliminate the problems presupposed by policies of toleration, see Jon Parkin, 'Toleration', in *The Oxford Handbook of British Seventeenth Century Philosophy*, ed. Peter Anstey (Oxford: Oxford University Press, 2013), 620–1.

[55] For the best account of this exchange, see Jeffrey Collins, 'Christian Ecclesiology and the Composition of *Leviathan*: A Newly Discovered Letter to Thomas Hobbes', *Historical Journal* 43.1 (2000), 217–31; cf. Parkin, *Taming*, 68–9.

[56] Collins, 'Christian Ecclesiology', 230.   [57] Ibid., 231.

episcopacy a feature of *Leviathan*. Hobbes's answer appears to have been that although he had no problem with episcopacy per se, he would not give it a privileged role in his theoretical work, a position consistent with the thought that the arguments in *Leviathan* were designed to appeal to a variety of Christian denominations.

Another example might be the relationship between Hobbes and the interregnum Independents. As with the case of Episcopalianism, Hobbes had left space in *Leviathan* for positions that might appeal to Independents, not least in his allusion to Independency in chapter 47. Jeffrey Collins has made a convincing case for seeing a number of Independent writers developing arguments which not only parallel Hobbesian ideas, but which arguably owed much to them.[58] Despite some evident nervousness about Hobbes's deeply ambiguous theology, John Owen, the Independent leader, famously described *Leviathan* as 'most full of excellent remarks', a view that probably reflected an appreciation of the Erastian and anti-Presbyterian resources in Hobbes's work.[59] As Collins suggests, Owen's *Of Schism* at times not only echoes Hobbes but also appears to articulate the thought that the English church could only be understood as the totality of subjects gathered under a sovereign, in ways that seem to owe something to Hobbes's formula.[60] Similarly Louis du Moulin, a writer who privately acknowledged the usefulness of Hobbes's religious doctrines in the 1660s, can be found in the 1650s expressing both his distaste for ecclesiological dualism and his support for the thought that 'Every Christian commonwealth is a church and every Christian Church a Commonwealth'.[61] The connections here are suggestive of the thought that elements of Hobbesian ecclesiology may well have started to inform the articulation of Independent arguments about the relationship between church and state, in ways that may have helped to entrench Hobbesian blocks within certain kinds of Independent discourse. Independent writers may not have agreed with everything that Hobbes had to say, but distinctive elements of the Hobbesian project were being picked up and used.

What these examples suggest is that Hobbes's work clearly did allow a variety of readers to engage with recognizably Hobbesian principles and to assimilate them in a variety of very different denominational settings. My suggestion is that this outcome was to some extent something that Hobbes had in mind in writing in the way that he did, and that this intention informed his approach to the presentation of his materials. Hobbes's distinctively paradoxical 'blocking manoeuvres' were clothed in ambiguous and minimalist formulae designed to make them available, adaptable, and useful to users of religious language. So we might also suggest that what actually happened in terms of the broad assimilation of Hobbesian principles was what Hobbes, to some extent, saw as the future of religion: a situation in which various forms of Christianity

---

[58] Collins, *Allegiance*, especially chapter 6.   [59] C, p. 459.   [60] Collins, *Allegiance*, 234–5.

[61] In 1669 Du Moulin remarked to Richard Baxter that Hobbes came 'nearer the truth than many good men'. Letter quoted in Mark Goldie, 'Priestcraft and the Birth of Whiggism', in *Political Discourses in Early Modern Britain*, ed. Nicholas Phillipson and Quentin Skinner (Cambridge: Cambridge University Press, 1993), 231.

could be remodelled along Hobbesian lines, infiltrated by Hobbesian ideas, and worked out in a variety of different ways. Religious discourse would thus be made consistent with the requirements of sovereignty, removing a major source of political instability and providing a more durable foundation for peace.

For all the sophistication of the strategy, Hobbes would not have seen the actual course of the reception of his ideas as a stunning success. Indeed, we know that it fell a long way short of the ambitions that he had. Perhaps the most important of these was his near-obsession with establishing his doctrine in the universities. If one wanted to reboot Christianity in early modern England, Hobbes was clear that the best way to do this institutionally was to uninstall the disastrous cocktail of Hellenized Christianity that constituted scholastic university teaching.[62] Educational reprogramming was fundamental to ensuring that the clergy occupying parish pulpits were more likely to promote stability rather than disorder. Of course, this would involve the application of Hobbesian doctrine, but again, intriguingly in the light of this discussion, not a full curriculum but a Hobbesian algorithm adapted by the universities themselves.[63] Hobbes's enemies during the 1650s sometimes alluded to a concern that tutors in Oxford and Cambridge were reading Hobbes to impressionable young students,[64] but Hobbes was unsuccessful in his repeated attempts to secure the kind of institutional presence that might secure the immediate reform of religion. Indeed, towards the end of his life, with his reputation blackened, with the paradoxical wonders of *Leviathan* now represented as unambiguous signs of atheism, Hobbes might have reflected that

---

[62] L, 'Review, and Conclusion', pp. 1140–1.

[63] When Hobbes discusses the application of Hobbesian doctrine in the 1650s he is careful to distinguish between the idea that his doctrine should be taught, but not *Leviathan*: 'For wiser men may so digest the same Doctrine as to fit it better for a publique teaching'. *Six Lessons to the Professors of the Mathematiques* (London, 1656), 60. The same thought seems to be envisaged in Hobbes's recommendations for the reform of the universities in *Behemoth*. The way that Hobbes frames the discussion it is clear that Hobbes's blocking manoeuvres should structure/discipline the syllabus generally rather than prescribing the content: 'That the Polyticks there taught be made to be (as true Polyticks should be) such as are fit to make men know that it is their duty to obey all laws whatsoever that shall by the Authority of the King be enacted . . . such as are fit to make men understand, that the Civill Laws are Gods Laws, as they that make them are by God appointed to make them; and to make men know, that the People and the Church are one thing, and have but one Head, the King, and that no man has title to govern under him, that has it not from him. That the King ows his Crowne to God onely, and to no man Ecclesiastick or other. And that the Religion they teach there, be a quiet waiting for the comming againe of our blessed Saviour, and in the mean time a resolution to obey the Kings Laws (which also are Gods Laws); to injure no man, to be in charity with all men, to cherish the poor and sick, and to live soberly and free from scandall. Without mingling our Religion with points of naturall Philosophy, as freedom of Will, incorporeall substance, everlasting Nows, ubiquities, Hypostases which the people understand not, nor will ever care for. When the Universities shall be thus disciplin'd, there will come out of them from time to time, well principled Preachers, and they that are now ill principled from time to time fall away.' B, pp. 182–3.

[64] See Ross, *Leviathan Drawn out*, Sig A3r; George Lawson, *An Examination of the Political Part of Mr. Hobbs his Leviathan* (London, 1657), Sig A2r–v; Peter Barwick, *The Life of the Reverend Dr John Barwick* (London, 1724), 430–1, quoting Edward Hyde. It is worth noting that the text and its presentational strategies are perhaps calibrated to work best on the young, who seem to have constituted most of Hobbes's target audiences. Most identifiable 'Hobbists' tend to be in their late teens and twenties when they became interested in Hobbes.

his own attempt to refound Christianity had ultimately suffered the same fate as that of all the other religions that he had described in chapter 12. But then again, perhaps he also looked around at the latitudinarians and the deists of those times, thinkers in their own ways still grappling with the ambiguous and paradoxical formulae of Hobbesian arguments, and saw in each of them signs of Hobbesian futures.[65]

---

[65] As one writer put it in *An Elegie on Mr Thomas Hobbes of Malmesbury* (London, 1679): 'Leviathan the Great is faln! But see | The small *Behemoths* of his Progenie | Survive to duel all *Divinitie*'. For the senses in which early English deist thought constituted one possible Hobbesian future, see Elad Carmel's chapter, 'Hobbes and Early English Deism', in this volume.

12

Hobbes and Early English Deism

Elad Carmel

In 1754 the Presbyterian minister John Leland published a book called *A View of the Principal Deistical Writers that Have Appeared in England in the Last and Present Century*.[1] Leland was determined to provide a thorough account of those whom he considered to be the prominent English deists, their writings, and the controversies in which they were involved. The deists, according to Leland, 'reject all revealed religion, and discard all pretences to it as owing to imposture or enthusiasm'.[2] Their aim, therefore, is 'to set aside revelation, and to substitute mere natural religion, or … no religion at all, in its room'.[3]

Leland's list starts with Lord Herbert of Cherbury, 'the first remarkable Deist in order of time'.[4] The second figure on Leland's list of deistical writers is Thomas Hobbes. Leland explained that there 'have been few persons, whose writings have had a more pernicious influence in spreading irreligion and infidelity than his'.[5] According to Leland, Hobbes took Scripture as the word and the law of God on the one hand but ridiculed inspiration and revelation on the other; and he sometimes saw inspiration as a supernatural gift but also described the pretence to it as a sign of madness.[6] Leland's attack on Hobbes touched on a range of issues in his theory, such as the authority of Scripture being dependent on the authority of the sovereign, the questioning of aspects in the old and new testaments, the denial of our ability to know any more about God than that He exists, and so on. Leland argued that 'Hobbes's scheme strikes at the foundation of all religion, both natural and revealed' and that 'it tendeth not only to subvert

---

[1] John Leland, *A View of the Principal Deistical Writers that Have Appeared in England in the Last and Present Century* (London, 1754). A second volume was published in the following year.

[2] Ibid., 3. [3] Ibid., p. v.

[4] Ibid., 4. Herbert's main contribution to deism was in his theory of the common notions of religion that are rationally, naturally, and universally true. See Edward Herbert, *De Veritate*, ed. and trans. Meyrick H. Carré (Bristol: J. W. Arrowsmith, 1937), especially 291–307. Recent scholarship has shown, however, that although the common notions were *also* influential for deism, there is not enough evidence to suggest that they were in themselves deistic. See R. W. Serjeantson, 'Herbert of Cherbury before Deism: The Early Reception of the *De veritate*', *The Seventeenth Century* 16.2 (2001), 217–38.

[5] Leland, *A View*, 40. [6] Ibid., 41.

the authority of the scripture, but to destroy God's moral administration'.[7] Leland concluded:

the manifold absurdities and inconsistence of his scheme, and the pernicious consequences of it to religion, morality and the civil government, have been so well exposed, and set in a clear light, that there are not many of our modern Deists that would be thought openly to espouse his system in its full extent. And yet it cannot be denied, that there are not a few things in their writings borrowed from his; and that some of them have chosen rather to follow him than Lord Herbert in several of his principles; and particularly in asserting the materiality and mortality of the human soul, and denying man's free agency.[8]

According to Leland, the deists borrowed much from Hobbes, and in some ways more than they did from Herbert, who Leland himself considered to be the first English deist. They did so, however, without always declaring they were adopting Hobbes, due to his dubious reputation at the time. Particularly in his materialism, Leland argued, Hobbes had gone further than Herbert and had subsequently been followed by the 'modern deists'.

Leland seems right to have acknowledged the complexity of Hobbes's position, holding that 'none of his treatises are directly level'd against revealed religion'.[9] But was Leland also right in recognizing that Hobbes was in fact, alongside Herbert, one of the fathers of English deism, at least in some respects?

The relevant scholarship takes Hobbes to be influential for the English deists of the late seventeenth century to some extent.[10] However, the full scope and the precise nature of the relationship between Hobbes and the deists remains a puzzle. It is arguable that Hobbes inspired them with his anticlericalism, his sceptical and even mocking attitude towards revelation and miracles, and his thorough exegesis of Scripture, including his questioning of its authorship and authority. At the same time, it would be slightly anachronistic to identify Hobbes himself as a deist, nor is there any historical evidence for such a claim. Moreover, there are several reasons to separate him from these 'radicals', mainly his alleged pessimism regarding human nature and consequently his absolutist

---

[7] Ibid., 46.   [8] Ibid., 47–8.   [9] Ibid., 40.

[10] Jon Parkin has argued that 'Hobbes's critical treatment of religion could be added to a deist's conceptual toolkit', *Taming the Leviathan: The Reception of the Political and Religious Ideas of Thomas Hobbes in England, 1640–1700* (Cambridge: Cambridge University Press, 2007), 405–6. See also Justin Champion, *The Pillars of Priestcraft Shaken: The Church of England and its Enemies 1660–1730* (Cambridge: Cambridge University Press, 1992), 133–7. For other brief (and sometimes hesitant) suggestions in this direction, see Peter Gay, *Deism: An Anthology* (Princeton, NJ: Van Nostrand, 1968), 22–4; Margaret Jacob, *The Radical Enlightenment: Pantheists, Freemasons and Republicans* (London: Allen & Unwin, 1981), 75–7; Richard Tuck, *Hobbes: A Very Short Introduction* (Oxford: Oxford University Press, 2002), 91; Edwin Curley, ' "I durst not write so boldly" or, How to Read Hobbes' Theological-Political Treatise', in *Hobbes e Spinoza*, ed. D. Bostrenghi (Napoli: Bibliopolis, 1992), 572. Finally, see Patricia Springborg's illuminating paper where she focuses on Hobbes's possible reception as a deist based on some heterodox aspects which she identifies particularly in his 'long-neglected *Historia Ecclesiastica*', namely, '1) his equation of God and Nature; 2) his materialist epistemology and atomist ontology; and 3) his theory of representation, in particular his doctrine of the Trinity'. See Patricia Springborg, 'Hobbes the Atheist and his Deist Reception', in *I filosofi e la società senza religione*, ed. Marco Geuna and Gianbattista Gori (Bologna: Il Mulino, 2011), especially 150–1.

political theory, or alternatively his voluntarist theology.[11] This has led some scholars, most recently and famously Jonathan Israel, to claim that it was Spinoza, rather than Hobbes, who was the main influence on the 'radical enlightenment', English deism included.[12]

In the first part of this chapter I will show that Hobbes was a significant influence for subsequent deists and that this can be clearly inferred from many of their texts.[13] I will focus on the core figures of English deism from its early stages in the 1670s until its peak in the early eighteenth century, namely Charles Blount, John Toland, Matthew Tindal, and Anthony Collins. In the second part I will go back to Hobbes and suggest that in some important respects he anticipated the deist project—mainly in his anti-clericalism alongside his hope for natural reason—even if in other respects he was more traditional or conservative than the later deists. Accordingly, Leland's assessment was far from being mistaken: Hobbes was indeed a father of English deism.

12.1   The Deists and Hobbes

12.1.1   Charles Blount

Some—usually denunciatory—references to the deists were made in England from the late sixteenth century.[14] Yet it took another century for the debate on the phenomenon called deism to gather momentum, first in England and later on the Continent. It is from the late 1670s, with the appearance of the writings of the young political activist, Charles Blount (1654–93), that we can date this development.

There is some evidence that from an early stage Blount was drawing on Hobbes. In 1678 he sent Hobbes a copy of his publication *Anima Mundi*, in which he explored various ancient views on the immortality of the soul. Accompanying this work, Blount sent Hobbes a letter, praising the manuscript of his 'Treatise of Heresie' that would eventually be published posthumously as *An Historical Narration Concerning Heresie*

---

[11]   See for example Jeffrey Barnouw, 'The Separation of Reason and Faith in Bacon and Hobbes, and Leibniz's Theodicy', *Journal of the History of Ideas* 42.4 (1981), 618; Wayne Hudson, *The English Deists: Studies in Early Enlightenment* (London: Pickering & Chatto, 2009), 76. Furthermore, it is arguable that Hobbes's God was the philosophical God as a first cause *and* the historical God as a person. For this distinction, see for example George Wright, *Religion, Politics and Thomas Hobbes* (Dordrecht: Springer, 2006).

[12]   Jonathan Israel, *Radical Enlightenment: Philosophy and the Making of Modernity 1650–1750* (Oxford: Oxford University Press, 2001), 599–627. See also Rosalie Colie, 'Spinoza and the Early English Deists', *Journal of the History of Ideas* 20.1 (1959), 23–46.

[13]   Demonstrating intellectual influence requires some caution. See Quentin Skinner, *Visions of Politics*, i: *Regarding Method* (Cambridge: Cambridge University Press, 2002), 74–6. Here I will rely on cases where there is definite textual evidence of the deists having engaged with Hobbes, following Parkin, *Taming the Leviathan*, 12. I am grateful for the comments that I received from the participants of the workshop 'Thomas Hobbes and the Politics of Religion', King's College London (April 2015), which made me rethink this methodological issue.

[14]   For the earliest mention of the 'deists' in England, see Josias Nichols, *An Order of Houshold Instruction* (London, 1595).

in 1680.[15] Blount wrote in the letter that Hobbes had provided 'a more accurate and faithful Account of the Nicene Council…than is any where else to be met with'.[16] To Blount, Hobbes was 'the great instructor of the most sensible Part of Mankind in the noble Science of Philosophy'.[17]

In his *Historical Narration*, Hobbes returned to the primitive church and the problem of the Trinity to give an account of the events that had led to the Council of Nicaea. Hobbes emphasized the role that Constantine the Great had played as the sovereign in making Christianity the public religion and settling the disputes over its creed, first and foremost the one that was provoked by Arius who claimed that Jesus was inferior to God and in fact not divine. The Council of Nicaea decided against the Arians.

In his letter, Blount also went back to the primitive church. His aim was to expose the cynical political interests behind the major Christian debates. He argued that Constantine had treated the Arians as Louis XIV treated the Huguenots: he supported them as long as he needed them in order to gain power, but then he turned against them to assure that their own power was restricted. Blount concluded that 'there is as little Trust to be reposed in General councils, who have been Guilty of so much Ignorance and Interest, as well as so frequently contradicting one another'.[18]

Blount did not attribute this view to Hobbes, but he presumably felt that Hobbes would be sympathetic. In one thing Blount clearly followed Hobbes's position: 'You your self have very well observed, when Reason is against a Man, a Man will be against Reason; and therefore 'tis no wonder to see, from several Interests, so many Opinions and Animosities arise'.[19] This is a paraphrase on Hobbes's statements in *The Elements of Law* and *Leviathan*.[20] In both cases, Hobbes argued that truth might be in danger once certain interests are at stake. The context was clearly anticlerical. The implication was a strong position against persecution of heresies, since declaring a doctrine as heresy was itself the machinations of clerical interests. Another implication—although much less straightforward—could be a call for toleration of dissenters.[21] This was arguably also the message of his *Historical Narration*.[22] Clearly familiar with these texts, Blount

---

[15] C, p. 759.   [16] C, p. 759.   [17] C, p. 763.

[18] C, p. 762. As Jeffery Collins argues, Blount's letter drew on 'the subversive account of the Nicene Council found in the *Historical Narration*', which can serve to show how Hobbes's writing of sacred history 'prefigured the deism and anticlericalism of the early Enlightenment'. See Jeffrey Collins, 'Thomas Hobbes's Ecclesiastical History', in *The Oxford Handbook of Hobbes*, ed. A. P. Martinich and Kinch Hoekstra (Oxford: Oxford University Press, 2016), 541–2.

[19] C, p. 759.   [20] EL, 'Epistle Dedicatory'; L, 11, p. 158.

[21] Indeed, this Hobbesian quote had already been used in 1668 by MP Edward Seymour to support toleration: he mentioned 'the strictness of the institution of the Spanish Inquisition, one of the greatest causes of the decay of that Monarchy', and added: 'Mr Hobbes says, That when reason is against a man, a man is against reason—Why should we proceed in a way, that answers not our end?' See Anchitell Grey, *Debates of the House of Commons, From the Year 1667 to the Year 1694* (London, 1763), i, 103–4. See Parkin, *Taming the Leviathan*, 243; Parkin, 'Baiting the Bear: The Anglican attack on Hobbes in the Later 1660s', *History of Political Thought* 34.3 (2013), 445–6. See also Richard Tuck, 'Hobbes and Locke on Toleration', in *Thomas Hobbes and Political Theory*, ed. Mary G. Dietz (Lawrence, KS: University Press of Kansas, 1990), 153–71.

[22] Hobbes redefined heresy historically as 'no more than a private Opinion', and argued that there was no English law against it, a tactic that was presumably meant to defend toleration, if not his own fate.

used precisely these arguments, analysing religion primarily in terms of interests, and priestly interests in particular. In another letter of 1678, Blount stated 'that a Temporal Interest was the great Machine upon which all human Actions moved; and that the common and general pretence of Piety and Religion, was but like Grace before a Meal'.[23] In *A Just Vindication of Learning* (1679), he similarly argued that 'Faction and Heresie were things unknown in the World, till the increase of Interest, and abatement of Christian Simplicity'.[24] Interestingly, however, in this tract Blount combined this Hobbesian idea with others, derived primarily from Milton, in order to argue for freedom of the press, a cause which Hobbes himself hardly championed.

In 1680 Blount subsequently published two works that presented organized religion in a dubious light, in one of which—his translation of the *Life of Apollonius*—he cited passages from *Leviathan*.[25] He encouraged an impartial inquiry of religion, emphasizing that people do not usually see beyond their interests: 'self-love is so predominant in mankind' and so 'Most men are apt to flatter their own Party, calling that Religion in themselves which in others they term Irreligion or Superstition'.[26] He followed Hobbes's naturalization, or rather humanization, of religion in order to show that it had come to be nothing but a social convention.[27]

Blount's subsequent two works were both published in 1683. In *Religio Laici* he followed Herbert in formulating the common notions of religion. This text corresponded to a text by John Dryden from a year earlier with an identical title, which was a defence of revealed religion and an open attack on those who were trying to diminish it in favour of natural religion, namely the deists.[28] Blount's response to Dryden was thus arguably the first public declaration of deism. Here, too, there are loud echoes of Hobbes. For example, Blount's sceptical argument that miracles can be pretended 'by Confederacy, where one helps the other to abuse the People' is essentially the same one made in *Leviathan*.[29] But the influence became even clearer in the second work that Blount published in that year, *Miracles No Violations of the Laws of Nature*. His message there is that the laws of nature are themselves the decree of God and, therefore, there is no reason to believe that God would work above or contrary to them, that is, in the

---

See *An Historical Narration Concerning Heresie, And the Punishment Thereof* (London, 1680), 3; Richard Tuck, *Philosophy and Government 1572–1651* (Cambridge: Cambridge University Press, 1993), 335–45.

[23] Charles Blount, *Oracles of Reason...In Several Letters to Mr. Hobbs and other Persons of Eminent Quality, and Learning* (London, 1693), 156.

[24] Charles Blount, *A Just Vindication of Learning, or, An Humble Address to the High Court of Parliament, In behalf of the Liberty of the Press* (London, 1679), 15.

[25] Charles Blount, *Great is Diana of the Ephesians, or, The Original of Idolatry Together with the Politick Institution of the Gentiles Sacrifices* (London, 1680); Blount, *The Two First Books of Philostratus, Concerning the Life of Apollonius Tyaneus: Written Originally in Greek, and Now Published in English* (London, 1680). Also published in the same year, *The Last Sayings, or Dying Legacy of Mr. Thomas Hobbes of Malmesbury* (London, 1680) was a short collection of Hobbes's more critical and radical statements, mainly on religion. Blount was thought to be its author, but recently it has been suggested that he was only connected to the authors. See Noel Malcolm, 'Charles Blount', in C, pp. 793–4.

[26] Blount, *Books of Philostratus*, 5–6.   [27] Ibid., 28–9, 32–3, 151–2, 212.

[28] John Dryden, *Religio Laici, or, A Laymans Faith. A Poem* (London, 1682).

[29] Charles Blount, *Religio Laici Written in a Letter to John Dryden, Esq.* (London, 1683), 36. Cf. L, 37, p. 692.

form of miracles. Consequently, one should not look for God's dominion or providence in supernatural phenomena, but rather in the immutable and fixed order of nature, namely, the ordinary course of causes and effects. This argument was copied from the sixth chapter of Spinoza's *Tractatus: Of Miracles*.[30] To that, Blount added other passages from Hobbes, borrowing his extreme scepticism towards the possibility of the occurrence of present miracles. For example, Blount inserted a passage from *Leviathan* in which Hobbes argued that admiration is a function of experience, and therefore phenomena like the eclipses of the sun and the moon were considered miracles only until more knowledge became available.[31]

While relying upon Herbert, Spinoza, and Hobbes, Blount structured his deism as natural religion combined with a systematic attack on priestcraft. But it was ten years later, in 1693, the year of his death, that Blount's most famous book was published. There Blount's admiration for Hobbes finally became public and explicit, as indicated by its full title, *Oracles of Reason . . . In Several Letters to Mr Hobbs and other Persons of Eminent Quality, and Learning*. The *Oracles* included the letter that Blount had sent to Hobbes, but this is not the only place where he paid respect to Hobbes. Another example is found in the first letter in the collection, in which Blount mentioned the 'late and great Modern Philosopher of this Nation', according to whom 'It is not an Argument sufficient to prove those Books were written by Moses, because they are call'd the Five Books of Moses'. Blount repeated the arguments and examples given by Hobbes in *Leviathan* to question Moses' authorship, for example, the claim that the section on Moses' sepulchre must have been written after his death.[32]

Hobbes clearly inspired Blount's scepticism and anticlericalism, as well as his approach to Scripture and its treatment as a historical document. Hence, Blount recruited Hobbes for his cause, even if Hobbes's claims were sometimes not as explicit as Blount's. He took the issues that were raised by Hobbes and others further, developing his version of deism through them. In some cases, Blount did not have to radicalize Hobbes but simply to follow him and Spinoza where they had already been radical enough, as with the case of the Pentateuch. In these instances, Blount was simply a transmitter of ideas and, as his critics recognized, quite an efficient one.

The *Oracles* became the most notorious deistic tract of the early 1690s, provoking numerous responses by outraged Anglicans. The critics of the emerging deism did not miss the links to Hobbes. Sometimes they emphasized these to discredit deism through association with Hobbes, or alternatively, to use deism to discredit Hobbes. The combined attacks on deism and Hobbes—made consistently in the Boyle Lectures for example—emphasized the influence of Hobbes's work upon the emergence of deism. Perhaps they even drew the attention of the 'radicals' themselves to

---

[30] Benedict de Spinoza, *Theological-Political Treatise*, ed. and trans. Jonathan Israel and Michael Silverthorne (Cambridge: Cambridge University Press, 2007), 81–96.

[31] Charles Blount, *Miracles No Violations of the Laws of Nature* (London, 1683), 2–3. Cf. L, 37, p. 684.

[32] Blount, *Oracles of Reason*, 16–18. Cf. L, 33, pp. 590–2. See also Noel Malcolm, *Aspects of Hobbes* (Oxford: Clarendon Press, 2000), 429.

their closeness to some Hobbesian ideas.[33] As we shall see next, deism developed in a number of directions in the early eighteenth century and Hobbes's footprints can be traced in many of them.

12.1.2 John Toland

In the case of John Toland (1670–1722), deism is at best a partial label for his somewhat eclectic work. He combined republicanism with pantheism, anticlericalism with a call for a civil religion.[34] His most famous text, *Christianity Not Mysterious* (1696), sent a clear message to the readers: they must not believe in things they cannot conceive by their own reason, as the gospels are not contrary to, nor above, reason.[35] In doing so, *Christianity Not Mysterious* stated boldly what Blount had suggested earlier and, consequently, it was perceived as an escalation of the attack on revealed religion.

Toland's main point was that Christianity in its original and uncorrupted form, as found in Jesus's teachings and the gospels, had been simple and plain. Mysteries were introduced later by the Jews and Gentiles, and were maintained by the ambition and craft of the priests, with the assistance of philosophers, or 'divinity schools'. Eventually, Christianity ceased to be intelligible and degenerated into mere paganism, consisting of ridiculous and foolish rituals and ceremonies.[36] Some of these arguments follow Hobbes's anticlericalism closely. Like Hobbes, Toland saw the actions of the clergy as 'Usurpations upon Mankind' and believed that it was this political interest that led the clergy to keep for themselves the sole right to interpret Scripture and, most importantly, to claim infallibility.[37] Indeed, Toland explicitly acknowledged his debt to Hobbes elsewhere. In an essay 'Concerning the Rise, Progress, and Destruction of Fables and Romances' (1695), Toland similarly investigated the historical origins of fables 'thought necessary to sweeten and allure the minds of men, naturally Superstitious and Credulous'.[38] This time, however, he credited Hobbes openly:

To this Essay of Fables and Romances, the History of Daemonology doth properly belong, with all the terrible troops of Spirits and Witches; but I find this Part is so Judiciously and Learnedly Treated of by our Countryman Mr. Hobbs in that Book of his Leviathan, called the Kingdom of Darkness.[39]

Toland also identified his biblical criticism with Hobbes's. He believed that the reading of Scripture had to be adjusted to reach a better, more natural, understanding of the

---

[33] See for example Humphrey Prideaux, *A Letter to the Deists* (London, 1696); William Stephens, *An Account of the Growth of Deism in England* (London, 1696). See also Parkin, *Taming the Leviathan*, 391–6.

[34] For a thorough account of Toland's project, see Justin Champion, *Republican Learning: John Toland and the Crisis of Christian Culture, 1696–1722* (Manchester: Manchester University Press, 2003).

[35] John Toland, *Christianity Not Mysterious, or, A Treatise Shewing That There Is Nothing in the Gospel Contrary to Reason, Nor Above It: and That No Christian Doctrine can be Properly Call'd a Mystery* (London, 1696).

[36] For example, ibid., 141–2, 151–69.   [37] Ibid., 166. Cf. L, 47, p. 1108.

[38] L. P. [John Toland], *Two Essays Sent in a Letter from Oxford to a Nobleman in London* (London, 1695), 29.

[39] Ibid., 35.

world. Indeed, people like Galileo, Descartes, Mersenne, and Gassendi made new discoveries, and yet, they were 'not esteem'd the worse Christians, because they contradict the Scriptures in Physical or Mathematical Problems'.[40] Clearly, however, this development was still disputed: 'The Philosophick History of the Bible, is not always to be embraced; for what an outcry against Mr. Hobs! because he describ'd God Almighty as Corporeal, though Moses and the Scriptures had done so before him'.[41] For Toland, Hobbes's materialist position was not only compatible with flourishing natural philosophy but also with Scripture once thoroughly investigated. Furthermore, Toland's explanation for the attacks on Hobbes was no less interesting, in that he explained them in terms of sectarian interests: 'Things are denominated Heresie and Atheism, not by any certain Rules of Truth, or Falshood, but according to the Caprice, or Interests of Sects and Parties'.[42] As we have seen, this was the precise view of both Hobbes and Blount.

Thus, Hobbes's materialism and his biblical criticism, combined together, were powerful tools for subsequent deists who dared to question the unquestionable. As John Harris argued in one of his Boyle Lectures, 'there must be some substantial Reason why Deists and Antiscripturists are always Corporealists'.[43] For Harris, Hobbes and Spinoza were the greatest corporealists, and consequently atheists, of all; deism was nothing but another manifestation of the same dangerous approach.

12.1.3 Matthew Tindal

During the 1690s, the lawyer and All Souls fellow Matthew Tindal (1657–1733) frequented the London coffeehouses and became a strong critic of the Church of England's clergy.[44] Tindal's reputation was dubious at the Oxonian college, where it was said posthumously that he had attempted 'to cultivate and improve what Mr. Hobbs and his Disciples had begun'. Tindal, according to this anonymous report, 'was desirous, that the Generality of Mankind should imagine he had stopt short at Deism; but he was too reserved and cunning to profess himself a Deist in an explicit and open manner'.[45] Using Hobbes, or deism, to stain a person's reputation was not an original trick. Nor was it a groundless accusation.

In 1706 Tindal published his most notorious work, *The Rights of the Christian Church Asserted*. Like previous deists, Tindal believed that the clergy had complicated and mystified religion to gain an independent power in church matters. He argued that people should make their own judgement in religious matters unrelated to the public interest, including the manner in which they worship God or even the religion they choose. Moreover, the magistrate must protect the subjects' conscience as a natural

---

[40] Ibid., p. ii.   [41] Ibid., pp. ii–iii.   [42] Ibid., p. iii.

[43] John Harris, *The Atheist's Objections, Against the Immaterial Nature of God, and Incorporeal Substances, Refuted* (London, 1698), 50.

[44] B. W. Young, 'Tindal, Matthew (*bap.* 1657, *d.* 1733)', *Oxford Dictionary of National Biography*, <http://www.oxforddnb.com/view/article/27462>, accessed 16 June 2017.

[45] [Anon.], *The Religious, Rational, and Moral Conduct of Matthew Tindal, L.L.D.* (London, 1735), 19–20.

right and forbid any act of persecution, which Tindal considered a severe crime.[46] At the same time, Tindal argued that the civil magistrate should have the supreme power in all religious matters insofar as they affect the public good. It is here that the link to Hobbes becomes apparent.

Like Hobbes, Tindal reached an Erastian position driven by a strong anticlerical motivation.[47] He argued fiercely against the coexistence of two independent powers in society: magisterial and ecclesiastical, precisely those that Hobbes identified as the danger of 'seeing double'.[48] Tindal was aware of this resemblance, and he acknowledged that the exclusive power that he gave to the sovereign could seem 'as great a power as Hobbs complemented him with'.[49] At the same time, however, he distanced himself from Hobbes because he wanted to leave greater room for people to act upon their own judgement than he thought Hobbes had granted. This was no negligible difference. Tindal genuinely disagreed with Hobbes on this issue. Nonetheless, he also recognized that he had arrived at a result that was in a sense rather Hobbesian. Both Tindal and Hobbes despised the political aspirations of the clergy. As a solution they made the civil magistrate the superior authority in the religious matters that they perceived as relevant for the public good. The disagreement was on what constituted the public good—but that, both agreed, is ultimately left for the sovereign to decide.

Tindal quoted Hobbes favourably, but without giving him the credit. In his *Christianity as Old as the Creation*, also known as the 'bible of deism', he argued against those 'who, on Pretence of magnifying Tradition, endeavour to weaken the Force of Reason; (tho' to be sure they always except their own;)'. But, he added, 'as long as Reason is against Men, they will be against Reason. We must not, therefore, be surpris'd, to see some endeavour to reason Men out of their Reason; tho' the very Attempt to destroy Reason by Reason, is a Demonstration Men have nothing but Reason to trust to'.[50] As Blount had done before him, Tindal used this Hobbesian quote in 1730 to argue against priestcraft, which threatened to suppress human reason. Even when the deists disagreed with substantial parts of Hobbes's political theory, then, they nevertheless recognized him as a most resourceful ally in their urgent campaign to undermine the power of the priests.

12.1.4 Anthony Collins

Another figure central to these debates was Anthony Collins (1676–1729). Collins knew Toland and Tindal personally and was also known for his close friendship with

---

[46] Matthew Tindal, *The Rights of the Christian Church Asserted, Against the Romish, and All Other Priests Who Claim an Independent Power over It* (London, 1706), 17–20.

[47] Erastianism is taken here as the doctrine according to which the church should be entirely subordinated to, and controlled by, the state. On the association between Tindal's Erastianism and Hobbes see also Mark Goldie, 'The Reception of Hobbes', in *The Cambridge History of Political Thought 1450–1700*, ed. J. H. Burns with Mark Goldie (Cambridge: Cambridge University Press, 1991), 612–15.

[48] L, 39, pp. 732–4.   [49] Tindal, *Rights*, 28.

[50] Matthew Tindal, *Christianity as Old as the Creation: Or, the Gospel, a Republication of the Religion of Nature* (London, 1730), 179.

John Locke.[51] Collins's philosophical work included a theory of materialism and determinism, which he presented fully in his *Philosophical Inquiry concerning Human Liberty* (1717). Collins attempted to prove that man is 'a necessary agent', thereby rejecting free will. He argued that God's prescience must suppose the necessity of the existence of all future things and hence could not be reconciled with free will.[52] It is clear that this position was deeply influenced by Hobbes.[53] Joseph Priestley, who followed Collins in converting to determinism, mentioned in the preface to his edition of the *Philosophical Inquiry* that 'Mr. Hobbes... was the first who, in this, or any other country, rightly understood, and clearly stated, the argument; but he wrote nothing systematical, and consequently nothing that could be of much use to a student. For this purpose this treatise of Collins is excellent'.[54]

Collins identified himself as a freethinker. In *A Discourse of Free-thinking* (1713), he argued that everyone is capable of freethinking in matters of religion by their own reason: it is our right and duty to perform such thinking for our own sake as well as for the sake and progress of the whole society. The aim of freethinking is to expose superstitious beliefs that otherwise cause dangerous and unnecessary fears. Collins followed earlier deists and Hobbes in asserting that priests do not necessarily teach the truth as such, but doctrines that serve their own interests, hence the differences between the teachings of the various sects in Christianity, and consequently, the need for free and individual inquiries.[55]

Collins took the deistic criticism of the church and channelled it into a manifesto for freedom of thought and belief, and for religious toleration. He sided with the deists against the church and recruited Hobbes for his justification of freethinking. He praised Hobbes as 'a great instance of Learning, Virtue and Free-Thinking' despite his 'several false Opinions, and his High-Church Politicks'.[56] Elsewhere, he went so far as to describe Hobbes as one 'of the greatest Droles and Wits that any Age ever produc'd', who surrounded King Charles II during his education.[57]

Freethought was not a common position to attribute to Hobbes, who was perceived even by deists like Tindal as someone who allowed the sovereign a certain degree of control over the subjects' thoughts.[58] Collins's case, however, shows that the deists and their allies could still relate to Hobbes and even use him for some proto-liberal arguments. Once again, the responses were quick to appear. In the *Remarks Upon a Late Discourse of Free-thinking*, Richard Bentley argued against Collins:

---

[51] J. Dybikowski, 'Collins, Anthony (1676–1729)', *Oxford Dictionary of National Biography*, online: <http://www.oxforddnb.com/view/article/5933>, accessed 19 June 2017.

[52] Anthony Collins, *A Philosophical Inquiry Concerning Human Liberty* (London, 1717), 82–4.

[53] James O'Higgins, *Anthony Collins: The Man and His Works* (The Hague: Martinus Nijhoff, 1970), 96–107. See this position in Hobbes's debate with Bramhall, EW 5, pp. 17–18.

[54] Anthony Collins, *A Philosophical Inquiry Concerning Human Liberty, Republished with a Preface by Joseph Priestley* (Birmingham, 1790), pp. iii–iv.

[55] Anthony Collins, *A Discourse of Free-thinking* (London, 1713), 38–61.   [56] Ibid., 170–1.

[57] Anthony Collins, *A Discourse Concerning Ridicule and Irony in Writing* (London, 1729), 43.

[58] See also Teresa M. Bejan's chapter in this volume, 'First Impressions: Hobbes on Religion, Education, and the Metaphor of Imprinting'.

O the glorious Nation you would be! If…Free-thinkers appointed Tutors to your young Nobility and Gentry. How would Arts, Learning, Manners and all Humanity flourish in an Academy under such preceptors? Who instead of your Bible should read Hobbes's Leviathan; should instill early the sound doctrines of the Mortality of the soul, and the sole Good of a voluptuous Life.[59]

Bentley was certainly right in at least one respect: in the academy of the freethinkers and the deists, *Leviathan* was indeed an obligatory book.

We can conclude that Hobbes was a significant influence for early English deism. The deists were familiar with Hobbes's texts. Not only did they follow some of his ideas and methods, but they also made approving references to him despite the dangers of doing so. Together with various other sources, such as Herbert and Spinoza, Hobbes's contribution was crucial for the development of deism. He was influential for early deism in his religious scepticism and anticlericalism; in his careful and arguably subversive reading of Scripture; in his historical account of Christianity, especially in tracing elements that had been brought into it from the heathens; in his psychological analysis of the origins of religion; in his preference for the natural over the supernatural, and adherence to natural law; and in his materialism, with its implications for questions regarding the role of God, the immortality of the soul, and the existence, or lack thereof, of free will. Hobbes's Erastianism was also linked to deism, aspiring to undermine the power of the corrupt clergy. Finally, the 'absolutist' Hobbes was even employed as a freethinker known for his clear and witty writings.

An anonymous book from 1704, *Visits from the Shades*, contained a fictional dialogue between Hobbes and an interlocutor, in which the latter tells Hobbes: 'had you not writ at all, I question whether the *Oracles of Reason*, or *Christianity Not Mysterious*, had ever seen the Light'.[60] Indeed, both the deists and their critics acknowledged this debt. Here I have attempted to emphasize how significant and deep this debt was.

12.2   Hobbes

As we have seen, there is enough evidence to suggest that the deists knowingly took much from Hobbes, and that in this sense they saw him as one of their predecessors. However, there are still obvious objections to the association of Hobbes with deism in particular, and the 'radical enlightenment' in general, as set forth by Jonathan Israel:

But in the final analysis, Hobbes could not serve as the philosophical underpinning of a broad-based philosophical radicalism opposed to all existing structures of authority and tradition, ecclesiastical power, and the existing social hierarchy, as well as divine-right monarchy, precisely because of his anti-libertarian politics, High Church sympathies, and support for rigorous political and intellectual censorship. Hobbes was an absolutist in politics and a pessimist about human nature, on top of which he admitted (however half-heartedly) miracles and Revelation, and temporized on the immortality of the soul.[61]

---

[59]   Richard Bentley, *Remarks Upon a Late Discourse of Free-thinking* (London, 1713), 18–19.
[60]   [Anon.], *Visits from the Shades* (London, 1704), 34.   [61]   Israel, *Radical Enlightenment*, 602.

For Israel, radical deism and atheism alike provided the framework for the revolutionary ideas of the 'radical enlightenment', which sought to sweep away the existing institutions and the existing civil order.[62] Israel thus disqualifies Hobbes from serving as an influence upon the 'radicals'. Instead, he argues that it was Spinoza who 'emerged as the supreme philosophical bogeyman of Early Enlightenment Europe' and that '[n]o one else during the century 1650–1750 remotely rivalled his notoriety'.[63]

There are a few objections to Israel's argument. First, that Spinoza was a key influence upon the deists and others does not necessarily exclude others from being influential as well. Indeed, as we have seen, in some instances it was the combination of a few sources which shaped the new positions formulated by the deists. Second, Hobbes's politics—even if we accept that it was more authoritarian or conservative than that of subsequent deists—need not disqualify him from being influential in other fields of his thought, especially his critical approach to religion, which was clearly notorious enough. As we have seen, both the deists and their critics recognized in Hobbes much more scepticism about revelation and miracles, and about the immortality of the soul, than Israel allows. Third, the deists themselves were arguably not as radical as Israel suggests. They certainly rejected ecclesiastical authority insofar as it sought to be independent—as we have seen in the case of Tindal—but it is far from clear that their positions were aimed either against the monarchy or against religion as such.[64]

There are therefore two answers to arguments like Israel's. The first, 'softer', answer is that the deists could pick and choose what they took from Hobbes, ignoring his absolutism and taking other aspects from his writings that they found more compelling. As we have seen, this is certainly the case, but I will argue here for another, 'stronger', answer: that is, even politics would not necessarily have been a point of contention between Hobbes and the subsequent deists. I will suggest that we need to read Hobbes's theory as *primarily* anticlerical both on the religious and the political levels. When understood as such, Hobbes's absolutism can be seen as part of a more complex story which was meant to deal with the problem of religion out of control. Furthermore, once natural reason is free from suppression by clerics, and the primary obstacle to peace and stability is thus removed, Hobbes's theory could offer some 'enlightened' elements that bring him even closer to the ideas of the freethinkers.

It is worth stressing that anticlericalism was not the preserve of deism and freethinkers alone, and I do not mean to suggest that identifying these features in Hobbes

---

[62] Ibid., 11–12.   [63] Ibid., 159.

[64] For the first two objections, see Malcolm, *Aspects of Hobbes*, especially 535–7; for the third objection, see Jeffrey R. Wigelsworth, *Deism in Enlightenment England: Theology, Politics, and Newtonian Public Science* (Manchester: Manchester University Press, 2009), especially 206–7. See also Parkin, *Taming the Leviathan*, 402–9. Finally, also criticizing Israel's interpretation of Hobbes, Edwin Curley notes that Israel told him in personal communication that he had modified his reading of Hobbes's religious views: 'He now thinks he was inclined to take Hobbes's statements about religion too literally when he dismissed him as a radical Enlightenment figure'. See Curley, 'Hobbes and the Cause of Religious Toleration', in *The Cambridge Companion to Hobbes's Leviathan*, ed. Patricia Springborg (Cambridge: Cambridge University Press, 2007), especially 329, n. 23.

is sufficient to classify him as a (proto-)deist. My 'stronger' answer to Israel instead involves narrowing the gap between Hobbes's and the deists' politics, such that the deists might be seen as developing a broadly Hobbesian approach to the politics of religion. As Wayne Hudson has recently argued, 'the term "deism" has different meanings in different contexts and no one knows a priori what any particular deist believed'.[65] In light of the preceding survey, however, a few general—even if slightly simplified—points can be made to further the comparison with Hobbes. The deists in question all subscribed to natural religion, while discarding almost entirely the *need for* revealed religion. In doing so, the deists went further than most other anticlerical thinkers of their time. Natural reason alone became sufficient to know all we need in order to live, including our religious duties. Accordingly, no religious doctrine should be mysterious, or above or contrary to reason; hence the grave suspicion towards any phenomenon claimed to be supernatural, including present miracles, prophecies, and revelation. Furthermore, Scripture should be seen as a historical document subject to rational examination, which should not be a prerogative of the church. Finally, freethinking and religious toleration are crucial for the prosperity of any society, whereas persecution of opinions and beliefs is the biggest danger to society.

Indeed, Hobbes's theory was more complex than simply subscribing to mere natural religion, and his tolerationist tendencies were at best questionable. Yet, in what follows I will argue that Hobbes's anticlericalism could pave the way to the more radical positions of the deists. Furthermore, Hobbes's belief in the important role that natural reason could play, once liberated from the harmful influence of interested parties, and his later arguments against persecution of so-called heresies—all clearly structured against the dangerous political aspirations of the clergy—can make him look more like a proto-deist than is usually appreciated.

Hobbes's anticlericalism—famously directed at the 'unpleasing priests'[66]—was quite straightforward, as evident for example in the second half of *Leviathan*. He made extremely harsh accusations against the clergy for attempting to gain independent political power, but he did not argue against Christianity as such. Rather, quite realistically, Hobbes admitted that religion is inherent to human nature, and that it is human curiosity that leads men to derive rationally the existence of God.[67] Hobbes's anticlericalism was perhaps radical but not atheistic: as Sarah Mortimer puts it, Hobbes 'did not want to throw the Christian baby out with the clerical bathwater'.[68] Similarly, Hobbes's notorious arguments about Moses and Jesus as political rulers who also represent the persons of God were clearly heterodox, but more than anything else, their purpose was to deliver the message that God was, and will be, a sovereign in His own kingdom

---

[65] Wayne Hudson, 'Atheism and Deism Demythologized', in *Atheism and Deism Revalued*, ed. Wayne Hudson, Diego Lucci, and Jeffrey R. Wigelsworth (Burlington: Ashgate, 2014), 19.

[66] L, 12, p. 186.   [67] L, 12, pp. 164–6.

[68] Sarah Mortimer, 'Christianity and Civil Religion in Hobbes's *Leviathan*', in *The Oxford Handbook of Hobbes*, 517.

properly speaking, but He is not at the moment.[69] Presently, God works only through His natural kingdom, governing mankind through the natural dictates of reason, which in turn should guide men to obey their earthly sovereign.[70] Additionally, Hobbes notably reduced the faith required for salvation to 'the only necessary article', according to which 'Jesus is the Christ'.[71] This article has the virtue of being relatively easy 'For if an inward assent of the mind to all the Doctrines concerning Christian Faith now taught, (whereof the greatest part are disputed,) were necessary to Salvation, there would be nothing in the world so hard, as to be a Christian'.[72] It is in light of this article that one should examine any prophecy in which one is asked to believe, using natural reason, to determine whether it is true or false.[73] Hobbes's version of Christian faith was thus minimalistic and rationalistic. The main message was about the need to question any pretended prophet while, at the same time, always obeying the civil sovereign. But even the sovereign may at no point take away one's natural reason:

we are not to renounce our Senses, and Experience; nor (that which is the undoubted Word of God) our naturall Reason. For they are the talents which he hath put into our hands to negotiate, till the coming again of our blessed Saviour; and therefore not to be folded up in the Napkin of an Implicite Faith, but employed in the purchase of Justice, Peace, and true Religion.[74]

Hobbes's anticlericalism was closely related to his hope for human rationality. He believed that 'The Ecclesiastiques take from young men, the use of Reason, by certain Charms compounded of Metaphysiques, and Miracles, and Traditions, and Abused Scripture, whereby they are good for nothing else, but to execute what they command them'.[75] Hobbes's project was aimed precisely at fixing that: as Malcolm puts it, in this sense it was a project of liberation from falsehood and from the groups that manipulate falsehood for their own ends.[76] For Hobbes, it is our own reason—given to us by God and nature—that we must follow and that must be protected from the clergy who attempt to take it away in order to make us 'natural fools'.[77] It is no exaggeration to say that this precise conviction lay at the heart of English deist ideas. Moreover, the deist principle according to which individual inquiries should lead to true religious judgements and beliefs can already be found in Hobbes's famous statement that 'there ought to be no Power over the Consciences of men, but of the Word it selfe'.[78] The word of God, namely natural reason, was the medicine against the most dangerous illness that threatened the safety of society, that is, the power-hungry clerical establishment. In developing this idea, the deists were Hobbes's immediate successors.

It is true that life under a Hobbesian magistrate might not be the ideal of freedom. However, here too, the picture is clearly more complex. Hobbes supported censorship imposed by the magistrate—although only in matters of peace and defence.[79] He argued

---

[69] L, 40–1, pp. 736–72.   [70] L, 31, p. 556; 43, p. 932.   [71] L, 43, p. 938.
[72] L, 43, p. 940.   [73] L, 36, pp. 676–80.   [74] L, 32, p. 576.   [75] L, 47, p. 1120.
[76] Malcolm, *Aspects of Hobbes*, 544.   [77] L, 47, p. 1120.
[78] L, 47, p. 1116.   [79] L, 18, pp. 270–2.

that the magistrate should determine the form of the worship of God—although only in public—and that a citizen should obey even religious dictates from an infidel sovereign—although only in words.[80] Hobbes was certainly more concerned with issues of life and death rather than with matters such as freedom of the press that preoccupied some of the subsequent deists. But he also maintained that private thoughts and consciences were not subject to any civil law, an argument made explicitly against attempts of 'Inquistion'.[81] Thus, we can identify in Hobbes an early, even if underdeveloped, version of the call for freethinking.[82] For him, as for Tindal and Collins, the basis for this position was a deep sense of anticlericalism, and an attempt to elevate human reason as an answer to superstitions maintained by priestcraft. This was also the motive for all of them to take an extremely strong position against persecution. Hobbes believed that truth was being suppressed but he was not without hope for the future: the knots on liberty had been untied, and religion could be brought back to take a stabilizing, rather than destabilizing, role in the commonwealth.[83]

Hobbes was not simply authoritarian nor was he a typical tolerationist. As Jon Parkin has shown, his reception demonstrates that his theory was used to support both—somewhat opposite—positions.[84] We can at least say that Hobbes's absolutism need not *always* imply authoritarian measures and *could* be consistent with the subjects enjoying various liberties. He clearly thought that appropriate limits on liberty depended on the circumstances.[85] A strong form of authoritarianism was at present the most effective way to neutralize the disruptive power of religion; but once peace was established, natural reason was liberated, and philosophy and science flourished, a brighter future would await.[86] There is good reason to believe that in such a peaceful and stable situation, when individuals are more rational and less superstitious, we might need a sovereign who is less authoritarian, and who might not even need to exercise his or her right of censorship very often. In this sense, Hobbes's theory contained elements that could lead to something approaching a deist future.[87]

[80] L, 31, p. 570; 42, p. 784.   [81] L, 46, p. 1096.

[82] See also Franck Lessay's chapter in this volume, 'Tolerance as a Dimension of Hobbes's Absolutism'.

[83] L, 47, pp. 1114–16. It is this line of argument that has led some to claim that Hobbes's project was meant to bring about a 'cultural transformation', and to identify proto-liberal and even utopian elements in Hobbes's thought. A few prominent examples are David Johnston, *The Rhetoric of Leviathan: Thomas Hobbes and the Politics of Cultural Transformation* (Princeton, NJ: Princeton University Press, 1986); Alan Ryan, 'Hobbes, Toleration, and the Inner Life', in *The Nature of Political Theory*, ed. David Miller and Larry Siedentop (Oxford: Clarendon Press, 1983), 197–218; Ryan, 'A More Tolerant Hobbes?', in *Justifying Toleration*, ed. Susan Mendus (Cambridge: Cambridge University Press, 1988), 37–59; Richard Tuck, 'The Utopianism of *Leviathan*', in *Leviathan After 350 Years*, ed. Tom Sorell and Luc Foisneau (Oxford: Oxford University Press, 2004), 125–38; Malcolm, *Aspects of Hobbes*, 27–52; and the additional works by Malcolm, Curley, and Tuck cited in notes 10, 21, 22, and 64. On the other hand, it is important not to make Hobbes more 'tolerant' than he really was, since establishing uniformity—rather than embracing diversity and promoting the freedoms of worship and association—was his main goal. This position is well summarized in Glen Newey, *The Routledge Guidebook to Hobbes' Leviathan*, 2nd edition (London: Routledge, 2014), 231–53.

[84] See for example Parkin, *Taming the Leviathan*, 242–4.   [85] L, 21, p. 340.

[86] '*Leasure* is the mother of *Philosophy*; and *Common-wealth*, the mother of *Peace*, and *Leasure*'. L, 46, p. 1054.

[87] See also Jon Parkin's chapter in this volume, 'Hobbes and the Future of Religion'.

Hobbes and the deists did not hold precisely the same political positions. We have seen that there are *some* political ideas that they had in common, such as their thoughts on the nature of what constituted heresy and their consequent objection to persecution. Perhaps most important, however, is the fact that all of them shared a common goal. As Hobbes's friend, the poet Edmund Waller, once commented about him, 'what was chiefly to be taken notice of in his elogie was that he, being but one, and a private person, pulled-downe all the churches, dispelled the mists of ignorance, and layd-open their priest-craft'.[88] Early English deism followed Hobbes precisely in this task.

12.3 Conclusion

Hobbes and the deists were often accused by contemporaries—and indeed, they are still sometimes interpreted accordingly—of being covert atheists.[89] But their philosophy and theology were much more sophisticated than this accusation suggests. Moreover, once seen in their full complexity, the positions of Hobbes and the deists are close in many respects. Hobbes cast serious doubt on our ability to believe in revelations that take place in present times. Anyone who pretends to have had a revelation might lie, and people would lie as it serves their interests. The deists continued this line of thought and radicalized it. The very fact of present revelation became questionable. Moreover, it became redundant. Revelation could only confirm what natural reason tells us. If there is a contradiction, reason should always take priority. This argument was much more explicitly heterodox than Hobbes's. The motive, however, was precisely the same. The fairy tales of revelation were part of priestcraft and, as such, they were used by the corrupt clergy who endlessly sought to gain and maintain an independent power. The deists' war against priestcraft was Hobbes's war against the kingdom of darkness taken one step further.[90] At the same time, none of them was trying to deny the existence of God, nor, in fact, His providence. Their goal was one: to disprove any *story about* God that could benefit only the storyteller.

Hobbes could not know with any certainty who would benefit from his doctrine, but he did know that it was innovative. The deists, indeed, identified everything that was innovative in Hobbes. He was their resource and ally in the historic battle against priestcraft. Together with others, and primarily Spinoza, Hobbes was *one* of the fathers of deism; and deism was *one* possible highway to what may be called a multifaceted *Hobbesian enlightenment*. It was an enlightenment that combined traditional with

---

[88] John Aubrey, *Brief Lives, Chiefly of Contemporaries*, ed. Andrew Clark (Oxford: Clarendon Press, 1898), i, 358.

[89] See, for example, David Berman, *A History of Atheism in Britain: From Hobbes to Russell* (London: Routledge, 1990); Berman, 'Deism, Immortality and the Art of Theological Lying', in *Deism, Masonry, and the Enlightenment*, ed. J. A. Leo Lemay (Newark, NJ: University of Delaware Press, 1987), 61–78.

[90] A similar argument leads Mark Goldie to suggest that 'it does not require much foreshortening of historical explanation to say of Hobbes that, ecclesiologically, he was a Whig'. See Goldie, 'Priestcraft and the Birth of Whiggism', in *Political Discourses in Early Modern Britain*, ed. Nicholas Phillipson and Quentin Skinner (Cambridge: Cambridge University Press, 1993), 217.

unusual premises. It was not necessarily Israel's 'radical enlightenment', but also not exactly a 'clerical enlightenment'.[91] Theirs was an *anticlerical enlightenment*: an enlightenment that was aimed principally against the self-interested priests.

Thus, the English deists were not wrong in identifying the various anticlerical elements in Hobbes, and Leland was not wrong at all in asserting that some of the deists chose to follow Hobbes in several principles. In fact, they may have understood him better than many of the interpretations that we still encounter today.

[91] For the idea of a clerical or conservative English enlightenment, see for example Roy Porter, 'The Enlightenment in England', in *The Enlightenment in National Context*, ed. Roy Porter and Mikulás Teich (Cambridge: Cambridge University Press, 1981), 1–18.

13

All the Wars of Christendom
Hobbes's Theory of Religious Conflict

Jeffrey Collins

The claim that Thomas Hobbes, along with the other major early modern political theorists, devised modern understandings of sovereignty in response to the so-called age of religious war is a historical commonplace. The idea has long been engrained in the mythology of modern liberalism, but in recent decades it has enjoyed an accentuated emphasis. Several contextual factors—most notably 9/11 and its aftermath, but also the Iranian Revolution and the Balkan Wars—have riveted contemporary attention on the question of religious politics and religious violence.[1] In these contexts it is not unusual to find geopolitical debate littered with references to the Reformation or the Crusades.[2] The self-understanding of liberalism, including its internal historical mythologies, has been recast in the light of these political preoccupations.

The regnant secularization theories of the twentieth century have largely collapsed.[3] And if we can no longer equate modernity with an irreligious secularization, or portray religion as an atavism, then religion proves to have a surprisingly durable capacity to inform politics and war.

On the other hand, our very fascination with religious war (indeed our understanding of it) perhaps emerged from a differently understood process of secularization. If modern secularization does not mean the receding of religion or the rise of unbelief, but rather 'the freeing of successive sectors of social life and thought from ecclesiastical oversight and religious concepts',[4] then secularization (so defined) is in some sense the precondition for any notion of 'religious war'. War, as such, becomes the proper domain

---

[1] José Casanova, *Public Religions in the Modern World* (Chicago, IL: University of Chicago Press, 1994), 3–6.

[2] Ayaan Hirsi Ali, *Heretic: Why Islam Needs a Reformation Now* (New York: Harper, 2015); Carole Hillenbrand, *The Crusades: Islamic Perspectives* (Edinburgh: Edinburgh University Press, 1999); Jonathan Riley-Smith, *The Crusades, Christianity, and Islam* (New York: Columbia University Press, 2011).

[3] David Martin, *On Secularization: Towards a Revised General Theory* (Aldershot: Ashgate, 2005), 7–12; Charles Taylor, *A Secular Age* (Cambridge, MA: Belknap Press of Harvard University Press, 2007), introduction *et passim*.

[4] Martin, *Secularization*, 187.

of vocational politicians and statesmen acting according to an autonomous political logic. 'Religious war' then becomes a dangerous hybrid, requiring differentiation.

A raft of books has appeared over the past few decades using religious warfare as a historical foil for the Enlightenment and the modern state. The histories of the Enlightenment by Jonathan Israel and Anthony Pagden, for instance, credit atheistic Enlightenment ideas and the secular state for short-circuiting the European cycle of religious violence.[5] Mark Lilla's *The Stillborn God* offered a history of liberalism which attributed prosperity and stability to the 'separation' of religious belief from public life. 'Political theology', according to Lilla—transcendent and salvic—necessarily breeds violence and fanaticism. Liberal political philosophy, by contrast, supposedly pro-motes peaceful stability.[6] Hobbes, Lilla wrote, believed that Christian theology sus-tained a 'kingdom of darkness' prone to disastrous violence. Only absolute political sovereignty could control religion, and only if a strict separation was initiated dividing religious life from political life. Hobbes initiated this 'Great Separation', which would eventually empower a neutral sovereign and privatize religion, thereby pacifying the latter.[7] John Rawls himself located the origins of liberalism in the wars of religion, and in the political difficulties posed by the supposed tendency of historic Christianity to strive for a coercive domination.[8] Hobbes played a pivotal role in his account, as devisor of a purely 'secular political and moral system' built on the proposition that religion conflicts with those rational principles 'necessary for the peace and concord of society'.[9]

Hobbes has become fixed in historical memory as a modern, secular theorist who helped to resolve the problem of religious warfare. This chapter will comment on this commonplace, and expose its partiality. A more nuanced grasp of how Hobbes under-stood the phenomenon of religious violence suggests broader interpretive correctives as regards modern liberalism's mythologies of origin. In historical terms, the concept of a European age of religious war is both indispensable and highly problematic. 'Religious war' is not so much a clear historical phenomenon as an ideologically freighted observer's category with varied frames of reference. The problematic nature of 'religious war' as a covering concept has recently been subject to considerable critical scholarship.

For historians of Europe the primary context for these issues is invariably the post-Reformation period, the era of the 'wars of religion' ending with the Peace of Westphalia. The French civil wars of the latter sixteenth century constitute the gravita-tion centre of this historical period, which extends back to the German Reformation

[5] Jonathan Israel, *Radical Enlightenment: Philosophy and the Making of Modernity, 1650–1750* (Oxford: Oxford University Press, 2001), 4; Anthony Pagden, *The Enlightenment and Why It Still Matters* (Oxford: Oxford University Press, 2013), 34–5.

[6] Mark Lilla, *The Stillborn God: Religion, Politics, and the Modern West* (New York: Knopf, 2008).

[7] Lilla, *Stillborn God*, chapter two.

[8] John Rawls, *Political Liberalism* (Cambridge, MA: Belknap Press of Harvard University Press, 2005), 476–7.

[9] John Rawls, *Lectures on the History of Political Philosophy*, ed. Samuel Freeman (Cambridge, MA: Belknap Press of Harvard University Press, 2007), 27–8.

conflicts, and forward to the Dutch Revolt, England's conflicts with Spain, the Thirty Years War, and the civil wars of Britain. Though Crusades preceded this period and Holy Alliances followed it, the 'textbook' era of European religious war ran from the Reformation through the Thirty Years War. The Reformation itself generated moral disagreement and panic. Both 'bottom-up' religious revolts and 'top-down' religious repressions form part of the story, which is largely narrated as an intra-Christian drama of internal strife. This was the era in which religion made Europe a 'killing ground'.[10] Heroic roles are played throughout by *politiques* and sovereignists. In this form, the European 'age of religious war' constitutes the narrative spine of the 'early modern' historical period itself. It is a historical schematic containing considerable truth. Nevertheless, scholars in recent years have begun to lay bare the limitations of the historical accounts of religious war which play such an outsized role in liberalism's foundational mythology.

This critique is largely based on an 'anti-essentialist' theorization of religion itself, which traces back to the foundational writings of Wilfred Cantwell Smith and has continued in the work of scholars such as Talal Asad and Daniel Dubuisson.[11] These theorists, aided by contextualist intellectual historians such as Peter Harrison, have unpacked our concept of 'religion' and linked it to the rise of social scientific disciplines such as sociology and anthropology. Rather than treat any specific religion as a set of contestable philosophical, ethical, or historical truth claims, social scientists deploy psychological or social laws to construct 'functionalist' theories of all religions. Religion, per se, emerges from the fear of death, is projected from scientific ignorance, channels superstition, sacralizes political, social, or sexual hierarchies, and so forth. To sustain these claims, scholars construct 'sets' of religions in which are grouped phenomena as disparate as Christian denominations, Buddhism, Islam, Confucianism, paganism, polytheism, monotheism, sometimes atheism, and even political ideologies such as Communism and Fascism.[12] During the 'age of reason', writes Peter Harrison, 'religion' was increasingly used as a 'framework for classifying particular aspects of human life', often as 'an outsider's description of a dubious theological enterprise'.[13] Twentieth-century sociology advanced this effort, formalized it, stripped it of its polemical context and varnished it with the veneer of scientific fact. Max Weber's

---

[10] Padgen, *Enlightenment*, 33–41.

[11] Wilfred Cantwell Smith, *The Meaning and End of Religion: A New Approach to the Religious Traditions of Mankind* (New York: Macmillan, 1962); Talal Asad, 'The Construction of Religion as an Anthropological Category', in his *Genealogies of Religion: Discipline and Reasons of Power in Christianity and Islam* (London and Baltimore, MD: Johns Hopkins University Press, 1993); Daniel Dubuisson, *The Western Construction of Religion: Myths, Knowledge and Ideology*, trans. William Sayers (London and Baltimore, MD: Johns Hopkins University Press, 2003).

[12] Jonathan Israel has recently recast Robespierre as some kind of dictatorial theocrat, thus managing the trick of explaining the Terror of the French Revolution as a fundamentally religious phenomenon. See his *Revolutionary Ideas: An Intellectual History of the French Revolution* (Princeton, NJ: Princeton University Press, 2004).

[13] Peter Harrison, *'Religion' and the Religions in the English Enlightenment* (Cambridge: Cambridge University Press, 1990), 1–2.

classic *The Sociology of Religion* capped the process, offering an influential 'typology' of human religious experience which arrayed it on a developmental scale from elementary magical and charismatic forms to modern, 'rationalized', symbolic forms.[14]

'Religion', in Latinate traditions, once denoted a realm of deep obligation or rules, duties to family, nation, or cult.[15] Early Christianity tended to construe it as the realm of the divine and of individual connection to the divine. *Religio* marked piety, but not institutional rites, ecclesial organization, or a discreet social activity found across cultures. Our more modern, comparative theories of religion require that the religious and the secular be starkly demarcated, that religion be cordoned and defined so that its presence in various human cultures might be compared, and its underlying function distinguished from its specific outward forms. To some extent, these distinctions (of spiritual and secular) were intrinsic to ecclesial Christianity, and accentuated by Reformation theology.[16] But the full emergence of religion as a distinct category of social analysis was driven by the rise of social science.

The category of 'religious war' is parasitic on this concept. Like the category of 'religion', 'religious war' entails the creation of a distinct set of phenomena found in diverse historical settings, with a core definitional stability that prevails beneath contingencies. To the extent that moderns have often defined religion itself as a repository for irrationalism, superstition, or violence, religious war becomes its natural consequence.[17] Religious institutions are understood as efforts to channel these destabilizing impulses. Religious war results from the failure of such institutions to perform this function.

These interpretive habits pose apparent dangers. A psychologized or social-functional interpretation of religion, for one thing, short-circuits philosophical, ethical, or political critiques of particular orthodoxies. These are rendered superfluous, in that religious claims are now understood only in light of their particular psychological or social effects.[18] This reductive approach to the truth claims of religions, masquerading as a 'neutral' scientific perspective, thus carries philosophical costs. But more relevant to the present concerns of this chapter is the potential of the category 'religious war' to distort the history of human violence. The possibility that the idea of religious war might work as a foil within efforts to legitimize violence according to alternate logics is

---

[14] Max Weber, *The Sociology of Religion*, trans. Talcott Parsons (Boston, MA: Beacon Press, 1993). For critique see Pierre Manent, *The City of Man*, trans. Marc A. LePain (Princeton, NJ: Princeton University Press, 1994), 67–81.

[15] Brent Nongbri, *Before Religion: A History of a Modern Concept* (New Haven, CT: Yale University Press, 2013), 26–34.

[16] Larry Siedentop, *Inventing the Individual: The Origins of Western Liberalism* (London: Allen Lane, 2014), 349–63.

[17] William Cavanaugh, *The Myth of Religious Violence* (Oxford: Oxford University Press, 2009), 57–120; the vogue for sociobiology has produced pseudo-scientific accounts of religious belief as a coping mechanism or 'meme'. See Daniel Dennett, *Breaking the Spell: Religion as a Natural Phenomenon* (New York: Penguin, 2007).

[18] Mark Goldie, 'Ideology', in *Political Ideology and Conceptual Change*, ed. Terrance Ball, James Farr, and Russell L. Hanson (Cambridge: Cambridge University Press, 1989), 266–91.

one that has been explored in recent scholarship.[19] We will leave aside the most absurd examples of this tendency, though these can be revelatory in the manner of any *reductio ad absurdum*.[20] Nevertheless, even as regards the 'classic' European religious wars, the best recent scholarship has pressured the implication that these wars were fundamentally or entirely religious in nature. Attributing early modern warfare to religion as such, and its supposed disruption of the *politique* state, does not fare well among historians of the 'confessionalization' process.[21] If the old age of religious war is recast as an age of confessionalization, during which religious differences were codified and lashed to political identity, 'religious war' must in some measure be attributed to the very rise of the sovereign state. Religion became a central cause of conflict precisely because 'confession' had become central to order. The best studies of conflicts such as the French civil wars and the Thirty Years War attribute them to a complex interaction of political and religious causation.[22]

To treat these conflicts as particular examples of the inherent violence of religion (or monotheistic religion,[23] Christianity,[24] or Trinitarianism[25]) is facile. Such interpretations echo Enlightenment era 'philosophical' histories, where the entire 'era of religious war' was first devised, and where it developed in tandem with proto-psychologized or sociological interpretations of 'religion' itself. As J. G. A. Pocock has put it, the preoccupation with 'ecclesiastical authority and religious warfare is so far recurrent in all the phenomena we term Enlightened that it may be used in organizing and explaining them'.[26] The original, Enlightened thesis of religious war was often undergirded by a deep hostility to Christian orthodoxy in particular, and this polemical purpose can often inform modern deployment of the notion.

But even among historians not prone to philosophical advocacy, the concept of 'religious war' can obscure more than it reveals. Disparate conflicts are forced together under this umbrella concept. A religious war might include conflicts fought to protect sacred sites or claim sacred territory (the ancient Greek 'sacred wars' or the medieval

[19] Cavanaugh, *Myth of Religious Violence*; Karen Armstrong, *Fields of Blood: Religion and the History of Violence* (New York: Knopf, 2014), introduction.
[20] It is perhaps best to be politely silent, for instance, when atheistic Stalinism or Nazism are understood as a species of religious violence. Christopher Hitchens, *God is Not Great: How Religion Poisons Everything* (New York: Warner Twelve, 2007), 230–44.
[21] As pioneered by Heinz Schilling. See, for example, *Confessionalization in Europe, 1555–1700: Essays in Honor and Memory of Bodo Nischan*, ed. John M. Headley, Hans J. Hillerbrand, and Anthony J. Papalas (Aldershot: Ashgate, 2004); Philip Gorski, *The Disciplinary Revolution: Calvinism and the Rise of the State in Early Modern Europe* (Chicago, IL: University of Chicago Press, 2003).
[22] Peter Wilson, *The Thirty Years War: Europe's Tragedy* (London: Penguin, 2009); Thomas Brady, *German Histories in the Age of Reformations* (Cambridge: Cambridge University Press, 2009); Mack Holt, *The French Wars of Religion, 1562–1629* (Cambridge: Cambridge University Press, 1995), introduction.
[23] Regina Schwartz, *The Curse of Cain: The Violent Legacy of Monotheism* (Chicago, IL: University of Chicago Press, 1997).
[24] Perez Zagorin, *How the Idea of Religious Toleration Came to the West* (Princeton, NJ: Princeton University Press, 2003) promoted the view of Gibbon that Christianity was the most violent religion in world history.
[25] Lilla, *Stillborn God*, 35 et passim.
[26] J. G. A. Pocock, *Barbarism and Religion* (Cambridge: Cambridge University Press, 1999), ii, 19.

Crusades). It might entail war against the enemies of a particular religion, fought to expand that religion's reach. It might be waged, bottom-up, as a religiously inspired rebellion: either to secure religious freedom or to establish a different confessional identity for a refashioned polity. Alternatively, a religious war might target such an uprising in defence of an established church-state. A religious war might attack a secularist regime, or seek to secure one. In specifying any given conflict, historians will rarely be served by such generalized tropes as 'religious war'. Such reasoning through analogy often breeds fallacy.

The remainder of this chapter will examine Hobbes's account of religious warfare, keeping a close eye on its specificity. Hobbes offered a lurid, conspiratorial account of religious warfare within Christendom. The ideological purposes of this account have been veiled by the historical mythology of a generic 'age of religious war'. It will further be argued that, while Hobbes often described religious war in highly specific (and Christian) terms, in other places he advanced a psychological and proto-sociological account of religious conflict that foreran the modern mindset on the subject. 'Enlightened' liberalism finds the *generic* notion of religious warfare a useful marker of barbarity and an irresistible foil for secularism. But the general critique often masks more targeted hostility towards particular orthodoxies and forms of ecclesial organization. Hobbes's theory of religious war anticipated this pattern by containing both particular and generic dimensions.

The English Civil War was of course the particular conflict which occasioned *Leviathan*, and also constituted the subject of Hobbes's most important work of history, *Behemoth*. Together, these texts made a sustained early effort to interpret the Civil War as a war of religion. Though there has been a long subsequent history of such interpretation, Hobbes's early account is often overlooked.

Clarendon's influential history of the 'rebellion' heaped enormous opprobrium on the preachers and zealots of the era, but he largely viewed them as pious frauds, manipulating religion in order to justify sedition. Political and social rebellion propelled the civil wars; religious fakery served as rhetorical window dressing. David Hume was more inclined to see an honest religious 'fanaticism' at work in the conflict. His Civil War was fought by Puritan enthusiasts, fired by an incandescent anticlericalism. But Hume too doubted religion as a real cause of the war. Much of the era's religious passion he dismissed as 'counterfeit', a mixture of 'fraud and ardour' covering the 'familiar motives of interest and ambition'. For both men, constitutional issues played a predominant role in the war. This became the dominant view; the Civil War's 'religious parties' were mere 'surrogates for political parties'.[27] When edited in the eighteenth century, memoirs and diaries of the Civil War often had their religious dimensions stripped away.[28] The standard Victorian history of S. R. Gardiner, though it followed

[27] Glenn Burgess, 'Introduction: Religion and the Historiography of the English Civil War', in *England's Wars of Religion Revisited*, ed. Charles Prior and Glenn Burgess (Aldershot: Ashgate, 2011), 3–5.
[28] Blair Worden, *Roundhead Reputations: The English Civil Wars and the Passions of Posterity* (London: Penguin, 2001).

Thomas Carlyle in speaking of a 'Puritan Revolution', viewed the revolution as a constitutional revolt against absolute monarchy. As one historian has written of Gardiner's work, 'the cunning of history had made Puritans the servants of political liberty'.[29]

Twentieth-century historians of the Civil War developed their own logic for treating religion as epiphenomenal. Weberian sociology and Marxist theory weighed heavily on these accounts. Puritanism was thus construed as an imaginative, psychological, and rhetoric resource for a rising bourgeoisie, and radical religious sectarianism as the vehicle for a nascent proletariat. 'Class antagonism' and 'social pressures' replaced constitutional struggles in these histories, but religion continued to play a subordinate role.[30]

American study of seventeenth-century Puritanism offered the first compelling accounts of the English Revolution as a 'religious war'. William Haller and Michael Walzer refused to read religious language as mere 'code used to talk about other more important matters'.[31] They understood Puritanism's radical potential as a theological matter, driven by concepts such as covenant, providence, discipline, and conscience.[32] They developed a more thoroughgoing account of the Revolution as a 'religious war', one caused by tensions within Christian theology and practice.

Later twentieth-century scholarship continued to operate with these assumptions. 'Revisionist' scholarship of the 1970s and 1980s qualified the idea of 'revolutionary Puritanism' by unearthing the more conservative and consensus-oriented aspects of Puritanism, and the political activism of Church of England episcopalianism. For scholars such as John Morrill, Nicholas Tyacke, and Jonathan Clark, the Civil War was no revolution, but a Reformation-style religious war pitting reformed versus 'Catholic' (or prelatical) parties (and often casting the latter as the instigators).[33] The Civil War became a distant consequence of the 'crisis of Reformation politics', without even unintentional secularizing or modernizing consequences.[34]

Clearly the English Civil War offers a useful illustration of the point that the concept of 'religious war' can do both too much and too little interpretive work. Disparate interpretive possibilities, often incompatible, have sheltered under the category. Locating Hobbes's account of the war amidst the range of possibilities thus requires specificity.

---

[29] Burgess, 'Introduction', 8.

[30] Christopher Hill, *The World Turned Upside Down: Radical Ideas During the English Revolution* (London: Maurice Temple Smith, 1972) is a classic example of this tradition.

[31] Burgess, 'Introduction', 11–14.

[32] William Haller, *Liberty and Reformation in the Puritan Revolution* (New York: Columbia University Press, 1953); Michael Walzer, *The Revolution of the Saints: A Study of the Origins of Radical Politics* (Cambridge, MA: Harvard University Press, 1965).

[33] John Morrill, 'The Religious Context of the English Civil War', *Transactions of the Royal Historical Society*, 5th series, 34 (1984), 155–78; Nicholas Tyacke, *Anti-Calvinists: The Rise of English Arminianism, c.1590–1640* (Oxford: Clarendon Press, 1987).

[34] Michael Braddick, *God's Fury, England's Fire: A New History of the English Civil Wars* (London: Penguin, 2008), pp. xxiii, xxvi.

A few interpretive avenues can be closed at once. Hobbes, by and large, did not share Clarendon's view that the 'hot Protestant' cause was a pretext for ambitious rebels motivated by baser interests. Hobbes was, of course, perfectly aware that generals and statesmen might strike pious postures, or dress up their motives and actions with religious veils. In *Behemoth* he quite strongly suggested that Cromwell was such an ambitious masquerader (playing, for instance, the 'sects' as his 'best cards'[35]). But where this kind of public falseness was in operation, Hobbes was more prone than Clarendon to sympathize with it as a Machiavellian strategy of stabilization. In any case, Hobbes did not, by and large, argue that religion served as a mere pretext among Civil War actors. And though Hobbes passingly gestured towards class motives that might have accelerated the war, he never mapped these onto religious factions.[36] In short, he did not prefigure either the Whig or the Marxist interpretations of the Civil War's religious parties, subordinating them to either constitutionalist or bourgeoisie interests.

Nor can we say that Hobbes anticipated accounts of the war according to which his own modernized sovereignty sought to replace an unstable and retrograde divine right account of monarchy. Hobbes certainly denied that any polity other than ancient Israel could be directly modelled on revelation or scriptural injunction.[37] This provoked Robert Filmer, among others.[38] But *Leviathan* expended little effort riposting the divine right monarchists. He was more provoked by the royalists' strategic embrace of mixed constitutionalism, a position not notably advanced by the Laudian church.[39] Though Hobbes, as we shall see, kept a wary eye on the bishops, he did not view the Civil War as the product of a dangerous 'throne and altar' alliance.

Hobbes presented the Civil War not as a generic 'war of religion', but as a conflict endemic to Christianity. He repeatedly argued that 'the dispute for precedence betwene the *spirituall* and *civill power*, has of late, more then any other thing in the world, bene the cause of *civill warres*, in all *places of Christendome*.'[40] He also stated that *Leviathan* had been 'caused' by his 'consideration of what the Ministers before, and in the beginning of the Civill War, by their preaching and writing did contribute thereunto'.[41] The book was written in the conviction that the Civil War was caused by 'nothing other than the quarrelling, first between the Roman Church and the Anglican, and then within the Anglican Church between the Episcopalian and Presbyterian pastors, about theological issues'.[42] If we are to grasp the historic implications of *Leviathan*, these explanatory comments by its author—and not our own more capacious and schematic understanding of 'religious war'—must guide us in the first instance.

---

[35] B, pp. 290–1.   [36] B, pp. 110–11.   [37] L, 31, p. 556; 35, pp. 636–44.

[38] Robert Filmer, *Observations Concerning the Originall of Government* (London, 1652), preface and 1–2; Casare Cuttica, *Sir Robert Filmer and the Patriotic Monarch* (Manchester: Manchester University Press, 2015).

[39] David Smith, *Constitutional Royalism and the Search for Settlement, 1640–1649* (Cambridge: Cambridge University Press, 2002), 248–53.

[40] C, p. 120; DCv, 6.11; L, 14, p. 216.

[41] *Six Lessons to the Professors of the Mathematiques* (London, 1656), 56.

[42] LLA, p. 1226.

Hobbes offered two possible theories of the Civil War as a war of religion: the first presenting the war as an uprising of the 'conscientious'; the second presenting it as an elite conspiracy caused by the division of temporal and spiritual authority. The first account tended to present England's hot Protestant reformers as the malevolent agents of the war. The second trained its fire on Britain's established, corporate churches: the Scottish Kirk and the episcopal Church of England. Hobbes's relative preference between these two accounts shifted throughout his experience of the Civil War and its aftermath.

13.1 The Civil War as a War of Conscientious Rebels

Hobbes's concern about the political implications of unbridled individual conscience was a consistent feature of his writing. When discussing beliefs that tended to dissolve sovereignty, Hobbes condemned the doctrine that anything done in violation of individual conscience constituted sin.[43] In the revised version of *De Cive*, he wrote that this aspect of the book (the 'taking away of individual conscience') had been 'sharply criticized' by 'Sectarians'.[44]

In the first dialogue of *Behemoth* Hobbes provided a list of the 'seducers' who had set the Kingdom against Charles I. The first identified are 'Ministers of Christ' ('pretending to have a right from God to governe every one his Parish; and their Assembly the whole nation'). Hobbes identifies these as the Presbyterians. He then adds to his roster of rebels those who 'shortly after' the start of the war 'declared themselves for a Liberty in Religion, and those of different opinions one from another; some of them (because they would have all congregations free and independent upon one another) were called *Independents*'. Others, he writes, were called Anabaptists, others Quakers, and so forth. These were 'divers Sects' who 'arose against his Majesty from the private interpretation of the Scripture exposed to every mans scanning in his Mother tongue'.[45]

This chronology attributed the original troubles of the Long Parliament to Presbyterians looking to reshape the official church. Such aspirations explained the initial revolt of Scotland and the factionalizing of the parliament. Thereafter, sectarian advocates for religious liberty swept into action, peddling 'obscure' doctrine devised by private scriptural interpretation. This was a standard royalist interpretation of the rebellion, placing blame for the initial civil war on Presbyterians, but blame for the regicide on the Independents. It locates the religious zeal behind the war firmly on the side of Parliament and opponents of the Church of England.

Leviathan broadcast Hobbes's suspicion of Presbyterianism and sectarianism when discussing the nature of sovereignty. *Leviathan* insisted that political covenants could only exist between individuals in a state of nature. Humans could not covenant directly with God (barring some supernatural revelation). This stricture targeted the Scottish National Covenant—the 'confession' of faith binding the Scots to defend the reformed

---

[43] EL, 26.2; DCv, 12.2.   [44] DCv, 'Preface to the Readers'.   [45] B, pp. 109–10.

Kirk against the 'popish' innovations of Charles I's government. Throughout the initial narrative of *Behemoth* Hobbes condemns the divine right claims of Presbyterian church government, and those who had rebelled to protect them.[46]

As for the Independents and the sects, who clamoured for a Congregational model of church government and for a high degree of free conscience, *Leviathan* argued against their position as well. In chapter 29, Hobbes rejected, as dangerous to sovereignty, the doctrines that '*every private man is Judge of Good and Evill actions*' and that '*whatsoever a man does against his Conscience, is Sinne*'.[47] Hobbes thus presented the epistemology of radical Protestantism (this sectarian or individual religious 'seeking') as a cause of religious rebellion.

Remarkably, in *Behemoth* Hobbes attributed sedition to the translation of the Bible. This permitted 'every man, nay every boy and every wench that could read English' to think 'they spoke with God Almighty and understood what he said, when by a certain number of chapters a day, they had read the Scriptures once or twice over.'[48] By 1651 these sentiments would have seemed remarkably retrograde. The translation of the Bible was hardly a controversial development by this time. So close does this complaint come to a reactionary Catholic point of view that sarcasm may have been at work. Hobbes also blamed radical Presbyterianism on the Marian exiles of the sixteenth century, and on the appeal of Presbyterianism to those also attracted to 'popular' government in the state. The 'Presbyterians' since Queen Elizabeth's day had gone abroad 'preaching into most of the Market townes of England' against supposed tyranny in church and state affairs.[49]

Hobbes often wrote as one whose outlook might have been fixed in the sixteenth century, when Calvinist resistance theory was produced in both France and Scotland. Calvinist resistance theory was based upon contract theory—the proposition that political sovereignty emerged from a joint contract guaranteed by sovereign, people, and God himself. The failure to uphold true religion would mark a failure of this contract, and would justify resistance.[50] Hobbes sought to distance his very different form of contractual theory from this resistance tradition. Thus he disavowed the claim that conscience must be acted upon outwardly, or that God was ever a direct party to a religious covenant.

In offering this account of the war, Hobbes participated in what would be a long line of interpretation, which attributed the religious upheaval of the civil wars to the uncompromising zeal of the 'Puritan' or anti-Laudian cause.

[46] B, pp. 145, 172, 181, 210, 214, *et passim*.
[47] L, 29, p. 502.   [48] B, p. 135.   [49] B, p. 137.
[50] Exemplars include Hotman's *Francogallia* (1573), Beza's *Du droit des magistrats* (1575), and the *Vindiciae contra Tyrannos* (1579). For an introduction to the Calvinist and Catholic variants of contractual resistance theory, see Robert M. Kingdon, 'Calvinism and Resistance Theory, 1550–1580', and J. H. M. Salmon, 'Catholic Resistance Theory, Ultramontanism, and the Royalist Response, 1580–1620', both in *The Cambridge History of Political Thought 1450–1700*, ed. J. H. Burns with Mark Goldie (Cambridge: Cambridge University Press, 1991).

However, Hobbes's tendency to blame the war on individual 'conscientious' religious actors was surprisingly muted. There was a broad royalist tendency to blame the war on reforming zealots, loosed from all church authority. Hobbes, for his part, did not attach himself to a strong version of this thesis of the war. Indeed, as is well known, *Leviathan* made significant concessions to the demands of individual conscience.

The Latin term *conscientia* contained certain ambiguities that were reflected in early modern usage. Conscience had a pre-Christian meaning, of either 'knowledge with another' or 'knowledge within oneself'. It could denote (in a scholastic setting) an inner comprehension of something like natural law; within Christianity it was often associated with movements of the Holy Spirit. Conscience was not radically free. It was limited to those open to the guidance of Scripture and revelation. The category of a 'false conscience' could be invoked against those presumed to be acting out of an ill will.

Hobbes had long written in a negative vein about conscientious action, but in *Leviathan* he introduced positive discussion of the concept. Again, the Latin term carried two possible meanings, knowledge within oneself or with others. Hobbes explicitly defined conscience in the latter way:

When two, or more men, know of one and the same fact, they are said to be CONSCIOUS of it one to another; which is as much as to know it together. And because such are fittest witnesses of the facts of one another, or of a third; it was, and ever will be reputed a very Evill act, for any man to speak against his *Conscience*; or to corrupt, or force, another to do so…Afterwards, men made use of the same word metaphorically, for the knowledge of their own secret facts, and secret thoughts; and therefore it is Rhetorically said, that the Conscience is a thousand witnesses.[51]

Here we do find some deference to free conscience, but a definition of it which accentuates publicity and thus distances it from individual arbitration. Communication and consensus create conscience. A free conscience existed only where conditions of clear fact and public communication structured it. This definition was explicitly sceptical of inner conscience.[52]

But Hobbes usually deployed the more standard definition of conscience, defining it as an individual perception. In the *Elements of Law* every man has his 'own conscience', and in *Leviathan* Hobbes refers to conscience as 'private Reason'.[53] Hobbes generally wrote of conscience operating in an 'inner' court ('*foro interno*'), not an 'outer one' ('*foro externo*'). And in *Leviathan*, Hobbes adopted a language of *free*, inner conscience. He condemned the extension of 'the Law, which is the Rule of Actions only, to the very Thoughts, and Consciences of men'.[54] He cautioned against burdening 'good & pious

---

[51] L, 7, p. 100.
[52] This reading is foregrounded in Johan Tralau, 'Hobbes Contra Liberty of Conscience', *Political Theory* 39.1 (2011), 58–84.
[53] L, 37, p. 696.   [54] L, 46, p. 1096.

conscience' with unnecessary doctrine.[55] He wrote that 'there ought to be no Power over the Consciences of men, but of the Word it selfe, working Faith in every one'.[56]

To some extent, these comments merely reflected Hobbes's view that force could not change inner belief, but only outward obedience. When it came to inner conscience, might could not become right. Free conscience, in light of this, might be purely internal, and thus quite meagre. Hobbes indeed used this deep disjuncture, between inner belief and outer profession or action, to justify a high level of sovereign spiritual control. He wrote that a Christian might worship pagan gods because such actions of obedience to sovereigns—important in other respects—could not touch the conscience. (Clergy, as evangelists, he wryly observed, might have some duty to martyr themselves.) Free conscience could thus denote a strictly inner freedom that was in fact a valuable adjunct to outward obedience.[57]

However, Hobbes did at times concede that certain political arrangements and real-world effects might follow from the inviolability of conscientious belief. First, the need for free conscience should result in a minimal public theological doctrine. Complex orthodoxy was a burden to the conscience. Second, Hobbes used the notion of free conscience to attack 'praeterpolitical' church government. In the final pages of *Leviathan* Hobbes condemned Catholicism, the episcopal Church of England, and Presbyterianism as successive usurpations of sovereign right. Cromwell's 'Independent' church of atomized congregations under sovereign jurisdiction was partly justified by Hobbes as a shrewd political model, but also as a boon to conscientious religion.[58] A respect for conscience could thus have outer effects. It could inform an anticlerical

---

[55] L, 42, p. 802. There is not present space to consider the ambiguities of Hobbes's position. His chief targets in these passages are the traditional agents of religious coercion: clergy armed with churchly orthodoxy. Sovereign states enjoyed more latitude to define the ambit of public doctrine and encourage its inculcation. Teresa Bejan's article in the present volume, 'First Impressions: Hobbes on Religion, Education, and the Metaphor of Imprinting', explores this question with insight. See also R. W. Serjeantson, 'Hobbes, the Universities and the History of Philosophy', in *The Philosopher in Early Modern Europe: The Nature of a Contested Identity*, ed. Conal Condren, Stephen Gaukroger, and Ian Hunter (Cambridge: Cambridge University Press, 2006), 113–39.

[56] L, 47, p. 1116.

[57] L, 42, pp. 786–90. The complexities of Hobbes's account of conscience, given his 'mechanistic, anti-Aristotelian account of deliberation' are treated in Mark Hanin, 'Thomas Hobbes's Theory of Conscience', *History of Political Thought* 33.1 (2012), 55–85. The complexities of the Hobbesian conscience in the Christian and Jewish cases are explored in Richard Tuck, 'Hobbes, Conscience, and Christianity', in *The Oxford Handbook of Hobbes*, ed. A. P. Martinich and Kinch Hoekstra (Oxford: Oxford University Press, 2016), 481–500.

[58] L, 47, pp. 1114–16. Hobbes's endorsement of Independency has been subject to considerable debate. My own work and that of Richard Tuck has emphasized it. Scholars such as Johann Sommerville and A. P. Martinich have treated it as a misleading anomaly. Franck Lessay's chapter in the present volume, 'Tolerance as a Dimension of Hobbes's Absolutism', offers a version of this sceptical position. There is not space here to debate the point. Suffice it to say that Sommerville and Lessay, in my view, confuse the question by offering a composite portrait of revolution 'Independency' that amounts to a fallacy of composition. Hobbes endorsed the ecclesial form of Independency for his own reasons (as did James Harrington, Henry Stubbe, and others). We need not require of him enthusiasm for separatism, providentialism, radical anti-formalism, theories of the anti-Christ, or other beliefs held by some—but certainly not all—Independents.

politics, a minimalist theological programme of public doctrine, and a church model of magisterial Independency.

The advocacy of an atomized church establishment of independent congregations was unheard of among prominent early modern political philosophers. Many modern commentators have sought to render Hobbes's endorsement of Independency suspect by noting its 'provisional' nature.[59] Hobbes did require that members of Independent congregations not engage in contention, or measure Christian doctrine according to their devotion to individual ministers. Crucially, however, these were not self-defeating, provisional conditions of Hobbes's own invention. They were themselves extracted from Congregationalist polemic, where they served to explain why Paul was reproving the Corinthians (for a lack of charity) without falling into the traditional view that he was angry at their schismatic affront to primitive episcopal authority. In a text Hobbes commended, for instance, John Owen made exactly this point in order to protect the Congregational way from charges of schism as traditionally understood.[60] And when James Harrington was accused of following Hobbes in promoting the Congregational way, he addressed the relevant passages from Corinthians: 'Nor doth Paul blame the Congregations of Apollos and Cephas (1 Cor. 1) in that they were gathered, but in that they put too much upon them that gathered them.'[61] Paul, in other words, denounced schism defined as contention, *rather than* schism defined as congregational autonomy. This was a standard *apologetical* point. Hobbes's provisos, in other words, did not qualify his endorsement of Independency but constituted further evidence of it.

By endorsing the ecclesial preferences of the more mainstream Independents, and by adopting in part their rhetoric of free conscience, Hobbes effectively distanced himself from what would be the primary royalist account of the Civil War as a war of religion.[62]

We should thus not be surprised that when Hobbes came to write Restoration era accounts of *Leviathan* and its effort to resolve religious war, he rarely mentioned sectarians or the cause of free conscience. He instead foregrounded the dangers of clerical authority, autonomous church power, and the machinations of the episcopalians and Presbyterians. If Hobbes's concern with the revolt of individual conscience receded

---

[59] Jon Parkin, following Alan Cromartie, makes this claim in his chapter in this volume, 'Hobbes and the Future of Religion'. Hobbes's provisos have been emphasized most insistently by Teresa M. Bejan, 'Difference without Disagreement: Rethinking Hobbes on "Independency" and Toleration', *The Review of Politics* 78.1 (2016), 1–25. She views them as conditions of Hobbes's own devising.

[60] John Owen, *Of Schisme, The True Nature of it Discovered and Considered, With Reference to the present Differences in Religion* (Oxford, 1657), 26–8. For Hobbes's praise of this book, see C, p. 449. For the more traditional view, see Robert Baillie, *A Dissuasive from the Errours of the Time* (London, 1645), 218–19; John Bastwick, *The Utter Routing of the whole Army of all Independents and Sectarians* (London, 1646), 262–3.

[61] James Harrington, *Pian Piano* (London, 1656), 4, 66–7. The high-churchman Henry Ferne specifically attributed Harrington's views on this point to Hobbes.

[62] The Independents function as the primary agents of radicalization and regicide in the histories of Heylin, Fuller, Clarendon, and others. Revealingly, relative to Hobbes they are more harshly treated in James Heath's *A Chronicle of the Late Intestine War in the Three Kingdoms* (London, 1676), which was Hobbes's main source for historical detail in his own *Behemoth* (see B, pp. 119, 127, 133–4, 139, 143, 163, *et passim*).

somewhat during the course of the Civil War and after it, his obsession with the dangers of corporate ecclesial authority moved in the opposite direction.

13.2 The Civil War as a Conspiracy of Priests

On several occasions Hobbes stated that the civil wars (across Europe) were generated by hierarchical churches seeking authority for themselves which justly belonged to sovereigns. Most royalists rallied to the old proposition of James I: 'no bishop, no King'. They understood themselves duty-bound to uphold at once the monarchical constitution of the nation and the episcopal constitution of the church. These institutions were construed as partners, upholding order and justice against the radical religious individualism of the sects. Hobbes rejected this view, and understood the crown and the church to be rivals for power. The church might ally with the monarchy for its own self-interest, but it fundamentally thirsted after autonomous power. To the extent that it did so, the church divided sovereignty, distracted the allegiance of subjects, and created the potential for civil war.

Hobbes had first developed this theory of the Civil War before its inception. In the summer of 1641, as the Long Parliament was moving forward with a radical plan for parliamentary committees to assume episcopal authority, Hobbes wrote to the earl of Devonshire that the deprivation of the bishops might be justified. 'I am sure', he wrote, 'that Experience teaches, thus much, that the dispute for precedence betwene the *spirituall* and *civill power*, has of late, more then any other thing in the world, bene the cause of *civill warres*, in all *places of Christendome*.'[63] Hobbes would repeat this claim in both *De Cive* and in *Leviathan*. In *De Cive* he explicitly linked the usurpation of sovereignty authority to the behaviour of the episcopal Church of England, and asked 'what war ever broke out in the Christian world that did not spring from this root or was fed by it?'[64] In correspondence with his friend Robert Payne during the composition of *Leviathan* Hobbes made clear that he viewed clerical power seeking as a primary cause of religious war—and he insisted that the Church of England could be indicted on this score.[65] Several passages in *Leviathan* make clear that Hobbes did not look upon the religious policies of the Laudian church with favour. He was hostile to the proposition that bishops enjoyed authority over the church by divine right. In chapter 29, on things that lead to the dissolution of commonwealths, Hobbes included the teaching that '*Soveraign Power may be divided*'. The division that particularly concerned him was between temporal authority and spiritual authority, whereby churches could set up a '*Supremacy* against the *Soveraignty*; *Canons* against *Lawes*; and a *Ghostly Authority* against the *Civill*'. These divisions, whereby one authority had the power to declare 'what is Sinne' and another 'what is Law', blinded subjects to their true obedience.

---

[63] C, pp. 120–1.   [64] DCv, 6.11.
[65] Jeffrey Collins, 'Christian Ecclesiology and the Composition of *Leviathan*: A Newly Discovered Letter to Thomas Hobbes', *Historical Journal* 43.1 (2000), 217–31.

The division of spiritual authority from temporal was a particularly dangerous division (worse than a division of authority between Parliament and King), because spiritual power claimed to control the afterlife, while sovereigns could only deal in earthly punishment.[66]

Behemoth most clearly revealed Hobbes's view that the English bishops had been responsible for weakening the Stuart dynasty and encouraging rebellion. One of the oddities of *Behemoth* for modern readers is the first dialogue of the work. This section seems tangential, digressing deep into the history of clerical usurpation during the age of the medieval papal monarchy. Hobbes understood this as the primal political struggle of European civilization, and *Behemoth* casts the Civil War as an episode in this history—another effort to beat back the power claims of hierarchical, 'divine right' clergy. That Hobbes understood Catholicism in this way was not surprising, but that he presented the Church of England as heir to this tradition of sedition was remarkable. Hobbes viewed the conduct of the Laudian Church of England as a revival of the medieval outrages of Catholic dualism—whereby spiritual sovereignty claimed pride of place over the mere temporal authority of kings. Capping his condemnation of the Catholic tendency to split sovereignty, Hobbes wrote: 'this Power not only the Pope pretends to in all Christendome; but most bishops also in their severall Dioceses, Jure Divino, that is, *immediately from Christ*'.[67] Hobbes went on to condemn Archbishop Laud specifically for imposing the prayer book on Scotland, for encouraging debased theology in the interest of church power, and for undermining the Royal Supremacy by claiming episcopal divine right.[68] Hobbes expressed a remarkable sympathy with the Long Parliament's war against 'Ecclesiasticall Tyranny and Usurpation'. Many of the bishops, he said, had acted in their own private interests—'indiscreetly, and perhaps wickedly'.[69] They 'carried themselves as if they owed their greatnesse not to the King's favour and to his Letters Patents' but to their own merit and dignity.[70]

There is a great deal more in *Behemoth* against the episcopal church than against the radical sects. It offered a theory of the Civil War as a religious war in which the Caroline bishops played the role of the medieval Catholics, betrayers of their royal master and usurpers of legitimate sovereignty.

Thus, while Hobbes was convinced that the Civil War was a religious war, in analysing the specifics of that war he offered duelling theories. On the one hand, he condemned the Civil War as a religious rebellion, fuelled by spiritual individualism and the radical levelling propensities of low-church Protestantism. This was a familiar theory of religious war during the age of Reformation, used to explain the German Peasants' War, the Anabaptists of Münster, and the Huguenot resistance. On the other hand, Hobbes also cast the high-church Anglicans as the villains of the Civil War—responsible for usurping the unified authority of the King, dividing and thus dooming his sovereignty, governing in their own interests, and stirring the Presbyterian revolt. This

[66] L, 29, pp. 506–10.   [67] B, p. 113.   [68] B, pp. 143–5, 187–8, 201–4.
[69] B, pp. 213–14.   [70] B, p. 224.

account spoke for a long-standing resistance to clerical authority that also marked the Magisterial Reformation, but was older than that and not limited to the Protestant world. It was a top-down theory of religious war, blaming it on the divided sovereignty cultivated by Roman Catholicism and by Protestant churches insufficiently purged of Catholicizing tendencies.

In *Behemoth* Hobbes's account of the English Civil War expanded into an account of Christian civil war as such. Formulated in *Leviathan*, and elaborated in Restoration texts such as the *Historia Ecclesiastica*, Hobbes's account of Christian religious war relentlessly targeted organized clerical power. (The sectarians of the past—Hussites, Waldensians, and so forth—are more often commended than condemned.) Hobbes's sacred history was carried forward with a tone of relentless cynicism, and with a lurid conspiratorial mindset. Trinitarianism was reduced to a manipulative kind of intentional obscurantism; clerical celibacy and the mendicant orders into strategies for developing loyal, papal drones; and so forth. All of the bombastic polemics of the Enlightenment are prefigured in Hobbes's writings. His concern, to reiterate, is not a throne and altar alliance but a throne and altar rivalry. The 'divine' powers of monarchy may have been dubious to the Hobbesian science of politics, but did not divide sovereignty as the 'divine' powers of the priesthood often did.[71]

If we wish to accurately reconstruct Hobbes's rejection of 'sacred' politics, we must read him not against the patriarchal monarchism of Filmer, but against the churchly piety of Charles I. *Leviathan*'s great counterpoint is not *Patriarcha* but the *Eikon Basilike*. From the scaffold Charles had urged: 'You must give God His due by regulating rightly his Church (according to His Scripture) which is now out of order. For to set you in a way particularly, now I cannot; but only this: a national synod freely called, freely debating among themselves, must settle this...'[72] The 'free' church was in many ways Charles I's only immovable political priority. Charles's speech, and the wildly popular *Eikon Basilike*, set the agenda and tone for post-regicidal royalism. In these texts Charles did not assert, explicitly, the divine right of kings and tended towards constitutional royalism. But he did espouse the sacred rights of the episcopal church. The Root and Branch petition had constituted a 'sacrilegious' attack on the bishops. Charles defended his refusal to dismantle the 'Primitive, Apostolicall, and anciently Universall Government of the Church by Bishops'.[73] It was in this context that the King most regularly appealed to the image of ultimate, Christly sacrifice. Of his efforts to defend the 'rights of the church' he prayed to God: 'Better they destroy Me, than Thou shouldst damn Me.'[74] Charles esteemed 'the Church above the State, the glory of Christ

[71] Patricia Springborg, 'Hobbes, Heresy, and the *Historica Ecclesiastica*', *Journal of the History of Ideas* 55.4 (1994), 553–71; Jeffrey Collins, 'Thomas Hobbes's Ecclesiastical History', in *The Oxford Handbook of Hobbes*, 520–44.

[72] *The Trial of Charles I: A Documentary History*, ed. David Lagomarsino and Charles T. Wood (Hanover, NH: University Press of New England, 1989), 140–3.

[73] *Eikon Basilike: The Pourtraicture of His Sacred Majestie in His Solitudes and Sufferings* (London, reprinted 1648/9), 41.

[74] Ibid., 26, 44–5.

above my Own: and the salvation of men's Souls above the preservation of their Bodies and Estates'.[75]

The *Eikon Basilike* defended the 'rights of the church' not as an adjunct to sovereignty, but as the inheritance of an autonomous corporation. 'No men have been more injuriously used, as to their Legal Rights, than the Bishops and the churchmen', wrote Charles. He avowed that he would rather live on the church's alms than raid the clergy to strengthen the state.[76] Against both fractious 'reformers' and the 'covetousness of some States and Princes',[77] Charles wrote:

> I am so much a friend to all Churchmen that have anything in them beseeming that sacred function, that I have hazarded my own interests, chiefly upon Conscience and Constancy to maintain their Rights.[78]

All of this represented unadulterated Laudianism, and would lash post-regicidal royalism tightly to episcopal, liturgical piety. (The *Eikon Basilike* was produced—or edited—by the moderate churchman John Gauden, though its more high-church chapters were reportedly written by Brian Duppa and reflected the King's own confessional posture.)[79] The sacred monarchy of Charles I was not the Davidic Godly kingship of his father, fusing temporal and spiritual power, but instead cast the monarchy as the loyal, suffering servant of the church. Hobbes was profoundly hostile to this aspiration, and *Leviathan* was determined to expose it—despite its thematic centrality to royalism—as the root cause of the English Civil War.

The bishops did not appreciate this treatment. When Hobbes tried to publish *Behemoth* in the 1660s, they recoiled.[80] Hobbes tried to suppress some of the passages of *Behemoth* most offensive to episcopal sentiment, but even this effort did not avail him. *Behemoth* was not authorized for publication during his lifetime.

Hobbes's opposition to clerical authority provided him with a theory of religious sedition, but did not by any means make him a religious pacifist. Hobbes's prescription for the political pacification of religion was two-pronged. He advised a certain deference to individual conscience, and a determined protection of the state's monopoly over ecclesiastical authority. Atomization and coercion would operate in concert. Securing these conditions would not necessarily be easy, and Hobbes did not flinch from the need to exert violence in order to achieve them. His early hostility to the episcopal church, for instance, made him favourable to the reform efforts of the Long Parliament during a time it was extensively impeaching and imprisoning the bishops of the church, ramping up a purge of the pulpits, and preparing for the fatal trial of Archbishop Laud. Charles I, from his different perspective, characterized this 'secular

---

[75] Ibid., 73; Kevin Sharpe, 'Private Conscience and Public Duty in the Writings of Charles I', *Historical Journal* 40.3 (1997), 643–65.

[76] *Eikon*, 80.   [77] Ibid., 102–3.   [78] Ibid., 145.

[79] Bryan D. Spinks, 'Gauden, John (1599/1600?–1662)', *Oxford Dictionary of National Biography*, <http://www.oxforddnb.com/view/article/10456>, accessed 16 June 2017.

[80] Jeffrey Collins, *The Allegiance of Thomas Hobbes* (Oxford: Oxford University Press, 2005), 85–7.

violence' as a 'religious Reformation by the sword'.[81] When the earl of Clarendon read *Leviathan*, he denounced it for justifying those who had led the churchmen to the scaffold and left them to 'welter in their own blood'.[82] Or consider the chilling passage of *Behemoth*, in which Hobbes asserted that it would have been better for Charles I to have killed 1000 clergymen, if it would have prevented the Civil War.[83] In some ways Hobbes was a critic of religious war, but he was willing to justify state violence to excise the threat of religious rebellion or usurpation. We thus glimpse in Hobbes one of the paradoxes mentioned at the start of this chapter. For those inclined to attribute human violence to religion and human stability to secular sovereignty, it is important to recognize that the most clear-eyed apologists for sovereignty usually did not indulge in such comforting polarities. Hobbes was under no illusion that securing the power of sovereignty over religion would always be a peaceful affair. And of course, European history from the Reformation to the Jacobin Revolution to the Nazi and Communist regimes of the twentieth century bears this out. Modern states have cultivated a mythology of religious sedition and war in part to justify their own exercise of violence. We can glimpse the shape of this ideological project in Hobbes.

13.3 Hobbes and Modernity's 'Wars of Religion'

There is one final consideration required if we are to do justice to the Hobbesian theory of religious war. This chapter has argued that generic or sociological theories of 'religious war' confuse historical understanding more than they clarify it. But if quasi-scientific and trans-historical accounts of religious violence have, in Hobbes's case, dulled our understanding of the sharp specifics of his own account of Christian religious violence, there is perhaps some justice in that. There are, in fact, aspects of *Leviathan* where the modern understanding of religious war—embedded within psychology and sociology rather than history, ecclesiology, and theology—is anticipated.[84] Religion, for modernity, becomes an abstract, functionally understood aspect of the human mind or of human societies. Broadly defined in this way, it can be detached from specific doctrines and at times associated with a general propensity to irrationality, superstition, or violence. Religion as such becomes a cause of war. Secularity and scientific rationality are thus vindicated by comparison, but the comparison is in some sense rigged.

---

[81] *Eikon*, 101–2.

[82] Edward Hyde, *A Brief View and Survey of the Dangerous and Pernicious Errors to Church and State in Mr. Hobbes's Book Entitled Leviathan* (Oxford, 1676), 305.

[83] 'It had been (I confesse) a great Massacre, but the killing of a hundred thousand is a greater', B, p. 231.

[84] Not that there were no ancient and early modern anticipations of these theories. Hobbes's account of religion's fearful origins—and the way that priests could play on this fear—likely owed something to the Epicurean tradition. On which see Gianni Paganini, 'Hobbes, Gassendi and the Tradition of Political Epicureanism' and Patricia Springborg, 'Hobbes and Epicurean Religion', both in *Der Garten und die Moderne: Epikureische Moral und Politik vom Humanismus bis zur Aufklärung*, ed. Gianni Paganini and Edoardo Tortarolo (Stuttgart: Fromman-Holzboog, 2004).

For early moderns, religious wars would have been differentiated—as Anabaptist rebellions, for instance, or as Muslim Jihads, or as Catholic Crusades. They would have understood such wars as related, for good or ill, to specific doctrines and practices. Religion as such was rarely thought about in the abstract, and certainly not primarily as a repository for human irrationality and violence. Politics, therefore, could not be justified in all its ways simply by virtue of being secular.

If we were to identify a thinker who begins to move us from one shore to the other on this question, Hobbes would be a very good candidate. Alongside Hobbes's more contextually oriented theories of religious war, he offered a generic, abstract, psychologized account of religion. In many places, as I have argued, he blamed religious war on specific doctrines of various Christian factions: on providentially inspired resistance, on an inflated privileging of conscience, on disordered prophecies, on perverse readings of Scripture, and above all on arguments for the divine right of clerical powers.

But in other passages, Hobbes anticipated the more sweeping modern arguments about religious war, and generated a sense that religion—understood abstractly—was a primary source of dangerous irrationality and violence. We find this most clearly in the remarkable twelfth chapter of *Leviathan*. The chapter proceeds to define religion (as such) as an ingrained propensity of humans, an impulse born of natural ignorance and anxiety. Hobbes offered a precocious 'projection' theory of religion that would have been worthy of Freud. Humans desire to know the first cause of all things and the final effect—but their minds cannot know these things. Ignorance breeds 'anxiety', an anxiety with no clear object and thus projected onto an 'invisible' agent endowed with enormous power. The same mechanisms undergirded the ancient polytheisms and Judeo-Christian monotheism. Hobbes drew no principled distinction other than the judgement of the state.[85]

We find here religion reduced to psychology and sociology—religion born of innate fear of death and of scientific ignorance. Crucially, this account of religion implicated a theory of religious war. Religion, as a human impulse, required external government. Religious impulses could be channelled towards state purposes, to ensure obedience and allegiance, as at the direction of the ancient 'Founders, and Legislators' of commonwealths, who crafted civil religions governed by the state and social hierarchy. Or, they could be governed by outsiders, by prophets and prognosticators, by reckless clergy seeking their own power. Statesmen would ensure that subjects were taught to believe 'that the same things were displeasing to the Gods, which were forbidden by the Lawes'.[86] Prophets and clergy did not always show this caution, and set up their own religious power against state power. This created upheaval and violent change. In this chapter, Hobbes in fact offered a compressed account of religious violence, whereby the 'first seeds' of religion remained engrained, but their manifestation in specific religions changed through the ages. Several factors drove this process according to Hobbes: the tendency of clergy to propagate 'impossible' doctrines; the tendency

---

[85] L, 12, pp. 164–70.   [86] L, 12, pp. 176–8.

of clergy to use 'religion' to hide their own avarice and ambition; the tendency of natural science to undermine miracles. All of these factors, Hobbes argued, eventually exposed the contradictions and absurdities of any religion and caused the 'people to revolt' against the churches, 'either against the will of their own Princes, as in *France*, and *Holland*; or with their will, as in *England*'.[87] Here we find a generic theory of religion that becomes a generic theory of religious war—theories that might be equally applied to pagan or Christian societies.

With the twelfth chapter of *Leviathan* distinctive views of modernity round into view. Hobbes had prevised Durkheim, and Weber, and Freud—he devised an account of religion which made no reference to its truth, but understood it as a psychological and social category, compelled by the weakness of the human mind: inescapable but dangerous, the dumping ground for all things irrational, superstitious, unscientific, and violent. This version of Hobbes has enjoyed a telling influence among sociobiologists such as Steven Pinker, who has celebrated Hobbes for crafting an interest-oriented sovereignty capable of suppressing our primal religious tribalism.[88]

We are now in a position to see why Hobbes, for all of his cynicism about humanity, and despite the absolutism of his political model, has proven so attractive as a thinker to modern theorists and historians such as Rawls, Lilla, or Pagden. We can see rather more clearly why Hobbes must play a role, as he does for Pagden, in the process whereby European politics freed itself of the 'murderous tendencies' of 'religion'. There was a direct line of descent from Hobbes to figures such as d'Holbach and Voltaire, who cast European history as one plagued by 'religious violence' and redeemed only by the invention of secular sovereignty. The Enlightenment essentially defined the Middle Ages and the early modern centuries as ages of barbarity driven by religious violence. This somewhat simplistic historical interpretation was wedded, in the minds of the philosophes, to a quasi-sociological and psychological understanding of religion. This conjuncture of a simplified historical mythology and a quasi-scientific understanding of religion would prove a powerful combination in justifying the rise of sovereignty in Europe. It was a constellation of ideas anticipated in the writings of Thomas Hobbes.[89]

Hobbes's theory of religious war was thus at once a highly partisan account rooted in a particular interpretation of Christianity, and a nascent generic, rationalized account of religious violence that would—in its mature form—help to hide that very partisanship under the veil of a neutral, scientific rhetoric.

---

[87] L, 12, p. 184.

[88] Steven Pinker, *The Better Angels of our Nature: Why Violence Has Declined* (New York: Allen Lane, 2011), chapter 2.

[89] Hobbes is left out of this process in Nongbri, *Before Religion*, and included but somewhat minimally in Gary Stroumsa, *A New Science: The Discovery of Religion in the Age of Reason* (Cambridge, MA: Harvard University Press, 2010), 23, 140.

14

Religious Conflict and Moral Consensus

Hobbes, Rawls, and Two Types of Moral Justification

Daniel Eggers

The claim that Hobbes's political theory was shaped by the experience of the English Civil War and the political and religious conflicts that preceded it is arguably the main commonplace about his philosophy. Both within and without Hobbes scholarship more narrowly construed, the idea that the appearance of his theory is the result of the mixture of political and religious strife witnessed during his lifetime has countless times been repeated and hardly ever been challenged.

Yet, there are different ways in which the experience of the political and religious struggles shaped Hobbes's theory, as there are obviously quite different strategies by which one can respond to such struggles, and to the challenge posed by religious pluralism in particular. One strategy was for Hobbes to directly engage in theological discussion and provide his own interpretations of the key tenets of Christian religion. A related strategy was to provide scriptural interpretations and to demonstrate that his moral and political teachings are compatible with the teachings of the Bible. As many Hobbes scholars have emphasized, there is a lot of evidence that he pursued both these strategies. We find in all his major political works explicit discussions of theological concepts and explicit efforts to identify his moral and political doctrine as one that any true believer can accept.

However, it is natural to think that the experience of religious struggle should also have shaped Hobbes's political doctrine, and the moral theory underlying it, in a more direct manner. Given that the experience characteristic for Hobbes and his time was that of the *conflict* between different groups of citizens and their diverging religious

For helpful comments on earlier drafts of this chapter, I would like to thank Laurens van Apeldoorn, Adrian Blau, Alexandra Chadwick, Robin Douglass, and Johan Olsthoorn.

convictions, we might expect him to have tried to devise a moral and political theory that is equally acceptable to readers of diverse religious and ideological backgrounds.

That Hobbes pursued this third and somewhat autonomous strategy is an idea we find in Hobbes scholarship, too. What makes this strategy especially interesting is that it has been taken up by modern Hobbesians such as David Gauthier and Peter Stemmer, who develop their moral theories with the explicit aim of overcoming problems of religiously motivated moral disagreement in the modern world.[1] As commentators have sometimes pointed out, what is characteristic of Hobbes's political argument is that it starts from relatively modest and widely acceptable anthropological assumptions, most notably the assumption that human beings have a strong or even overriding interest in their own preservation (at least insofar as they are rational).[2] It then ventures to show that quite considerable normative constraints on human behaviour can be derived from these assumptions, constraints that must rationally be accepted by anyone who accepts the original starting point. It is this idea which we find exemplified in Gauthier's and Stemmer's theories and which they present as a crucial element of their Hobbesian heritage.[3]

In the wake of Rawls's *Political Liberalism*, it has become customary to describe consensualist strategies in moral and political philosophy as the attempt to found an overlapping consensus between different conceptions of the good. However, the general strategy of appealing to a moral consensus that can ground one's political argument in the face of religious pluralism is not confined to the context of Rawls's theory of justice and should therefore not be confused with his particular version of it. My aim in this chapter is to analyse the way in which Hobbes pursues a consensualist approach and to contrast it with Rawls's quite different effort. My reasons for choosing Rawls's theory as a foil of comparison are threefold. First, as just indicated, the notion of a moral consensus is more closely associated with Rawls than with any other philosopher in the current philosophical debate; second, like Hobbes, Rawls attempts to establish such a consensus within the general philosophical framework of contract theory; third, Rawls pursues a consensualist approach that is interestingly and importantly different from Hobbes's approach in that it relies on a different idea of moral justification. Since Rawls's theory, therefore, demonstrates that (and how) an appeal to moral consensus different from the one pursued by Hobbes is possible, and possible within a broadly

---

[1] See David Gauthier, *Morals by Agreement* (Oxford: Oxford University Press, 1986); and Peter Stemmer, *Handeln zugunsten anderer* (Berlin and New York: De Gruyter, 2000). Stemmer explicitly emphasizes that people's diverging ethical views are largely the result of different religious assumptions (p. 204) and that, in response to this, his objective is one of devising a moral theory that applies to all rational human beings in the same way (p. 210).

[2] See, for example, Konrad Ott, *Moralbegründungen zur Einführung* (Hamburg: Junius, 2001), 123–4. The view is also implicitly suggested by Gauthier, *Morals*, 17; and Robert Sugden, 'Rationality and Impartiality: Is the Contractarian Enterprise Possible?', in *Rationality, Justice and the Social Contract: Themes from Morals by Agreement*, ed. David Gauthier and Robert Sugden (New York and London: Harvester Wheatsheaf, 1993), 157–8.

[3] See, in particular, Gauthier, *Morals*, 17.

contractarian framework, it can help us both to systematically classify Hobbes's approach and to identify its possible weaknesses.

In section 14.1, I first provide textual evidence that Hobbes's moral theory appeals to a *consensus omnium* and then classify his argument as an instance of what I refer to as extra-moral justification. In section 14.2, by contrast, I briefly describe Rawls's theory as an instance of intra-moral justification. In the third section, I defend this way of contrasting Hobbes's and Rawls's justificatory strategies against an objection that might be raised on the basis of Lloyd's recent interpretation of Hobbes's moral theory. In the final section, I critically assess the potential of the Hobbesian strategy for grounding a moral consensus under conditions of religious diversity. My tentative conclusion will be that the possible philosophical advantages of the fundamental justification provided by Hobbes and modern Hobbesians do not make up for the losses that a Hobbesian moral theory incurs in terms of compatibility with common-sense morality. While Rawls's appeal to a moral consensus may face problems in its own right, the more modest idea of moral justification on which it relies, and which is explicitly rejected by Gauthier and Stemmer, provides no reasons for thinking that the quite different Hobbesian appeal must ultimately yield better results.

14.1 Hobbes's Appeal to a *consensus omnium*

In all his major political works Hobbes's political argument begins with a description of the state of nature that is meant to provide the basis for his political conclusions by showing that no human being can rationally desire to live in a state that lacks the characteristic structures of civil society. This account of the natural condition of mankind is in various ways designed to be able to claim wide or even universal acceptance. Hobbes's ultimate argument for why individuals need to leave the state of nature is that it is a state of war and hence ultimately incompatible with the goal of self-preservation.[4] That this aim is one we can attribute to all human beings, at least in so far as they are rational, is repeatedly claimed in all of Hobbes's works.[5] Moreover, Hobbes infers from the pivotal role assigned to the goal of self-preservation that his state of nature argument is one that no reader can reasonably reject. According to Hobbes, nobody

---

[4] It has been suggested that Hobbes presents peace as intrinsically good and that the requirement to leave the state of nature might therefore be independent of any desire to preserve oneself. See, for instance, Bernd Ludwig, *Die Wiederentdeckung des Epikureischen Naturrechtes* (Frankfurt am Main: Klostermann, 1998), 374. However, there is ample evidence that Hobbes takes the value of peace to be an instrumental value that consists in what peace contributes to the shared but individual aim of personal survival. See, for example, Hobbes's claim that 'reason dictates to every man *for his own good* to seek after peace'. EL, 15.2 (my emphasis); see also L, 15, p. 242. Note also that the requirement to seek peace is explicitly qualified and applies only where individuals can do so without putting their preservation at risk (see L, 14, p. 198). Moreover, in describing the duties of the sovereign, which are grounded in the laws of nature, Hobbes does not refer to the goal of peace, but to the 'Preservation' of the subjects and 'other Contentments' (L, 30, p. 520) of their lives.

[5] See EL, 14.6, 14.12, 14.13, 17.14; DCv, 1.7, 2.3. Hobbes goes as far as to describe the desire to avoid violent death as one of the two most certain postulates of human nature, DCv, 'Epistle Dedicatory'.

can deny that the state of nature necessarily turns into a state of war, nobody will view such a state as a good for himself, and everybody will consider it advisable to leave the state of nature.[6]

The derivation of the state of war itself is also laid out in a way that is meant to ensure the assent of different groups of readers. It is developed out of a handful of empirical assumptions about the physical and psychological features of human beings and their natural living conditions that are presented by Hobbes as beyond dispute. His initial assumption is that human beings are relevantly equal to one another with regard to their physical and mental capacities. Though he admits that there are considerable differences in individual abilities, he argues that most human beings are sufficiently similar to serve as a threat to one another and concludes from this that everyone is well advised to conceive of others as equal and treat them accordingly.

Kinch Hoekstra has recently suggested that, instead of being derived from the equality of men's natural abilities, the requirement to acknowledge others as equal logically precedes and, in fact, grounds Hobbes's claims about natural equality.[7] However, Hoekstra's account ultimately collapses into the standard position he strives to reject. According to Hoekstra, the reason why we should acknowledge others as equal is that this is necessary for peace because failing to do so would increase the probability of violent conflict. However, if—as we have already seen—peace is introduced by Hobbes not as an end in itself but only as a necessary means to self-preservation, then it seems that the requirement to acknowledge others as equal cannot ground Hobbes's claim about natural equality because it presupposes it. If it were not for relevant natural equality and the fact that 'the weakest can kill the strongest', individuals would simply have insufficient reasons to fear and avoid violent confrontation.

Hobbes's assumption of relevant equality is then hooked up with the claim that certain internal and external conditions of human life in the state of nature actually lead the individuals into conflict with one another. As I have tried to demonstrate elsewhere,[8] Hobbes's description of the two main sources of conflict—competition and anticipation—is dependent on the relatively modest and defensible presupposition that the state of nature is a condition of uncertainty and moderate scarcity. His description of the third source of conflict—glory—is bound to be slightly more controversial. It needs to be emphasized, however, that Hobbes does not allege an active disposition to extort respect from others wherever this is possible, but the more passive disposition to defend one's reputation *if* it is challenged. Moreover, though Hobbes suggests that this disposition is one every individual possesses, he leaves open whether

---

[6] See DCv, 1.12, 3.31. See also Hobbes's remarks that the state of war is a state which all men by nature abhor and that all men want to leave the state of nature once they realize the evils that necessarily attach to it, DCv, 'Epistle Dedicatory'.

[7] See Kinch Hoekstra, 'Hobbesian Equality', in *Hobbes Today: Insights for the 21st Century*, ed. S. A. Lloyd (Cambridge: Cambridge University Press, 2012), 112.

[8] See Daniel Eggers, 'Hobbes and Game Theory Revisited', *Southern Journal of Philosophy* 49.3 (2011), 199–206.

it is equally strong in everybody. It is also important to note that, in order for his ultimate conclusion to go through, he does not need to put much emphasis on the third source of conflict in the first place: Hobbes explicitly describes the state of war as consisting not in constant actual fighting, but only 'in the known disposition thereto, during all the time there is no assurance to the contrary,'[9] and the first two sources are sufficient to turn the natural state into a state of this kind.

To say that Hobbes may legitimately view his derivation of the state of war as resting on an uncontroversial anthropological foundation, however, is not to say that the message was well received by his readers. It is this part of the argument that, up to this day, has led people to criticize Hobbes for expounding an overly negative view of human nature. Yet, the way Hobbes responds to this objection only goes to confirm his interest in appealing to a *consensus omnium*. In the second edition of *De Cive*, he tries to dispel the worry that his argument presents human beings as evil by nature and to identify his anthropological assumptions as ones which his readers accept for themselves—if not by word, then by deed. Hobbes reminds his readers of the fact that, though living in the relative safety of civil society, they usually do not travel without a weapon or go to bed without locking their doors, just as commonwealths defend their borders with garrisons of soldiers, even when they are at peace with their neighbours—which would all be irrational if one were to deny that certain aspects of human psychology or human social life make violent conflict probable.[10] We find a further response in the fact that Hobbes significantly revises his derivation of the state of war in his later works. The text of *Leviathan*, on which I relied above, is already the result of some important modifications in Hobbes's description of the several sources of conflict that all tend to stress the role of the rational pursuit of self-preservation over the role of anti-social human inclinations.

That Hobbes is interested in securing the uncontroversial character of his argument cannot only be seen from the way he describes and revises his derivation of the state of war, but also from the way in which he sets up his doctrine of natural right and natural law. In justifying the initial right to self-preservation in the *Elements*, Hobbes claims that it is not against reason that an individual should try to defend his life and limbs and adds: 'that which is not against reason, men call RIGHT'.[11] Moreover, even after arriving at the radical conclusion that every man has a natural right to all things, Hobbes attempts to class his position as part of (philosophical) common sense, by adding '[a]nd for this cause it is rightly said: *Natura dedit omnia omnibus*'.[12] We find almost identical statements in the corresponding passages of *De Cive*,[13] and in *Leviathan* we have a similar appeal to common sense in Hobbes's discussion of the necessity of anticipatory violence, where Hobbes remarks that if an individual strikes out pre-emptively against others, 'this is no more than his own conservation requireth, and is generally allowed'.[14]

[9] L, 13, p. 192.   [10] See L, 13, p. 194.   [11] EL, 14.6.
[12] EL, 14.10.   [13] See DCv, 1.7, 1.10, 2.1.   [14] L, 13, p. 190.

As far as the doctrine of the laws of nature is concerned, the appeal to a universal consensus is most visible in Hobbes's more general descriptions of his own doctrine. In the 'Epistle Dedicatory' of the *Elements*, Hobbes alludes to previous controversies about morality and justice and affirms his intention to build the laws of nature, 'which hitherto have been built in the air', on safe and uncontroversial principles 'till the whole be inexpugnable'.[15] That the laws of nature he subsequently formulates actually meet this standard is argued in the concluding passages of chapter 17. Hobbes emphasizes that every individual must call good what contributes to his preservation and must therefore also approve of the ways of behaviour laid out by the laws of nature. According to Hobbes, the actions commanded or forbidden by the laws of nature are 'that good and evil, which not every man in passion calleth so, but all men by reason'.[16] Again, we find very much the same claims in *De Cive* and in *Leviathan*, which emphasizes that 'all men agree on this, that Peace is Good, and therefore also the way, or means of Peace, which (as I have shewed before) are *Justice, Gratitude, Modesty, Equity, Mercy*, & the rest of the Laws of Nature, are good'.[17]

As with his description of the various sources of conflict in the state of nature, Hobbes's attempt to identify his doctrine of natural right and natural law as one that is fully in line with what people ordinarily think was hardly successful with regard to his contemporary readers. Yet, since at least the late 1960s, there has been a tendency in Hobbes scholarship to assess his discussion of natural right and natural law much more charitably. Moreover, as already indicated, modern contractarians like Gauthier and Stemmer have taken up Hobbes's argumentative strategy and have done so just because of the moderate and uncontroversial assumptions on which this strategy rests.

If we try to characterize generally the kind of moral justification that Hobbes provides us with, then the justification of the various laws of nature is a form of extra-moral justification in that Hobbes attempts to derive the moral necessity of certain forms of behaviour from wholly non-moral premises. The purpose of his discussion of morality is not merely to apply given moral principles to particular situations or to specific challenges that arise as part of human life, nor is it to justify some key moral principles by deriving them from a more general moral principle or from the moral standpoint as such. Rather, he wants to demonstrate that it is rationally necessary to act in accordance with certain moral principles without already drawing on any genuinely moral perspective or any genuine moral assumptions, such as those grounded in certain religious views of his time.

Though Hobbes himself may not describe his methodological approach in exactly these terms, there is sufficient evidence that he, like modern Hobbesians,[18] conceives of it in this way and that his reliance on a form of extra-moral justification results from

---

[15] EL, 'Epistle Dedicatory'.   [16] EL, 17.14.
[17] L, 15, p. 242. See also DCv, 'Epistle Dedicatory', 3.31–2.
[18] See, in particular, Gauthier, *Morals*, 4, 9–10.

a conscious decision on his part. He explicitly describes the state of nature argument, which grounds his moral theory, as an 'Inference, made from the Passions' and thus as a piece of descriptive anthropology.[19] In accordance with this, both Hobbes's claim that human beings are relevantly similar in their physical and mental abilities and his various claims about the internal and external sources of conflict are descriptive claims that do not yet contain any commitment to particular moral principles or even as much as a moral standpoint. The same applies to his treatment of the fundamental desire for self-preservation from which Hobbes's laws of nature derive their normative authority.

14.2 Moral Consensus in Rawls

Compared to the preceding discussion of Hobbes's moral theory, my treatment of Rawls will be fairly brief. The main reason for this is that there is no real need to verify the consensualist credentials of Rawls's theory: that Rawls aims at an overlapping consensus is not only explicitly emphasized by him, but also unanimously acknowledged among Rawls scholars. Rather than trying to substantiate a consensualist interpretation of Rawls's theory, then, we can focus on the specific nature of the Rawlsian consensus and on his justification of it.

The idea of an overlapping consensus is developed in a 1987 paper with the very same title and plays a crucial role in the argument of *Political Liberalism*, originally published in 1993. Rawls takes up the idea of an overlapping consensus because of certain problems with the original version of his theory.[20] However, the fact that Rawls develops the idea of an overlapping consensus only after the publication of *A Theory of Justice* should not mislead us into thinking that the idea of a moral consensus plays no role in his original theory. The difference between *A Theory of Justice* and *Political Liberalism* is that the former relies on the optimistic view that all or nearly all citizens may agree on one reasonable comprehensive doctrine of justice, while the latter admits that agreement will extend only to a political conception of justice more narrowly construed. What distinguishes the two theories, then, is not that one conceives of the acceptance of the principles of justice in terms of an underlying moral consensus while the other does not. It is rather that the consensus in question is conceived of differently. Accordingly, there is talk of consensus, and even of overlapping consensus, in *A Theory of Justice*.[21] In its introduction, Rawls even sets out his programme in a way that is reminiscent of the kind of consensualist strategy I have attributed to Hobbes.[22] For the purposes of this chapter, I will therefore understand the

---

[19] L, 13, p. 194.

[20] For Rawls's own account of these problems, see John Rawls, *Political Liberalism* (New York: Columbia Press, 2005), pp. xv–xviii.

[21] See, for example, John Rawls, *A Theory of Justice* (Cambridge, MA: Belknap Press of Harvard University Press, 1971), 387–8, 581–2.

[22] Ibid., 18.

idea of a moral consensus in a somewhat broader sense that can encompass the efforts made by Rawls in *A Theory of Justice*.

The general purpose of Rawls's theory is to formulate principles of justice for the basic structure of a well-ordered society. The focus of the justification of Rawls's two principles is provided by the question of why we can expect citizens with diverging comprehensive theories of the good to equally accept these two principles and, in particular, the list of basic liberties which complements them. The justification of *A Theory of Justice* draws heavily on the idea that there are such things as all-purpose means, i.e. goods which any individual having a theory of the good or a rational plan of life will necessarily desire. This idea lies at the heart of Rawls's theory of 'primary social goods' in its original version.[23] Primary goods, as introduced in *A Theory of Justice*, are 'things it is supposed a rational man wants whatever else he wants',[24] and the examples given by Rawls include rights, liberties, powers, opportunities, income, wealth, and the social bases of self-respect. His theory of the primary goods represents an important element of the argument from the original position: Given the veil of ignorance, which denies the parties any knowledge of their personal features or talents and their particular theories of the good, it is only in virtue of the presupposed desire for primary goods that the parties are in a position to choose any specific principles of justice at all.

In contrast, the justification of *Political Liberalism* crucially relies on two ideas that linger in the background of *A Theory of Justice*: the idea of society as a fair system of cooperation and the idea of the person. A person, according to Rawls, is 'someone who can be a citizen, that is, a normal and fully cooperating member of society over a complete life'.[25] In order to be a normal and fully cooperating member of society, an individual needs to have what Rawls refers to as the two 'moral powers':[26] a capacity for a sense of justice and a capacity for a conception of the good. According to Rawls, it is in virtue of these two powers that we conceive of persons as free and rational. Moreover, having these powers to the requisite degree in order to be a fully cooperating member of society is what makes people equal in the relevant political sense.

Rawls's conception of the two moral powers introduces an additional criterion that guides the parties in the original position.[27] In Rawls's view, we can legitimately attribute to all citizens a higher-order interest in the development and full exercise of their two moral powers, given that these powers are what makes them fully cooperating members of society and free and equal persons. As the Rawls of *Political Liberalism* claims, it is this higher-order interest in the development and full exercise of the two moral powers that initially explains the citizens' interest in the various primary goods and that also allows them to weigh these goods against one another.

As with Hobbes, there are certainly different ways to characterize the type of moral justification we encounter in Rawls's argument. The point that I would like to focus on is that Rawls does not provide an extra-moral justification, but only what we may

---

[23] Ibid., 90.   [24] Ibid., 92.   [25] Rawls, *Liberalism*, 18.
[26] Ibid., 19.   [27] For the following, see ibid., 75–6, 178–9.

describe as an intra-moral justification. It is important to recognize that this is true of Rawls's argument in both its original and its revised form. The desire for primary goods is *prima facie* not so different from the kind of self-interest on which Hobbes's argument relies. However, given the veil of ignorance, which ensures that the decision made by the parties in the original position is unaffected by any differences in the individuals' natural assets or their particular positions in society, Rawls's argument is by no means morally neutral. In its original form, therefore, Rawls's justification appeals to a consensus in two ways: by positively basing the choice of the principles of justice on a shared thin conception of the good (represented by the universal desire for primary goods); and by negatively excluding contingent differences in power or natural talent from providing reasons for choice because this would violate our considered judgements about fairness. While the former consensus may entirely be constituted by non-moral assumptions, the latter is clearly not.

In the revised argument in *Political Liberalism*, the moral basis for the justification of the two principles of justice is even more visible. The idea of the person and the idea of the two moral powers are just as morally tinted as the fundamental idea of society as a fair system of cooperation. Accordingly, the universal interests that guide the choice of the parties in the original position are not non-moral interests, but presuppose the recognition of general moral principles of reciprocity or fairness. This is also emphasized by the fact that the consensus Rawls describes is one between *reasonable* comprehensive doctrines, not one between rational comprehensive doctrines. According to the explicit distinction offered in *Political Liberalism*, individuals act reasonably, as opposed to merely rationally, if they accept fundamental ideas of fairness and reciprocity and 'desire for its own sake a social world in which they, as free and equal, can cooperate with others on terms all can accept'.[28]

14.3 The 'Reciprocity Interpretation' of Hobbes's Moral Philosophy

The way Rawls appeals to a moral consensus, therefore, appears to be decidedly different from Hobbes's way. However, before assessing the respective merits of the two types of moral justification, I would like to take up the possible objection that Hobbes is in fact much more of a Rawlsian than I allow. According to the 'reciprocity interpretation of Hobbes's moral philosophy' recently advocated by S. A. Lloyd, Hobbes's moral theory appeals to a Rawlsian notion of reciprocity in a way that makes it an instance of intra-moral rather than extra-moral justification.[29] In Lloyd's view, Hobbes's doctrine of the laws of nature is neither based on the non-moral desire for self-preservation nor on considerations of self-interest more generally. Rather, Hobbes's point of departure is a

---

[28] Ibid., 50.
[29] S. A. Lloyd, *Morality in the Philosophy of Thomas Hobbes* (Cambridge and New York: Cambridge University Press, 2009), 7.

conception of ourselves as rational agents and persons, according to which a person is somebody who is generally willing and able to offer justifying reasons for his behaviour. As Lloyd claims, the central idea of Hobbes's moral theory is then provided by a 'reciprocity theorem', according to which offering certain considerations as justifying reasons for one's actions commits oneself to accepting the same considerations as justifying the like actions of others.[30] Hobbes thereby provides 'an early articulation and defense'[31] of the idea of reasonableness we find in Rawls, and in particular 'an insistence on the irreducibility of... the reasonable to the rational'.[32]

Lloyd is not always entirely clear on whether she understands the reciprocity theorem as a substantial moral principle demanding fairness and impartiality or merely in terms of the kind of conceptual principle usually referred to as the principle of universalizability. However, both the analogy with Rawls and her emphasis on Hobbes's use of the Golden Rule (which goes beyond mere universalizability and clearly is a substantial moral principle) strongly suggest the former. Therefore, if Lloyd's interpretation were correct, it would seem that my characterization of extra-moral justification does not provide an appropriate account of Hobbes's theory.

While a detailed discussion of Lloyd's book is beyond the scope of this chapter, I think there are strong reasons to stick to the more common interpretation of Hobbes, even in the face of the evidence Lloyd provides in support of her interpretation.[33] Though there are several passages in Hobbes's works about equality, about the need to acknowledge others as equal, and even about some kind of reciprocity, we find him, in virtually all of these cases, offering a prudential rationale for why individuals should allow others equal treatment, a rationale that crucially appeals to the self-preservation of the agent.

Thus, as we have seen, the explanation given by Hobbes for why individuals in the state of nature should conceive of each other as equal is simply that they are sufficiently similar in their physical and psychological properties to serve as a threat to one another's safety. Similarly, Hobbes's justification of the laws of nature requiring equity and prohibiting arrogance and pride appeals to the strategic idea that without acknowledging others as equal, other individuals would not be willing to enter into the kind of cooperative enterprise that is needed for securing one's long-term survival. In *The Elements*, Hobbes explicitly emphasizes that nature has ordained the law 'for peace sake... *That every man acknowledge other for his equal*'.[34] In *De Cive* and *Leviathan*, Hobbes makes it even clearer that the requirement follows from the possible threat others pose to the self-preservation of the agent, by explicitly linking it to his previous discussion of the physical and psychological equality of human beings,[35] by pointing

---

[30] Ibid., 4, 220.   [31] Ibid., p. xvi.
[32] Ibid., 226–7. It deserves to be noted that Rawls himself does not conceive of Hobbes's theory in this way. According to Rawls, Hobbes explains the reasonable wholly in terms of the rational and, as a result, has no place for any moral rights or duties in the ordinary sense of these words. See John Rawls, *Lectures on the History of Political Philosophy*, ed. Samuel Freeman (Cambridge, Mass.: Belknap Press of Harvard University Press, 2007), 54–8.
[33] See, for instance, Lloyd, *Morality*, 14–15.   [34] EL, 17.1.   [35] DCv, 3.13; L, 15, p. 234.

out that violation will result in a contest for dominion,[36] and by emphasizing that an unwillingness to acknowledge others as equals will deprive these others of their willingness to enter into a peaceful state in the first place.[37]

Moreover, in his references to the Golden Rule, Hobbes avoids any appeal to substantial moral reasons. The Golden Rule is introduced only as a rule of thumb by which individuals may identify the morally advisable course of action without having to enter into the sophisticated argument on which Hobbes's derivation of the laws of nature relies.[38] The Golden Rule, then, is not presented as an independent foundation or even a negative constraint on the laws of nature, but merely as a practical guide to identify what the laws of nature, and the prudential rationale behind these laws, require in a given situation.

In accordance with this, Hobbes does not seem to have any genuinely moral concept of human dignity or moral worth that could ground a non-prudential moral obligation to treat others as free and equal persons. As Hobbes infamously claims in chapter 10 of *Leviathan*, 'The *Value*, or WORTH of a man, is [...] his Price; that is to say, so much as would be given for the use of his Power: and therefore is not absolute; but a thing dependent on the need and judgement of another.'[39] While we may certainly give this definition a somewhat broader interpretation, it would be quite a stretch to attribute to Hobbes anything like Rawls's decidedly moral conception of persons as free and equal. Furthermore, if an asymmetrical solution to the predicament of the state of nature in which some individuals retain their right to all things should be unacceptable to Hobbes in virtue of the reciprocity theorem,[40] why should he specifically examine the question of whether the submission of others or the formation of defensive alliances could provide a remedy for the problem of the state of nature and reject these possibilities on purely pragmatic grounds?[41]

However, the main problem with Lloyd's interpretation is not that there are no passages in Hobbes's works that allow for it, or even, if considered in isolation, suggest it. There is wide agreement among commentators that Hobbes is not always consistent and that we can find isolated evidence for almost any interpretation, especially if we are willing to stray from the main road of Hobbes's argument. The problem is rather to then give a satisfactory account of all the opposed statements and to make sense of the overall structure of his argument. If we take Hobbes's moral theory to depend on the desire for self-preservation (or on self-interest more generally), there are two main explanations we can give for those passages that do not sit well with this interpretation. One is that Hobbes introduced traditional moral vocabulary in order for his theory to be acceptable to a wider audience; the other is that he did so in order for himself to escape prosecution. To some commentators, such explanations may appear ad hoc. However, as I have demonstrated in the first section, it cannot be denied that Hobbes

---

[36] DCv, 3.13.   [37] DCv, 3.14; L, 15, p. 234.   [38] EL, 17.9–10; DCv, 3.26–7; L, 15, pp. 240–1.
[39] L, 10, p. 134.   [40] For this claim see Lloyd, *Morality*, 25.
[41] See EL, 19.3; DCv, 2.5; and L, 17, p. 256.

appeals to a universal consensus, and given some passages in his autobiographical writings,[42] there can hardly be any doubt that he worried about his safety, either. Moreover, the idea that he was not therefore willing to give up on *all* revisionary strands in his theory, which he might rightfully have perceived as comprising much of what was original about his theory, is clearly one we need to take seriously. In contrast with this, the commentators who want to turn Hobbes into a more traditional moralist do not provide an equally plausible explanation for the role of self-preservation in Hobbes and for quite a few revisionary statements which make Hobbes appear to be a radical, a pessimist, and perhaps even an atheist when it comes to morality.

What remains to be seen is whether Hobbes is well advised to pursue his justificatory strategy, given his obvious interest in basing his political theory on a consensualist moral theory that allows readers with conflicting religious views to converge on the bare necessities of political life, and the necessity of civil obedience in particular. The *prima facie* counter-intuitive answer, for which I argue in the final section of this chapter, is that it is because of his fundamental approach to justification and his misinterpretations of human nature that Hobbes spoils the potential benefits of his appeal to common sense.

14.4 Moral Justification and the Challenge of Religious Pluralism

It is natural to think that when it comes to grounding a moral consensus that can further agreement between groups with different religious or ideological backgrounds, a fundamental extra-moral justification of the kind provided by Hobbes should yield the best results. As long as the descriptive assumptions from which the justification proceeds are as uncontroversial as the human interest in survival (and not as controversial as, for example, the belief in genuine altruistic human motivation), and as long as the ultimate moral conclusions are convincingly derived from these assumptions, it seems that any form of intra-moral justification must stand at a disadvantage—because it takes certain moral principles for granted and we must expect the religious or ideological differences between different groups of readers to include distinct moral convictions.

However, in what follows I want to argue that, if something like this is the idea behind Hobbes's moral theory, he has importantly misjudged both human nature and the demands of moral justification in the political arena. The main advantage that a Hobbesian approach to moral justification can claim over examples of intra-moral justification is that such an approach, if otherwise successful, can persuade the radical moral sceptic who does not yet accept any fundamental moral principles or even as much as a moral standpoint. The figures traditionally cited as proponents of such a radical scepticism include Plato's Thrasymachus, Hume's sensible knave, and Hobbes's

---

[42] See EW, 4, p. 414; OL, 1, p. xv.

'Foole'. Modern examples of Hobbesian contractarianism are explicitly designed as attempts to convince the moral sceptic of the non-moral necessity of moral behaviour.[43]

Yet, as far as moral justification in the political arena is concerned, the crucial task is rarely, if ever, one of providing an ultimate justification of morality or a refutation of radical moral sceptics. When moral justification becomes a public issue, we are typically dealing with individuals who share some fundamental moral ideas or are at least equally willing to assume a general moral standpoint, since it is this standpoint that gives rise to the need for justification in the first place. To cite a contemporary example, those engaged in modern debates about applied ethics, whose different religious views often bear directly on the issues in question, are not usually worried about the question of whether there are any moral distinctions at all, or whether there is an ultimate rational basis for expecting others to act in a particular manner. Rather, they are discussing what the basic moral ideas or values that most of us share and figure to *some* extent in all major religions or religious moralities (equality, reciprocity, the value of life, etc.) can be taken to prescribe with regard to concrete and often unprecedented practices. In a similar manner, we may want to argue that the contentious issue in Hobbes's England was not so much whether civil society is necessary or whether there is any duty of civil obedience whatsoever, since these were points Hobbes's contemporaries widely accepted, their different religious faiths notwithstanding. It was rather to whom such obedience is primarily due and whether it is dependent on any further conditions.

That the ultimate argumentative foundation of moral doctrines is not what decides their public acceptance is also suggested by current research in social psychology. As recent experiments by Jonathan Haidt and his collaborators suggest, 'moral dumbfounding', i.e. clinging to substantial moral convictions in the absence of rational justification, is quite a common phenomenon.[44] Whatever we may think of Haidt's quite far-reaching anti-rationalist conclusions, the least his findings can be taken to indicate is that many are unshaken in their adherence to deeply held moral convictions despite their inability to come up with a convincing rationale for those views. If this is correct, however, then it seems that where the idea is to appeal to some kind of universal consensus, a moral doctrine such as Hobbes's will hardly be able to compensate for deviations from the substance of common-sense morality by offering a more fundamental justification of the substantial moral principles it actually endorses.

Moreover, it also seems to be a common experience that human beings tend to evaluate moral positions not so much in terms of whether the explicit moral claims associated with this position are in some way consistent with their own convictions, but rather in terms of whether their convictions and their way of life are positively *affirmed* by the position in question. Human beings frequently display hostility

---

[43] See Stemmer, *Handeln*, 17–20. See also Ann Cudd, 'Contractarianism', *Stanford Encyclopedia of Philosophy*, <http://plato.stanford.edu/entries/contractarianism/>, accessed 16 June 2017.
[44] Jonathan Haidt, *The Righteous Mind* (London: Penguin, 2013), 43.

towards moral principles that are purely permissive and merely *allow* certain practices, sexual or otherwise, without in any way demanding them. What this suggests is that the property of being less demanding and more tolerant, which we may ascribe to the kind of minimum morality constituted by a Hobbesian approach, does not necessarily add to the social acceptability of a moral doctrine. This also seems true with regard to those anthropological assumptions on which Hobbes's moral theory is founded. In order for people to accept a proposed view of human nature, it will be insufficient to define human nature in terms of qualities that are generally included among the qualities of human beings, such as the desire for self-preservation; rather, it will be necessary to include *all* (or almost all) the qualities that others take to be definitive of human nature and to thereby positively affirm their view of what being human is all about.

All this suggests that the fate of the *consensus omnium* envisaged by Hobbes very much hinges on how far his ultimate conclusions positively affirm common-sense views on human nature and morality. However, his partial conformity with common-sense morality notwithstanding, Hobbes's moral theory is clearly in contradiction with some of our most fundamental intuitions or considered judgements. One important difficulty results from the fact that the moral obligation imposed by the laws of nature is a prudential obligation, whereas we ordinarily conceive of being imprudent and being immoral as two different things. According to common-sense morality, the immorality of immoral behaviour is typically linked to disadvantages suffered by others and somehow grounded in their persons and the legitimate claims they have on us. The Hobbesian approach, however, suggests that what is problematic about behaving immorally has not to do, or at least not primarily, with the interests, desires, rights, or even the dignity of others, but with the agent and his own advantage.[45]

A second but related difficulty consists in the fact that the scope of Hobbesian morality seems to be seriously limited, a fact that is explicitly conceded by modern Hobbesians,[46] and, at least implicitly, by Hobbes as well. Even if we accept Hobbes's claim of relevant equality as far as is needed for a basic defence of the state of nature argument, the rationale behind the laws of nature and their obligatory force does not seem to extend to important groups of human beings which, despite our possibly diverse religious and ideological backgrounds, we all ordinarily take to be members of the moral community. For example, Hobbes's argument fails to securely ground any moral obligations towards children or the disabled, a consequence that is implicitly acknowledged by Hobbes himself.[47] These deviations from ordinary morality derive from the kind of non-moral justification on which Hobbes relies, which does not award human beings any fundamental moral worth or moral dignity from the start, and they are therefore to be found in a similar way in the theories of Gauthier and

---

[45] See also Nicholas Southwood who develops his 'normativity objection' against Hobbesian approaches to morality along similar lines, *Contractualism and the Foundations of Morality* (Oxford: Oxford University Press, 2010), 34.

[46] See, for instance, Gauthier, *Morals*, 268; Stemmer, *Handeln*, 257–64.

[47] See EL, 4.3, 10.8; DCv, 9.2, 17.12; L, 20, p. 310.

Stemmer.[48] If what was said above is correct, however, such deviations pose serious problems when it comes to appealing to a universal consensus, problems that are not outweighed by the possible advantages of Hobbes's approach.

We can sum up these considerations and return to the aspect of religious diversity by appealing to the Golden Rule which is explicitly acknowledged by Hobbes as a valid principle. As is impressively demonstrated by recent literature, the Golden Rule is part of the teachings of all major religions. Not only do we find ideas resembling the proverbial dictum *Quod tibi fieri non vis, alteri ne feceris* (on which Hobbes mainly relies) in the Old and New Testaments,[49] we also find them in the Talmud,[50] in the works of influential Christian theologians such as Augustine, Anselm of Canterbury, Abelard, Duns Scotus, Thomas Aquinas, and Martin Luther,[51] in the Qur'an, in the *hadith* of Muhammad and in Islamic mysticism,[52] as well as in Buddhism,[53] Hinduism,[54] Confucianism,[55] and Zoroastrianism.[56]

A fundamental idea of equality or reciprocity, then, is recognized by both the various Christian sects which contributed to religious strife in Hobbes's lifetime and by those religions to which any modern-day Hobbesian needs to appeal, even though the exact role and import of this element strongly differ—from one religion or religious sect to another as well as from one era in the history of a religion to another. As I have argued, the fact that Hobbes explicitly includes the Golden Rule in his discussion of the laws of nature can be seen as an expression of his consensualist strategy. Yet, as I have also emphasized, what Hobbes attempts, very much in accordance with his extra-moral approach to justification, is to provide a prudential rationale for the Golden Rule and to thus justify it on non-moral grounds. If the claims I have defended in this section are anywhere near the truth, then it should be extremely doubtful whether this brings Hobbes closer to the objective of establishing a moral consensus than if he had simply presupposed the validity of these fundamental moral ideas and worked himself from this presupposition to a more demanding morality with a wider scope. The reactions to Hobbes's theory—and to modern examples of Hobbesian moral theory—strongly suggest that a prudential justification of the Golden Rule will rather repel those who acknowledge the validity and religious dignity of this fundamental ethical principle, especially since this prudential justification has the

---

[48] See Gauthier, *Morals*, 268; Stemmer, *Handeln*, 261.   [49] Cf. Matt. 7:12 and Luke 6:31.

[50] Jacob Neusner, 'The Golden Rule in Classical Judaism', in *The Golden Rule: The Ethics of Reciprocity in World Religions*, ed. Jacob Neusner and Bruce D. Chilton (London: Continuum, 2008), 59. See also Jeffrey Wattles, *The Golden Rule* (New York and Oxford: Oxford University Press, 1996), 42–3.

[51] See Wattles, *Golden Rule*, 70–3.

[52] See Th. Emil Homerin, 'The Golden Rule in Islam', in *Golden Rule: The Ethics*, 102, 104–5.

[53] See Kristin Scheible, 'The Formulation and Significance of the Golden Rule in Buddhism', in *Golden Rule: The Ethics*, 117, 119. See also Charles Hallisey, 'The Golden Rule in Buddhism', in *Golden Rule: The Ethics*, 131.

[54] See Richard H. Davis, 'A Hindu Golden Rule, in Context', in *Golden Rule: The Ethics*, 147.

[55] See Mark A. Csikszentmihalyi, 'The Golden Rule in Confucianism', in *Golden Rule: The Ethics*, 157–69. See also Wattles, *Golden Rule*, 15–26.

[56] See Mahna Moazami, 'The Golden Rule in Zoroastrianism', in *Golden Rule: The Ethics*, 65–75.

implication of excluding children and disabled people from the range of the Golden Rule altogether; beings, that is, who, from a religious perspective, are the workmanship of God in just the way healthy mature people are.

The upshot of this is that Hobbes's striving for a moral consensus tends to be ultimately at odds with his idea of establishing a *scientia moralis*. It is plausible to think that his reliance on a variant of non-moral justification is not only fuelled by his striving for a moral consensus but also by his preoccupation with the emerging natural sciences and his enthusiasm about the geometrical method. His overall aim is to develop a *scientia moralis* that is well-integrated into an overall scientific system and can perhaps even be derived from a materialist *prima philosophia*, and it seems that the most promising way to realize this aim might be to build one's moral theory on certain non-moral anthropological assumptions. Contrary to what Hobbes might have thought, however, his two purposes are not equally furthered by one and the same justificatory strategy: the best scientific theory of morality is not necessarily the one that can most easily claim universal acceptance and gain political influence.

My conclusion, then, which in the absence of comprehensive empirical research into the issues in question must obviously remain tentative, is that Hobbes misses the target he himself identifies for his moral theory, by relying on an idea of moral justification that is not well suited to the aim of grounding a moral consensus in the face of religious pluralism and by underestimating the alternative potential of intra-moral justification. In contrast to what Hobbes and modern Hobbesians suggest, it is doubtful whether being able to proceed from uncontroversial non-moral assumptions represents a relevant virtue when it comes to dealing with religious and non-religious pluralism and whether Rawls's commitment to some kind of moral starting point constitutes any relevant disadvantage.

This is not to say, of course, that the particular way in which Rawls develops his intra-moral approach to justification and incorporates the fundamental ideas of equality and reciprocity is the best one can do. It is a much-discussed question whether Rawls's argument establishes the kind of overlapping consensus between reasonable comprehensive doctrines that it is designed to establish. Moreover, some of the worries concerning the limited scope of Hobbes's morality have been expressed with regards to Rawls's conception of justice as well, if in an importantly qualified way. By interpreting personhood in terms of the idea of society as a system of fair cooperation, Rawls too, seems to exclude all beings that are permanently incapable of being fully cooperating members of society from the sphere of justice. It is important to note, however, that this does not apply to children (since they have the potential to develop a sense of justice and a conception of the good) and that even those beings who *are* excluded from the sphere of justice are not thereby excluded from the sphere of morality altogether. As Rawls himself emphasizes, non-fully cooperating members of society may impose genuine duties on us—if not duties of justice, then duties of compassion or humanity.[57]

---

[57] See Rawls, *Theory*, 512.

Moreover, even if Rawls may not be in a position to grant children and certain other beings the exact moral role we ordinarily attribute to them, his possible failure in establishing a moral consensus would not be due to the fact that he relies on intra-moral justification, but on the fact that he appeals to the wrong considered judgements or interprets them in an inappropriate manner. The way to improve on Rawls's account, then, would not be to resort to a more Hobbesian approach, but to come up with a more convincing strategy for intra-moral justification. Whether there is such a strategy, and what it looks like, are questions that very much deserve to be discussed in their own right.

15

Hobbes on the Duty Not to Act on Conscience

S. A. Lloyd

Hobbes lists among those doctrines 'repugnant to civil society' because they create destabilizing conflict the doctrine that *whatsoever a man does against his conscience is sin*. On the contrary, he argued, in some cases we have a duty *not* to act on our consciences. Specifically, when we conscientiously judge that we should disobey a civil law or sovereign command, we morally ought not to act on that judgement. We ought instead to obey, although we think the commanded action is wrong.[1] This is a striking position. It seems to imply a principle repudiated at Nuremberg, namely, that one should follow wrongful orders.

I shall explain how Hobbes arrives at this suspect principle and what role it plays in his larger project, and offer a preliminary assessment of its defensibility. I shall offer reasons for thinking that there is something right in the reasoning that leads Hobbes to it, something that any defensible position on political obligation will have to accommodate. If that reasoning relies on ineliminable theological premises, his political theory will not be defensible on purely secular assumptions. That would be a surprising, and possibly troubling, finding, particularly to those who cling to the notion that religion is irrelevant to Hobbes's political philosophy, but even to those who think Hobbes offers a theory intended to have universal appeal. This investigation will not settle the question of the dependence of Hobbes's theory on religious assumptions, but will suggest a direction of research to do so.

---

[1] The 'true liberties of subjects' discussed in chapter 21 of *Leviathan* do not represent exceptions to this rule. Those liberties merely immunize us from moral blame for failing to obey commands that we nevertheless may be legitimately punished for failing to obey. This class is picked out by our survival needs rather than by any judgement that the commanded actions are morally wrong.

15.1 Transcendent Interests in Acting on Religious Conscience Undermine Civil Stability

Hobbes devoted his political works to theorizing a solution to the problem of social disorders—sedition, rebellion, and civil war. Very often these result from conflicting demands on citizens by religious authorities and secular authorities. Hobbes insisted that the English Civil War was fuelled by the claims of various religious factions that they were administering a presently existing kingdom of God and had authority to determine the profession and practice required of Christian subjects, that civil commands contrary to God's law were not to be obeyed, and that it was a sin, punishable by damnation, to act contrary to correct religious conscience.[2] These conflicting demands are destabilizing because religious believers may be moved to act on their perceived religious duty in defiance of the civil authority's commands and irrespective of its threatened punishments. Some believers have transcendent religious interests for the sake of which they are willing to risk or even to sacrifice their lives if necessary. Hobbes warns that in a commonwealth where secular and religious authority are divided, 'if one command somewhat to be done under penalty of natural death, another forbid it under pain of eternal death . . . it will follow that . . . the city itself is altogether dissolved. For no man can serve two masters; nor is he less, but rather more a master, whom we believe we are to obey for fear of damnation, than he whom we obey for fear of temporal death'.[3] Hobbes is prepared to grant the reasonableness in principle of privileging religious duty, writing that 'when a man receiveth two contrary Commands, and knows that one of them is Gods, he ought to obey that, and not the other, though it be the command even of his lawfull Soveraign'.[4] Indeed, if civil obedience would result in the loss of eternal life, it would be 'madnesse to obey'.[5] Yet when the requirements of religious duty are determined by anyone other than the civil authority, and especially when it is up to the conscientious judgements of each individual to determine what those requirements are, disagreements about religious duty are bound to undermine social order. Because 'Eternall life is a greater reward, than the life present; and Eternall torment a greater punishment than the death of Nature',[6] Christians will have to be assured that God will not punish them for acting contrary to their consciences. It is essential then to Hobbes's project that he refute the contention that one sins if one obeys the civil authority's commands contrary to one's conscience.

---

[2] Roberto Farneti discusses the role of the desire to achieve salvation in the English Civil Wars in 'Hobbes on Salvation', in The Cambridge Companion to Hobbes's Leviathan, ed. Patricia Springborg (Cambridge: Cambridge University Press, 2007), 291–308. Gerald Gaus points out that Hobbes faulted the religious interpretations of Puritans and Fifth Monarchy Men (who denied the legitimacy of all states between the Roman Empire and the Reign of Christ) as leading to the war. See his 'Hobbes's Challenge to Public Reason Liberalism: Public Reason and Religious Convictions in Leviathan', in Hobbes Today: Insights for the 21st Century, ed. S. A. Lloyd (Cambridge: Cambridge University Press, 2007), 155–77. Behemoth presents a long list of guilty factions.

[3] Philosophical Rudiments Concerning Government and Society, 6.11, in EW 2.   [4] L, 43, p. 928.

[5] L, 43, p. 930; cf. DCv, 17.25, 18.14.   [6] L, 38, p. 698.

15.2 The Epistemic Status of Claims of Conscience

Hobbes argues that the conscience is 'nothing else but a man's settled judgment and opinion'.[7] Opinions and judgements are species of belief; and whatever we believe, we believe to be true, even when our belief does not rise to the level of knowledge. When settled, these beliefs are convictions. The convictions we term our conscience often concern matters of right and wrong. When we feel certain about the truth of our belief that some behaviour is morally or religiously required or prohibited, we defend that claim as a matter of conscience. However, notwithstanding our certainty, those beliefs may be false. As the judgement may err, so too may the conscience.[8]

A person's conscience being merely the set of her own private judgements in which she has full confidence, its content is determined by the facts of her biography that produce that confidence. People's opinions are a function of a complex interaction of their personal experiences, bodily constitution, the teachings or hearsay evidence of others they have absorbed, and (less often) their reasoning. Direct perception grounds some of our beliefs, while most of the others are taken on authority. Religious conscience is not all that different, except that for most of us our religious beliefs reflect only what we have been taught or have come to accept on the authority of others, and not any immediate religious experiences.

It is especially evident in matters of religion that what we believe is primarily a matter of whom we believe. '[A]ll formed Religion', Hobbes notes, 'is founded at first, upon the faith which a multitude hath in some one person, whom they believe ... to be a holy man, to whom God himselfe vouchsafeth to declare his will supernaturally'.[9] With different founders believed, we see different doctrines accepted. Most religious faith arises from the mundane process of hearing and learning, and not from either immediate supernatural experience or divine 'infusion' or 'inspiration'. Most people have never experienced any direct supernatural personal revelation; they take their religious beliefs entirely on authority from parents, one or another church, their pastors or preachers, texts deemed by authorities to be sacred, or from their social group. This entails that the religious conscience of most people (their settled opinions about the truth of their religious duties) reflects contingencies of their immediate social environment rather than some direct font of cosmic truth. Christians may imagine that in holding their beliefs they are believing God, or believing Jesus, but having had no immediate contact with either, they are at most believing only what some other men have said was said by God or by Jesus, at a very far remove of stories passed down over generations.

---

[7] EL, 25.12.

[8] Hobbes writes 'Another doctrine repugnant to Civill Society, is, that *whatsoever a man does against his Conscience, is Sinne;* and it dependeth on the presumption of making himself judge of Good and Evill. For a mans Conscience, and his Judgement is the same thing; and as the Judgement, so also the Conscience may be erroneous.' L, 29, p. 502.

[9] L, 12, p. 180.

Some few people do form their religious opinions on the basis of direct supernatural experiences. Presumably Adam, Abraham, and Moses had religious convictions grounded on direct perceptual experiences. Hobbes concedes that the rare person who has experienced divine revelation ought to act on their resulting private conscience: 'God is the Soveraign of all Soveraigns; and therefore, when he speaks to any Subject, he ought to be obeyed'.[10] However, when God communicates in this way he does not oblige others to believe those who claim to have received his positive laws through revelation. Most dreams and visions have naturalistic causes, so that 'though God Almighty can speak to a man, by Dreams, Visions, Voice, and Inspiration; yet he obliges no man to beleeve he hath so done to him that pretends it; who (being a man) may erre, and (which is more) may lie'.[11]

Another mode of direct experience that may influence the formation of religious belief is the perception of miracles. A miracle is an extraordinary event caused directly by God circumventing ordinary physical laws, and intended to procure credit to his prophet. Witnessing a miracle can cause a person to believe something with great conviction. But, Hobbes warns, we should be sceptical of alleged miracles. What we see may be the product of fraud or of entirely natural causes we simply do not understand. To perceive what one thinks to be a miracle may give rise to a conviction, without justifying that conviction. Hobbes ventures that miracles have now ceased, so this potential source of religious conscience is as practically irrelevant as direct revelation.

By Hobbes's analysis, to have a general duty to act on conscience would be to be required to act on one's own private judgement, or private opinion, concerning every matter. One could not have such a duty unless one also had a right to act on one's own private judgement. This is why Hobbes ties the doctrine of duty to act on conscience to another 'error' disruptive to social stability, namely that every person is judge of good and evil. This is an elliptical formulation of the claim that each individual has the right to act on their personal judgements of right and wrong.[12] Hobbes ventures that when his countrymen, acting on the 'poisonous doctrine' of Greek and Latin philosophers they learned in the universities, 'each made up his mind about what is good, bad, just or unjust, about the laws, and about religion, as he pleased', that is, each according to his own discretion, 'this was the beginning of our trouble'.[13] Hobbes's state of nature

[10] L, 33, p. 586.   [11] L, 32, p. 580.

[12] That Hobbes does not mean to claim that sovereigns define 'good' and 'evil' is shown by his insistence that sovereigns may *err* in their moral judgements of equity—'there is no Judge Subordinate, nor Soveraign, but may erre in a Judgement of Equity' (L, 36, p. 432)—and of good legislation, making laws 'which he ought not to' (L, 42, p. 894). Moral error would be impossible if sovereign judgement defined good and evil. And because sovereigns are normatively fallible, the distinction between private conscience and the public conscience expressed in the sovereign's laws cannot be a distinction between fallible opinion and infallible knowledge, as Mark Hanin appears to suppose. See his 'Thomas Hobbes's Theory of Conscience', *History of Political Thought* 33.1 (2012), 78. The error involved in the claim that every person is judge of good and evil is to think that subjects are entitled to act on their own judgements of good and evil contrary to those of their sovereign.

[13] LL, 46, p. 1097.

argument reveals what happens when we posit a right of each to act on his own discretion, conscience, or private judgement.

15.3 Morality Requires Forgoing the Right to Act on Private Judgement

Hobbes's state of nature argument is meant to show that a condition in which all may permissibly act on their own private judgements so undermines our ability to achieve our ends that any rational agent must abhor and seek to avoid it. A state of nature is a situation of universal private judgement; when 'private Appetite is the measure of Good, and Evill' men are in the 'condition of meer Nature'.[14] When each person insists on their own private judgements of right and wrong, good and bad, just and unjust, righteous or sinful, honourable and dishonourable, and every other question, the prospects of mutual interference and insecure control of resources make it very uncertain that we will be able to make our agency effective in pursuit of any of our ends, whatever those ends may be. No rational person can willingly choose to live in the sort of agency-voiding environment created by the exercise of a universal right of private judgement. Therefore, any rational person must demand that the people whose actions can most affect himself (community members) relinquish their right to act on their own private judgements.

However, morality dictates that whatever we require of others we too must do. The core requirement of the laws of nature is *reciprocity*, the requirement that we hold ourselves to the same standards we impose on others.[15] We are to treat them as equals, equitably. Hobbes summarizes these immutable moral laws accessible by the exercise of natural reason as demanding that '*Whatsoever you require that others should do to you, that do ye to them.*'[16] Because we must insist that others lay down some portion of their right to act on their private judgement (particularly over contested questions that affect others) and agree to abide by the judgement of a public authority, reciprocity requires that we lay down the corresponding portion of our own right.[17] This requirement that we subordinate our private judgement to a public judgement is tantamount to a *duty not to act on conscience* contrary to the public judgement.

---

[14] L, 15, p. 242.

[15] For the derivation of this reciprocity requirement as a theorem of reason, see S. A. Lloyd, *Morality in the Philosophy of Thomas Hobbes: Cases in the Law of Nature* (Cambridge: Cambridge University Press, 2009), 219–20.

[16] L, 14, p. 200. As formulated in the tenth law of nature, reciprocity requires that '*at the entrance into conditions of Peace, no man require to reserve to himselfe any Right, which he is not content should be reserved to every one of the rest*'. L, 15, p. 234.

[17] How much private judgement we jointly undertake to subordinate, and over which matters, is worked out through applications of the reciprocity requirement to our judgements of what it is reasonable to require of ourselves, resulting in the limited set of retained rights to act on private judgement covered by what Hobbes terms 'the true liberties of subjects'. See Lloyd, *Morality*, 28–30.

The moral law of nature requiring reciprocity is also divine law in God's natural kingdom, and confirmed by divine positive law in Scripture. Hobbes writes,

[That] law of nature, which commands every man to allow the same rights to others they would be allowed themselves, and which contains in it all the other laws besides, is the same which Moses set down (Levit. Xix.18): *Thou shalt love thy neighbor as thyself.* And our Saviour calls it *the sum of the moral law:* Math. Xxii. 36–40.[18]

It follows that by the same argument, Jews and Christians have a religious duty, as well as a moral duty, not to act on their private consciences in defiance of public authority.

In addition to natural law, Scripture as properly interpreted instructs Christians to obey princes and civil magistrates generally, and to do so from duty and not just as a matter of personal prudence: 'The Holy Scriptures teach that Christian subjects should obey their kings and sovereigns, and their ministers, even if they are heathen, not only for fear, but for conscience's sake, as ordained by God for our benefit.'[19] Citing Peter's admonition to obey the king and his governors, *'for so is the will of God'*, and Paul's instruction to *'Put men in mind to be subject to Principalities, and Powers, and to obey Magistrates'* even though they were infidels, Hobbes argues that Scripture established that Christians are to recognize the judgements of their civil sovereigns in all matters, religious and civil, as authoritative, whether those judgements are ultimately correct or incorrect. Furthermore, Hobbes argues, the Christian's prospects for salvation depend on the effort to fulfil their duty under natural law to obey the civil sovereign.[20] Christians not only may permissibly, but must as a matter of duty, obey secular authorities, even in religious matters for the sake of conscience, those having been ordained by God for our good.

15.4 Christians Are Not Subject to Special Obligations to Act on Conscience

Hobbes must show that his general argument for a duty not to act on conscience is not undermined by a set of special duties imposed on Christians. Citing scriptural evidence and church history, Christians may maintain that they are under special obligations (a) to believe that Jesus is the Christ, (b) to bear witness and to refuse to deny the same, (c) not to commit idolatry or to worship improperly, and (d) to accept martyrdom if necessary for fulfilling obligations (a) through (c). Hobbes replies that none of these claims is true of Christians living in his own time. A civil command not to believe would have no effect, because belief is not subject to the will; and because we can be responsible only for what is subject to our will, we can have no duties to believe anything. Faith is a gift of God which can be neither instilled nor taken away by means of

---

[18] *Philosophical Rudiments*, 4.12. Cf. L, 42, p. 786.   [19] LL, 46, p. 1095.
[20] L, 43, pp. 930, 932.

commands. Further, no one can bear witness to events at which he was not present, including the Resurrection. And one's killing will count as martyrdom only if one personally witnessed the Resurrection, was formally commissioned by the appropriate authority to bear witness to it, and did so to those who did not already believe.[21] So Christians other than a very few persons living in Jesus's day can have no special exemption from the duty not to act on conscience on those grounds.

The prohibition on idolatry can be observed consistent with whatever the sovereign commands, because genuine idolatry requires believing that the idol worshipped is a God, which the Christian does not. To answer the claim that Christians must conscientiously refuse commands to worship falsely, Hobbes cites Scripture in support of a permission to do so:

[A] Christian, holding firmly in his heart the Faith of Christ, hath the same liberty which the Prophet Elisha allowed to Naaman the Syrian ... [W]hatsoever a subject, as Naaman was, is compelled to in obedience to his Soveraign, and doth it not in order to his own mind, but in order to the laws of his country, that action is not his, but his Soveraigns; nor is it he that in this case denyeth Christ before men, but his Governour, and the law of his countrey.[22]

Hobbes may sense that it would be unwise to rest his argument on his interpretation of Elisha's words 'Go in peace' as a permission to worship by whatever rites one's sovereign commands.[23] What he needs is a principled argument that does not depend on a controversial interpretation of a single Scriptural verse; and he begins to develop that argument in the passage quoted.

15.5 Merely Obedient Subjects Are Not Morally Liable for What Is Done at the Sovereign's Command

The grand philosophical argument Hobbes constructs to answer residual qualms of conscience applies across the board, to Christians and non-Christians alike. It aims to establish that when, contrary to private conscience, subjects obey commands to do wrongful actions, they bear no responsibility for the wrongs done. This is so because first, what the *merely obedient* subject does (the subject who does what is commanded 'not in order to his own mind' but only because it was lawfully commanded) is the action of the sovereign only. An action belongs to the person who commands that it be done, whereas those duty-bound to carry out the command are mere instruments. Second, moral responsibility attaches only to the natural will. The content of a sovereign command is provided by the natural will of the person or

[21] L, 42, pp. 786, 788.   [22] L, 42, p. 784.
[23] Prior to *Leviathan* Hobbes had argued that if one occupied a leadership position such that one's wrongful public worship would scandalize believers or shake their faith, one ought to refuse to obey commands so to worship.

persons who are sovereign. The natural will of the merely obedient subject acting contrary to conscience is innocent of willing wrongdoing. Hobbes insists that:

[T]he externall actions done in obedience to [laws], without the inward approbation, are the actions of the Soveraign, and not of the Subject, which is in that case but as an instrument, without any motion of his owne at all; because God hath commanded to obey them.[24]

An action done *only* in obedience to a command one is obligated to obey is the act of the authority who commanded it. So far, we might say that it is the sovereign's will that is being acted on when obeying a law, with the obedient subject being used as the means (Hobbes says 'instrument') by which that will is carried out. Hobbes repeatedly likens the sovereign to the 'soul' of the commonwealth, giving it life and motion by providing its will and judgement, while subjects are the 'limbs' moved by it. Subjects are conceived as having given up their right to resist the uses the sovereign makes of their '*strength*' (abilities) and '*means*' (assets) '*as he shall think expedient*'.[25]

The quoted passage asserts that if one *disapproves* of the commanded action, one's obedient performance of it is the sovereign's action. This leaves open the possibility that if the subject approves of the commanded action, her performance of it is the joint action of herself and the sovereign, or that there are two actions in a single event here; the subject's action on her private judgement, and the sovereign's action by means of the subject's instrumentality. This general analysis of the ownership of actions is instantiated in Hobbes's explanation of why it is permissible for Christians, as it was for Naaman, to engage in heathen practices should their sovereign so command. The idolatrous action performed in such a case is the sovereign's, and not the merely obedient subject's.

What about immoral or sinful actions? Sin is the violation of God's laws, including the laws of nature. Based on his position that the commanded action done through the instrumentality of the merely obedient subject is the action of the sovereign only, we would expect Hobbes to conclude that if that action is sinful, the sin belongs to the sovereign alone. That is in fact what we find:

Commands may be sometimes contrary to right reason, and therefore sins in them who command them; yet are they not against right reason, nor sins in subjects; whose right reason, in points of controversy, is that which submits itself to the reason of the city.[26]

If someone sins at another's command, both sin, since neither did right; *unless*, by chance, the *state* commanded it to be done, *so that the actor ought not to refuse*.[27]

When the [subject] doth any thing against the Law of Nature by command of the [sovereign], if he be obliged by former Covenant to obey him, not he, but the [sovereign] breaketh the Law

---

[24] Hobbes introduces this claim in explaining why Christians should obey their sovereign's erroneous religious commands. He prefaces the quoted remark: '[A Christian king] cannot oblige men to beleeve; though as a Civill Soveraign he may make Laws suitable to his Doctrine, which may oblige men to certain actions, and sometimes to such as they would not otherwise do, and which he ought not to command; and yet when they are commanded, they are Laws'. L, 42, p. 894.
    [25] L, 17, p. 262.   [26] *Philosophical Rudiments*, 15.18.   [27] DH, 15.2 (emphasis added).

of Nature: for though the Action be against the Law of Nature; yet it is not his: but contrarily, to refuse to do it, is against the Law of Nature, that forbiddeth breach of Covenant.[28]

The sin belongs to the person who commands the sinful action, because the content of the command is supplied by the natural will of the person commanding, and responsibility attaches only to a natural will. Hobbes specifies that 'in a monarchy, if the monarch make any decree against the laws of nature, he sins himself; because in him the civil will and the natural are all one'.[29] In the case of a sovereign assembly, only the members who voted on their natural wills in favour of a sinful measure are guilty, for 'an offense issues from an expression of natural will not from a political will, which is artificial'.[30] In the case of a civil command to do something contrary to natural law, 'yet is not the injustice of the decree the injustice of every particular man, but only of those men by whose express suffrages, the decree or command was passed... [T]o make a particular man unjust, which consisteth of a body and soul natural, there is required a natural and very will.'[31] What is true for minority members of an assembly that votes to command an iniquitous action, is also true for the merely obedient subjects carrying out that command. Because the command does not express their natural wills, but rather opposes them, they are not responsible.[32]

Hobbes's distinction between a natural will and an artificial will parallels his distinction between private and public conscience. The will is the last appetite in deliberation, and the judgement, or conscience, is the last opinion in the search for truth.[33] Just as the commonwealth's laws serve as the artificial will of the subject, so does the judgement that they are to be obeyed serve as the artificial judgement of the subject. Hobbes writes that in obeying his sovereign, a man does act 'according to his conscience and judgment, as having deposited his judgment in all controversies in the hands of the sovereign power'.[34] But we must distinguish:

For the conscience being nothing else but a man's settled judgment and opinion, when he hath once transferred his right of judging to another, that which shall be commanded, is no less his judgment, than [it is] the judgment of that other. So that in obedience to laws, a man doth still according to his own conscience, *but not his private conscience*.[35]

---

[28] L, 16, p. 246. The substitution of 'subject' for 'Actor' and 'sovereign' for 'Author' is licensed not only by Hobbes's text, but by the logic of this passage: because sovereigns have made no covenant to obey anyone, the referent of 'he' (which stands in for 'Actor') in 'if he be obliged by former Covenant to obey him' can only be the subject. And because only sovereigns command, 'by the command of the Author' cannot mean by command of the subject. Ministers exercising sovereign power by appointment, when carrying out commands, are also actors, and themselves subjects. For confirmation that Hobbes's conception of authorization, introduced in *Leviathan*, does not alter his argument insulating subjects from moral responsibility for merely obedient responses to their sovereign's commands, see S. A. Lloyd, 'Authorization and Moral Responsibility in the Philosophy of Hobbes', *Hobbes Studies* 29.2 (2016), 169–88.

[29] *Philosophical Rudiments*, 7.14.   [30] DCv, 7.14.   [31] EL, 21.4.

[32] The individuals who are subjects of a commonwealth are both natural persons and artificial persons. For a fuller discussion of what this fact entails for their moral responsibilities, see Lloyd, 'Authorization'.

[33] L, 7, p. 98.   [34] EL, 27.5.   [35] EL, 25.12 (emphasis added).

He acts according to his own *public conscience*. The issue then is not whether we should obey the law in violation of conscience; the law accords with our conscience, that is, with our public conscience, the judgement of the public person (the commonwealth) whose actions we implement. The issue is whether, when our private conscience diverges from our public, we *sin* in following the dictates of our public conscience. To this Hobbes answers categorically: 'whatsoever is done contrary to private conscience, is then a sin, when the laws have left him to his own liberty, *and never else*'.[36]

This is a subtle position. It is no sin to violate your private conscience by obeying a legitimate law you believe to command something wrongful. This is because you have a controlling duty to subordinate your private judgement to the public judgement, as expressed in the law. In a case like this, you have a duty *not* to act on private conscience. But, to do the thing you believe to be wrong *absent* the law commanding it *would* be a sin. This will be true whether or not the action is *actually, objectively* wrong, because to willingly do what one believes is contrary to God's law is to show contempt for the law and a willingness to break the law, thwarted only by one's ignorance of what the law is. God, who reads hearts, takes the will for the deed. To choose, not in response to an obligation of obedience, to do what one believes to be wrong is to act 'with a seared conscience', which is a sin. So to do what one believes to be wrong is as blameworthy as to do what is actually wrong, when, but only when, the judgement of right and wrong is up to oneself.[37]

It is important to appreciate that Hobbes is arguing, not that we sometimes have a duty to act against conscience, but rather that acting in obedience to law in fact *accords* with our conscience. It is not just that we *substitute* the sovereign's conscience in place of our own. We ourselves judge it to be our duty under natural law to prioritize the public judgement over our private judgements, and this judgement *makes* the public conscience our own.[38] We acknowledge something similar when we take the will of the majority to be our practical will even though we voted the minority position; or when we willingly defer to the decision of the Supreme Court even in cases that it has decided wrongly in our private judgement. We distinguish between our *substantive* private will, and our *procedurally ascertained* public will.[39] Rousseau's familiar view that the general

---

[36] Ibid., (emphasis added).

[37] Hobbes explains in DCv 12.2, 'a distinction must be made: my sin is what I as agent regard as a sin on my part; but what I regard as a sin in someone else, I may sometimes do without committing sin myself. For if I am told to do something which it is a sin for the person to tell me to do, I commit no sin in doing it, provided that the person who tells me to do it is my Lord by right...Those who do not observe this distinction will find themselves committed to sin whenever they are ordered to do anything illicit—or which seems so to them.' I discuss in section 15.7 the dilemma (Hobbes here alludes to) that would arise were we to have a duty always to act on private conscience.

[38] For this reason, it is misleading to speak, as Hanin does, of a 'taxing and unstable...combination of external submission and internal dissent' in Hobbes's political system, as if the judgement that she ought to submit were not the subject's own conscientious judgement. See Hanin, 'Hobbes's Theory of Conscience', 81.

[39] Why we might do that is the issue Hobbes is engaging. If we give priority to our public will—to procedure over substance—for principled moral or religious reasons, our commitment to doing so will be much more stable than if it is based on calculations of relative power to impose our substantive preferences. Hobbes is arguing that we do in fact have such reasons.

will is our authentic will, and to be acted on in preference to our competing corporate or private wills, articulates an idea in some respects similar to Hobbes's.[40]

At this point, a question naturally arises. That actions done merely obediently at the command of the sovereign and in violation of natural law are the sovereign's actions, and the sovereign's sin, rather than the subjects', is clearly Hobbes's position. But we might wonder how this can be consistent with his view in chapters 17 and 18 of *Leviathan* that subjects 'own and authorize' the actions of their sovereigns. The idiosyncratic conception of authorization Hobbes uses confers immunity on sovereigns without ascribing moral liability to subjects.[41] By 'seating the legislative power' or 'ratifying the people's [commonwealth's] acts in general', subjects commit to treating *all* the sovereign's judgements as controlling, and would do wrong, Hobbes insists, to then refuse to treat *some* of them (those of which they disapprove) as controlling. But subjects do not command or commission the sovereign to do any specified or particular actions. To say that an action is done by authority is to say that it is 'done by Commission, or Licence from him whose right it is',[42] and 'unless he that is the author hath the right of acting himself, the actor hath no authority to act'.[43] No one, neither sovereign nor subject, has any right to sin. So subjects cannot transfer to their sovereign any right to sin, nor are they authors of sinful actions commanded by the sovereign. Hobbesian authorization involves undertaking to privilege the sovereign's public judgement over the subject's private judgement, and immunizing the sovereign from complaints by the subject, but Hobbesian authorization does not make subjects morally responsible for the sovereign's commands or actions done only in obedience to those commands.[44] Hobbes insists in the passages we earlier surveyed that moral responsibility attaches to the person or persons whose natural will provided the content of the command, and not to the unwilling but obedient subject used as an instrument to carry out that command.

15.6 Hobbes's Hierarchy of Responsibility

The moral responsibilities of sovereigns and subjects differ, and may be organized into what I have termed a *hierarchy of responsibility*. Sovereigns are required under the law of nature to do all they can to secure the common good, and are accountable to God

---

[40] Clearly not in all. Rousseau's general will requires that all participate in determining the law, that the law apply to all, and that the law be decided on the basis of whether it advances the goods citizens hold in common. These conditions restrict the kind of procedure that can reveal the general will. But the general will is ascertained through a public decision procedure, as is the public judgement by a Hobbesian sovereign; and that procedure takes precedence over the private conscience (for Rousseau the equivalent would be the corporate or personal will) of the individual as a matter of right.

[41] This technical understanding of authorization is documented and discussed in Lloyd, 'Authorization'.

[42] L, 16, p. 244.   [43] DH, 15.2.

[44] It is a common mistake among commentators to suppose that because our own notion of authorization allows for the commissioning of actions one has no right to perform and assigns responsibility for those actions to the authorizer, that Hobbes's notion of authorization does the same. It does not. For the full argument, with textual support, see Lloyd, 'Authorization'.

for any failure to do so.[45] The eternal and immutable laws of nature bind sovereigns just as stringently as they do everyone else, and so the required acts of good governance 'are the duties of sovereigns, and required at their hands to the utmost of their endeavour, by God Almighty, under pain of eternal death'.[46] Sovereigns' duties of good governance are owed directly to God, and not to subjects. Subjects are duty-bound to obey their sovereign's commands. This is primarily a duty of equity or fairness owed to their fellow subjects whose like obedience to the sovereign they demand for the sake of their own safety.[47] Subjects are accountable to God for the performance of their duty of obedience to their sovereign, also on pain of eternal death, for as we saw earlier, the effort to fulfil one's duties under the law of nature is one of the two necessary conditions for salvation. Thus subjects are responsible to God for their obedience to the sovereign's commands, whereas sovereigns are responsible to God for the content of their commands.

We may also picture these responsibilities hierarchically: 'Subjects owe to sovereigns simple obedience',[48] and sovereigns owe to God simple obedience. Subjects are to obey their sovereign's laws, and their sovereigns are to obey God's laws. This *allocation of accountability* entails a corresponding allocation of immunity. Sovereigns are immune from censure by their subjects no matter the content of their commands, because 'God has commanded [subjects] to obey them'. And subjects are immune from censure by God for obeying the sovereign's commands no matter their content for the same reason, because 'God has commanded to obey [sovereigns]'. Thus a subject who acts conscientiously in obedience to her sovereign's commands, even against her private judgements of right and wrong, has done nothing wrong. Indeed, she has fulfilled her duty not to act on conscience.

15.7 In Favour of Hobbes's Position, It Avoids Tragic Dilemmas

I said at the beginning that there might be a Nuremberg sort of worry about this position, that it too easily excuses wrongdoing on the ground that one was just following orders. We do not want to excuse those who obey the law when it commands them to do something clearly iniquitous, say to kill all the babies or firstborns in the land. Suppose then, that things were otherwise than Hobbes says. Suppose we have a moral duty to act on private conscience, so that we would be appropriately liable to moral censure, ostracism, shaming, and feelings of guilt and remorse if we obeyed a law we thought wrong. That means that we must choose between being punished by the state

---

[45] L, 30, p. 520.   [46] EL, 28.1.

[47] It may also be a duty of gratitude owed to the sovereign who maintains the orderly environment they enjoy; and if they have made a promise to their fellow subjects or to the sovereign to obey, obedience will be owed as a matter of justice as well as equity.

[48] L, 31, p. 554. Hobbes continues, 'in all things, wherein their obedience is not repugnant to the Lawes of God'.

for disobeying the law, or suffering those consequences of moral condemnation for obeying the law. Suppose further that we are religiously required to act according to our private conscience, even in violation of civil law, and that we would then be liable to divine punishment, including eternal damnation, if we obeyed any law against our conscience. That means we must choose between being punished by the state for disobeying, or punished by God for obeying. Suppose finally that state punishment for disobeying the law is serious—death, say;[49] and that the state is effective and so can reliably carry out its threatened punishments.

On these suppositions, we face a tragic dilemma. When we have the bad fortune to *think* that a law is wrong (whether or not it really is wrong) we have no choice but to obey it anyway and be punished by moral censure and damned by God for acting with a seared conscience, or to disobey it, and be killed by the state. Moral pariah, damned sinner, or executed criminal: these are our choices. There is no choice we can make that will let us just get on with the lives we value and were trying to live. Hobbes was sensitive to this prospect of a dilemma. He writes 'All men therefore that would avoid, both the punishments that are to be in this world inflicted, for disobedience to their earthly Soveraign, and those that shall be inflicted in the world to come for disobedience to God, have need be taught to distinguish well between what is, and what is not Necessary to Eternall Salvation.'[50] What is necessary is a good faith effort to honour our natural law duty to obey the sovereign; what is not necessary is indulging the promptings of our private conscience.

Imposing on people a stringent duty to act on conscience makes them inordinately vulnerable to the vicissitudes of fortune. If they are unlucky enough to live under a political regime that makes bad laws enforced by draconian punishments, they cannot escape life ruination. Another unwelcome consequence of this strong position is that because the dilemma emerges only when the citizen's private judgements diverge from the law's requirements, the more effectively the state propagandizes its citizens into internalizing its requirements as a matter of conscience, the more rarely will they face a dilemma, and so the safer they will be from untimely death, or dishonour, or damnation. This would count in favour of invasive state formation of citizen's moral views, but we may rightly object to that.

The position that one is required always to act on conscience no matter what the consequences is overly demanding. So if this is what is meant by the claim that a man sins in acting contrary to his conscience, the standard for avoiding sin looks unreasonably high. Would a loving, merciful God impose such a standard? The worry that God imposes tyrannical demands becomes exponentially more acute when we combine the duty to act on private conscience with our duty under the law of nature to defer to public judgement. Hobbes has offered a demonstration that the reciprocity requirement of the

---

[49] That supposition is not far-fetched, because the laws that are most likely to engage conscientious objection are often the laws the state feels the need most rigorously to enforce.

[50] L, 43, p. 930.

law of nature demands that we submit disputes among our private judgements to the judgement of a public authoritative arbitrator and defer to its decisions. Further, Hobbes has offered evidence to show that Scripture confirms this natural law requirement to obey the civil authority. Sin being a violation of God's law, it is a sin to act on private judgement in defiance of public law. So if it were also a sin to act against private con-science, *we would sin no matter which we did*, whether we obeyed the law or defied the law. God would have imposed on us a set of commandments that cannot be jointly obeyed in circumstances of conflict; and whether those circumstances obtain is not within our control. We are trapped like rats in the maze of the evil scientist who mines every path with an electric shock. Except that God is made to be the evil scientist.

We arrived at this repugnant conclusion by denying Hobbes's assertion that subjects are not required to act on their private consciences. The hierarchy of responsibility Hobbes defends on both philosophical and scriptural grounds dissolves the dilemma and absolves God of the charge of tyranny. That should count in favour of Hobbes's understanding. We cannot, consistently with our intention to honour God,[51] think of God as systematically forcing us to face tragic choices, especially if damnation looms for whichever choice we make. Hobbes removes one horn of the dilemma by showing that the duty to act on private conscience is limited to cases in which it does not con-flict with civil obedience. God does not require us to act on our private conscience in defiance of civil law, so we commit no sin in obeying.

An alternative way to resolve the dilemma would be simply to deny that God's natural or positive laws require us to obey kings and magistrates and to submit to public authority. Maybe there is no call on us to submit to government in the first place. If God does not require the subordination of private judgement to public, we never sin in following our private conscience. Against this suggestion, Hobbes's state of nature argument shows that individual self-rule by private judgement undermines our ability to achieve our human ends. Unlike the communities of bees and ants and other naturally sociable creatures whose hardwired consensus in private judgements enables them to cooperate without government,[52] large-scale anarchic human communities are unsus-tainable and incompatible with our good. This being so, all except principled anarchists are likely to grant Hobbes's conclusion that we are morally required to join with others in submitting to some sort of government. Further, our human need for government will suggest to the believer that in designing us with the nature we have, God must have willed that we submit to government.[53] So this alternative path for avoiding the dilemma meets with an insurmountable roadblock. Short of radically altering human

---

[51] This entails thinking as highly as possible of his goodness, and his care for us. L, 31, p. 560.

[52] L, 17, p. 258.

[53] Aquinas had offered an argument similar in outline, that human nature requires government to real-ize our good. True, he thought subjects should obey only civil commands consistent with religious duty, as determined by the church, the proper public judgement in religious matters. But he argued against self-rule by individual private judgement on much the same ground that Hobbes did.

nature so as to homogenize our private judgements, we must posit a duty to submit to some government.

Another hope for avoiding the dilemma would be to weaken each prong: we have a duty to obey the laws only when we do not think them egregiously immoral, and we have a duty to act on our private conscience only when egregious immorality is at stake (and otherwise may not act on private conscience). One difficulty with taking this alternative is that private conscience will sometimes demand not just personal disobedience to some laws but active resistance to eliminate those laws, or even revolution against the entire government. (It may require, for instance, violation of secrecy laws, aid to the enemy in unjust wars, bombing abortion clinics or killing abortionists, imposition of religious intolerance, of rigid gender roles, economic redistribution or collectivization, or dismantling the system altogether.) The political system is not insulated from possible destruction by the conscientious private judgements admitted by this alternative. So whatever argument there is in favour of having functional government speaks against permitting conscientious action on any strongly held private conviction regardless of its content.

As the examples suggest, individuals disagree radically in their judgements of which laws are egregiously immoral. Such disagreements are seemingly unbounded.[54] Equity demands that if we afford anyone the right to act on their judgements regarding egregious immorality, we must afford everyone that right (otherwise we are guilty of what John Stuart Mill termed the logic of persecutors, that we may persecute others because we are right, while they may not persecute us because they are wrong). Allowing a right to disobey means granting immunity from prosecution, that is, exempting from punishment those people whose disobedience is conscientious. If we allow the right to everyone, how much instability will be introduced? If tremendous instability would result, we have to weigh our desire to maintain our peaceful society in the face of what we regard as the incorrect moral or religious zealotry of others, against our willingness to risk civil collapse so that we can follow our own conscientious convictions.

So Hobbes has given formidable reasons for declining to take either of those alternative routes to resolving the dilemma. Anyone who wishes to do so bears the burden of explaining how decent human lives could be lived in the absence of effective government, or of fashioning some system of effective government in which everyone reserves the right still to act on their private judgement at their discretion while enjoying the benefits of government. As a last resort, one might argue that morality does not in fact require reciprocity, and that stability could be maintained were we to permit conscientious exemptions only for ourselves and those who share our opinions. We could try to defend the logic of persecutors.

It is worth noting that Hobbes's system is not necessarily incompatible with a complex system of government that contains checks and balances, so long as the system as a

---

[54] Gerald Gaus explains the ideas of insulation and unbounded disagreement in 'Hobbes's Challenge to Public Reason Liberalism'.

whole exercises all the rights of sovereignty and is internally ordered so as to produce a fully determinate resolution to every dispute.[55] We can even permit to everyone a right of conscientious objection on some grounds in some matters. For instance, exemptions from combat service, and from being called to testify against family members are explicitly approved by Hobbes. He argues that under the law of nature sovereigns are required to preserve all harmless liberties for their subjects; it would follow that the sovereign has moral reason to allow conscientious exemptions *whenever* they do not much affect stability. Indeed doing so would positively contribute to stability by reducing two of the three necessary conditions for rebellion: citizen discontent, and also pretence of right, or justification, for rebelling.[56] This consideration provides the sovereign with a prudential reason to accommodate harmless conscientious objection, to supplement the moral reason provided by the law of nature. But this more palatable political regime still resolves the dilemma in favour of public judgement, as Hobbes insists it should.

15.8 A Question Concerning the Dispensability of Religious Argument to Hobbes's Political Theory

Does Hobbes's argument that we do no wrong in obeying commands that conflict with our private conscience depend essentially on religious premises? This argument is crucial to the justification of his political theory. Without it he cannot demonstrate that subjects have a general, indefeasible, and overriding duty to obey political authority. Nor can he expect to motivate religious readers to comply with his theory's prescriptions. From the twentieth century onwards much Hobbes interpretation by philosophers has insisted that his political theory could be understood as entirely secular, with the religious parts of his works treated as optional addenda. It would be ironic if it turned out that the theory in fact depends essentially on religious premises. The arguments we have seen for his assertion that Christians are to obey civil authorities 'for conscience sake, as ordained by God for their good' do depend on both scriptural support and on thinking of the laws of nature as divine laws enforced by divine sanctions. So it is worth considering whether his position can be adequately supported without these religious assumptions.

If we remove from Hobbes's theory the claims that God exists and that Scripture contains God's word, he loses the divine backing of the laws of nature, and scriptural supports for his argument like the divine permission allowed to Naaman. He also loses a potentially tremendous source of motivation to defer to the sovereign's commands, namely, the desire to avoid eternal death. On the flip side of the coin, gone along with religion would be a huge potential source of motivation to *defect* from civil obedience. Without religion as an independent font of normative claims on subjects, they would

---

[55] See S. A. Lloyd, 'Locating Sovereignty in Complex Systems', in *Sovereignty and the New Executive Order*, ed. Claire Finkelstein (Oxford: Oxford University Press, forthcoming).

[56] EL, 27.1.

have fewer competing demands on themselves, and no fear of damnation if they complied with sovereign commands. What would remain from this excision of religion is a secular moral argument that treating other people fairly and as our equals requires us to submit our disputes with them to the judgement of some authoritative arbitrator and then to stand to its decision, even if that decision goes against us. The only fair alternative to this would be to let everyone act on their own private judgement, and we are not willing to allow that. But if we are thus *morally required* to defer to the public judge, it is unreasonable to *morally fault* us for doing so. To fault us for failing to insist on our private conscience in defiance of the public judgement is to fault us for doing what it would be immoral of us to refuse to do. We would be guilty of immorality whichever way we act. (This is the secular version of the dilemma that Hobbes's conception allows us to avoid.) In addition to this argument from fairness, Hobbes would still have his conceptual distinctions assigning responsibility for actions done by the merely obedient subject to the sovereign alone.

Is this secular argument supported by Hobbes's distinctions good enough to answer the Nuremberg objection? There remains a psychological gap between prioritizing our duty to act on the procedural requirement that we submit to public authority, and our fervent desire to act on whatever substantive moral requirement we think directs us not to submit to the public authority in the case at hand. This is the very problem that confronts liberal theories of justice, including Rawls's, that demand that citizens prioritize public principles of procedural fairness over substantive moral requirements given them by their comprehensive doctrines. Perhaps, if the argument is good enough, we should try to adjust our psychology. If the secular argument is not good enough, it may possibly be reinforced using a religious argument of the sort Hobbes advanced. If it turns out that the plausibility of the central Hobbesian argument for submitting private conscience to public authority depends on religious assumptions, Hobbes will be a political theorist who should be of interest *only* to religious believers. Wouldn't that be ironic?

Bibliography

Manuscripts

British Library, Evelyn MS 39a, fo. 128: Evelyn to Sprat, 31 October 1664.
British Library, Harley MS 6796, fo. 297: 'Short Tract'.
Hardwick Hall, MS E1A: book list Hardwick Hall.
Hartlib Papers, 62/30/3b–4a: Rand to Hartlib, 18 July 1651.

Primary Texts

Adams, Thomas, *Commentary or, Exposition upon the Divine Second Latin Epistle General, Written by the Blessed Apostle St. Peter* (London, 1633).
Ambrose, St, *Christian Offices Crystal Glass* (London, 1637).
Ames, William, *Conscience with the Power and Cases thereof Devided into V. books* ([Leyden and London], 1639).
Ames, William, *The Marrow of All Theology* (Durham, NC: Labyrinth Press, 1968).
[Anon.], *Discourse presented to those Who Seek Reformation of the Church of England* (London, 1642).
[Anon.], *Mercurius Davidicus, or A Patterne of Loyall Devotion* (Oxford, 1643).
[Anon.], *An Elegie on Mr Thomas Hobbes of Malmesbury* (London, 1679).
[Anon.], *The Last Sayings, or Dying Legacy of Mr. Thomas Hobbes of Malmesbury* (London, 1680).
[Anon.], *Visits from the Shades* (London, 1704).
[Anon.], *The Religious, Rational, and Moral Conduct of Matthew Tindal, L.L.D.* (London, 1735).
[Anon.], 'Illustrations of the State of the Church during the Great Rebellion', *The Theologian and the Ecclesiastic* 9 (1850), 294–5.
[Anon.], *Vindiciae, Contra Tyrannos*, ed. and trans. George Garnett (Cambridge: Cambridge University Press, 1994).
Aquinas, Thomas, *Summa Theologica*, trans. Fathers of the English Dominican Province (New York: Benziger Brothers, 1947), <http://www.dhspriory.org/thomas/summa/index.html>, accessed 19 June 2017.
Aquinas, Thomas, 'Aquinas: Psalm 4', trans. F. F. Reilly, n.d. <http://dhspriory.org/thomas/PsalmsAquinas/ThoPs4.htm>, accessed 19 June 2017.
Aristotle, *De Memoria*, trans. G. R. T. Ross (Cambridge: Cambridge University Press, 1906).
Arrowsmith, John, *Armilla Catechetica. A Chain of Principles* (London, 1659).
Aubrey, John, *Brief Lives, Chiefly of Contemporaries*, ed. Andrew Clark, 2 vols (Oxford: Oxford University Press, 1898).
Augustine, St, *On the Free Choice of the Will, On Grace and Free Choice, and Other Writings*, ed. and trans. Peter King (Cambridge: Cambridge University Press, 2010).
Ayre, G. E., C. R. Rivington, and H. R. Plomer (eds), *A Transcript of the Register of the Worshipful Company of Stationers from 1640–1708* (London, 1913–14).

Baillie, Robert, *A Dissuasive from the Errours of the Time* (London, 1645).

Barckley, Richard, *A Discourse of the Felicitie of Man, or his 'Summum bonum'* (London, 1603).

Barwick, Peter, *The Life of the Reverend Dr John Barwick* (London, 1724).

Bastwick, John, *The Utter Routing of the whole Army of all Independents and Sectarians* (London, 1646).

Bayle, Pierre, *A Philosophical Commentary on These Words of the Gospel, Luke 14.23: 'Compel Them to Come In, That My House May Be Full'*, ed. John Kilcullen and Chandran Kukathas (Indianapolis, IN: Liberty Fund, 2005).

Bellarmine, Robert, *Disputationum...de controversiis Christianae fidei, adversus huius temporis hereticos*, iv (Ingolstadt, 1601).

Bellarmine, Robert, *Opera Omnia*, 6 vols (Naples: Josephum Giuliano, 1856–62).

Bentley, Richard, *Remarks Upon a Late Discourse of Free-thinking* (London, 1713).

The Bible, King James Version, with the Apocrypha (London: Penguin Classics, 2006).

Blaising, Craig A. and Carmen S. Hardin (eds), *Psalms 1–50* (Downers Grove, IL: InterVarsity Press, 2008).

Blount, Charles, *A Just Vindication of Learning, or, An Humble Address to the High Court of Parliament, In behalf of the Liberty of the Press* (London, 1679).

Blount, Charles, *Great is Diana of the Ephesians, or, The Original of Idolatry Together with the Politick Institution of the Gentiles Sacrifices* (London, 1680).

Blount, Charles, *The Two First Books of Philostratus, Concerning the Life of Apollonius Tyaneus: Written Originally in Greek, and Now Published in English* (London, 1680).

Blount, Charles, *Miracles No Violations of the Laws of Nature* (London, 1683).

Blount, Charles, *Religio Laici Written in a Letter to John Dryden, Esq.* (London, 1683).

Blount, Charles, *Oracles of Reason...In Several Letters to Mr. Hobbs and other Persons of Eminent Quality, and Learning* (London, 1693).

Bramhall, John, *The Catching of Leviathan* (London, 1657).

Bramhall, John, *Castigations of Mr. Hobbes His Last Animadversions in the Case Concerning Liberty and Universal Necessity Wherein All His Exceptions About That Controversie Are Fully Satisfied* (London, 1658).

Bramhall, John, *Schism Guarded and Beaten Back upon the Right Owners* (London, 1658).

Bramhall, John, *The Works of the Most Reverend Father in God, John Bramhall*, iv (Oxford, 1854).

Buchanan, George, *A Dialogue on the Law of Kingship among the Scots*, ed. and trans. Roger A. Mason and Martin S. Smith (Aldershot: Ashgate, 2004).

Calendar of State Papers, Domestic, 1666–1667 (London, 1907).

Calvin, John, *Opuscula omnia in unum volumen collecta* (Geneva, 1552).

Calvin, John, *Institutes of the Christian Religion* (Geneva, 1559).

Calvin, John, *The Institution of Christian Religion*, trans. Thomas Norton (London, 1561).

Calvin, John, *Institutes of the Christian Religion*, ed. John T. McNeill, trans. Ford Lewis Battles (Philadelphia, PA: Westminster Press, 1960).

Calvin, John, *Institutes of the Christian Religion*, trans. Henry Beveridge (Peabody, MA: Hendrickson Publishers, 2008).

Camden, William, *The Abridgment of Camden's Britania* (London, 1626).

Cartwright, Christopher, *A Practical and Polemical Commentary or Exposition on the Whole Fifteenth Psalm* (London, 1658).

Cheynell, Francis, *The Rise, Growth and Danger of Socinianisme* (London, 1643).

Chillingworth, William, *The Religion of Protestants* (London, 1638).

Church, Henry, *Miscellanea Philo-theologica. Or, God, & Man* (London, 1637).

The Collegiat Suffrage of the Divines of Great Britaine (London, 1629).

Collins, Anthony, *A Discourse of Free-thinking* (London, 1713).

Collins, Anthony, *A Philosophical Inquiry Concerning Human Liberty* (London, 1717).

Collins, Anthony, *A Discourse Concerning Ridicule and Irony in Writing* (London, 1729).

Collins, Anthony, *A Philosophical Inquiry Concerning Human Liberty, Republished with a Preface by Joseph Priestley* (Birmingham, 1790).

Cumberland, Richard, *A Treatise of the Laws of Nature*, ed. Jon Parkin, trans. John Maxwell (Indianapolis, IN: Liberty Fund, 2005).

Davenant, William, *A Discourse upon Gondibert* (London, 1650).

Descartes, René, *Œuvres de Descartes*, ed. Charles Adam and Paul Tannery (Paris: Leopold Cerf, 1904).

Dryden, John, *Religio Laici, or, a Laymans Faith. A Poem* (London, 1682).

Duppa, Brian, *The Correspondence of Bishop Brian Duppai*, ed. G. Isham (Northampton: Northamptonshire Record Society, 1951).

Eachard, John, *Some Opinions of Mr. Hobbs Considered* (London, 1673).

Eikon Basilike: The Pourtraicture of His Sacred Majestie in His Solitudes and Sufferings (London, reprinted 1648/9).

Epiphanius, *The Panarion of St. Epiphanius, Bishop of Salamis, Selected Passages*, ed. Philip R. Amidon (Oxford: Oxford University Press, 1990).

Erastus, Thomas, *The Nullity of Church-Censures* (London, 1659).

Ferne, Henry, *A Reply unto Severall Treatises Pleading for the Armes Now Taken Up by Subjects in the Pretended Defence of Religion and Liberty* (Oxford, 1643).

Field, Nathaniel, *Some Short Memorials Concerning the Life of that Reverend Divine Richard Field* (London, 1717).

Filmer, Robert, *Observations Concerning the Originall of Government* (London, 1652).

Filmer, Robert, *Observations Concerning the Originall of Government*. In *Patriarcha and Other Writings*, ed. J. P. Sommerville (Cambridge: Cambridge University Press, 1991), 184–95.

Filmer, Robert, *Patriarcha*. In *Patriarcha and Other Writings*, ed. J. P. Sommerville (Cambridge: Cambridge University Press, 1991), 1–68.

Gay, Peter, *Deism: An Anthology* (Princeton, NJ: Van Nostrand, 1968).

Gill, John, *The Cause of God and Truth*, 4 vols (London, 1737).

Gillespie, George, *A Late Dialogue Betwixt a Civilian and a Divine Concerning the Present Condition of the Church of England* (London, 1644).

Greenhill, William, *The Axe at the Root, a Sermon Preached before the Honorable House of Commons* (London, 1643).

Grey, Anchitell, *Debates of the House of Commons, From the Year 1667 to the Year 1694*, i (London, 1763).

Grotius, Hugo, *De Imperio Summarum Potestatum Circa Sacra*, trans. Harm-Jan Van Dam (Leiden: Brill, 2001).

Hall, Edmund, *Lazarus's Sores Licked* (London, 1650).

Hammond, Henry, *A Letter of Resolution to Six Quaeres* (London, 1653).

Harrington, James, *Pian Piano* (London, 1656).

Harrington, James, *Pian Piano*. In *The Political Works of James Harrington*, ed. J. G. A. Pocock (Cambridge: Cambridge University Press, 1977).

Harrington, James, *The Art of Lawgiving*. In *The Political Works of James Harrington*, ed. J. G. A. Pocock (Cambridge: Cambridge University Press, 1977), 599–704.

Harrington, James, *The Commonwealth of Oceana*. In *The Political Works of James Harrington*, ed. J. G. A. Pocock (Cambridge: Cambridge University Press, 1977), 155–359.

Harrington, James, *The Prerogative of Popular Government*. In *The Political Works of James Harrington*, ed. J. G. A. Pocock (Cambridge: Cambridge University Press, 1977), 389–498.

Harris, John, *The Atheist's Objections, Against the Immaterial Nature of God, and Incorporeal Substances, Refuted* (London, 1698).

Heath, James, *A Chronicle of the Late Intestine War in the Three Kingdoms* (London, 1676).

Herbert, Edward, *De Veritate*, ed. and trans. Meyrick H. Carré (Bristol: J. W. Arrowsmith, 1937).

Heylyn, Peter, *Cyprianus Anglicus* (London, 1668).

Hildersham, Arthur, *CLII Lectures upon Psalme LI preached at Ashby-Delazouch in Leicester-shire* (London, 1635).

Hobbes, Thomas, *Of Libertie and Necessitie* (London, 1654).

Hobbes, Thomas, *Questions Concerning Liberty, Necessity, and Chance* (London, 1656).

Hobbes, Thomas, *Six Lessons to the Professors of the Mathematiques* (London, 1656).

Hobbes, Thomas, *Mr Hobbes Considered in his Loyalty, Religion, Reputation and Manners* (London, 1662).

Hobbes, Thomas, *Thomae Hobbesii Malmesburiensis Vita* (London, 1679).

Hobbes, Thomas, *An Historical Narration Concerning Heresie, And the Punishment Thereof* (London, 1680).

Hobbes, Thomas, *Thomae Hobbes Angli Philosophi Vita* (London, 1681).

Hobbes, Thomas, *The English Works of Thomas Hobbes of Malmesbury*, ed. William Molesworth, 10 vols (London: John Bohn, 1839–45).

Hobbes, Thomas, *Thomae Hobbes malmesburiensis opera philosophica quae latine scripsit omnia*, ed. William Molesworth, 5 vols (London: John Bohn, 1839–45).

Hobbes, Thomas, *De Cive*, ed. Sterling P. Lamprecht (New York: Appleton-Century-Crofts, 1949).

Hobbes, Thomas, *Leviathan: Parts One and Two*, ed. Herbert W. Schneider (New York: Liberal Arts Press, 1958).

Hobbes, Thomas, *Léviathan Traité de la matière, de la forme et du pouvoir de la république ecclésiastique et civile*, ed. François Tricaud (Paris: Sirey, 1971).

Hobbes, Thomas, *Critique du De Mundo de Thomas White*, ed. Jean Jacquot and Harold Whitmore Jones (Paris: J. Vrin, 1973).

Hobbes, Thomas, *Thomas White's De Mundo Examined*, ed. and trans. Harold Whitmore Jones (London: Bradford University Press, 1976).

Hobbes, Thomas, *Storia Ecclesiastica, narrata in forma di carmine elegiaca*, trans. G. Invernizzi and A. Lupoli, in Thomas Hobbes, *Scritti teologici* (Milan: Franco Angeli, 1988).

Hobbes, Thomas, *Man and Citizen (De Homine and De Cive)*, ed. Bernard Gert (Indianapolis, IN: Hackett, 1991).

Hobbes, Thomas, 'The 1668 Appendix to *Leviathan*', in George Wright, 'Thomas Hobbes: The 1668 Appendix to *Leviathan*', *Interpretation* 18.4 (1991), 324–413.

Hobbes, Thomas, *The Correspondence*, ed. Noel Malcolm, 2 vols (Oxford: Clarendon Press, 1994).

Hobbes, Thomas, *The Elements of Law, Natural and Politic: Part I, Human Nature, Part II, De Corpore Politico; with Three Lives*, ed. J. C. A. Gaskin (Oxford: Oxford University Press, 1994).

Hobbes, Thomas, *On the Citizen*, ed. and trans. Richard Tuck and Michael Silverthorne (Cambridge: Cambridge University Press, 1998).

Hobbes, Thomas, *Writings on Common Law and Hereditary Right*, ed. Alan Cromartie and Quentin Skinner (Oxford: Clarendon Press, 2005).

Hobbes, Thomas, *Historia Ecclesiastica*, ed. and trans. Patricia Springborg, Patricia Stablein, and Paul Wilson (Paris: Champion, 2008).

Hobbes, Thomas, *Behemoth or The Long Parliament*, ed. Paul Seaward (Oxford: Clarendon Press, 2010).

Hobbes, Thomas, *Leviathan: The English and Latin Texts*, ed. Noel Malcolm (Oxford: Clarendon Press, 2012).

Hobbes, Thomas and John Bramhall, *Hobbes and Bramhall on Liberty and Necessity*, ed. Vere Chappell (Cambridge: Cambridge University Press, 1999).

Hooker, Richard, *Of the Laws of Ecclesiastical Polity*, ed. Arthur Stephen McGrade (Cambridge: Cambridge University Press, 1989).

Hooker, Richard, *Of the Laws of Ecclesiastical Polity*, ed. Arthur Stephen McGrade, 3 vols (Oxford: Oxford University Press, 2013).

House of Commons Journals: Volume 8, 1660–1667 (London, 1802).

Hyde, Edward, *A Brief View and Survey of the Dangerous and Pernicious Errors to Church and State, in Mr. Hobbes's Book, Entitled Leviathan* (Oxford, 1676).

James VI and I, *The Trew Law of Free Monarchies*. In *King James VI and I: Political Writings*, ed. J. P. Sommerville (Cambridge: Cambridge University Press, 1994), 62–84.

The Judgement of the Synode holden at Dort (London: John Bill, 1619).

Kennett, White, *A Sermon Preach'd at the Funeral of the Right Noble William Duke of Devonshire: With some memoirs of the family of Cavendish* (London, 1708).

Lagomarsino, David and Charles T. Wood (eds), *The Trial of Charles I: A Documentary History* (Hanover, NH: University Press of New England, 1989).

Lawson, George, *An Examination of the Political Part of Mr. Hobbs his Leviathan* (London, 1657).

Leibniz, Gottfried, 'The Common Concept of Justice', in Gottfried Leibniz, *Political Writings*, ed. Patrick Riley (Cambridge: Cambridge University Press, 1988), 45–64.

Leland, John, *A View of the Principal Deistical Writers that Have Appeared in England in the Last and Present Century* (London, 1754).

Lilburne, John, *The Free-man's Freedom Vindicated* (London, 1646).

Lipsius, Justus, *Two Books of Constancie*, ed. Rudolf Kirk, trans. Sir John Stradling (New Brunswick, NJ: Rutgers University Press, 1939).

Locke, John, *An Essay Concerning Human Understanding*, ed. Peter Nidditch (Oxford: Clarendon Press, 1975).

Locke, John, *Some Thoughts Concerning Education*, ed. Jean S. Yolton and John W. Yolton (Oxford: Clarendon Press, 1989).

Lucian, *Works*, vii, ed. M. D. Macleod (London: Heinemann, 1961).

Luther, *De servo arbitrio*. In *Luther and Erasmus: Free Will and Salvation*, ed. and trans. Philip S. Watson (London: SCM, 1969).

Machiavelli, Niccolò, *Discourses on Livy*, ed. and trans. Harvey C. Mansfield and Nathan Tarcov (Chicago, IL: University of Chicago Press, 1996).

Maro, Virgilius, *Opera P. Virgilii Maronis* (Cambridge, 1632).

Mede, Joseph, *Diatribae: Discourses on Divers Texts of Scripture* (London, 1642).

Milton, John, *Pro Populo Anglicano Defensio* (London, 1651).

Milton, John, *The Poetical Works of John Milton*, iv, ed. Edward Hawkins (Oxford: J. Parker, 1824).

Milton, John, *A Defence of the People of England*. In *Complete Prose Works of John Milton*, ed. Don M. Wolfe, trans. Donald C. Mackenzie (New Haven, CT: Yale University Press, 1966), iv, 301–537.

More, Henry, *The Immortality of the Soul, So farre forth as it is Demonstrable from the Knowledge of Nature and the Light of Reason* (London, 1659).

Moulin, Peter du, *The Buckler of the Faith* (London, 1620).

The New Oxford Annotated Bible, College Edition, 3rd edition (New York: Oxford University Press, 2001).

Nichols, Josias, *An Order of Houshold Instruction* (London, 1595).

Owen, John, *Of Schisme, The True Nature of it Discovered and Considered, With Reference to the present Differences in Religion* (Oxford, 1657).

Pagett, Ephraim, *Heresiography, or, a Description and History of the Hereticks and Sectaries Sprang Up in these Latter Times* (London, 1645).

Parker, Henry, *Observations upon Some of His Majesties Late Answers and Expresses* (London, 1642).

Pemble, William, *Vindiciae fidei* (Oxford, 1625).

Pepys, Samuel, *The Diary of Samuel Pepys*, ed. Robert Latham and William Matthews, 11 vols (London: Bell and Hyman, 1970–83).

Perkins, William, *A Golden Chaine* (Cambridge, 1595).

Perkins, William, *A Reformed Catholike* (Cambridge, 1598).

Perkins, William, *A Christian and Plaine Treatise of the Manner and Order of Predestination*, trans. Francis Cacot and Thomas Tuke (London, 1606).

Pierce, Thomas, *Autokatakrisis, or Self-Condemnation Exemplified* (London, 1658).

Pighius, Albertus, *De libero hominis arbitrio et divina gratia* (Cologne, 1542).

Plato, *Complete Works*, ed. John M. Cooper (Indianapolis, IN: Hackett, 1997).

Plato, *Theaetetus and Sophist*, ed. Christopher Rowe (Cambridge: Cambridge University Press, 2015).

Prideaux, Humphrey, *A Letter to the Deists* (London, 1696).

Reynolds, Edward, *A Treatise on the Passions and Faculties of the Soule of Man* (London, 1640).

Ross, Alexander, *Leviathan Drawn out with a Hook* (London, 1653).

Rousseau, Jean-Jacques, *Du contrat social; ou principes du droit politique* (Amsterdam, 1762).

Salwey, Arthur, *Halting Stigmatiz'd in a Sermon Preached to the Honorable House of Commons* (London, 1644).

Scudder, Henry, *Gods Warning to England by the Voyce of His Rod ... A Sermon Preached ... before the Honourable House of Commons* (London, 1644).

Sidney, Algernon, *Court Maxims*, ed. Hans W. Blom, Eco Haitsma-Mulier, and Ronald Janse (Cambridge: Cambridge University Press, 1996).

Sidney, Algernon, *Discourses Concerning Government*, ed. Thomas G. West (Indianapolis, IN: Liberty Fund, 1996).

Spinoza, Benedict de, *Theological-Political Treatise*, ed. and trans. Jonathan Israel and Michael Silverthorne (Cambridge: Cambridge University Press, 2007).

Stephens, William, *An Account of the Growth of Deism in England* (London, 1696).

Suarez, Francesco, *Varia opuscula theologica* (Moguntiae, 1600).

Suarez, Francesco, *Metaphysicarum Disputationum Tomi Duo* (Moguntiae, 1614).

Templer, John, *Idea theologiae Leviathanis* (Cambridge, 1673).

Tenison, Thomas, *The Creed of Mr. Hobbes Examined* (London, 1670).

Tindal, Matthew, *The Rights of the Christian Church Asserted, Against the Romish, and All Other Priests Who Claim an Independent Power over It* (London, 1706).

Tindal, Matthew, *Christianity as Old as the Creation: Or, the Gospel, A Republication of the Religion of Nature* (London, 1730).

L. P. [Toland, John], *Two Essays Sent in a Letter from Oxford to a Nobleman in London* (London, 1695).

Toland, John, *Christianity Not Mysterious, or, A Treatise Shewing That There Is Nothing in the Gospel Contrary to Reason, Nor Above It: And That No Christian Doctrine Can be Properly Call'd a Mystery* (London, 1696).

Twisse, William, *The Doctrine of the Synod of Dort and Arles Reduced to the Practise. With a consideration thereof* (Amsterdam, 1631).

Twisse, William, *The Riches of Gods Love unto the Vessells of Mercy* (Oxford, 1653).

Wallis, John, *Elenchus Geometriae Hobbianae* (Oxford, 1655).

Wallis, John, *Hobbius Heauton-timoroumenos. Or a consideration of Mr. Hobbes his dialogues. In an epistolary discourse, addressed to the Hon. R. Boyle* (London, 1662).

Ward, Seth, *In Thomae Hobbii Philosophiam Exercitatio Epistolica* (Oxford, 1656).

Ward, Seth and John Wallis, *Vindiciae academiarum* (Oxford, 1654).

Williams, John, *Great Britains Salomon* (London, 1625).

Zanchi, Girolamo, *Hieronymi Zanchii Tractationum theologicarum volumen* (Neostadii Palatinatus, 1603).

Secondary Texts

Abizadeh, Arash, 'The Representation of Hobbesian Sovereignty: *Leviathan* as Mythology'. In *Hobbes Today: Insights for the 21st Century*, ed. S. A. Lloyd (Cambridge: Cambridge University Press, 2013), 113–52.

Abizadeh, Arash, 'Publicity, Privacy, and Religious Toleration in Hobbes's *Leviathan*', *Modern Intellectual History* 10.2 (2013), 261–91.

Abizadeh, Arash, 'Hobbes's Conventionalist Theology, the Trinity, and God as an Artificial Person by Fiction', *The Historical Journal* 60.4 (2017), 915–41.

Allen, Danielle, *Why Plato Wrote* (Chichester: John Wiley & Sons, 2010).

Allison, C. F., *The Rise of Moralism: The Proclamation of the Gospel from Hooker to Baxter* (London: SPCK, 1966).

Arendt, Hannah, 'Truth and Politics'. In Hannah Arendt, *Between Past and Future* (New York: Penguin, 2006), 223–59.

Armstrong, Karen, *Fields of Blood: Religion and the History of Violence* (New York: Knopf, 2014).

Asad, Talal, 'The Construction of Religion as an Anthropological Category'. In Talal Asad, *Genealogies of Religion: Discipline and Reasons of Power in Christianity and Islam* (London and Baltimore, MD: Johns Hopkins University Press, 1993).

Attridge, Harold (ed.), *HarperCollins Study Bible* (New York: Harper One, 2006).

Bagby, Laurie M. Johnson, *Thomas Hobbes: Turning Point for Honour* (Plymouth: Lexington Books, 2009).

Baldini, Artemio Enzo, 'Censures de l'Eglise romaine contre Hobbes: *De Cive* et *Léviathan*', *Bulletin Hobbes XIII, Archives de Philosophie* 64.2 (2001), 2–7.

Barnouw, Jeffrey, 'The Separation of Reason and Faith in Bacon and Hobbes, and Leibniz's Theodicy', *Journal of the History of Ideas* 42.4 (1981), 607–28.

Barry, Brian, 'Warrender and His Critics', *Philosophy* 43.164 (1968), 117–37.

Baumgold, Deborah, *Hobbes's Political Thought* (Cambridge: Cambridge University Press, 1988).

Beiner, Ronald, 'Machiavelli, Hobbes, and Rousseau on Civil Religion', *The Review of Politics* 55.4 (1993), 617–38.

Beiner, Ronald, *Civil Religion: A Dialogue in the History of Political Philosophy* (Cambridge and New York: Cambridge University Press, 2010).

Beiner, Ronald, 'James Harrington on the Hebrew Commonwealth', *The Review of Politics* 76.2 (2014), 169–93.

Bejan, Teresa M., 'Teaching the *Leviathan*', *Oxford Review of Education* 36 (2010), 607–26.

Bejan, Teresa M., 'Difference without Disagreement: Rethinking Hobbes on "Independency" and Toleration', *The Review of Politics* 78.1 (2016), 1–25.

Bejan, Teresa M., *Mere Civility: Disagreement and the Limits of Toleration* (Cambridge, MA: Harvard University Press, 2017).

Berman, David, 'Deism, Immortality and the Art of Theological Lying'. In *Deism, Masonry and the Enlightenment*, ed. J. A. Leo Lemay (Newark, NJ: University of Delaware Press, 1987), 61–78.

Berman, David, *A History of Atheism in Britain: From Hobbes to Russell* (London: Routledge, 1990).

Bobbio, Norberto, *Thomas Hobbes and the Natural Law Tradition*, trans. Daniela Gobetti (Chicago, IL: University of Chicago Press, 1993).

Bourdin, Bernard, *La genèse théologico-politique de l'Etat moderne: La controverse de Jacques Ier d'Angleterre avec le cardinal Bellarmin* (Paris: Presses Universitaires de France, 2004).

Braddick, Michael, *God's Fury, England's Fire: A New History of the English Civil Wars* (London: Penguin, 2008).

Bradshaw, Paul F., *Rites of Ordination: Their History and Theology* (Collegeville, MN: Liturgical Press, 2013).

Brady, Thomas, *German Histories in the Age of Reformations* (Cambridge: Cambridge University Press, 2009).

Brandon, Eric, *The Coherence of Hobbes's 'Leviathan': Civil and Religious Authority Combined* (London: Continuum, 2007).

Brietz Monta, Susannah, 'Rendering unto Caesar: The Rhetorics of Divided Loyalties in Tudor England'. In *Martyrdom and Terrorism: Pre-Modern to Contemporary Perspectives*, ed. Dominic Janes and Alex Houen (Oxford: Oxford University Press, 2014), 59–86.

Brito Vieira, Mónica, *The Elements of Representation in Hobbes: Aesthetics, Theatre, Law, and Theology in the Construction of Hobbes's Theory of the State* (Leiden and Boston, MA: Brill, 2009).

Bulman, William, 'Hobbes's Publisher and the Political Business of Enlightenment', *The Historical Journal* 59.2 (2016), 339–64.

Burgess, Glenn, 'The Divine Right of Kings Reconsidered', *The English Historical Review* 425 (1992), 837–61.

Burgess, Glenn, 'Introduction: Religion and the Historiography of the English Civil War'. In *England's Wars of Religion Revisited*, ed. Charles Prior and Glenn Burgess (Aldershot: Ashgate, 2011), 1–25.

Button, Mark E., *Contract, Culture, and Citizenship: Transformative Liberalism from Hobbes to Rawls* (University Park, PA: Pennsylvania State University Press, 2010).

Casanova, José, *Public Religions in the Modern World* (Chicago, IL: University of Chicago Press, 1994).

Cavanaugh, William, *The Myth of Religious Violence* (Oxford: Oxford University Press, 2009).

Champion, Justin, *The Pillars of Priestcraft Shaken: The Church of England and its Enemies 1660–1730* (Cambridge: Cambridge University Press, 1992).

Champion, Justin, *Republican Learning: John Toland and the Crisis of Christian Culture, 1696–1722* (Manchester: Manchester University Press, 2003).

Champion, Justin, 'Decoding the *Leviathan*: Doing the History of Ideas through Images, 1651–1714'. In *Printed Images in Early Modern Britain: Essays in Interpretation*, ed. Michael Cyril William Hunter (Farnham: Ashgate, 2010), 255–76.

Chestnut, Glenn F., *The First Christian Histories: Eusebius, Socrates, Sozomen, Theodoret and Evagrius* (Paris: Editions Beauchesne, 1986).

Coleman, Frank M., 'Thomas Hobbes and the Hebreic Bible', *History of Political Thought* 25.4 (2004), 642–69.

Colie, Rosalie L., 'Spinoza and the Early English Deists', *Journal of the History of Ideas* 20.1 (1959), 23–46.

Collins, Jeffrey, 'Christian Ecclesiology and the Composition of *Leviathan*: A Newly Discovered Letter to Thomas Hobbes', *The Historical Journal* 43.1 (2000), 217–31.

Collins, Jeffrey, *The Allegiance of Thomas Hobbes* (Oxford: Oxford University Press, 2005).

Collins, Jeffrey, 'Silencing Thomas Hobbes: The Presbyterians and *Leviathan*'. In *The Cambridge Companion to Hobbes's Leviathan*, ed. Patricia Springborg (Cambridge: Cambridge University Press, 2007), 478–500.

Collins, Jeffrey, 'Thomas Hobbes, Heresy, and the Theological Project of *Leviathan*', *Hobbes Studies* 26.1 (2013), 6–33.

Collins, Jeffrey, 'Thomas Hobbes's Ecclesiastical History'. In *The Oxford Handbook of Hobbes*, ed. A. P. Martinich and Kinch Hoekstra (Oxford: Oxford University Press, 2016), 520–44.

Collins, John, *Introduction to the Hebrew Bible* (Minneapolis, MN: Fortress Press, 2004).

Conrad, Joseph, *The Complete Works of Conrad: Lord Jim* (New York: Doubleday, 1925).

Cooper, Julie E., *Secular Powers: Humility in Modern Political Thought* (Chicago, IL: Chicago University Press, 2013).

Craig, Leon, *The Platonian Leviathan* (Toronto: University of Toronto Press, 2013).

Crignon, Philippe, 'L'altération du christianisme. Hobbes et la trinité', *Les études philosophiques* 81.2 (2007), 235–63.

Cromartie, Alan, 'The God of Thomas Hobbes', *The Historical Journal* 51.4 (2008), 857–79.

Cromartie, Alan and Quentin Skinner, 'General Introduction'. In *Thomas Hobbes: Writings on Common Law and Hereditary Right*, ed. Alan Cromartie and Quentin Skinner (Oxford: Clarendon Press, 2005).

Crowley, Weldon S., 'Erastianism in England to 1640', *Journal of Church and State* 32.3 (1990), 549–66.

Csikszentmihalyi, Mark A., 'The Golden Rule in Confucianism'. In *The Golden Rule: The Ethics of Reciprocity in World Religions*, ed. Jacob Neusner and Bruce D. Chilton (London: Continuum, 2008), 157–69.

Cudd, Ann, 'Contractarianism', *Stanford Encyclopedia of Philosophy*, <http://plato.stanford.edu/entries/contractarianism/>, accessed 16 June 2017.

Curley, Edwin, '"I durst not write so boldly" or, How to Read Hobbes' Theological-Political Treatise'. In *Hobbes e Spinoza*, ed. D. Bostrenghi (Napoli: Bibliopolis, 1992), 497–593.

Curley, Edwin, 'Purposes and Features of this Edition'. In Thomas Hobbes, *Leviathan: With Selected Variants from the Latin Edition of* 1688, ed. Edwin Curley (Indianapolis, IN: Hackett, 1994), pp. lxxiii–lxxiv.

Curley, Edwin, 'Calvin and Hobbes, or Hobbes as an Orthodox Christian', *Journal of the History of Philosophy* 34.2 (1996), 257–71.

Curley, Edwin, 'The Covenant with God in *Leviathan*'. In *Leviathan After 350 Years*, ed. Tom Sorell and Luc Foisneau (Oxford: Clarendon Press, 2004), 199–216.

Curley, Edwin, 'Hobbes and the Cause of Religious Toleration'. In *The Cambridge Companion to Hobbes's Leviathan*, ed. Patricia Springborg (Cambridge: Cambridge University Press, 2007), 309–34.

Curley, Edwin, 'Spinoza's Exchange with Albert Burgh', in *Spinoza's 'Theological-Political Treatise': A Critical Guide*, ed. Yitzhak Melamed and Michael Rosenthal (Cambridge: Cambridge University Press, 2010), 11–28.

Cuttica, Casare, *Sir Robert Filmer and the Patriotic Monarch* (Manchester: Manchester University Press, 2015).

Cuttica, Cesare and Glenn Burgess (eds), *Monarchism and Absolutism in Early Modern Europe* (London: Pickering & Chatto, 2015).

Dagron, Robert, 'Orient-Occident: Césaro-papisme et théorie des deux pouvoirs face à la modernité', *Revue d'éthique et de théologie morale* 227 (2004), 143–57.

Damrosch, Leopold, Jr, 'Hobbes as Reformation Theologian: Implications of the Free-Will Controversy', *Journal of the History of Ideas* 40.3 (1979), 339–52.

Daniell, David, *The Bible in English* (New Haven, CT: Yale University Press, 2003).

Davis, Richard H., 'A Hindu Golden Rule, in Context'. In *The Golden Rule: The Ethics of Reciprocity in World Religions*, ed. Jacob Neusner and Bruce D. Chilton (London: Continuum, 2008), 146–56.

Deckard, Michael Funk, 'A Sudden Surprise of the Soul: The Passion of Wonder in Hobbes and Descartes', *The Heythrop Journal* 49.6 (2008), 948–63.

Deigh, John, 'Reply to Martinich', *European Hobbes Society*, <http://www.europeanhobbessociety.org/newpublications/debate-martinich-deigh-on-law-2-deigh/>, accessed 16 June 2017.

Dennett, Daniel, *Breaking the Spell: Religion as a Natural Phenomenon* (New York: Penguin, 2007).

Douglass, Robin, 'The Body Politic "is a fictitious body": Hobbes on Imagination and Fiction', *Hobbes Studies* 27.2 (2014), 126–47.

Douglass, Robin, *Hobbes and Rousseau: Nature, Free Will, and the Passions* (Oxford: Oxford University Press, 2015).

Dubuisson, Daniel, *The Western Construction of Religion: Myths, Knowledge and Ideology*, trans. William Sayers (London and Baltimore, MD: Johns Hopkins University Press, 2003).

Dybikowski, J., 'Collins, Anthony (1676–1729)', *Oxford Dictionary of National Biography*, <http://www.oxforddnb.com/view/article/5933>, accessed 16 June 2017.

Dyzenhaus, David, 'Hobbes and the Legitimacy of Law', *Law and Philosophy* 20.5 (2001), 461–98.

Dyzenhaus, David, 'The Genealogy of Legal Positivism', *Oxford Journal of Legal Studies* 24.1 (2004), 39–67.

Dyzenhaus, David and Thomas Poole (eds), *Hobbes and the Law* (Cambridge: Cambridge University Press, 2012).

Eggers, Daniel, 'Hobbes and Game Theory Revisited', *Southern Journal of Philosophy* 49.3 (2011), 193–226.

Eisenstein, Elizabeth L., *The Printing Revolution in Early Modern Europe* (Cambridge: Cambridge University Press, 2012).

Elazar, Daniel J., 'Hobbes Confronts Scripture', *Jewish Political Studies* 4.2 (1992), 3–24.

Eppley, David, 'Royal Supremacy'. In *A Companion to Richard Hooker*, ed. Torrance Kirby (Leiden and Boston, MA: Brill, 2008), 503–34.

Farneti, Roberto, 'Hobbes on Salvation'. In *The Cambridge Companion to Hobbes's Leviathan*, ed. Patricia Springborg (Cambridge: Cambridge University Press, 2007), 291–308.

Farr, James, 'Atomes of Scripture: Hobbes and the Politics of Biblical Interpretation'. In *Thomas Hobbes and Political Theory*, ed. Mary Dietz (Lawrence, KS: University Press of Kansas, 1990), 172–96.

Ferrero, Guglielmo, *Principles of Power: Great Political Crises of History* (Westport, CT: Greenwood Press, 1984).

Figgis, J. Neville, 'Erastus and Erastianism', *Journal of Theological Studies* 2.5 (1900), 66–101.

Flathman, Richard E., *Thomas Hobbes: Skepticism, Individuality, and Chastened Politics* (Lanham, MD: Rowman & Littlefield, 2002).

Foisneau, Luc, *Hobbes et la Toute-Puissance de Dieu* (Paris: Presses Universitaires de France, 2000).

Fontaine, Lauréline (ed.), *Droit et légitimité* (Paris: Anthémis, 2011).

Frost, Samantha, 'Faking It: Hobbes's Thinking-Bodies and the Ethics of Dissimulation', *Political Theory* 29.1 (2001), 30–57.

Frost, Samantha, *Lessons from a Materialist Thinker: Hobbesian Reflections on Ethics and Politics* (Stanford, CA: Stanford University Press, 2008).

Garfinkle, Steven, 'Ancient Near Eastern City-States'. In *The Oxford Handbook of the State in the Ancient Near East and Mediterranean*, ed. P. Fibiger Bang and W. Scheidel (New York: Oxford University Press, 2013), 94–119.

Garsten, Bryan, *Saving Persuasion: A Defense of Rhetoric and Judgment* (Cambridge, MA: Harvard University Press, 2006).

Garsten, Bryan, 'Religion and Representation in Hobbes'. In *Leviathan*, ed. Ian Shapiro (New Haven, CT: Yale University Press, 2010), 519–46.

Gaus, Gerald, 'Hobbes's Challenge to Public Reason Liberalism: Public Reason and Religious Convictions in *Leviathan*'. In *Hobbes Today: Insights for the 21st Century*, ed. S. A. Lloyd (Cambridge: Cambridge University Press, 2007), 155–77.

Gauthier, David, *The Logic of Leviathan* (Oxford: Oxford University Press, 1969).

Gauthier, David, *Morals by Agreement* (Oxford: Oxford University Press, 1986).

Gauthier, David, 'Hobbes: The Laws of Nature', *Pacific Philosophy Quarterly* 82.3–4 (2001), 258–84.

Geering, Lloyd, *Christianity Without God* (Santa Rosa, CA: Polebridge, 2002).

Gibson, John, *Genesis*, i (Edinburgh: The St. Andrew Press, 1981).

Gierke, Otto von, *Natural Law and the Theory of Society, 1500–1800*, i, trans. Ernest Barker (Cambridge: Cambridge University Press, 1934).

Glover, Willis B., 'God and Thomas Hobbes'. In *Hobbes Studies*, ed. K. C. Brown (Oxford: Blackwell, 1965), 141–68.

Goldie, Mark, 'Ideology'. In *Political Ideology and Conceptual Change*, ed. Terrance Ball, James Farr, and Russell L. Hanson (Cambridge: Cambridge University Press, 1989), 266–91.

Goldie, Mark, 'The Reception of Hobbes'. In *The Cambridge History of Political Thought 1450–1700*, ed. J. H. Burns with Mark Goldie (Cambridge: Cambridge University Press, 1991), 589–615.

Goldie, Mark, 'Priestcraft and the Birth of Whiggism'. In *Political Discourses in Early Modern Britain*, ed. Nicholas Phillipson and Quentin Skinner (Cambridge: Cambridge University Press, 1993), 209–31.

Gorski, Philip, *The Disciplinary Revolution: Calvinism and the Rise of the State in Early Modern Europe* (Chicago, IL: University of Chicago Press, 2003).

Green, Michael J., 'Authorization and Political Authority in Hobbes', *Journal of the History of Philosophy* 53.1 (2015), 25–47.

Gregory, Brad S., *Salvation at Stake: Christian Martyrdom in Early Modern Europe* (Cambridge, MA: Harvard University Press, 1999).

Guibbory, Achsah, *Christian Identity, Jews, and Israel in Seventeenth-Century England* (Oxford: Oxford University Press, 2010).

Haidt, Jonathan, *The Righteous Mind* (London: Penguin, 2013).

Haller, William, *Liberty and Reformation in the Puritan Revolution* (New York: Columbia University Press, 1953).

Hallisey, Charles, 'The Golden Rule in Buddhism'. In *The Golden Rule: The Ethics of Reciprocity in World Religions*, ed. Jacob Neusner and Bruce D. Chilton (London: Continuum, 2008), 129–45.

Hammill, Graham, *The Mosaic Constitution: Political Theology and Imagination from Machiavelli to Milton* (Chicago, IL: University of Chicago Press, 2012).

Hampton, Jean, *Hobbes and the Social Contract Tradition* (Cambridge: Cambridge University Press, 1986).

Hampton, Jean, 'Hobbes and Ethical Naturalism', *Philosophical Perspectives* 6 (1992), 333–53.

Hanin, Mark, 'Thomas Hobbes's Theory of Conscience', *History of Political Thought* 33.1 (2012), 55–85.

Harris, James A., *Of Liberty and Necessity: The Free Will Debate in Eighteenth-Century British Philosophy* (Cambridge: Cambridge University Press, 2005).

Harrison, Peter, *'Religion' and the Religions in the English Enlightenment* (Cambridge: Cambridge University Press, 1990).

Headley, John M., Hans J. Hillerbrand, and Anthony J. Papalas (eds), *Confessionalization in Europe, 1555–1700: Essays in Honor and Memory of Bodo Nischan* (Aldershot: Ashgate, 2004).

Hill, Christopher, *The World Turned Upside Down: Radical Ideas During the English Revolution* (London: Maurice Temple Smith, 1972).

Hill, Christopher, *The English Bible and the Seventeenth-Century Revolution* (London: Penguin Press, 1993).

Hillenbrand, Carole, *The Crusades: Islamic Perspectives* (Edinburgh: Edinburgh University Press, 1999).

Hirsi Ali, Ayaan, *Heretic: Why Islam Needs a Reformation Now* (New York: Harper, 2015).

Hitchens, Christopher, *God is Not Great: How Religion Poisons Everything* (New York: Twelve, 2009).

Hoekstra, Kinch, 'Tyrranus Rex *vs.* Leviathan', *Pacific Philosophical Quarterly* 82.3–4 (2001), 420–46.

Hoekstra, Kinch, 'The *de facto* Turn in Hobbes's Political Philosophy'. In *Leviathan After 350 Years*, ed. Tom Sorell and Luc Foisneau (Oxford: Clarendon Press, 2004), 33–74.

Hoekstra, Kinch, 'Disarming the Prophets: Thomas Hobbes and Predictive Power', *Rivista di Storia della Filosofia* 59.1 (2004), 97–153.

Hoekstra, Kinch, 'Hobbesian Equality'. In *Hobbes Today: Insights for the 21st Century*, ed. S. A. Lloyd (Cambridge: Cambridge University Press, 2012), 76–112.

Holden, Thomas, 'Hobbes's First Cause', *Journal of the History of Philosophy* 53.4 (2015), 647–67.

Holt, Mack, *The French Wars of Religion, 1562–1629* (Cambridge: Cambridge University Press, 1995).

Homerin, Th. Emil, 'The Golden Rule in Islam'. In *The Golden Rule: The Ethics of Reciprocity in World Religions*, ed. Jacob Neusner and Bruce D. Chilton (London: Continuum, 2008), 99–115.

Hood, F. C., *The Divine Politics of Thomas Hobbes: An Interpretation of Leviathan* (Oxford: Clarendon Press, 1964).

Hudson, Wayne, *The English Deists: Studies in Early Enlightenment* (London: Pickering & Chatto, 2009).

Hudson, Wayne, 'Atheism and Deism Demythologized'. In *Atheism and Deism Revalued*, ed. Wayne Hudson, Diego Lucci, and Jeffrey R. Wigelsworth (Burlington: Ashgate, 2014), 13–23.

Israel, Jonathan, *Radical Enlightenment: Philosophy and the Making of Modernity 1650–1750* (Oxford: Oxford University Press, 2001).

Israel, Jonathan, *Revolutionary Ideas: An Intellectual History of the French Revolution* (Princeton, NJ: Princeton University Press, 2004).

Jackson, Nicholas D., *Hobbes, Bramhall and the Politics of Liberty and Necessity: A Quarrel of the Civil Wars and Interregnum* (Cambridge: Cambridge University Press, 2007).

Jacob, Margaret, *The Radical Enlightenment: Pantheists, Freemasons and Republicans* (London: Allen & Unwin, 1981).

Jesseph, Douglas, *Squaring the Circle: The War Between Hobbes and Wallis* (Chicago, IL: University of Chicago Press, 1999).

Jesseph, Douglas, 'Hobbes's Atheism', *Midwest Studies in Philosophy* 26 (2002), 140–66.

Johnston, David, *The Rhetoric of Leviathan: Thomas Hobbes and the Politics of Cultural Transformation* (Princeton, NJ: Princeton University Press, 1986).

Jones, G. Lloyd, *The Discovery of Hebrew in Tudor England: A Third Language* (Manchester: Manchester University Press, 1983).

Jones, Meirav, ' "My Highest Priority Was to Absolve the Divine Laws": The Theory and Politics of Hobbes' *Leviathan* in a War of Religion', *Political Studies* 65.1 (2017), 248–63.

Jue, Jeffrey K., *Heaven Upon Earth: Joseph Mede (1586–1638) and the Legacy of Millenarianism* (Dordrecht: Springer, 2006).

Kingdon, Robert M., 'Calvinism and Resistance Theory, 1550–1580'. In *The Cambridge History of Political Thought 1450–1700*, ed. J. H. Burns with Mark Goldie (Cambridge: Cambridge University Press, 1991), 193–218.

Kristiansson, Magnus and Johan Tralau, 'Hobbes's Hidden Monster: A New Interpretation of the Frontispiece of *Leviathan*', *European Journal of Political Theory* 13.3 (2014), 299–320.

Lake, Peter and Steve Pincus, 'Rethinking the Public Sphere in Early Modern England', *Journal of British Studies* 45.2 (2006), 270–92.

Leijenhorst, Cees, *The Mechanisation of Aristotelianism* (Leiden: Brill, 2002).

Lessay, Franck, 'Le vocabulaire de la personne'. In *Hobbes et son vocabulaire: études de lexicographie philosophique*, ed. Yves Charles Zarka (Paris: Vrin, 1992), 155–86.

Lessay, Franck, 'Hobbes and Sacred History'. In *Hobbes and History*, ed. G. A. J. Rogers and Tom Sorell (London: Routledge, 2000), 147–59.

Lessay, Franck, 'Hobbes's Covenant Theology and Its Political Implications'. In *Cambridge Companion to Hobbes's Leviathan*, ed. Patricia Springborg (Cambridge: Cambridge University Press, 2007), 243–70.

Lewalski, Barbara K., *Protestant Poetics and the Seventeenth-Century Religious Lyric* (Princeton, NJ: Princeton University Press, 1979).

Lewalski, Barbara K., *The Life of John Milton: A Critical Biography*, revised edition (Oxford: Blackwell Publishing, 2003).

Lilla, Mark, *The Stillborn God: Religion, Politics, and the Modern West* (New York: Knopf, 2008).

Lloyd, S. A., *Ideals as Interests in Hobbes's 'Leviathan': The Power of Mind over Matter* (Cambridge: Cambridge University Press, 1992).

Lloyd, S. A., 'Coercion, Ideology, and Education in Hobbes's *Leviathan*'. In *Reclaiming the History of Ethics*, ed. A. Reath, B. Herman, and C. Korsgaard (Cambridge: Cambridge University Press, 1997), 32–65.

Lloyd, S. A., *Morality in the Philosophy of Thomas Hobbes: Cases in the Law of Nature* (Cambridge: Cambridge University Press, 2009).

Lloyd, S. A., 'Authorization and Moral Responsibility in the Philosophy of Hobbes', *Hobbes Studies* 29.2 (2016), 169–88.

Lloyd, S. A., 'Locating Sovereignty in Complex Systems'. In *Sovereignty and the New Executive Order*, ed. Claire Finkelstein (Oxford: Oxford University Press, forthcoming).

Lubienski, Zbigniew, *Die Grundlagen des ethisch-politischen System von Hobbes* (Munich: E. Reingardt, 1932).

Ludwig, Bernd, *Die Wiederentdeckung des Epikureischen Naturrechtes* (Frankfurt am Main: Klostermann, 1998).

Malcolm, Noel, 'Thomas Hobbes and Voluntarist Theology', PhD thesis, University of Cambridge, Cambridge (1982).

Malcolm, Noel, *Aspects of Hobbes* (Oxford: Clarendon Press, 2002).

Malcolm, Noel, '*Leviathan* and Biblical Criticism'. In *Leviathan After 350 Years*, ed. Tom Sorell and Luc Foisneau (Oxford: Oxford University Press, 2004), 241–64.

Malcolm, Noel, 'General Introduction'. In *Leviathan*, i, ed. Noel Malcolm (Oxford: Clarendon Press, 2012).

Malcolm, Noel, 'Textual Introduction'. In *Leviathan*, i, ed. Noel Malcolm (Oxford: Clarendon Press, 2012).

Manent, Pierre, *The City of Man*, trans. Marc A. LePain (Princeton, NJ: Princeton University Press, 1994).

Martin, David, *On Secularization: Towards a Revised General Theory* (Aldershot: Ashgate, 2005).

Martinich, A. P., *The Two Gods of Leviathan: Thomas Hobbes on Religion and Politics* (Cambridge: Cambridge University Press, 1992).

Martinich, A. P., 'On the Proper Interpretation of Hobbes's Philosophy', *Journal of the History of Philosophy* 34.2 (1996), 272–83.

Martinich, A. P., 'The Interpretation of Covenants in *Leviathan*', in *Leviathan After 350 Years*, ed. Tom Sorell and Luc Foisneau (Oxford: Clarendon Press, 2004), 217–40.

Martinich, A. P., *Hobbes* (London: Routledge, 2005).

Martinich, A. P., 'Hobbes's Erastianism and Interpretation', *Journal of the History of Ideas* 70.1 (2009), 143–63.

Martinich, A. P., 'On Hobbes's English Calvinism: Necessity, Omnipotence, and Goodness', *Philosophical Readings* 4.1 (2012), 18–30.

Martinich, A. P., 'L'auteur du péché et les démoniaques'. In *Jean Calvin et Thomas Hobbes: Naissance de la modernité politique*, ed. Oliver Abel, Pierre-François Moreau, and Dominique Weber (Geneva: Labor et Fides, 2013), 43–71.

Martinich, A. P., 'Law and Self-Preservation in *Leviathan*: On Misinterpreting Hobbes 1650–1700'. In *The Persistence of the Sacred in Modern Thought*, ed. Chris L. Firestone and Nathan A. Jacobs (South Bend, IN: University of Notre Dame Press, 2013), 38–65.

Martinich, A. P., 'Authorization and Representation in Hobbes's *Leviathan*'. In *The Oxford Handbook of Hobbes*, ed. A. Martinich and K. Hoekstra (New York: Oxford University Press, 2016), 315–38.

Martinich, A. P., 'The Laws of Nature are the Laws of God in *Leviathan*', *European Hobbes Society*, <http://www.europeanhobbessociety.org/newpublications/debate-martinich-deigh-on-law-1-martinich/>, accessed 16 June 2017.

McGee, J. Sears, 'On Misidentifying Puritans: The Case of Thomas Adams', *Albion* 30.3 (1998), 401–18.

McGee, J. Sears, 'Thomas Adams', in *The Dictionary of National Biography*, <http://www.oxforddnb.com/index/0/101000131>, accessed 16 June 2017.

McNeilly, F. S., 'Egoism in Hobbes', *The Philosophical Quarterly* 16 (1966), 193–206.

Michael, Emily, 'Renaissance Theories of Body, Soul, and Mind'. In *Psyche and Soma: Physicians and Metaphysicians on the Mind–Body Problem from Antiquity to Enlightenment*, ed. John P. Wright and Paul Potter (Oxford: Clarendon Press, 2000), 147–72.

Milton, Philip, 'Hobbes, Heresy and Lord Arlington', *History of Political Thought* 14.4 (1993), 501–46.

Mintz, Samuel I., *The Hunting of Leviathan* (Cambridge: Cambridge University Press, 1962).

Mitchell, Joshua, 'Luther and Hobbes on the Question: Who Was Moses, Who Was Christ?', *The Journal of Politics* 53.3 (1991), 676–700.

Moazami, Mahna, 'The Golden Rule in Zoroastrianism'. In *The Golden Rule: The Ethics of Reciprocity in World Religions*, ed. Jacob Neusner and Bruce D. Chilton (London: Continuum, 2008), 65–75.

Morrill, John, 'The Religious Context of the English Civil War', *Transactions of the Royal Historical Society*, 5th series, 34 (1984), 155–78.

Morris, Christopher W., *An Essay on the Modern State* (Cambridge: Cambridge University Press, 1998).

Morris, Christopher W., 'The State'. In *The Oxford Handbook of the History of Political Philosophy*, ed. George Klosko (Oxford: Oxford University Press, 2011), 544–60.

Mortimer, Sarah, 'Kingship and the "Apostolic Church", 1620–1650', *Reformation & Renaissance Review* 13.2 (2011), 225–46.

Mortimer, Sarah, 'Christianity and Civil Religion in Hobbes's *Leviathan*'. In *The Oxford Handbook of Hobbes*, ed. A. P. Martinich and Kinch Hoekstra (Oxford: Oxford University Press, 2016), 501–19.

Mortley, Raoul, *The Idea of Universal History from Hellenistic Philosophy to Early Christian Historiography* (Lewiston, NY: Edwin Mellen Press, 1996).

Muller, Richard A., *Post-Reformation Reformed Dogmatics: The Rise and Development of Reformed Orthodoxy, ca.1520 to ca.1725* (Grand Rapids, MI: Eerdmans, 2005).

Murphy, Mark, 'Hobbes on the Evil of Death', *Archiv für Geschichte der Philosophie* 82.1 (2000), 36–61.

Nauta, Lodi, 'Hobbes on Religion and the Church between *The Elements of Law* and *Leviathan*: A Dramatic Change of Direction?', *Journal of the History of Ideas* 63.4 (2002), 577–98.

Nelson, Eric, *The Hebrew Republic: Jewish Sources and the Transformation of European Political Thought* (Cambridge, MA: Harvard University Press, 2010).

Nelson, Eric, 'Translation as Correction: Hobbes in the 1660s and 1670s'. In *Why Concepts Matter: Translating Social and Political Thought*, ed. Martin Burke and Melvin Richter (Leiden and Boston, MA: Brill, 2012), 119–39.

Neusner, Jacob, 'The Golden Rule in Classical Judaism'. In *The Golden Rule: The Ethics of Reciprocity in World Religions*, ed. Jacob Neusner and Bruce D. Chilton (London: Continuum, 2008), 55–64.

Newey, Glen, *The Routledge Guidebook to Hobbes' Leviathan*, 2nd edition (London: Routledge, 2014).

Newey, Glen, 'First Politics, Second Nature: Political Representation in Hobbesish Mode', working MS.

Nichols, John, *The Progresses and Public Processions of Queen Elizabeth* (London: John Nichols and Son, 1823).

Nirenberg, David, *Anti-Judaism: The Western Tradition* (New York: W. W. Norton & Co., 2013).

Nongbri, Brent, *Before Religion: A History of a Modern Concept* (New Haven, CT: Yale University Press, 2013).

Oakeshott, Michael, *On History and Other Essays* (Indianapolis, IN: Liberty Fund, 1999).

O'Higgins, James, *Anthony Collins: The Man and His Works* (The Hague: Martinus Nijhoff, 1970).

Olsthoorn, Johan, 'Worse than Death: The Non-Preservationist Foundations of Hobbes's Moral Philosophy', *Hobbes Studies* 27.2 (2014), 148–70.

Osborn, Eric, *Tertullian: First Theologian of the West* (Cambridge: Cambridge University Press, 1997).

Ott, Konrad, *Moralbegründungen zur Einführung* (Hamburg: Junius, 2001).

Overhoff, Jürgen, *Hobbes's Theory of the Will* (Lanham, MD: Rowman & Littlefield, 2000).

Owen, J. Judd, 'The Tolerant Leviathan: Hobbes and the Paradox of Liberalism', *Polity* 37.1 (2005), 130–48.

Owen, J. Judd, *Making Religion Safe for Democracy* (Cambridge: Cambridge University Press, 2014).

Pacchi, Arrigo, 'Hobbes and Biblical Philology in Service of the State', *Topoi* 7.3 (1988), 231–9.

Pacchi, Arrigo, 'Hobbes and the Problem of God'. In *Perspectives on Thomas Hobbes*, ed. G. A. J. Rogers and Alan Ryan (Oxford: Oxford University Press, 1988), 171–88.

Paganini, Gianni, 'Hobbes, Gassendi and the Tradition of Political Epicureanism'. In *Der Garten und die Moderne: Epikureische Moral und Politik vom Humanismus bis zur Aufklärung*, ed. Gianni Paganini and Edoardo Tortarolo (Stuttgart: Fromman-Holzboog, 2004), 113–37.

Pagden, Anthony, *The Enlightenment and Why It Still Matters* (Oxford: Oxford University Press, 2013).

Parkin, Jon, *Science, Religion and Politics in Restoration England: Richard Cumberland's 'De legibus naturae'* (Woodbridge: The Boydell Press, 1999).

Parkin, Jon, *Taming the Leviathan: The Reception of the Political and Religious Ideas of Thomas Hobbes in England, 1640–1700* (Cambridge: Cambridge University Press, 2007).

Parkin, Jon, 'Baiting the Bear: The Anglican Attack on Hobbes in the Later 1660s', *History of Political Thought* 34.3 (2013), 421–58.

Parkin, Jon, 'Toleration'. In *The Oxford Handbook of British Seventeenth Century Philosophy*, ed. Peter Anstey (Oxford: Oxford University Press, 2013), 609–26.

Parkin, Jon, 'Hobbes and the Problem of Self-Censorship'. In *The Art of Veiled Speech: Self-Censorship from Aristophanes to Hobbes*, ed. Han Baltussen and Peter J. Davis (Philadelphia, PA: University of Pennsylvania Press, 2015), 293–317.

Parkin, Jon, 'Hobbes and the Reception of *Leviathan*', *Journal of the History of Ideas* 76.2 (2015), 289–300.

Parkin, Jon, 'Hobbes and Paradox'. In *The Oxford Handbook of Hobbes*, ed. A. P. Martinich and Kinch Hoekstra (Oxford: Oxford University Press, 2016), 624–42.

Pettit, Philip, *Made with Words: Hobbes on Language, Mind, and Politics* (Princeton, NJ: Princeton University Press, 2008).

Pilsner, Joseph, *The Specification of Human Actions in St Thomas Aquinas* (Oxford: Oxford University Press, 2006).

Pink, Thomas, 'Suarez, Hobbes and the Scholastic Tradition in Action Theory'. In *The Will and Human Action: From Antiquity to the Present Day*, ed. Thomas Pink and M. W. F. Stone (London and New York: Routledge, 2004), 127–53.

Pinker, Steven, *The Better Angels of our Nature: Why Violence Has Decline* (New York: Allen Lane, 2011).

Plamenatz, John, 'Mr. Warrender's Hobbes', *Political Studies* 5.3 (1957), 295–308.

Pocock, J. G. A., 'Time, History, and Eschatology in the Thought of Thomas Hobbes'. In J. G. A. Pocock, *Politics, Language, and Time* (New York: Athenaeum, 1971), 148–201.

Pocock, J. G. A., 'Historical Introduction'. In *The Political Works of James Harrington*, ed. J. G. A. Pocock (Cambridge: Cambridge University Press, 1977), 1–152.

Pocock, J. G. A., *Barbarism and Religion*, 6 vols (Cambridge: Cambridge University Press, 1999–2015).

Popkin, Richard, *The History of Skepticism*, revised edition (Oxford: Oxford University Press, 2003).

Porter, Roy, 'The Enlightenment in England'. In *The Enlightenment in National Context*, ed. Roy Porter and Mikulás Teich (Cambridge: Cambridge University Press, 1981), 1–18.

Prior, Charles W. A., 'Hebraism and the Problem of Church and State in England, 1642–1660', *The Seventeenth Century* 28.1 (2013), 37–61.

Purkiss, Diane, *The English Civil War* (New York: Basic Books, 2006).

Rawls, John, *A Theory of Justice* (Cambridge, MA: Belknap Press of Harvard University Press, 1971).

Rawls, John, *Political Liberalism* (New York: Columbia Press, 2005).

Rawls, John, *Lectures on the History of Political Philosophy*, ed. Samuel Freeman (Cambridge, MA: Belknap Press of Harvard University Press, 2007).

Reik, Miriam, *The Golden Lands of Thomas Hobbes* (Detroit: Wayne State University Press, 1977).

Riley-Smith, Jonathan, *The Crusades, Christianity, and Islam* (New York: Columbia University Press, 2011).

Robin, Corey, *The Reactionary Mind: Conservatism from Edmund Burke to Sarah Palin* (New York: Oxford University Press, 2011).

Rose, Jacqueline, *Godly Kingship in Restoration England: The Politics of the Royal Supremacy, 1660–1688* (Cambridge: Cambridge University Press, 2011).

Rosenberg, Roy, 'Yahweh Becomes King', *Journal of Biblical Literature* 85.3 (1966), 297–307.

Ryan, Alan, 'Hobbes, Toleration, and the Inner Life'. In *The Nature of Political Theory*, ed. David Miller and Larry Siedentop (Oxford: Clarendon Press, 1983), 197–218.

Ryan, Alan, 'A More Tolerant Hobbes?' In *Justifying Toleration*, ed. Susan Mendus (Cambridge: Cambridge University Press, 1988), 37–59.

Salmon, J. H. M., 'Catholic Resistance Theory, Ultramontanism, and the Royalist Response, 1580–1620'. In *The Cambridge History of Political Thought 1450–1700*, ed. J. H. Burns with Mark Goldie (Cambridge: Cambridge University Press, 1991), 219–53.

Scheible, Kristin, 'The Formulation and Significance of the Golden Rule in Buddhism'. In *The Golden Rule: The Ethics of Reciprocity in World Religions*, ed. Jacob Neusner and Bruce D. Chilton (London: Continuum, 2008), 116–28.

Schino, A. L., 'Tre lettere inedite di Gabriel Naudé', *Rivista di storia della philosophia* 4 (1987), 697–708.

Schmitter, Amy, 'Passions and Affections'. In *The Oxford Handbook of British Philosophy of the 17th Century*, ed. Peter R. Anstey (Oxford: Oxford University Press, 2013), 442–71.

Schuhmann, Karl, *Hobbes: Une chronique* (Paris: Vrin, 1998).

Schuhmann, Karl, 'Le Short Tract, première oeuvre philosophique de Hobbes'. In Karl Schuhmann, *Selected Papers on Renaissance Philosophy and on Thomas Hobbes*, ed. P. Steenbakkers and C. Leijenhorst (Dordrecht: Kluwer, 2004), 227–59.

Schwartz, Joel, 'Hobbes and the Two Kingdoms of God', *Polity* 18.1 (1985), 7–24.

Schwartz, Regina, *The Curse of Cain: The Violent Legacy of Monotheism* (Chicago, IL: University of Chicago Press, 1997).

Scodel, Joshua, 'The Cowleyan Pindaric Ode and Sublime Diversions'. In *A Nation Transformed: England after the Restoration*, ed. Alan Houston and Steve Pincus (Cambridge: Cambridge University Press, 2001), 180–210.

Scott, John T., 'The Illustrative Education of Rousseau's *Emile*', *American Political Science Review* 108.3 (2014), 533–46.

Serjeantson, R. W., 'Herbert of Cherbury before Deism: The Early Reception of the *De veritate*', *The Seventeenth Century* 16.2 (2001), 217–38.

Serjeantson, R. W., 'Hobbes, the Universities and the History of Philosophy'. In *The Philosopher in Early Modern Europe: The Nature of a Contested Identity*, ed. Conal Condren, Stephen Gaukroger, and Ian Hunter (Cambridge: Cambridge University Press, 2006), 113–39.

Serjeantson, R. W., 'The Soul'. In *The Oxford Handbook of Philosophy in Early Modern Europe*, ed. Desmond Clarke and Catherine Wilson (Oxford: Oxford University Press, 2011), 119–41.

Sharpe, Kevin, *The Personal Rule of Charles I* (New Haven, CT: Yale University Press, 1992).

Sharpe, Kevin, 'Private Conscience and Public Duty in the Writings of Charles I', *Historical Journal* 40.3 (1997), 643–65.

Siedentop, Larry, *Inventing the Individual: The Origins of Western Liberalism* (London: Allen Lane, 2014).

Skinner, Quentin, *Reason and Rhetoric in the Philosophy of Hobbes* (Cambridge: Cambridge University Press, 1996).

Skinner, Quentin, 'Hobbes and the Purely Artificial Person of the State', *Journal of Political Philosophy* 7.1 (1999), 1–29.

Skinner, Quentin, *Visions of Politics*, i: *Regarding Method* (Cambridge: Cambridge University Press, 2002).

Skinner, Quentin, 'Hobbes on Representation', *European Journal of Philosophy* 13.2 (2005), 155–84.

Skinner, Quentin, 'A Genealogy of the Modern State', *Proceedings of the British Academy* 162 (2009), 325–70.

Smith, David, *Constitutional Royalism and the Search for Settlement, 1640–1649* (Cambridge: Cambridge University Press, 2002).

Smith, Nigel, *Literature and Revolution in England 1640–1660* (New Haven, CT: Yale University Press, 1994).

Smith, Steven B., *Modernity and its Discontents* (New Haven, CT: Yale University Press, 2016).

Smith, Travis D., 'Forgiving Those Not Trespassing against Us'. In *Civil Religion and Political Thought*, ed. R. Weed and J. von Heyking (Washington, DC: Catholic University of America Press, 2010), 93–120.

Smith, Wilfred Cantwell, *The Meaning and End of Religion: A New Approach to the Religious Traditions of Mankind* (New York: Macmillan, 1962).

Sommerville, J. P., 'The Royal Supremacy and Episcopacy "Jure Divino", 1603–1640', *The Journal of Ecclesiastical History* 34.4 (1983), 548–58.

Sommerville, J. P., 'Richard Hooker, Hadrian Saravia, and the Advent of the Divine Right of Kings', *History of Political Thought* 4.2 (1983), 229–45.

Sommerville, J. P., *Thomas Hobbes: Political Ideas in Historical Context* (Basingstoke: Macmillan Press, 1992).

Sommerville, J. P., 'Hobbes, Selden, Erastianism, and the History of the Jews'. In *Hobbes and History*, ed. G. A. J. Rogers and Tom Sorell (London: Routledge, 2000), 160–88.

Sommerville, J. P., 'Hobbes and Independency'. In *Nuove prospettive critiche sul Leviatano di Hobbes nel 350° anniversario di pubblicazione/New Critical Perspectives on Hobbes's Leviathan upon the 350th Anniversary of its Publication*, ed. Luc Foisneau and George Wright (Milan: Franco Angeli, 2004), 155–73.

Sommerville, J. P., 'Leviathan and its Anglican Context'. In *The Cambridge Companion to Hobbes's Leviathan*, ed. Patricia Springborg (Cambridge: Cambridge University Press, 2007), 358–74.

Sorabji, Richard, *Aristotle on Memory* (Providence, RI: Brown University Press, 1972).

Sorabji, Richard, *Moral Conscience Through the Ages: Fifth Century BCE to the Present* (Oxford: Oxford University Press, 2014).

Sorenson, Roy, 'Fictional Theism', *Analysis* 75.4 (2015), 539–50.

Southwood, Nicholas, *Contractualism and the Foundations of Morality* (Oxford: Oxford University Press, 2010).

Spinks, Bryan D., 'Gauden, John (1599/1600?–1662)', *Oxford Dictionary of National Biography*, <http://www.oxforddnb.com/view/article/10456>, accessed 16 June 2017.

Springborg, Patricia, 'Hobbes, Heresy, and the *Historica Ecclesiastica*', *Journal of the History of Ideas* 55.4 (1994), 553–71.

Springborg, Patricia, 'Thomas Hobbes and Cardinal Bellarmine: *Leviathan* and the Ghost of the Roman Empire', *History of Political Thought* 16.4 (1995), 503–31.

Springborg, Patricia, 'Hobbes on Religion'. In *The Cambridge Companion to Hobbes*, ed. Tom Sorell (Cambridge, Cambridge University Press, 1996), 346–80.

Springborg, Patricia, 'Writing to Redundancy: Hobbes and Cluverius', *The Historical Journal* 39.4 (1996), 1075–8.

Springborg, Patricia, 'Hobbes's Theory of Civil Religion: The *Historia Ecclesiastica*'. In *Pluralismo e religione civile*, ed. Gianni Paganini and Edoardo Tortarolo (Milan: Bruno Mondatori, 2003), 61–98.

Springborg, Patricia, 'Hobbes and Epicurean Religion'. In *Der Garten und die Moderne: Epikureische Moral und Politik vom Humanismus bis zur Aufklärung*, ed. Gianni Paganini and Edoardo Tortarolo (Stuttgart: Fromman-Holzboog, 2004), 161–214.

Springborg, Patricia, 'Hobbes the Atheist and his Deist Reception'. In *I filosofi e la società senza religione,* ed. Marco Geuna and Gianbattista Gori (Bologna: Il Mulino, 2011), 145–63.

Springborg, Patricia, 'Hobbes and the Word'. In *Obbedienza religiosa e resistenza politica nella prima età moderna. Filosofi ebrei, cristiani e islamici di fronte alla Bibbia*, ed. Luisa Simonutti (Turnhout, Belgium: Brepols Publishers, 2015), 183–212.

Sreedhar, Susanne, *Hobbes on Resistance: Defying the Leviathan* (Cambridge: Cambridge University Press, 2010).

Stemmer, Peter, *Handeln zugunsten anderer* (Berlin and New York: De Gruyter, 2000).

Stoffell, Brian, 'Hobbes on Self-Preservation and Suicide', *Hobbes Studies* 4 (1991), 26–33.

Stone, Lawrence, 'The Educational Revolution in England, 1560–1640', *Past & Present* 28.1 (1964), 41–80.

Strauss, Leo, *Natural Right and History* (Chicago, IL: University of Chicago Press, 1953).

Strong, Tracy B., 'How to Write Scripture: Words, Authorities, and Politics in Thomas Hobbes', *Critical Inquiry* 20.1 (1993), 128–59.

Stroumsa, Gary, *A New Science: The Discovery of Religion in the Age of Reason* (Cambridge, MA: Harvard University Press, 2010).

Sugden, Robert, 'Rationality and Impartiality: Is the Contractarian Enterprise Possible?' In *Rationality, Justice and the Social Contract: Themes from Morals by Agreement*, ed. David Gauthier and Robert Sugden (New York and London: Harvester Wheatsheaf, 1993), 157–75.

Talaska, Richard A., *The Hardwick Library and Hobbes's Early Intellectual Development* (Charlottesville, VA: Philosophy Documentation Center, 2013).

Tarcov, Nathan, *Locke's Education for Liberty* (Lanham, MD: Lexington Books, 1999).

Tarlton, Charles, 'The Despotical Doctrine of Hobbes', *History of Political Thought* 23.1 (2002), 62–89.

Taylor, A. E., 'The Ethical Doctrine of Hobbes', *Philosophy* 13.52 (1938), 406–24.

Taylor, Charles, *A Secular Age* (Cambridge MA: Belknap Press of Harvard University Press, 2007).

Torrance Kirby, W. J., *Richard Hooker's Doctrine of the Royal Supremacy* (Leiden: Brill, 1990).

Tralau, Johan, 'Hobbes Contra Liberty of Conscience', *Political Theory* 39.1 (2011), 58–84.

Trompf, Garry W., *Early Christian Historiography: Narratives of Retributive Historiography* (London: Continuum, 2000).

Tuck, Richard, 'Warrender's *De Cive*', *Political Studies* 33.2 (1985), 308–15.

Tuck, Richard, *Hobbes* (Oxford: Oxford University Press, 1989).

Tuck, Richard, 'Hobbes and Locke on Toleration'. In *Thomas Hobbes and Political Theory*, ed. Mary G. Dietz (Lawrence, KS: University of Kansas Press, 1990), 153–71.

Tuck, Richard, 'The Civil Religion of Thomas Hobbes'. In *Political Discourse in Early Modern Britain*, ed. Nicholas Phillipson and Quentin Skinner (Cambridge: Cambridge University Press, 1992), 120–38.

Tuck, Richard, 'The "Christian Atheism" of Thomas Hobbes'. In *Atheism from Reformation to the Enlightenment*, ed. M. Hunter and D. Wootton (Oxford: Oxford University Press, 1992), 111–30.

Tuck, Richard, *Philosophy and Government 1572–1651* (Cambridge: Cambridge University Press, 1993).

Tuck, Richard, 'Introduction'. In *Thomas Hobbes: Leviathan*, revised student edition (Cambridge: Cambridge University Press, 1996), pp. ix–xlv.

Tuck, Richard, 'Hobbes on Education'. In *Philosophers on Education*, ed. Amelie Oksenberg Rorty (London and New York: Routledge, 1998), 147–56.

Tuck, Richard, *Hobbes: A Very Short Introduction* (Oxford: Oxford University Press, 2002).

Tuck, Richard, 'The Utopianism of *Leviathan*'. In *Leviathan After 350 Years*, ed. Tom Sorell and Luc Foisneau (Oxford: Oxford University Press, 2004), 125–38.

Tuck, Richard, 'Hobbes, Conscience, and Christianity'. In *The Oxford Handbook of Hobbes*, ed. A. P. Martinich and Kinch Hoekstra (Oxford: Oxford University Press, 2016), 481–500.

Tyacke, Nicholas, 'Puritanism, Calvinism, and Counter-Revolution'. In *The Origins of the English Revolution*, ed. Conrad Russell (London: Macmillan, 1973).

Tyacke, Nicholas, *Anti-Calvinists: The Rise of English Arminianism, c.1590–1640* (Oxford: Clarendon Press, 1987).

Vaughan, Geoffrey, *Behemoth Teaches Leviathan: Thomas Hobbes on Political Education* (Lanham, MD: Lexington Books, 2002).

Voegelin, Eric, 'The Political Religions'. In *Modernity Without Restraint*, ed. Manfred Henningsen (Columbia, MO: University of Missouri Press, 2000), 19–73.

Waldron, Jeremy, 'Hobbes: Truth, Publicity, and Civil Doctrine'. In *Philosophers on Education*, ed. Amelie Oksenberg Rorty (London and New York: Routledge, 1998), 139–46.

Walzer, Michael, *The Revolution of the Saints: A Study of the Origins of Radical Politics* (Cambridge, MA: Harvard University Press, 1965).

Walzer, Michael, *In God's Shadow: Politics in the Hebrew Bible* (New Haven, CT: Yale University Press, 2012).

Warrender, Howard, *The Political Philosophy of Hobbes: His Theory of Obligation* (Oxford: Clarendon Press, 1957).

Warrender, Howard, 'The Place of God in Hobbes's Philosophy', *Political Studies* 8 (1960), 48–57.

Watkins, J. W. N., 'Philosophy and Politics in Hobbes', *The Philosophical Quarterly* 5 (1955), 125–46.

Watkins, J. W. N., *Hobbes's System of Ideas* (London: Hutchinson & Co., 1965).

Wattles, Jeffrey, *The Golden Rule* (New York and Oxford: Oxford University Press, 1996).

Weber, Dominique, *Histoire du salut: Ce que le Christ fait au Léviathan de Hobbes* (Paris: Presses de l'Université Paris-Sorbonne, 2008).

Weber, Max, *The Sociology of Religion*, trans. Talcott Parsons (Boston, MA: Beacon Press, 1993).

Wigelsworth, Jeffrey R., *Deism in Enlightenment England: Theology, Politics, and Newtonian Public Science* (Manchester: Manchester University Press, 2009).

Wilson, Peter, *The Thirty Years War: Europe's Tragedy* (London: Penguin, 2009).

Worden, Blair, *Roundhead Reputations: The English Civil Wars and the Passions of Posterity* (London: Penguin, 2001).

Wright, George, *Religion, Politics and Thomas Hobbes* (Dordrecht: Springer, 2006).

Wright, George, 'Hobbes and the Economic Trinity'. In George Wright, *Religion, Politics and Thomas Hobbes* (Dordrecht: Springer, 2006), 175–210.

Wybrow, Cameron, 'Hobbes as an Interpreter of Biblical Political Thought'. In *Liberal Democracy and the Bible*, ed. Kim Ian Parker (Lewiston, NY: The Edwin Mellen Press, 1992), 39–71.

Yarnell, Malcolm B., III, *Royal Priesthood in the English Reformation* (Oxford: Oxford University Press, 2013).

Young, B. W., 'Tindal, Matthew (*bap.* 1657, *d.* 1733)', *Oxford Dictionary of National Biography*, <http://www.oxforddnb.com/view/article/27462>, accessed 16 June 2017.

Zagorin, Perez, *Ways of Lying: Dissimulation, Persecution and Conformity in Early Modern Europe* (Cambridge, MA: Harvard University Press, 1990).

Zagorin, Perez, *How the Idea of Religious Toleration Came to the West* (Princeton, NJ: Princeton University Press, 2003).

Zagorin, Perez, *Hobbes and the Law of Nature* (Princeton, NJ and Oxford: Princeton University Press, 2009).

Index

Adams, Thomas 30
Ambrose, Saint 38
Anglicanism 1, 7, 11n, 16, 46, 67, 74, 152, 168, 169n, 170, 171, 173, 174, 181–3, 186, 187, 198, 207, 226, 233
anticlericalism 8, 77, 190, 203, 207, 208, 210, 213–16, 224
Aquinas, Thomas 52, 86n, 89, 92, 253, 269n
Aristotle 2, 46, 50n, 53, 92, 145, 151, 160, 175n
Arminianism 96, 97, 110–12, 115, 165
Athanasian Creed 40, 180–1
atheism 5, 39, 56, 64, 70–1, 168, 171–2, 181n, 182, 185–6, 189–90, 196, 200, 209, 213, 214, 217, 221, 250
Aubrey, John 4, 48, 54, 155, 157, 167, 168, 170, 172
Augustine, Saint 52, 98–101, 111, 159, 181, 253
authorization 19–20, 26, 28, 65–6, 178–80, 183, 266

Bayle, Pierre 55–6, 69
Bellarmine, Robert 72–3, 77n, 102, 136n, 143–4, 153, 180
Bentley, Richard 211–12
Blount, Charles 204–8
Bramhall, John 3, 6, 11n, 13, 40, 42, 55, 58, 65, 66, 67n, 70, 74–5, 84, 90n, 92n, 97, 98, 101, 108–12, 114, 129, 133, 137n, 146, 148, 168, 174–5, 182

Calvin, John and Calvinism 6–7, 30, 31, 90, 92, 95–8, 100–15, 120, 137, 186, 228
Catholicism 39, 54, 61, 72, 74, 77n, 96, 103, 105, 107, 119, 137, 152, 159, 160, 191, 192, 230, 233–4
    anti-Catholicism 30, 141n, 190
Chillingworth, William 96
civic religion 185
civil war 58, 59, 81, 124, 136, 151, 154, 220–1, 223, 224–6, 236–8, 257
    English Civil War 1, 2, 3, 8, 39, 48, 77, 116–17, 121–2, 131, 141, 151–2, 166, 224–36, 239, 257
Collins, Anthony 204, 210–12, 216
conscience 8, 45, 60, 67–9, 76, 83, 85, 91–2, 148, 193, 209, 227–31, 235, 237, 256–72
Constantine 27, 69, 70, 148, 151, 161, 162, 163, 164, 180n, 205
corporation 22–3, 235

covenant 12, 19, 20–1, 23, 29n, 34n, 40–1, 58–9, 66, 123, 125, 182, 183n, 225, 227–8, 263–4
Cumberland, Richard 90
curiosity 147, 195–6, 214

Davenant, William 53, 196n
deism 8, 202–12, 212–14, 217
Descartes, René 85, 105, 209
determinism 6–7, 97–115, 211
disagreement 1, 5, 8, 82, 221, 240, 257, 270
divine right 12, 24, 25, 41, 63–4, 77, 126–7, 128–32, 212n, 226, 228, 232–4, 237
Dryden, John 206
Duppa, Brian 190, 235

Eachard, John 193
education 45–62, 104, 200
enlightenment 49, 57, 59–60, 212–13, 217, 220, 238
Epicureanism 105, 151, 154
Epiphanius 158, 165–6
equality 242, 248, 251, 252–3, 254
Erastus, Thomas and Erastianism 3, 5, 10–11, 12, 17, 19, 21, 23, 74, 133, 137, 152, 156, 194, 196, 199, 210, 212
evil, the problem of 36–9, 99–100

faith 18, 45–7, 54–5, 60–1, 69, 69n, 72, 82–3, 95, 96–7, 101, 192, 215, 258, 261–2
fear 65, 79n, 110, 130, 138, 145n, 148, 167, 221, 236n
Ferne, Henry 120, 231n
Filmer, Robert 120, 133, 140, 190, 226, 234
freedom 25, 46, 65–6, 101–4, 107, 111n, 112–13, 126n, 128, 211, 216, 224–5, 227, 230, 265
    free will 97, 98, 99, 101, 105, 109–10, 200n

Gill, John 97
Gillespie, George 112
Golden Rule 248–9, 253–4
Greenhill, William 123
Grotius, Hugo 120, 194

Harrington, James 123–4, 133, 134n, 230n, 231
Harris, John 209
Herbert, Edward 202–3, 206
Heresiographers 163–6
heresy 7, 35n, 61, 152, 153, 159, 162, 163–6, 169–72, 172–3, 179, 185, 197, 205, 217

Hildersham, Arthur 36n, 38
Hooker, Richard 15–16, 74–5, 120–1
Hyde, Edward 65n, 136, 137, 147, 171

Independency 24n, 45, 51, 57, 60, 75–7, 152,
    186, 191n, 192, 198n, 199, 230n, 231
Israel (Biblical) and Israelites 7, 39, 44, 74,
    116–34, 140, 142, 147n, 148, 177–8n, 226

James I 30, 43, 77n, 95, 121, 137, 232
Jesus Christ 16, 35, 67, 69, 72–3, 82, 83, 84,
    97, 138, 175, 179, 180, 194, 205, 214, 215,
    258, 261
Job 36–7, 144, 167

Latitudinarianism 201
Laud, William and Laudianism 32, 61, 122, 226,
    232, 233, 235
laws of nature 5, 29, 55, 75, 83, 194, 206, 212,
    229, 243–5, 247, 248–9, 252, 253, 260, 261,
    263–4, 265–7, 268–9, 271
Lawson, George 4, 34, 64n
Leland, John 202–4, 218
liberalism 219–21, 224, 240, 245–7
liberty see freedom
Lilburne, John 38
Lipsius, Justus 109
Locke, John 46–7, 51, 52, 69, 71n, 211
Lucian 53, 151, 158, 160, 174
Luther, Martin and Lutheranism 95–7, 99–100,
    102, 186, 253

martyrdom 6, 80–7, 262
materialism 3n, 6, 46, 79–80, 85–9, 91–4, 98,
    138, 193, 203, 209, 211, 212, 254
Mede, Joseph 7, 144–6
Milton, John 46, 124, 146, 147n, 155n, 206
miracles 130, 161, 163, 165, 168, 177n, 192,
    195–6, 203, 206–7, 213, 214, 238, 259
mortalism 173, 180
Moses 7, 58, 73, 117–18, 123–34, 140–1, 148,
    174–5, 177, 177–8n, 179, 207, 209, 214,
    259, 261

natural law see laws of nature
necessity 88n, 97–8, 100, 102n, 103, 106–8, 109,
    111–12, 113, 114, 211
Nicea, Council of 69, 151, 205
    creed of 40, 153, 161, 173n, 175, 179, 180, 205

obligation 9, 11, 17, 18, 33, 40–1n, 65, 66, 68,
    126, 222, 252, 261, 265
omnipotence 6, 29, 32–3, 34n, 35–8, 40n, 41–4,
    97, 99–100, 115
Owen, John 77, 190, 199, 231

Pagett, Ephraim 165
Parker, Henry 44, 128

Payne, Robert 105n, 198, 232
peace 5, 6, 11, 18, 24n, 36, 69, 77, 82, 84, 85n,
    93, 131, 149, 151, 164, 184, 195, 196,
    200, 213, 216, 220, 241n, 242, 244,
    248–9, 270
Pelagianism 99, 165
Pemble, William 104–5
Pepys, Samuel 171
Perkins, William 97, 98, 100, 102–3, 106, 108
personation 11–23, 24n, 25, 26n, 27–8, 34–6,
    40, 77, 169, 172, 174; see also representation
    God as a person by fiction 35–6, 171n, 175,
    177–83, 214, 265–6
Pierce, Thomas 111–12
Pighius, Albertus 101
Plato 47, 50–4, 56, 60, 62, 145, 250
predestination 38, 81n, 95–8, 101–12,
    103n, 104–5
Presbyterianism 1, 76–7, 83, 121, 152–3, 165–6,
    171, 173n, 187, 189–92, 199, 202, 226,
    227–33
prophesy 55, 73, 106, 124, 126, 131, 135,
    139–40, 144, 146, 177, 179, 195, 196, 214,
    215, 237, 259
Psalms 6, 30, 32, 34, 42–3, 52, 121, 142–3
punishment (divine) 36, 40, 56, 61, 70–1, 81,
    146, 161, 163, 164, 172, 233, 257, 268, 270

Rawls, John 4, 8, 220, 238, 240–1, 245–8, 249,
    254–5, 272
reciprocity 168–9, 247–50, 251, 253–4,
    260–1, 270
Reformation 18n, 26n, 95, 96–8, 101, 105,
    111–12, 118–19, 136, 187, 192, 219, 220–2,
    225, 233–6
representation 5, 11–12, 16, 17, 19–24, 26–8,
    29, 31, 32, 35, 41, 42, 71n, 77, 126, 131–2,
    169, 171n, 175–83, 187, 194, 203n, 214;
    see also personation
revelation 8, 100, 106, 135, 177, 178, 180,
    183, 186, 196, 202–3, 213–14, 217, 226,
    229, 258–9
Reynolds, Edward 90, 91–2
rhetoric 61n, 118, 126, 132–4, 144, 153, 162,
    224–5, 231, 238
Ross, Alexander 136, 138n, 147, 152, 165–6,
    188–9, 190, 197
Rousseau, Jean–Jacques 1, 62, 265–6

salvation 3, 6, 15, 21, 67, 69, 72–3, 79–80, 82–4,
    87, 89, 90, 93, 96, 99, 138n, 194, 195, 215,
    235, 257n, 261, 267–8
Salwey, Arthur 122
Scripture, Holy 2–3, 7, 11, 17–19, 55, 60, 76,
    83, 89, 96, 100, 127, 131, 135–9, 144–8,
    173, 174, 175, 178n, 179, 193–4, 196, 202–3,
    207–9, 212, 214–15, 229, 237, 261–2,
    269, 271

Scudder, Henry 123
sectarianism 151–2, 159, 163, 165, 209, 225,
    227–8, 231, 234
secularism 2, 4, 6, 7, 8, 9, 12, 49, 60, 63–6, 69,
    72–3, 77, 98, 106, 140, 219–25, 235–8,
    256–7, 271–2
self-preservation 6, 55, 66, 79–80, 84, 86–7, 90,
    185, 240–5, 247–50, 252
Sidney, Algernon 124
sin 36–7, 67–8, 70, 71n, 96–7, 99, 102, 108,
    110–13, 114–15, 124, 146, 227, 228, 232,
    256, 257, 260, 263–9
    Original Sin 37, 92, 97, 102, 103
sovereignty 1, 5–6, 7, 8, 10–12, 14–28, 29–32,
    37, 40–1, 43–4, 46–7, 57–60, 63–70, 72–5,
    77–8, 82–3, 85n, 118, 124–32, 137, 140,
    157, 169, 174, 182–3, 193, 199–200, 202,
    210–11, 215, 226–8, 230, 232–6, 238, 259n,
    261–7, 271–2
    natural sovereignty 5–6, 29–44, 214–15
Spinoza, Benedict de 148n, 168, 204, 207, 209,
    212–13, 217
state of nature 21, 32, 44, 59, 68, 128–9,
    140, 173, 182, 227, 241–5, 248–9, 252,
    259–60, 269

Suarez, Francesco 97, 106–7, 114, 145
subordinate systems 5, 11–12, 21–4, 26–8,
    131, 198

Tenison, Thomas 137, 168, 182, 193
Tertullian 159, 169, 173–4, 180–1, 197
Tindal, Matthew 204, 209–10, 211, 213, 216
Toland, John 204, 208–9, 210
toleration 6, 8, 23, 24n, 45–7, 55–60, 63, 68–70,
    76, 78, 152, 189–90, 198n, 205, 211, 214,
    216, 270
Trinity, Holy 3, 7, 27, 72, 163n, 168n, 169, 170,
    173–7, 179–82, 188, 203n, 205, 223, 234
Twisse, William 103

Verdus, François du 143, 156–8
virtue 51, 53–4, 61–2, 104, 128, 160, 211

Wallis, John 3n, 168, 183, 197
Ward, Seth 182, 189, 196
warrior god 43–4
White, Thomas 108, 170–1, 190
Williams, John 121

Zanchi, Girolamo 110